# TEACHING: AN INTRODUCTION

# TEACHING: AN INTRODUCTION

D. Cecil Clark          Beverly Romney Cutler

*Brigham Young University*

HBJ

**Harcourt Brace Jovanovich, Publishers**

San Diego   New York   Chicago   Austin   Washington, D.C.
London   Sydney   Tokyo   Toronto

Requests for permission to make copies of any part of the work should be mailed to: Copyrights and Permissions Department, Harcourt Brace Jovanovich, Publishers, Orlando, Florida 32887.

ISBN 0-15-586597-8

Library of Congress Catalog Card Number: 89-84247

Printed in the United States of America

---

All photographs are copyrighted and reprinted by permission. Permission to reprint the following is gratefully appreciated.

**Page 168.** From "Salaries and Shortages," Geraldine J. Clifford and James W. Guthrie, *Ed School 1988,* pp. 28–31; figure 3. Copyright © 1988 by University of Chicago Press. Reprinted by permission.

**Pages 219, 236–237.** From "Good Seeds Grow in Strong Cultures," Jon Saphier and M. King, *Educational Leadership,* March 1985, Vol. 42:6, pp. 67–74. Reprinted with permission of the Association for Supervision and Curriculum Development. Copyright © by ASCD. All rights reserved.

**Pages 238–241.** From "Ingredients of a Successful School Effectiveness Project," Maureen McCormack-Larkin, *Educational Leadership,* March 1985, Vol. 42:6, pp. 31–37. Reprinted with permission of the Association for Supervision and Curriculum Development. Copyright © by ASCD. All rights reserved.

**Pages 243–244, 303–307.** From *Handbook of Research on Teaching,* 3rd ed., M. C. Wittrock (editor), Table 20.1 (pp. 576–577); figure 9.1 (p. 257); figure 9.3 (p. 275). Reprinted with permission of Macmillan Publishing Company, a Division of Macmillan, Inc. Copyright © 1985 by the American Educational Research Association.

**Pages 256–257.** From *Classroom Management for Secondary Teachers,* E. T. Emmer, C. M. Evertson, J. P. Sanford, B. S. Clements, and M. E. Worsham. © 1984, pp. 95–96. Reprinted by permission of Prentice Hall, Inc., Englewood Cliffs, New Jersey.

**Pages 257–258.** From *Classroom Management for Elementary Teachers,* 2nd ed., C. M. Evertson, E. T. Emmer, B. S. Clements, J. P. Sanford, and M. E. Worsham. © 1989, pp. 17–18. Reprinted by permission of Prentice Hall, Inc., Englewood Cliffs, New Jersey.

**Page 260.** From Lee S. Shulman, "Knowledge and Teaching: Foundations of the New Reform," *Harvard Educational Review,* 57:1, pp. 1–22. Copyright © 1987 by the President and Fellows of Harvard College. All rights reserved.

Pages 290–292. Excerpts from *Looking in Classrooms,* 4th ed., Thomas L. Good and Jere E. Brophy. Copyright © 1987 by Harper and Row, Publishers, Inc. Reprinted by permission of the publisher.

**Page 406.** From "Rethinking the School Calendar," Charles Ballinger, *Educational Leadership,* February 1988, Vol. 45:5, pp. 57–61. Reprinted with permission of the Association for Supervision and Curriculum Development. Copyright © by ASCD. All rights reserved.

**Pages 409–411.** From "The New Moral Education," Kevin Ryan, *Phi Delta Kappa,* November 1986, pp. 229–233. Copyright © 1986 by Phi Delta Kappan. Reprinted by permission of Phi Delta Kappa and the author.

**Pages 432–437.** Margaret Treece Metzger and Clare Fox, "Two Teachers of Letters," *Harvard Educational Review,* 56:4, pp. 349–354. Copyright © 1986 by the President and Fellows of Harvard College. All rights reserved.

**Pages 437–439.** From Sophie Freud Lowenstein, "The Passion and Challenge of Teaching," *Harvard Educational Review,* 50:1, pp. 1–12. Copyright © 1980 by the President and Fellows of Harvard College. All rights reserved.

**Pages 442–443.** From Donald W. Thomas, "The Torpedo's Touch," *Harvard Educational Review,* 55:2, pp. 220–222. Copyright © 1985 by the President and Fellows of Harvard College. All rights reserved.

**Page 445.** From Vivian Gussin Paley, "On Listening to What the Children Say," *Harvard Educational Review,* 56:2, pp. 122–131. Copyright © 1986 by the President and Fellows of Harvard College. All rights reserved.

**Page 447.** From Anne Martin, "Back to Kindergarten Basics," *Harvard Educational Review,* 55:3, pp. 318–320. Copyright © 1985 by the President and Fellows of Harvard College. All rights reserved.

**Pages 447–448.** From Joseph McDonald, "Raising the Teacher's Voice and the Ironic Role of Theory," *Harvard Educational Review,* 56:4, pp. 355–378. Copyright © 1986 by the President and Fellows of Harvard College. All rights reserved.

**Pages 448–449.** From "Sketches toward a Profile of a Professional Teacher," K. Devaney, *Education and Urban Society,* May 1985, Vol. 17:3, pp. 269, 270, 274, 275, 281. Reprinted by permission of Sage Publications, Inc. Copyright © by Sage Publications.

# PREFACE

*We know in our bones that over the long haul
what we do in education has the greatest
relevance to building the kind of society we
want.—John Gardner*

With this book, the authors offer a conversation about the wondrous field of teaching—its challenges and frustrations, its joys and disappointments, its laughter and tears. Above all, we emphasize the fact that what *you* as a teacher do matters. Sometimes we enjoin you, providing armchair advice based on our experience, on available research, and occasionally on just our hopes. Sometimes we stand alongside, simply pointing out this tree or that boulder on the landscape of teaching. Sometimes we raise a question, as you confront a new valley, or provoke you to consider, as you climb a bluff. But always we pursue a single goal: to introduce you to the field of teaching, to paint as best we can a realistic picture of what your life as a modern-day teacher would be, and to excite you about the possibilities of becoming stunningly good at what you do. In doing so, we have tried to anticipate your feelings, your perceptions, your anxieties, and even your background. Furthermore, we have constantly pressed ourselves to select relevant topics and present them in meaningful ways, forever asking, "Why ought a new student of education learn about this topic?" As a result, we have omitted some topics traditionally addressed in introductory texts, while developing others in considerable detail. This book is well suited for an introduction-to-education course for students going into either elementary or secondary teaching. Indeed, it is appropriate for anyone interested in an overview of the field of teaching.

Our style is personal. We have resisted the temptation to write this book for our professional colleagues as well as for you. You have won out. We have stripped it of jargon and have tried to use plain, communicative language with some vitality to it. Introducing you to the field inescapably reveals our own values and beliefs about teaching. We believe, for example, that superbly good teachers become that way not so much because of native ability, or even training, but because of a passionate commitment to teaching. Uncommonly good teachers are not making small contributions to the lives of their students—they are making giant ones! Finally, the complexity of today's classroom invites, indeed demands, a higher level of professionalism in teachers than ever before.

Each chapter begins with a short list of Main Points and concludes with some Expansions, which mostly invite you to expand on the concepts presented in the chapter. Section I introduces you to the preparation required to enter your teaching life: your teacher education program and that ever-challenging first year. Section II takes you into your workplace: your school and your classroom. We introduce you to your students and your relationships as well as to the curriculum, governance, finance, and, very importantly, the law. Section III introduces you to emerging knowledge in the field, acquainting you with effective schools, effective classrooms, the study of teaching, and the use of technology in teaching. From this section we hope you will see that the art of teaching rests more and more solidly on a scientific basis. Finally, Section IV focuses on the professional and personal challenges facing you as a teacher. Throughout all thirteen chapters, we try to connect you with the topic—we discuss you and the law, your role in the governing and financing of your school, you and the effective school, and your role in the curriculum.

This book is full of examples and vignettes that provide glimpses into the lives of teachers. The vignettes are typically conversations, revealing the rich variety of perceptions, attitudes, and orientations that exist among teachers. We hope you focus on the tone of these conversations rather than on the specifics and that you think about how you would react in similar situations.

We express appreciation to our colleagues—Don Norton, Malia Howland, Reese Hansen, Paul Merrill, Rulon Garfield, and Richard Sudweeks—who provided valuable suggestions about content, order, and style and to our reviewers—Wallace Draper, Ball State University; Shari Hatch; Cynthia Ledbetter, Texas A&M University; James Leming, Southern Illinois University; and Peter Soderbergh, Louisiana State University. We are also grateful to Julia Berrisford for her gentle vigilance and continual support throughout the project; to Cece Munson for her superb and pleasant coordination of the production process; and to Meredy Amyx, whose editing taught us what truly good writing is all about. And we thank our families, who have spent many nights and Saturdays patiently going about their lives without a father and a mother. Beyond that, they have goaded, coaxed, and cheered us on when we felt overwhelmed, and provided unending love, regular encouragement, and total faith in our ability to complete the project.

D.C.C.
B.R.C.

# CONTENTS

# TEACHING: AN INTRODUCTION

# SECTION ONE

# THE JOURNEY

# CHAPTER 1

# YOUR ENTRANCE INTO TEACHING

*Education is too significant and dynamic an enterprise to be left to mere technicians; and we might as well begin now the prodigious task of preparing men and women who understand not only the substance of what they are teaching but also the theories behind the particular strategies they employ to convey that substance.—Lawrence A. Cremin*

**MAIN IDEAS**

- Teaching is at once a complex, multifaceted, and indeed wondrous activity.

- Current teacher education programs have been molded by trends and movements such as mastery learning, programmed instruction, and "back to basics."

- Teachers today leave their training programs with a general education background, knowledge of the subject matter to be taught, and pedagogical skill in teaching that subject matter.

- We are on the brink of a sweeping restructure of teacher education programs.

- Your first year of teaching is satisfying, frustrating, full of joy and anxiety, and, above all, utterly exhausting.

- Developing a can-do perspective enables you to reap the greatest success from your first year of teaching.

*The calling of a teacher is so intimate, its duties so delicate, the things in which a teacher might prove unworthy or would fail are so numerous that they are incapable of enumeration in any legislative enactment. His habits, his speech, his good name, his cleanliness, the wisdom and propriety of his unofficial utterances, his associations, all are involved. His ability to inspire children and to govern them, his power as a teacher, and the character for which he stands are matters of major concern in a teacher's selection and retention.—Board of Trustees v. Stubblefield, 1971*

• During this first year, some of your hopeful expectations are abandoned, others modified. Still others, tenaciously clung to, lead you to unanticipated successes.

• You face and work through culture shock during this first year: being a teacher rather than a student, starting up a complex classroom, burning the candle at both ends, feeling a sense of isolation, and entering challengingly different relationships.

• Getting off to a good start and moving positively through your first year is imperative; whether you continue teaching after the first year is at stake.

• You are socialized into your school culture. The environment will mold your ideas and ways of doing things and, believe it or not, *you* will have an impact on your school's culture.

# INTRODUCTION

You may now be sitting uneasily in your first education course, thinking, "What, *really*, am I doing here? Ought I to be back in my music (biology, English, history) major, where I feel at home? Have I made the right decision about going into teaching?" It is normal for students entering the study of any profession—engineering, nursing, psychology, medicine, law, and yes, education—to wonder about their vocational choice.

In this chapter, and throughout the book, we assume you have tentatively made up your mind that teaching is the field for you. Now that you have done so, jump into your training program with full commitment! This is your surest course of action at this point. Only by immersing yourself in your newly chosen field will you come to know with certainty whether you have made the right decision. Merely surveying the field, comfortably contemplating its possibilities from the outside, will not bring about a final decision. Making the commitment will force you to confront yourself—your own abilities, interests, and values. You may indeed change your mind about becoming a teacher. But for now, stepping in with an open and receptive mind will give you the experience and perspective you need in order to make an informed choice at the end, even if it's a decision *not* to go into teaching. If you decide to go ahead, you'll have the force of a wholehearted commitment behind you.

So plunge in. Anticipate. Discover the realities, the hardships, the joys that await you in a teaching career. Our role will be to introduce you to the life of teaching—to offer you a peek at its challenges, its complexities, and its wonders. We will acquaint you with its many facets by illustration rather than by exhaustive description.

To help crystallize your thinking as you begin, why not conduct a brief self-inventory of your current knowledge and feelings about teaching? Ask yourself these questions:

1.   What beliefs about teacher education do I bring with me?
2.   What, in my mind, distinguishes good teaching from poor?
3.   What characteristics did my own best teachers display?
4.   What emotions do I experience in approaching my teacher education program? confidence? fear? excitement? resolve? wariness?
5.   What are my expectations as I go into my teacher education program?

Probably the easiest of these questions is number 5, because the folk-lore of education still rings in your ears:

"Education courses are boring. They contain too much fluff."

"Education courses are overly theoretical. Where is the practical?"

"The courses you endure; the student teaching is the fun."

"Instructors have been out of classrooms for twenty years. They're oblivious to what takes place in the trenches."

And from students currently in the program you receive on-the-spot reports:

"Standing in front of twenty-two kids for fifteen minutes leaves me totally drained!"

"I can't believe the time I'm putting in on this one course—there is so much make-work involved."

"You learn rules about how to manage students, but you're on your own standing in front of that class!"

"Most of my education courses are a lot more informative and enjoyable than people said they'd be."

"One thing's for sure: classrooms are circuses. You're making decisions every minute—and they'd better be right!"

"I'll be so psyched up by the time I get to student teaching, I'll probably blow it when I get in front of the class."

# YOUR TEACHER EDUCATION PROGRAM

Let's start with a preview of what you may encounter in your teacher education program.

## Your Instructors

Teacher educators, those who will instruct you in your teacher education program, are not easily characterized as a group. Your professors of education probably entered teacher education later in life, usually after a teaching career in the classroom. In fact, 70 percent have held teaching positions in elementary and secondary schools before coming to teach in a school of education.

Among the responsibilities of your professors are the following:

1. to expose students to teaching theories and practices
2. to demonstrate teaching practices and help students acquire minimal competency in their use
3. to establish good relationships with principals, cooperating teachers, and others in the schools where their students will be training
4. to ensure that students are placed with cooperating teachers who will provide optimal learning
5. to help solve problems that arise during student teaching
6. to document the progress of the student during the program.

In all likelihood, your professors will be conservative in their training approaches. You will undoubtedly be schooled in the teaching techniques that your professors have used and found successful during their careers in the classroom. You will not likely be encouraged to try new and extreme approaches falling outside the usual ways of doing things. Likewise, your professors will tend to emphasize the practical over the theoretical; that is, acquiring specific skills and techniques and "getting the job done." This commitment to the practical grows out of their own experience as classroom teachers. They believe that specific help in day-to-day teaching will prepare their students to have the greatest positive effects in their own classrooms.[1]

## Your Fellow Students

Teacher education students coming into the program will generally have the same orientation as their education professors: a desire for concrete and practical training. They fully expect professors to tell and show them the "right way to teach." Their desires are reflected in comments and questions such as these:

"What is the best way to discipline students?"

"I'm not interested in theory; I need specific techniques."

"What's the best way to help kids learn to read?"

Incoming education students bring with them a set of expectations formed through their own schooling experiences. About 25 percent are confident of their ability to teach even before coming into the program. Their experiences as camp counselors, as Sunday school teachers, and even as students, have provided them (they feel) with a foundation of teaching skills. Further, these education students are convinced that most of their development will come through on-the-job "instincts and experiences" rather than through principles learned in their program. Greene echoes this sentiment:

> No matter how practical, how grounded our educational courses were, they suddenly appear to be totally irrelevant in the concrete situation where we find ourselves. This is because general principles never fully apply to new and special situations, especially if those principles are thought of as prescriptions or rules. Dewey spoke of principles as modes or methods of analyzing situations, tools to be used in "judging suggested courses of action." We forget that, for a rule to be universally applicable, all situations must be fundamentally alike; and, most of us know, classroom situations are always new and never twice alike. Even so, we yearn oftentimes for what might be called a "technology of teaching," for standard operating procedures that can be relied upon to "work." Devoid of these, we project our frustration back upon whatever teacher education we experienced.[2]

## Your Coursework

Historically, teacher education programs have been composed of general education, major and minor fields, and pedagogical work (courses related to the art and science of teaching). To a great extent they still are, although current trends are introducing some new emphases.

GENERAL EDUCATION   General education makes up approximately one-third of a total four-year college education. Nearly all teacher training institutions agree that an effective teacher needs to be a generally educated person, one prepared for a lifetime of learning, effective communication, and responsible action. General education is designed to increase the student's understanding of mankind's most valuable knowledge and achievements in the arts, letters, and sciences. Through a general education, the student learns about the development of civilization and culture and achieves an awareness of relationships among human activities, knowledge, and accomplishments. General education courses introduce a spectrum of fields, including humanities, social sciences, natural sciences, and mathematics. Education students take representative classes from each of these groups, usually completing these requirements by their junior year.

MAJOR AND MINOR   Traditionally, students planning to teach in the elementary grades have majored in elementary education, whereas students planning to teach at the secondary level select a "subject" major, such as history, music, English, or math, coupled with an education minor. Courses in the major and minor fields are designed to ensure that students acquire core knowledge in selected substantive areas for which they will have responsibility in their teaching.

PEDAGOGICAL COURSES   Educational foundations, teaching methods, and field experiences are the three main pedagogical areas. Combined, they represent about one-fifth of the secondary teacher's program and one-third of the elementary teacher's program. Courses in the pedagogical areas prepare the new teacher to provide appropriate learning opportunities for students, helping them to acquire knowledge and skills suited to their level of development.

Educational foundations include history of education, sociology of education, philosophy of education, educational psychology, learning theory, and educational measurement.

The history of education acquaints the student with great educators of the past and shows how education was conducted during previous eras. Through the study of history, students come to see the roots of today's educational practices, such as learning through direct experience, "time out" methods of discipline, guided practice, and computer-aided instruction.

Sociology classes reveal the classroom to be a miniature society. Included are topics such as how schoolchildren are socialized, how clique relationships develop in the classroom, how student attitudes are formed and modified, how student roles develop and change, how groups affect the student, and how group rewards and punishments affect the student's expectations and social development. By studying the classroom as a miniature society, the student of education comes to see the social forces that affect learning.

Philosophy courses focus on various schools of thought about human beings, the purposes of education, and the sources of knowledge. Teacher education students examine their own assumptions about teaching and learning and explore how these assumptions will affect their teaching performance. For example, if the teacher assumes that learning is fostered in a secure environment, his curriculum will contain activities to promote emotional well-being.

Educational psychology leads the education student through theories of child development, learning, and personality. Issues include the biological, social, emotional, cognitive, and moral development of the learner. The student is introduced to different types of learning, such as memory learning, concept formation, and discovery learning. Educational psychology also covers motivation, values, attitudes, emotional adjustment, perception, classroom management, exceptional students, and learning disabilities.

A course in measurement and evaluation, traditionally a part of educational psychology, encompasses such topics as evaluating teaching, preparing instructional objectives, constructing classroom tests, selecting standardized tests, grading, measuring special traits, interpreting test results, and talking with parents about student progress.

Methods courses fall into two categories: general and special. In general methods courses, students learn to manage a classroom, create objectives, write lesson plans, select teaching strategies, diagnose learning problems, and individualize instruction.

Special methods courses focus on the teaching of particular subjects such as English, social studies, and chemistry. In these classes instructors acquaint students with the nature of the subject, various techniques and approaches for optimal learning of the subject, and problems learners typically encounter when exposed to the subject.

Field experiences are the heart of teacher education. Students finally move out of the university and into the real world of teaching. Here they have an opportunity to work with young learners, teachers, the principal, and parents. There are two basic types: early field experiences and student teaching.

Early field experiences, coming after the introductory class in education, expose the student to the world of the classroom. After a brief period of observation, the student moves into the flow of teaching life by photocopying class assignments, helping individual members of the class with seatwork, and later on, giving a simple presentation in front of the class. Ideally, these early experiences serve several functions:

1.  helping students determine whether teaching is for them (and being plunged into the classroom early on will surely do it!)
2.  giving the education faculty a chance to look at the students' potential in the classroom
3.  sensitizing students to the need to develop instructional skills
4.  helping students learn to perceive classroom life in realistic ways
5.  helping the school and university work together more closely
6.  accelerating students' movement from one stage of training to another.

Student teaching is a more permanent assignment to a given classroom, generally for six to ten weeks. As a culminating experience in the training process, student teaching is the arena in which newly learned teaching skills are gathered together and tried out in a regular classroom. By observing the cooperating teacher (the permanent classroom teacher to whom the student is assigned, and who also acts as confidant and coach), the student learns which teaching practices are effective and which are not. Start-

*One must see that difference between the hampering, blinding, misleading instruction given by an inexperienced young new teacher and the developing, transforming, and almost creative power of an accomplished teacher—one must rise to some comprehension of the vast import and significance of the phrase "to educate"—before he can regard with a sufficiently energetic contempt that boast of Dr. Bell, "Give me 24 pupils today and I will give you back 24 teachers tomorrow."—John P. Gordy*

ing off modestly, with parts of lessons, the student teacher gradually takes over the planning and teaching of entire units. Throughout the experience, the cooperating teacher works closely with the student teacher, providing support, a shoulder to cry on, and sometimes enthusiastic encouragement. The college supervisor too is mostly supportive, providing thoughtful suggestions and assistance in reflecting upon teaching experiences just undergone. As required, the supervisor rates the student teacher's performance and notes his progress.

# FOUNDATIONS OF AMERICAN EDUCATION

## Beginnings

In the early 1600s, American colonial education varied with geography, local customs, and degree of settlement. Throughout the country, parents were primarily responsible for the early education of their children. Family education was often extended by an apprenticeship in a trade, which included learning how to read.

In New England, small children first learned the rudiments of reading and moral and religious precepts in "dame" schools held in private homes. "Town" schools began in the mid-1600s in accordance with a law of the Massachusetts Bay Colony, and traveling teachers conducted "moving" schools to serve children in less populous areas. Of paramount importance was literacy. Principal teaching materials—the Horn Book and primers such as the *New England Primer*—reflected the predominant goal of learning to read the Bible.

In the middle colonies, national and religious pluralism fostered the development of private schools licensed by the state and financed by the parents. In the South, wealthy families hired private live-in tutors; the poor relied on church and charity for their schooling.

In none of the early schools—the dame school, the town school, or the moving school—did teachers undergo any sort of formal training. Teachers were usually itinerant preachers, hoping to supplement their meager ministerial salaries, or simply the more widely read members of the community who were willing to share their knowledge. Teachers were also poorly paid and held in relatively low esteem. Nevertheless, they faced a demanding set of expectations, ranging from performing menial tasks of schoolhouse maintenance to fulfilling an assortment of public duties and serving as models of character, morality, and personal propriety. Few regarded teaching as a lifelong commitment; to most, it was temporary employment until something better came along.

## Evolution of Modern Education

By 1830, national recognition of the value of education for all children had given rise to the "common" schools, forerunners of modern elementary and middle schools, and created a demand for more and better trained teachers. Now, for the first time, the average child could attend school. At first, parents paid tuition, but eventually free public education became available to all.

Secondary education in America had its origins in the "Latin Grammar Schools," the earliest and most famous of which was Boston Latin Grammar School, founded in 1635. At the age of seven or eight, boys were sent to these schools for several years of study of Latin, Greek, Hebrew, and the New Testament in preparation for college entrance. After a time, "English" schools arose to serve both girls and boys who needed a more practical education, especially those who were not college bound. Their curriculum included vocational and other secular subjects, as well as social skills such as music and dance.

As needs changed, the academic curriculum of the Latin Grammar Schools was combined with the vocational curriculum of the English Gram-

*M. E. Warren Collection/From Photo Researchers, Inc.*

*It should be our goal in all of education to produce caring, moral persons,
but we cannot accomplish this purpose by setting an objective and heading
straight toward it. Rather we approach our goal by living with those whom
we teach in a caring community, through modeling, dialogue, practice, and
confirmation.—Nel Noddings*

mar Schools to form the "academy." In the century following the opening of
Benjamin Franklin's Philadelphia Academy in 1751, some 6000 academies
sprang up, many of which offered classical and commercial courses and even
teacher training.

The early curricular emphasis on "training of the mind" gave way to
the teaching of practical skills as an increasingly industrialized society
exerted its influence. Which skills are considered marketable may change
from one generation to the next—yesterday, clerical skills; today, computer
skills—but the principle of educating students to take their place in society
remains.

The philosophy of teaching has undergone a similar shift. Early programs focused on content, and teachers became experts in subject matter:
"The path to good teaching is to know your subject thoroughly so you can
teach it well." Gradually, the credibility of this focus eroded as it became
evident that knowing a subject is not the same thing as knowing how to
teach it. Now training programs stress methods: a how-to approach to
teaching. Later on, however, we will see that superb teaching involves considerably more than being a good technician in the classroom.

Character and morals have regained a prominent position in society's
expectations of education. Religious training was once a central feature of
the curriculum, and a teacher's moral character counted for far more than
professional preparation. Later, to avoid favoritism toward any religious
orientation, teachers taught moral values rather than doctrine. Backing off
one step further, educators subsequently discouraged the promulgating of
any particular brand of morality in the classroom. Yet today from many directions comes pressure to provide children with moral education in the
schools, and once again the character of the teacher becomes a significant
issue.[3]

## Historical Movements and Social Forces

Several historical movements and social forces continue to influence modern-day teaching practices. We believe that in one form or another they will
affect you as a teacher.

EXPERIMENTALISM   In the early 1900s, the philosophy of John Dewey was
formally labeled *experimentalism*. Still very much alive, experimentalism
manifests itself in approaches to curriculum, subject matter, and teaching

methods. Essentially Dewey's philosophy said that students should prepare to live in a society by solving problems in a miniature society—the school. His students solved social problems related to their own needs and interests, and they gained knowledge as a by-product. Further, the curriculum was experiential, involving the student directly with the real world, and open ended, allowing freedom to explore areas of interest. The experimentalist teacher would probably say, "I teach children, not mathematics." The project as a method of teaching was supreme. In today's classrooms, teachers show the experimentalist influence in stressing problem solving over memorization, arranging field trips and hands-on experience, and teaching concepts through real-world situations.

PROGRESSIVE EDUCATION MOVEMENT    Dewey's thinking significantly influenced the formation in 1919 of the Progressive Education Association (PEA), which asserted that interest should be the motive of all work. Students should be self-governing, not subject to arbitrary law, and should have the freedom to develop naturally, they said. The school is a laboratory, the teacher a guide rather than a taskmaster. Values of the progressive education movement that endure in today's classrooms include student independence, self-expression, and self-governance, an enriched physical environment, and freedom of movement and access to materials.

TESTING MOVEMENT    From about 1933 to 1945, a mania for testing swept the nation's schools. Thousands of students nationwide were administered "standardized tests" of intelligence, aptitude, achievement, and a variety of skills. Predictably, PEA members criticized this movement for placing a false emphasis on accomplishments that could be objectively measured at the expense of less quantifiable educational values. The controversy still rages, with teachers expressing views such as these:

"I hate multiple-choice tests. They measure only memorized bits of information. My students do well on them but still don't understand the concepts."

"Some of my most well-adjusted kids score low on the aptitude tests."

"My students have got to do well on their ACTs or they can't get into college. Never mind how they do in life-adjustment classes. Unless they score high in math and science, there's not much hope."

"I purposely teach for tests. People who are in the business of making tests know what's important for students to learn at this age. So I coach my students on what they have to know."

Today, testing has become an integral (and more balanced) part of every educational program. More than 100 million standardized tests are administered annually in schools across the country. Increasingly, teachers also use their own tests to guide their development and presentation of lessons and their work with students.

*The aim of education should be to teach us rather how to think than what to
think, rather to improve our minds, so as to enable us to think for ourselves,
than to load the memory with the thought of other men.—James Beattie*

LIFE-ADJUSTMENT MOVEMENT   The experiences of the Great Depression in
the 1930s and World War II in the 1940s had their effect on education,
arousing interest in a "life-adjustment" curriculum—one that would help
students function in society. Social offerings such as dancing and peer-group
encounters began appearing in schools. Attention to issues of coping with
real-life problems, communication in relationships, and tolerance of differing values reflect the influence of this movement.

SPUTNIK   By the 1950s, Americans were becoming restless with life-adjustment curricula. Sagging test scores among high school graduates growing up
on life-centered courses initiated an era of reform. The gradual movement
toward "hard-headed" curricula got a shot in the arm when, in 1957, the
Soviets announced their successful launching of Sputnik, the first man-made
satellite. Deeply shocked at being caught napping in the race for space, the
United States rushed to overcome its technological deficit. For the first time,
the federal government stepped aggressively into public education and infused huge sums of money into curricular reform during the 1950s and
1960s. Resulting programs such as "the new math" changed both what and
how children learned. The research-based approach to teaching is a vigorous survivor of that era.

WAR ON POVERTY   In the 1960s and 1970s, many people took another look
at the nation's social needs and asked, "What good is it to send people to the
moon and neglect the poor and uneducated on earth?" This view found expression in the War on Poverty, which gave birth to projects Head Start and
Follow Through for disadvantaged children. Grant-in-aid programs began
appearing for handicapped, vocational, ethnic, and bilingual education.
Teachers committed themselves to subject matter that treated races equally,
to experiences aimed at reducing prejudice, and to units on minority cultures.
Demands for equality of educational opportunity heightened educators' sensitivity to discriminatory materials, content, practices, and policies. Lingering anxieties about these issues will be discussed in later chapters.

RELEVANCE   Concurrently, in the late 1960s and 1970s, a demand for relevance arose from reactions to the war in Vietnam. Why were we involved in
a lingering, debilitating conflict on the other side of the world, committing
lives and resources to a quarrel not even our own? Angry cries of irrele-
vance—why do this? who benefits?—generalized to other areas of American life, including education. Whereas voices had called earlier for a relevant
curriculum, now they called stridently for a relevant society: "Is it relevant?

If not, throw it out!" They now wanted to get rid of the school subject if it was not relevant to the student's life. That is, they turned their guns on "irrelevant" educational subjects as well.

BEHAVIORAL OBJECTIVES   The same period gave birth to a behavioral objectives movement in education, aimed at replacing vague, general goals (for example, producing good citizens) with specific, measurable ones (for example, enabling the student to recite the major causes of the Civil War). Some teachers saw this trend as a long-overdue move toward greater accountability, and some objected that it defined success in terms of what could be measured while devaluing other qualitatively important learning, such as consideration for others. However, the tediousness of writing hundreds of detailed goals coupled with the lack of evidence that they produced better learning brought about widespread disenchantment with the approach by the early 1980s. A residue of the movement is apparent in efforts to define the intended purpose of lessons and to specify what students are expected to learn.

MASTERY LEARNING   Theoretically, if a teacher specifies learner outcomes and then provides relevant instruction, most students will achieve "mastery." Thus the behavioral objectives movement laid the groundwork for the mastery learning movement. Traditional wisdom says that about one-third of students will learn well, one-third will learn adequately, and one-third will fail or barely get by. In contrast, the mastery approach argued that upwards of 90 percent could learn successfully if certain conditions were met:

> If the students are normally distributed with respect to aptitude but the kind and quality of instruction and the amount of time available for learning are made appropriate to the characteristics and needs of *each* student, the majority of students may be expected to achieve mastery of the subject.[4]

Mastery learning, or at least the spirit behind it, can be readily observed in today's curricula and in teachers' comments:

"I want each of my students to perform to his or her fullest potential."

"Students shouldn't have to compete with each other, just with themselves."

"I can never bring myself to grade on a curve. If you tell students what you want them to do, and they do it, I feel obliged to give them all A's."

"If my students aren't learning, something's wrong with my instruction."

PROGRAMMED INSTRUCTION   Behavioral objectives and mastery learning provided the basis for modern programmed instruction. Simply stated, programmed instruction means arranging materials and the sequence of presentation so as to be optimally understandable to the reader.

Primitive teaching machines, developed as early as 1926, evolved by 1959 into "programmed" question-and-answer books. Eventually a large number of programmed texts in math and other subjects appeared on the market. They employed principles of learning that had been derived from a combination of animal and human experiments: small steps, immediate corrective feedback, and student-constructed responses.

INSTRUCTIONAL SCIENCE   The new interdisciplinary field of instructional science concerns itself with classroom applications of knowledge about how people learn. Sophisticated technology such as microcomputers and videodiscs are often enlisted to provide computer-aided instruction tailored to the subject matter and even adaptable to the needs of the individual class. The curriculum is affected too, as this sample of educational titles shows: *Instructional Technology, Electronic Learning, Teaching Computers to Teach, The Electronic Schoolhouse, What Curriculum for the Information Age?,* and *Instructional Design Theories and Models.*

COGNITIVE PSYCHOLOGY   Behavioral psychology's early influence on education has been replaced by more "cognitive" approaches. Cognitive psychologists have had profound effects on educators in reading, writing, and mathematics, which are now being seen more as thinking operations than as memory exercises. The field of cognitive psychology is helping to solve problems of student learning in the classroom, focusing on how people think and make decisions. It studies student problem solving, the kinds of conceptual errors students make, how they use symbols, the relationship between their thinking and their motivation, and sex and age differences in thinking. Research also explores how people learn to read and solve math problems, how they learn to learn, and how they memorize.

BACK TO BASICS   The "back to basics" movement emerged in partial response to high school students' declining scores on college entrance exams from the 1960s into the mid-1970s. This educational reform movement emphasized a return to math, science, reading, and other traditional disciplines. In 1983 the National Commission on Excellence in Education produced the report *A Nation at Risk.* This is a sample of its findings:

- Average achievement of high-school students on most standardized tests is now lower than twenty-six years ago when Sputnik was launched.

- The College Board's Scholastic Aptitude Tests (SAT) demonstrate a virtually unbroken decline from 1963 to 1980. Average verbal scores fell over fifty points and average mathematics scores dropped nearly forty points.

- Many seventeen-year-olds do not possess the "higher order" intellectual skills we should expect of them. Nearly forty percent cannot draw inferences from written material; only one-fifth can write a persuasive essay; and only one-third can solve a mathematics problem requiring several steps.[5]

In the wake of the report, a spate of national committees have met to confer, review, and make recommendations for educational reforms, and a wave of similar activity at the state and local levels has brought pressure for specific reforms. On the basis of first-hand observations and others' testimony, then—U.S. Secretary of Education William J. Bennett issued the 1986 report *First Lessons: A Report on Elementary Education in America,* which included the following recommendations for elementary schools:

- Every elementary school can and must teach all its students to read.
- Children should learn that writing is more than filling in blanks. Writing must be part of the whole curriculum, not just language arts.
- Mathematics should extend beyond simple computation and should emphasize problem solving.
- Children should gain a basic grasp of the uses and limitations of computers.[6]

# CURRENT TRENDS IN TEACHER EDUCATION PROGRAMS

Where is teacher education headed? Because of the pluralistic nature of our society, future programs will place greater stress on multicultural training for the new teacher. Likewise, increased sensitivity to the lifestyles and values of culturally different students will be essential. Teachers will undergo more careful training in recognizing and setting aside their own prejudices, in respecting values different from their own, and in communicating with students of differing backgrounds. Also, with greater numbers of bilingual students in the schools (those who speak one language in their homes and another at school), teachers will require at least some training in a second language.

Handicapped, learning disabled, gifted, and exceptionally slow learners are being integrated into regular classrooms. Being sensitive to this influx, future teachers will enter the schools prepared and confident to work with exceptional students.

The inevitable presence of computers in classrooms compels teachers to broaden their technological training. Teachers will need to be computer literate. At best, they will maximize the computer's ability to assist the learner in reading, writing, and problem-solving development. Administratively, teachers will use computers for testing, record keeping, and communicating with parents.

National studies reveal unrest and disruption in the nation's classrooms. Teachers can look forward to increased training in managing classrooms and disruptive behavior.

Increasing students' reading and comprehension skills is a national obsession. As the insistence on greater literacy escalates, national attention turns to the teacher, the one person most responsible for teaching students to read and write. Teachers' increased accountability for successful teaching shows itself in national teacher examinations administered to practicing teachers—exams designed to measure teaching competency. Although problems surround the construction, use, and interpretation of these exams, they do reflect a national commitment to ensuring strong reading and communications skills among teachers.

Training teachers to be "reflective practitioners" continues as a major thrust in training institutions. For generations, teacher education has focused on providing recipes for teaching; for instance, how to create a lesson plan, organize a classroom, ask questions, teach reading, and review newly learned material. These specific skills will always be taught and remain important. But now colleges of education are also training young teachers to be "reflective," to take time to think about teaching episodes just completed, to analyze what they did and how it affected student learning. Thus, teachers will become more efficient as learners, as career-long students of their craft.

Prestigious committees have met, continue to meet, and continue to urge reforms in teacher education. In 1983, the Holmes Group (an association of university deans) gathered to discuss plans for raising the standard of teacher education at their respective universities. A number of decisive goals grew out of the deliberations:

1. to ensure that teachers go into their classrooms with a better command of the subjects they will teach

2. to recognize differences in teachers' knowledge, skill, and commitment and distinguish between novices and professional leaders

3. to institute tougher standards for students entering teacher education

4. to make greater use of expert teachers in the training process

5. to create a better climate for teachers to learn in once they are in the schools.

Nearly one hundred institutions across the country have joined the Holmes Group crusade in the upgrading of teacher education programs.[7]

In 1986, a national task force on teaching as a profession produced a report titled *A Nation Prepared: Teachers for the 21st Century*. The task force called for "a profession of well-educated teachers prepared to assume new powers and responsibilities to redesign schools for the future."[8] Among its recommendations were the creation of a national board to certify teachers and establish high standards, the requirement of a bachelor's degree in the arts and sciences as a prerequisite for the teacher preparation program, and the preparation of more minority group teachers. These two reports, along with many others, portend a radical overhaul of teacher education.

# YOUR CHALLENGE

Your teacher education program has been forged by historical trends, social forces, educational movements, major events, and people. The result encompasses a set of beliefs about and standards for what teachers ought to know and be able to do in their classrooms. Prospective teachers complete a broad general education program with exposure to educational philosophies, learning theories, the history of education, and human development. Practical applications include early experience working with students in classrooms and culminate with student teaching. Reflective practice makes teacher education an ongoing process.

Although teacher education has been sculpted by many movements and people, there is a tradition and sameness from year to year: general methods precede special methods; pedagogy follows foundations; practice teaching is the apex. But change is brewing. Gradual reform has characterized teacher education throughout history; but we now are on the brink of a sweeping redesign. In the near future, teachers-to-be may be required to complete a full college education before entering a teacher education program; new graduates will have to be strikingly better qualified as they walk into classrooms; teacher licensing requirements will be similar to bar exams for lawyers and national boards for doctors.

How will these reforms affect you? Your own program may very well depart from the traditional program introduced in this chapter in ways intended to further these new goals. Further, in the classroom, your successful performance will require a deep and continuously updated knowledge of subject matter and social skills, an ability to transform that knowledge into learner-usable knowledge, and great skill in facilitating the student's learning of that knowledge. The challenge is before you.

# YOUR FIRST YEAR OF TEACHING

Ready to start your first teaching position, all your preparation behind you, you stand on a threshold, anxious, excited, and hopeful. We know the realities you will face, both welcome and unwelcome, and we will tell you about them as plainly as possible. Remember, though— it's not just your first-year experiences but *how you see them* that will significantly influence your entire teaching career.

## Stepping into the Realities of Teaching

It's normal to set out with high hopes, realistic or not. You go into your first classroom with expectations of doing well, with strong visions of the impact you will have on the lives of students. This is as it should be. Do let those dreams guide you, at least for the first day, if not for your whole career. Experience will tell you which to abandon or modify and which are beacons to steer by. Here is one teacher's unbridled expectation:

> I will be able to reach all students; I will not be boring like many of my own teachers; I will be a friend to and like all my students; my own enthusiasm for my subject will be contagious to students; students will be motivated by good

© Erika Stone 1986/Photo Researchers, Inc.

lessons; all kids are reachable; students will appreciate and recognize my extra work and efforts; students will like and respect me.[9]

Your new role may take you away from everything that's known and familiar, leaving questions in its place. Enthusiastic and nervous, you report for your first teacher orientation before school opens, expecting it to answer some of them—and maybe it doesn't. The administrators may concentrate on making sure each new teacher knows policies and procedures, whereas you are anticipating learning about your specific teaching responsibilities. Suddenly it's all up to you.

Keep your head—don't panic. People do survive it, and your colleagues can help. How you move through the first weeks of teaching and through your first complete year strongly affects your development as a teacher. Indeed, your adjustment during the first year will largely determine whether you will continue teaching. Getting off to a good start is imperative.

Both teachers and observers have described the first day and week and year as exciting, exhausting, frustrating, completely involving, satisfying, emotionally draining, and an emotional roller coaster. For many new teachers, the upheaval of this period is compounded by the culture shock of teaching in a community that is drastically different from their own background. And all may be floored by the amount and kind of paperwork and adminis-

*We must take every possible step to ensure that new teachers are successful
right from the beginning of their careers. To cope is not enough. Poor
attitudes and questionable practices acquired during the first years are habits
that are difficult to break. To discourage potentially gifted teachers because
they are unprepared and unsupported during their initial year is a grave loss
to our schools.—Kevin Ryan*

trative responsibility expected, from absence reports and schedule cards to
locker assignments and lost kids.

This initial chaos notwithstanding, most teachers anticipate a successful year and, indeed, a satisfying career. Feel the realistic optimism of this
teacher:

> It is working! My dreams are coming true. I found a teaching job and it's going
> well. Not perfectly, but well. I say things and they listen. I tell them to do
> things and they do them. I assign homework and it gets done. I ask them to
> stop talking or to lower their voices and they actually do it. Or at least most of
> them usually do it. I feel like I am becoming an adult, like I am taking my place
> in society. And after all the schooling and all the worries and dreaming, it feels
> good.[10]

## Clearing the Hurdles

MULTIPLE ROLES   Teachers are required to wear many hats, more by far
than they have been prepared for or have anticipated: counselor, comforter,
accountant, historian, police officer, legal interpreter, custodian, and lob-
byist, to name a few.

For some sixteen years you have assumed the role of student. From
that vantage point you have observed many teachers. Some have affected
your life greatly, and others have gone virtually unnoticed. Perhaps one or
two have even impeded your growth. Indeed, you are well acquainted with
the life of a teacher—from a student's point of view. Now, overnight, *you*
become the teacher! You have prepared yourself for the role, but never have
you been completely on your own in fulfilling it—at least not for an entire
year. Now, standing in front of your own class for the first time, you are
overwhelmed by the students' learning needs and your inadequacies. In addition, you have lunchroom duty, sponsorship of the drill team, foreign language committee work—and you also usher at basketball games. Your role
is awesome, draining.

Unlike medicine, law, and other fields, teaching has virtually no apprenticeship period, no gradual working into the profession, no step-by-step
shouldering of responsibility. As a new teacher, you carry the same teaching
load as a twenty-year veteran. With a few helpful though meager suggestions, you are left to your own resources. Consider the burden this new
teacher felt:

Not only am I asked to diagnose and deal with learning disabilities, but parents expect and need me to provide much more than math and science. We have a lot of single parents in our school and they seem to need and want support. . . . I don't know if it's appropriate for me to give advice and sometimes I don't feel like I have the knowledge or experience.[11]

HANDLING PAPERWORK    A teacher must be meticulous in record keeping. This responsibility is challenging because it is unexpected, comes without training, and is downright tedious, even on a computer. Daily you face a multitude of record-keeping projects. You record student homework, test scores, reading assignments, unit progress, report cards, tardiness, attendance, and locker assignments. Additionally, you are responsible for school lunch reports, district in-service reports, and responses to requests from the principal and the district, as well as for communicating with parents.

## The Hiring of a Teacher

Herman Krusi, who became Pestalozzi's main assistant, gives an account of his entrance into teaching in 1793:

Since my leaving the day school, where I had learned and practiced only reading, learning by rote, and mechanical copying, and while I was growing up to adult age, I had so far forgotten to write that I no longer knew how to make all the capital letters; my friend Sonderegger therefore procured me a copy from a teacher Altstattinn, well known as a writing master. This single copy I wrote over as often as a hundred times, for the sake of improving my handwriting. I had no other special preparation for the profession, but notwithstanding, I ventured, when the notice was given from the pulpit, to offer myself as a candidate for the place, with but small hopes of obtaining it, but consoling myself with the thought that at least I should come off without shame.

The day of examination came. An elder fellow-candidate was first called before the committee. To read a chapter in the new Testament and to write a few lines, occupied him a full quarter of an hour. My turn now came. The genealogical register, from Adam to Abraham, from the first book of Chronicles, was given me to read. After this, chairman Schlapfer gave me an uncut quill, with the direction to write a few lines. "What shall I write?" I said. "Write the Lord's Prayer, or whatever you like," was the answer. As I had no knowledge of composition or spelling, it may be imagined how my writing looked. However, I was told to retire. After a short consideration, I was to my wonder and pride, recalled into the room. Here chairman Schlapfer informed me that the whole committee were of the opinion that both candidates knew little; that the other was best in reading, and I in writing.

The other, however, being over forty years old, and I only eighteen, they had come to the conclusion that I should learn what was necessary sooner than he, and as moreover my dwelling-house (the commune had then no school-house of their own) was better adapted for a school-house than his, I should receive the appointment. I was dismissed with friendly advice, and encouraging hopes of increased pay, if my exertions should be satisfactory.

E. P. Cubberley, *Readings in the History of Education* (New York: Houghton Mifflin, 1920), pp. 372–374.

*I did not know the role I haphazardly tried to play. I had known tyrant-
teachers and pushovers, bright ones and ignorant ones; but I had not known
them as colleagues. I had known mischievous students and helpful ones,
vicious ones and apple-polishers, but I had not known them as students in a
class I was supposed to teach. In short, I saw strange faces because I looked
out through the strangely new eyes of a teacher.—A first-year teacher*

**SCRAMBLING TO BE PREPARED**   No other part of a new teacher's life is so
hectic and pressure filled as having to stand in front of a class—always prepared. Generally, you will start from scratch, developing your units for the
first time: concepts to be presented, sequencing of material, examples, visual
aids, seatwork assignments, practice exercises, homework. Meeting daily
deadlines is a rigorous activity for the most seasoned teacher; it may seem

*© Alan Carey/The Image Works*

impossible to the newcomer. Think about this sample of suggestions for the first week of school:

- Prepare an outline of the units you will be teaching each semester.
- Closely examine the first few lessons in each manual so that you will be well prepared at the beginning of the year.
- Lesson plans and activities: overplan. Too much is better than not enough.
- Prepare all bulletin boards so they are in season and attractive.
- Have on hand plenty of simple get-acquainted activities for the first week of school.[12]

**FATIGUE** Fatigue is a powerful contributor to stress and anxiety. As more research is conducted on teacher stress, fatigue emerges as one of the chief culprits. In the past, we have become accustomed to thinking of anxiety and pressure as *causing* fatigue. But the opposite is also true, particularly for new teachers. Staying up late to prepare night after night, then weathering the exhausting rigors of a full day's teaching, leave a new teacher frayed and depleted. When teachers are physically worn down, and remain so over time, stresses from teaching are amplified, and coping becomes a major project. A good night's sleep changes a teacher's perception of what loomed the night before as a monumental preparation task. Sleep is the first activity sacrificed by a driven teacher. Note the wearing nature of fatigue:

> For the last hour of the school day, I drag myself around. I can hardly be civil to the students by the end of the day. Sometimes I have a headache and sometimes it is sheer exhaustion. And often both.
>
> I never realized the strain involved in having to manage all that activity, all that raw energy. I leave school every day and drive home and crawl into my apartment. All I can think of doing is sleeping. I promise myself I'll only take a nap, but I don't wake up until ten. Then it's a quick TV dinner and lesson plans until the early hours. I don't know how long I can keep this up![13]

**CLASSROOM DISCIPLINE** Classroom discipline ranks high on a new teacher's worry list. Being able to achieve and then maintain classroom control is a daily goal. Losing the class is a fearsome possibility for any teacher. Comments that begin, "Unless I can control my class and get them doing what I want them to do," are frequently heard among unseasoned teachers.

Effective discipline is fundamental in establishing a healthy relationship between teacher and student. The following example reveals a teacher's personal struggle within herself—momentarily withdrawing from her responsibility as teacher—as she encounters her first need to discipline:

> I was reading a story. A girl that is always out of the room came in late after lunch while I was reading. The kids started laughing, and I thought it was this one boy behind me, making faces. I turned around and immediately without asking questions first said, "Why are you doing . . . ?" He said, "I didn't do

*You get all these ideas in your head of what makes a good teacher and you try to be all of those things all of the time and you can't. And that's your mistake—you have to kick yourself once in a while to realize that you can't be this perfect person all the time, and yet at least with me I keep feeling that I have to be and that if I do anything less, the kids are missing something.*
—*A first-year teacher*

anything, it was Alicia." So I said, "Alicia, you go outside and try to come back in again—better yet, just stay in the hall and think about how you're supposed to walk into the room." She went outside. The door was open, and she said some things very angrily. I never heard exactly what she said, but I sort of did. I'm not insecure, but I was just like struck down dead. I could not come back from it. I just walked outside, and I couldn't even say anything to her. I just looked at her and I walked back into the room. I couldn't go on. I said to the kids, "Just take out a book and read, quietly." And the worst thing was they all yelled. "Yea!" So I felt worse. . . . I cried a little. But I just sat at my desk and read a book. It was so quiet in the class you could have heard a pin drop.[14]

**HAVING TO BRING ABOUT LEARNING**   Through her research years ago, Fuller identified a series of concerns that characterize stages of teaching.[15] Recent research has built on her foundation. She writes that the concerns of

*Spencer Grant/Photo Researchers, Inc.*

Paul Conklin/Monkmeyer Press Photo Service

teachers-to-be are unrelated to their teaching activities ("I'm concerned about getting a date for Saturday night."). As the new teacher matures, the concerns shift to the *task* of teaching ("I'm having to work late into the night to prepare my lesson plans for tomorrow."). Finally, concerns focus on the teacher's *impact* on students ("Are the kids learning what they need?").

There is an important difference between presenting a lesson (task concerns) and producing learning in students (impact concerns). With alarming frequency, teachers present lessons and then have students engage in activities, with little or no learning occurring. Presenting well-integrated lessons is rather easy; indeed, teachers are prone to judge their success by the elegance of a lesson, seducing them away from going after changes in students. They are content merely to have a nice, shiny preparation that produces no results. However, bringing about changes in learners is quite a different matter—a tougher task. Predictably, new teachers are high on task concerns, seasoned teachers on impact concerns. Through experience, new teachers come to distinguish the difference between going through the motions and bringing about learning.

NEW RELATIONSHIPS   Foundational to the role of teacher are productive relationships, a topic discussed in detail in Chapter 3. Suppose a new teacher came to his first teaching position carrying an overall college GPA of 3.8, straight A's in education classes, and a marvelous skill for planning and organizing instruction. Even with all this preparation, he would fail if he could not establish productive relationships with the key players in his teaching life: parents, other teachers, administrators, and students.

Parents are sources either of support or of fear and anxiety. New teachers face the challenge of developing helpful relationships with a variety of parent personalities, some enormously taxing:

> My first Parents' Night was going quite well. I was outlining the English curriculum we were following and there was a lot of head nodding, which I took as approval. When I started talking about the writing program, a man in the back started waving his hand. . . . He wanted to know why I don't teach grammar. I told him I did and I would continue to; and before I explained my approach to grammar, he started in on what he called "the new no-fault grammar being peddled today" and how it was rotting students' minds. He was quite impressive, except for the rather important fact that it had nothing to do with my class. I was shocked and, I guess, a little flustered. I started to answer him, but the passing bell rang and all the parents had to go to the auditorium for the principal's yearly talk. I just stood there with egg on my face as the parents filed out of the room, no one even making eye contact with me.[16]

Other teachers are your peers. Going into a new school, you are eager to make friends. You want to be accepted by colleagues and be seen as making a contribution. You desire to fit in to the culture. For their part, more experienced teachers want to help you learn the ropes. The last thing you want to endure is a personality clash! As a result, you put your best foot forward. You adjust gracefully to the copy-machine schedule, tough it out on the frozen playing field, and volunteer to bring doughnuts to faculty meetings. New teachers have a tendency to worry excessively about other teachers' perceptions of them, forever trying to be seen as "having it all together" and well on the road to success.

How well you get on with administrators is certainly a factor in your career. The principal nearly always stands ready to help make life in the school satisfying for the new teacher, orienting new teachers and running interference for them. Newcomers are grateful for the help. However, the relationship becomes strained when personalities and philosophies clash on such topics as dress policy, arrival and dismissal times, classroom budget, loudspeaker interruptions, and pull-out instruction in the computer lab. Frequently, new teachers become disenchanted when they acknowledge that their friend and confidant also wears another hat. The principal bears responsibility for evaluating a new teacher's performance, the amount of progress made by her students, and her contribution to the school's goals. This new teacher's belated recognition of her principal's role as evaluator came as a rude awakening:

> He was terrific to me, especially in the beginning. He went way out of his way to help me get settled in the community and to make me a part of the faculty. Probably because he reminded me so of my father, I started running to him every time the slightest thing went wrong. . . . He is very low key; and after each of the classroom observations he made, he told me that I needed to give more attention to math skills in my class. Well, I've always hated math and I

*I have come to a frightening conclusion. I am the decisive element in the classroom. It is my personal approach that creates the climate. It is my daily mood that makes the weather. As a teacher I possess tremendous power to make a child's life miserable or joyous. I can humiliate or humor, hurt or heal. In all situations it is my response that decides whether a crisis will be escalated or de-escalated, and a child humanized or dehumanized.*
—Haim Ginott

guess I thought I would play to my strength, reading. Finally in late April, he called me into his office and told me he could not recommend that the district renew my contract. I was thunderstruck. He said he had to have someone strong in math and he could not in good conscience recommend me. He told me about a summer course that turned out to be terrific, and he helped me get another job. Although it was painful, the experience really made me grow up. And it taught me a lot about school administration.[17]

Students are the key to any teacher's success. No other success by a teacher can compensate for failure to bring about student learning and growth. Students can be guided—boosted—in their learning by your efforts, they can be treated custodially, or they can be impeded. The emotional peaks and valleys in your teaching life are generally by-products of your success and failure in relating to students.

MISASSIGNMENT   The difficulties a new teacher encounters are inevitably compounded if that teacher is misassigned. Teachers are often asked to teach a subject for which they are not prepared, or to teach at an age level inappropriate to their strengths and personality. Research shows that about 12 percent of newly hired teachers are not certified in the fields to which they are assigned.[18]

The misassignment problem is compounded because teachers with the most experience are sometimes given easier assignments, leaving more difficult ones to inexperienced teachers. New teachers often have a larger number of preparations, heavy extracurricular assignments, and the responsibility of developing new courses outside their areas of interest.

Principals are aware of the struggles of their new teachers and try to ease them into the rigors of school life. Still, circumstances arise over which principals themselves have little control. When students' needs conflict with budget constraints, the principal may have no alternative but to assign teachers to subjects for which they have almost no preparation. Here is the report of one misassigned teacher:

I showed up the first day prepared to teach what the principal had assigned me—Spanish. But to my shock, I discovered they had assigned me two English classes as well! My minor was biology, not English. The current unit in English was on adverbs, so I taught adverbs. The trick was to stay a chapter ahead of the students.

*As there is contagion in the study of great teachers in action, there is also amusement and consolation in discovering that our anxieties are not unique.*—Houston Peterson

So how did I survive? Every night I would prepare five lessons: Spanish I, II, III, English 8, and 8R (remedial). A senior teacher befriended me at lunch, my only break. She identified with my plight and told me just to relax and enjoy teaching. Every day at lunch I would tell her my woes and she would encourage and teach me an easier way to do things. The English Department also decided to teach *Lord of the Flies* and show the movie of the book. Lo and behold, I had already read the book and seen the movie. I was saved in English![19]

A SENSE OF ISOLATION    The fanfare that attends being a new teacher, being formally oriented and made a fuss over, lasts but a short time. As the first months pass, new teachers experience a sense of isolation. The morning bell rings, and the door is closed in elementary, middle school, and high school classrooms. When the school day ends, the exhausted teacher opens the door and leaves the building. Throughout the day, scarcely any time has been devoted to chatting with another adult, either in casual conversation or in serious discussion of school-related matters. Day after day this experience of isolation continues, relieved only by fleeting exchanges in the oasis of the teachers' lounge. These interactions, brief as they are, serve an important socializing function. Yet they fall short of providing sustained work contacts necessary to break down prolonged feelings of isolation and seldom offer opportunities to solve teaching/learning problems. You should expect some feelings of isolation and prepare to deal with them. The challenge before you is to find valuable moments in which to socialize, to receive emotional support, and to be helped instructionally by your colleagues.

FEELINGS OF LACK OF CONTROL    Teachers in all stages of their careers have expressed a sense of lack of control over their teaching: Which students will I have in my class? What subjects will I be able to teach? How much freedom will I have in teaching them? What interruptions will I have to plan for? Will I have any say about when students are taken out of class for reading lab? Here are comments from exasperated teachers:

"Just because of RB 236, I'm required to teach an additional course in remedial math—this on top of my full load of algebra. That means I have to give up my college prep course I so dearly love!"

"The Special Ed teacher works three months with Dawn. Then he expects me to mainstream her. Well, she is still different from other students. I give her twice as much time as any other student! She still needs more help. It's just not fair."

"The district wants greater computer literacy. So every Monday and Wednesday I give up my kids for an hour in the computer lab. That means I'm cutting out two hours of reading every week!"

"My room is Grand Central Station! Kids are coming and going all day long. There's Workshop Way, computer lab, practice for the Christmas program, Spanish in the portable. What do I do?"

Although it is true that teachers may not enjoy the level of control they would like, they do have considerable freedom. This fact is well characterized by a teacher's militant reply when asked how much control she had: "Once I shut my door, I am in *complete* control."

## Fitting In

SOCIALIZATION   The terms *socialization* and *induction* are often applied to the first year of teaching. Essentially, socialization is a process the new teacher goes through, learning new behaviors, unlearning old ones, adjusting here, adapting there, becoming acclimated. You undergo these changes to meet the expectations present in the environment of your school, expectations you are anxious to fulfill. You walk into a culture made up of traditions, rules, and routine ways of doing things. By culture we mean ways of behaving in the school; rules, policies, and procedures a teacher must follow; expectations placed on the teacher by students, other teachers, and administrators in the school; and customs of the school. Your principal and colleagues, wanting you to start off on the right foot, convey messages that amount to "This is the way things are done in our school." After teaching for six months, teachers are able with hindsight to recognize this socialization process:

"I soon found out that faculty meetings are not the place to air gripes. It's in the privacy of the principal's office."

"The custodian, bless his heart, spent the first three weeks training me in how to take care of my room and get the equipment I want."

"I learned quickly that you don't talk about other teachers behind their backs!"

"It took me three weeks to figure out that you go to your chairman, not the principal, when you have a problem."

The success with which new teachers become socialized very much determines the success of their first year. But becoming socialized into your school culture (and the profession in general) is a complex operation. Conflicts arise and disillusionments occur. Let's take a closer look.

Considerable research shows that the school presses a new teacher to conform to a whole set of traditions and values. These are examples of those imperatives: maintain an orderly classroom, do not become emotional when handling disruptive students, do not get carried away in political movements, maintain dignified conduct when talking with parents, be conservative in expressing your opinions in the classroom, and conform to the school district policy on dress and grooming.

At the same time, you bring with you unformed values about teaching (probably a bucketful), opinions, indecisions, and curiosities. You have a set of lofty goals for your students; you want to be democratic in establishing classroom rules; you may believe in being liberal in what students can do in your classroom; and you have a list headed "Things I Want to Try."

Further, ample research suggests that during this socialization process, many teachers undergo a shift in their attitudes. They want to fit successfully into the school culture and are willing to be molded to the realities of teaching. As a result of adapting themselves to fit into the school's expectations, teachers sometimes experience disillusionment and a loss of idealism about what they can accomplish and what they desire to accomplish. For example, after a period of time, new teachers tend to adopt attitudes that are reversals of their original, more idealistic orientations. They become more impersonal with students; that is, they show less warmth and keep a greater social distance. They are less permissive in allowing students freedom to make decisions about their learning, such as choosing their own resource unit. And their classrooms become less democratic; that is, they allow less participation in rule making.

More recently, research has suggested that beginning teachers are not quite so "vulnerable and unformed" nor so readily "cajoled and molded into shapes within their schools" as has been believed. New teachers apparently *participate* in their own socialization process, changing the environment as well as being changed by it. For example, suppose you are a middle school counselor committed to early career counseling. Your school's curriculum has never included vocational counseling or community work experiences. During your first year, you persuade the principal to let you offer a class in career selection for seventh graders. However, he continues to insist that bona fide work experiences should be postponed until high school. The two of you enter into a give and take. He presses you to be more realistic: you can have your class, minus the community work experience. However, you are able to engage in one-on-one career counseling as part of the class. Changes have been made in both you and the school.

Be alerted. Know that whatever school you enter will expect you to act in certain ways. The reasons are your own survival, the welfare of your students, and the simple fact that "that's the way we do it." Be optimistic. Most of your colleagues will welcome your fresh ambitions, your unbounded enthusiasm, your desire to try out new approaches. Principals, teachers, and even parents can be persuaded.

INDUCTION   Educators have long understood the challenges facing new teachers. The work is hard, simultaneously disappointing and satisfying. Having gone through the same struggles, experienced teachers befriend their new young colleagues. Increasingly, this informal help is being augmented by formal teacher induction programs. Induction teams made up of a support teacher, the principal, and the beginning teacher work together to ease this transitional phase. These are areas in which you can receive start-up help:

1.  Classroom management. Are you having problems getting your class started, keeping students on task, offering suitable rewards (and penalties), maintaining a work atmosphere, or establishing routines?

2.  Organizing instruction. Are you able to present material clearly, in an organized fashion, using good examples?

3.  Time management. Do you have enough time to accomplish everything you have planned?

4.  Content knowledge. Do you have a firm grasp of the subject you are teaching?

5.  Relationships. Are you comfortable working with other teachers? with parents?

A new teacher participating in a school-based induction program might, for example, engage in a simulation activity two weeks before parent–teacher night. Playing the role of a parent, the support teacher approaches the teacher with a variety of parent questions and concerns. After each interchange, they discuss how the parent might react and then suggest alternative responses.

A teacher who had worked with a support team made this report: "I felt like the first day was a success. I was very pleased. All the preparation the school put me through really paid off. . . . I also consider myself very fortunate to be in a system that is so willing to help me." Speaking of her support teacher, she said, "I can go to her, I do go to her, with curriculum problems, with class management problems, with everything."[20]

# CONCLUSION

We hope you will develop an informed eagerness for teaching. Your first year of teaching will be filled with successes, failures, adjustments, learning, and unlearning. Your visions and hopes will be altered by the realities of classroom life. Some may be dashed, others strengthened. New goals will emerge. You will acquire patience with students and with yourself. You will know for sure what teaching is like—at least the first year of teaching. Reflecting on that first year, one teacher said, "If you lose your vision, then you have lost the game. You do get a little disillusioned. Your dreams come down to earth a little bit more. But if you can keep the vision, you have goals to shoot for."[21]

Is there more to be said about the first year of teaching? Yes. Many of your career-long habits will be established during this first year. Unformed values will take shape and firm up, and they will drive your teaching. You will sense how long your teaching career will be—one year, three to five years, a lifetime. You will realize that effective teaching results from deep preparation, patience, emerging commitments, and hard work. You will have had a chance to live on a teacher's salary and to have others see you as a professional teacher. Most important, you will have watched yourself performing as a teacher. One thing is certain: you will not look back on this year and say, "This has been an uneventful year of my life."

## Expansions

1. We assume you have made your decision to go into teaching, tentative though it may be. What aspects of teaching attract you, and what aspects hold you back?

2. Observe in one or two classrooms. Can you identify any practices engaged in by the teacher that have their roots in one or more of the movements and social forces described in this chapter?

3. One of the social movements discussed in the chapter was a cry for relevance. In your years as a student you must have formed opinions about the relevance of certain classes and topics. Think back to a class that was especially relevant for you and explain why it was so. Do the same for a class that seemed largely irrelevant. (Focus on the subject matter, not the teacher.)

4. You may have heard about and perhaps had experience with behavioral objectives. From your point of view, can you list some advantages and disadvantages of using them?

5. Think ahead to student teaching and working with a cooperating teacher. Can you think of any cautions you might give yourself as you go into this experience?

6. In the future, students may be required to earn a bachelor's degree prior to entering their teacher education program. Can you think of any advantages and disadvantages of doing this?

7. Describe the kind of relationship you would like to have with your students. Name one aspect of relating to students that you anticipate will be especially difficult.

8. Interview two experienced teachers. Find out some of the expectations they had as they went into teaching. Which expectations were modified and which were confirmed during the first year?

9. Write down some ways of relating to students that will get you off to a good start in your first classroom.

10. In this chapter we introduced you to some challenges facing beginning teachers: multiple roles, paperwork, lesson preparation, fatigue, dis-

cipline, task and impact concerns, relationships, misassignment, isolation, lack of control, and learning to fit in. Select three and describe why you suspect they will be especially challenging for you. Select three that will not be a particular challenge for you. Explain.

11. Describe several teaching values (for instance, importance of correctly done homework, good study habits) that you will carry into your first classroom. Which do you anticipate modifying over time? Explain.

12. Suppose your principal assigned you to a mentor teacher, a person responsible for showing you the ropes. How would you respond to such an arrangement?

## Notes

1. J. Lanier and J. W. Little, "Research on Teacher Education," in M. C. Wittrock (Ed.), *Handbook of Research on Teaching,* (3rd ed). (New York: Macmillan, 1986), pp. 527–569.

2. M. Greene, "Teaching: The Question of Personal Reality," in A. Lieberman and L. Miller (Eds.), *Staff Development: New Demands, New Realities, New Perspectives* (New York: Teachers College Press, Columbia University, 1979), pp. 27–28.

3. S. S. Cohen, *A History of Colonial Education: 1607–1776* (New York: Wiley, 1974); S. Cohen (Ed.), *Education in the United States: A Documentary History* (New York: Random House, 1974); D. R. Warren, "History of Education," in H. E. Mitzel (Ed.), *Encyclopedia of Educational Research,* 5th ed. (New York: Free Press, 1982), 2:808–817; M. L. Borrowman, "Liberal Education and the Professional Education of Teachers," in M. L. Borrowman (Ed.), *Teacher Education in America: A Documentary History* (New York: Teachers College Press, Columbia University, 1965), pp. 1–53.

4. B. S. Bloom, J. T. Hastings, and G. F. Madaus, *Handbook on Formative and Summative Evaluation of Student Learning* (New York: McGraw-Hill, 1971), p. 45.

5. National Commission on Excellence in Education, *A Nation at Risk: The Imperative for Educational Reform,* a report to the nation and the Secretary of Education (Washington, D. C.: U.S. Government Printing Office, 1983), pp. 8–9.

6. W. J. Bennett, *First Lessons: A Report on Elementary Education in America* (Washington, D.C.: U.S. Government Printing Office, 1986), p. 2.

7. Holmes Group, *Tomorrow's Teachers: A Report of The Holmes Group* (East Lansing, Mich.: The Holmes Group, Inc., 1986).

8. Carnegie Forum on Education and the Economy, *A Nation Prepared: Teachers for the 21st Century,* report of the Task Force on Teaching as a Profession (Hyattsville, Md.: Carnegie Forum on Education and the Economy, 1986), p. 2.

9. J. H. Childers, Jr., and R. S. Podemski, "Confronting Idealistic Teacher Expectations: Strategies for Training Programs and School Districts," *Teacher Educator* 18(3) (1982–1983), pp. 2–10.

10. K. Ryan, *The Induction of New Teachers* (Fastback 237) (Bloomington, Ind.: Phi Delta Kappa Educational Foundation, 1986), p. 13.

11.   M. M. Cohn, R. B. Kottkamp, and E. F. Provenz, Jr., (1987). *To Be a Teacher: Cases, Concepts, Observation Guides* (New York: Random House, 1987), p. 423.

12.   J. Clarkson and R. J. Blass, *First Year Elementary Teacher's Manual* (ERIC Document Reproduction Service No. ED 261–998, 1985).

13.   Ryan, *Induction*, p. 17.

14.   Cohn, Kottkamp, and Provenz, *To Be a Teacher*, p. 421.

15.   F. F. Fuller, "Concerns of Teachers: A Developmental Conceptualization," *American Educational Research Journal*, 6(2) (1969), pp. 207–226.

16.   Ryan, *Induction*, pp. 22–23.

17.   Ibid., p. 25.

18.   R. A. Roth, "Emergency Certificates, Misassignment of Teachers, and Other 'Dirty Little Secrets'" *Phi Delta Kappan* 67(10) (1986), pp. 725–727.

19.   From the journal of a first-year teacher (personal communication).

20.   L. Huling-Austin and E. T. Emmer, *First Days of School: A Good Beginning* (R & D Report No. 7206) ( Austin, Tex.: Research and Development Center for Teacher Education, The University of Texas at Austin, 1985).

21.   Cohn, Kottkamp, and Provenz, *To Be a Teacher*, p. 422.

# SECTION TWO

# THE WORKPLACE

# CHAPTER 2

# YOUR STUDENTS

*To be educated is to know what depths await us underneath the surface of things, whatever those things may be. To shield our children from life's inevitable perplexities is to leave them at the mercy of their ignorance and to deny them the wonder that is the basis of everything we know.—Donald W. Thomas*

**MAIN IDEAS**

- Knowing how students differ—and how best to accommodate those differences in your teaching—maximizes your ability to bring about student learning.

- You teach in a pluralistic classroom. Each student is unique. Each comes with his or her cultural background, home environment, race, religion, personality, temperament, and values.

- Despite this uniqueness, you discover similar patterns of behavior and personality, the knowledge of which facilitates your effectiveness with all your students.

- Subgroups of your students may include typical, latchkey, handicapped, gifted, bilingual, drug abuser, and unwed mother. Each poses a special challenge.

- Some differences among students markedly affect both their learning and your ability to help them learn.

- The home creates, then amplifies, differences among your students. These differences add variety, spice, and excitement to your teaching—and also vexation.

# INTRODUCTION

The doctor has patients, the lawyer has clients, and you, the teacher, have your students. Your fundamental purpose as a teacher is to bring about student learning and growth. All you do should contribute to this end. Nothing dilutes it. Decorating bulletin boards, taking students to a play, holding parent–teacher night, reading themes, attending high school pep rallies, going to faculty meetings, ordering supplies—these are all enabling activities, facilitating your central purpose. Recognizing this, you announce: "I am not a mere teacher; I am a professional committed to bringing about student learning and growth."

In this chapter we introduce you to your students. We invite you to think about two issues: how students differ and how their differences can best be accommodated in your teaching to maximize student learning.

In order to accommodate differences, you must come to know your students. Knowing them optimizes your ability to bring about their learning. Observe how one teacher blunted her ability to cultivate growth by not taking the time to know her students:

> Kathy, at rope's end, sat despairingly in Mr. Anderson's office. She was an intelligent, well-trained, and vigorously organized science teacher.
>
> "I'm a failure! I do all the right things: I plan interesting units, I work out details, I give lively presentations, I fill my lessons with good examples, I'm forever supportive, and I give challenging but certainly do-able homework. Yet my kids aren't learning science. They flunk the quizzes. They do poorly on homework. They sit and stare at me like I was from outer space. What's wrong?"
>
> Mr. Anderson responded confidently, "Well, you've told me a few things. Why don't I come into your class and observe? Something has to be wrong with what you're doing. What you're telling me doesn't make sense."
>
> On Thursday Mr. Anderson sat in on Kathy's intermediate science class. He jotted down notes during the period and invited Kathy to come to his office after school.
>
> "Bingo! It was clear in a minute. You're over their heads. You've got to appreciate something. These kids don't have the background to understand science the way you're teaching it. I don't think they lack motivation—they're trying to learn. But you're using words right out of your college textbooks. These kids are bailing out on you after the first five minutes. Take the unit you were discussing today. At one point I wrote down what you said: 'Students, you need to be forming hypotheses about how plant bacteria multiply in this hostile environment.' Well, these kids come from lower socioeconomic homes. You would never hear their parents talking about 'hypotheses' or 'bacteria.' They would say, 'The bugs grow.' Jaron asked what a hypothesis was. You said

something like, 'The definition is right there in your book on page 49.' You might have said, 'Good question. Hypotheses are guesses. Guess what you will be having for supper tonight.' You need to talk their language. These kids understand guesses and supper and bugs, but not what you're telling them. If you understood them better, you could really facilitate their learning."

Kathy had the desire and preparation, but insufficient knowledge of her students. Had she known them—their home life, their out-of-school interests, their reading levels and habits, their casual conversations—she would not have missed the mark.

# THE ENORMOUS VARIETY

We live in a pluralistic society. Your students represent different homes, socioeconomic levels, cultures, races, and religions. Here is a glimpse of the variety found in a small northern California city:

Adjacent to the library bins were shelves in which the children's writing portfolios were kept, filed and labeled alphabetically by first name, and accessible to the children. I asked about the names that seemed strange to me. As she translated names into descriptions of children, I understood that to Naomi [their teacher] these small people were a dramatic cast of characters. "Mah-

© *Elizabeth Crews/The Image Works*

soud is Iranian. Vu is Chinese from Vietnam. Kori is black. James is Russian/ Romanian—when he came to kindergarten, English was his fourth language. Teha—fascinating child transferred from a Catholic school: she reads like an adult, but mechanically, understanding nothing. Reiko—Japanese—her father a microbiologist visiting the university. She is my disaster of the week. I'm just furious because she broke her arm on the playground, and the children didn't report it, and she didn't complain, so none of the adults knew about it until I noticed that she was writing and holding her arm funny." Naomi was dismayed by this incident, not only because of the child's pain and the school's liability but because she realized that her careful instruction to the children to watch out for each other had not met this test. Yet she understood that the lapse was explainable in terms of cultural diversity: the American girls were fooled by the stoicism that Reiko's family had taught her.[1]

Mrs. Schultz, a fifth-grade teacher from Anywhere, U.S.A., introduces you to a few of her students:

Predictably, Elijah will be at my desk the minute seatwork begins. I'll have to explain all over again what I have just said, then allow him to ask more questions—until he understands.

Rosemary is tense and aggressive. She forges into the assignment before I finish giving directions. She's swift and sure of herself. She never asks for help, zips through her work, and is off reading a book before the rest of the class is half finished.

Eric dawdles. Other students are well into their work before he opens his book. He writes his name, plugs through the first exercise, then pops up for a drink or to sharpen a pencil.

Sherry is erratic. One day she plunges in and finishes off the assignment well ahead of the class, and everything is done correctly. The next day she daydreams, unaware of my instructions. When I tell her to get on with the assignment, I'm confronted with a blank stare.

Rachel is a dream. She follows directions, works independently, stays on task, and is very accurate. She is neat but not overly fast. She learns from her mistakes.

Mr. O'Brian, a high school teacher from Anywhere, U.S.A., introduces you to Miguel, a "typical" senior at Adams High:

Sports are his passion, especially baseball. After-school practice and his computer software job take up much of his time. College looms on the horizon, but sports, dating, and earning money are in the foreground. Schoolwork is important to him, mainly because getting a good job or going to college depends on high school graduation. Still, he horses around, skips classes, dashes off assignments, crams for tests, and nurses a B average.

Miguel relates to all but two of our teachers, is well liked, and is sensitive to differences among other students at the school. He likes causes: donating blood, gathering food for Third World countries, registering voters. His moods are uneven, as are his turned-in assignments, best characterized as "just-getting-

*A classroom with different types of students can be a very important social
setting for learning lifelong lessons.—Virginia Richardson-Koehler*

by" efforts. Still, his intentions are to do well in school. Most of the time he is
cheerful, though occasionally sullen and depressed.

Finally, we introduce you to several students—special students—who
are interesting to us and, we hope, to you. Let them represent the great variety of students to be found in your classroom over the years.

## A Latchkey Student

Carrie, a fourth-grader, lives in a small apartment with her mother and teenage brother. Two years ago her parents were divorced, and each summer she
spends two weeks with her father, who lives in upstate New York. Her
mother, an executive secretary in a Philadelphia brokerage firm, seldom arrives home before 6:00 P.M. Carrie comes home at 3:30 P.M. to an empty
apartment. With her brother working and only teenagers in the neighborhood, Carrie either turns on TV or watches the afternoon's events unfolding
on her block. Her one close friend, Emily, lives two miles away. Mother arrives home exhausted. The family eats dinner in front of the evening's TV
shows. After three hours of television viewing, Carrie is too tired to work on
tomorrow's math assignment, and both she and her mother turn in.
At school Carrie is a loner. She seldom participates in playground activities, but seems content to watch from the sidelines. Though she yearns
for close friends, a lack of confidence prevents her from cultivating associations. She seldom reads at home, a fact that would help explain below-average reading skills. Her grades are low. She daydreams a great deal and
fails to hand in assignments on a regular basis. Carrie is anxious about the
fact that she is below average in her schoolwork. Lately, she has become
compulsive about neatness and, as a result, works painfully slowly, thus
compounding her problems. The teacher asks Carrie's mother if she can
spend more time working with Carrie. At each conference, commitments are
made, but they are soon forgotten.
Over the year, Carrie has become increasingly fearful about going
home to an empty apartment. She fears that someone will break in and kidnap her or that her mother will fall victim to an accident and not come home.

## A Learning-Disabled Student

Melanie is in third grade at Rock Park Elementary. Her work in math is
average, but in reading she stumbles over words, unable to pronounce or
recognize them. Having an unusually short attention span, she can hardly
handle seatwork assignments. Her gaze shifts from one scene to another and

she fidgets constantly. She is clumsy, dropping books and pencils and bumping into desks and people. On the playground she catches the kickball with her entire body. Attempts to run and jump reveal a distinct lack of coordination.

Melanie is easily discouraged and cries when she is unable to do a project such as cutting out patterns. Her memory is short, and relearning is an uphill effort. Letters and words are reversed: *p*'s become *b*'s, and "was" becomes "saw." She appears not to hear directions and makes mistakes in following them. When going to the library or bathroom, she is often disoriented and heads in the wrong direction.

## A Gifted Student

Marcel acts much older than his sixth-grade peers. Breezing through assignments, he is irritated with their simplicity. Thank heaven for the freedom to read while waiting for others to finish. Science fiction is a release from daily boredom. Marcel attacks work with a vengeance. He has an unquenchable thirst for learning and reads voraciously on all subjects. He plays the piano, collects snakes, and is on a neighborhood soccer team.

Mr. Barth is reading *David Copperfield* to the class. Marcel seizes details quickly, comments insightfully on themes, and is able to identify metaphors. He does not hesitate to voice an opinion and aggressively asks questions.

## A Socially Aggressive Student

Curtis is a Lakeridge seventh-grader whose reputation in elementary school has preceded him. He bullies one day and is aloof and withdrawn the next. Around girls he is verbally abusive, hurling insults spiced with vulgarities. His classroom behavior is best described as defiant, and his I-dare-you attitude in the principal's office is a source of constant concern. On occasion Curtis steals money from other students' desks and even from his teacher's purse. Curtis's parents are called repeatedly. Willing to help but feeling a loss of control, the mother and father turn the problem back to the teacher. Curtis resents his father, a cold-natured person who shows little affection for or involvement with his son. The mother is a patsy for Curtis's every whim.

The teacher and principal are on guard, taking decisive action each time he launches himself on a disruptive course of action. His behavior consumes large amounts of the energy of those who have to cope with it. Curtis's homework assignments, when handed in, are done hastily and superficially. Test scores reflect a serious lack of learning. He enjoys art. The themes in his drawings seethe with hostility. Allowing him into the library is like letting a wolf into the chicken coop. He refuses to settle into an activity, interferes with the work of others, defaces books, and feuds with the librarian.

## A Multicultural Student

Lu is an eighth-grader. Two years ago his family arrived from Laos. He is learning English at a snail's pace, and his written assignments are well below average for the class. In math his aptitude is high and his work is near the top of the class. Lu is nervous and shy, even though befriended by other students. When called upon in class, he responds with difficulty and embarrassment. Once in a while, a muffled wisecrack follows his stammering recitation. Reddening, Lu sinks into his seat and stares at the floor. In all subjects, there is a childlike freshness about his desire to learn, but the progress is slow. Mrs. Kubalski gives him more time than she can spare.

## A Drug Abuser

Mark is in his first year at Jefferson High. He was a high achiever in elementary and junior high. He enjoyed being around friends of both sexes. Over several months in junior high he was introduced to alcohol and marijuana. By the end of that school year he was using marijuana two or three times a week. In high school, some friends introduced him to cocaine. After a month of regular use, Mark became dependent on the drug.

His behavior at school changed, leaving him irritable and withdrawn. Formerly close friends were bothersome and noisy. Mark now sits in the back of the room, avoids people in the halls, and skips classes. When he is there, he never participates in discussions and avoids teacher questions. When called on, he apologizes for being unprepared and becomes irritable when the teacher persists. Frequently he slips out to the restroom and to the water fountain. There are physical symptoms: watery eyes, a distant gaze, perspiration, and an inability to sit still and focus on events in class.

Ms. Baines, one of Mark's teachers, confronts him about his poor performance. Mark instantly rationalizes: "My job takes all my study time. I'm worn out by the time I get home and can't sleep." A phone call to Mark's parents confirms all suspicions. "Yes, he's on drugs. We can't get him to talk about it, nor will he see the doctor. His boss called and asked why he wasn't coming in. Mark's excuse was an ulcer. But he doesn't have an ulcer."

## An Unwed Mother

Tiffany, a junior at Triad High, became pregnant last spring. She confided in her mother and best friend at the time. As her figure began to change, she had to tell others. They rallied to her support. Understanding teachers allowed her extra time to complete assignments. Friends continued to include her in social activities. John, the father of the baby, transferred to another high school, and other boys, though friendly, felt it inappropriate to ask her out. Even though Tiffany anticipated a decline in her social life, she was surprised at her loneliness. This loneliness, plus a growing sense of the responsibilities of motherhood, brought on feelings of depression. Tiffany has become confused about her identity. She is pregnant but not married; she is a student but must soon become a breadwinner.

Tiffany's parents are totally supportive. While her mother cares for the baby, she can either go to work or complete her schooling, or both. Despite this assurance, Tiffany feels a growing resentment toward John, who is now out of her life: "Why won't he come back and help take care of the baby? I have to spend my last year of high school cooped up—no parties, no dates, nothing." These intrusive realities dissolve any remaining commitment Tiffany feels toward school. Her attendance is spotty. Assignments are turned in incomplete; some are not turned in at all. Her test scores decline and grades sag. The teachers, though sympathetic, feel helpless.

# UNDERSTANDING STUDENTS

We have portrayed a sample of individual students. Each can represent a general category of students about which considerable knowledge is available. We offer a brief overview of several categories.

## "Typical" Students

In actuality, there are no typical students. Each student brings his or her own personality, temperament, and ability level into your classroom. Each has a unique history, family background, and set of cultural values. Still, regular patterns of behavior and personality are found in the great majority of students.

As children mature in kindergarten through high school, they exhibit an increasing richness in their use of symbols, concepts, and rules, leading to greater comprehension and retention. They form hypotheses to solve problems, become more aware of their own thoughts, and show increased flexibility in thinking. Older students think abstractly, process information rapidly, minimize distractions, and discard ineffective solutions. They work for best solutions and try to avoid error. Young children enjoy pleasing the teacher, to whom they turn for attention, directions, and assistance. Older students are interested in pleasing peers and meeting their expectations. Students during middle childhood avoid close interaction with peers of the opposite sex, but this state of affairs reverses itself convincingly in later years.

During the elementary years students move from a posture of self-centeredness to one of give and take among peers. Middle childhood is a critical stage for development of conscience. Adolescence is a period of intense introspection in which youngsters spend considerable time contemplating themselves and their friends. Teenagers look to friends as a source of standards and values.

You can apply the literature in human development to your lesson plans, always keeping the emotional, social, and other needs of your learners clearly before you. For example, in the cognitive area, you bear in mind that young children have short attention spans and think in concrete terms; therefore you keep your lessons short and filled with concrete illustrations. Older students can be presented with abstract concepts, longer assignments, complex choices, and more extended periods of independent work.

## Latchkey Students

So-called latchkey children are regularly left unattended or are watched over by an underage child. Most often, the parents work and the child is left unsupervised through the afternoon and perhaps the evening hours. Latchkey children generally care for themselves, play outside, stay home alone, join a gang, or engage in time-filling activities until parents return home. The number of latchkey children is increasing in schools across the country. Studies have shown that these children have a greater chance than others of becoming maladjusted, getting involved with drugs, being sexually abused, and experiencing learning problems in school.

## Handicapped Students

A handicap is any permanent physical or mental condition that inhibits the normal functioning of a student. Twelve to fifteen percent of the students in schools across the country have been diagnosed as handicapped. Going on the national average, you can expect two handicapped students in your class at any given time.

*Peter Vandermark/Stock, Boston*

The most comprehensive legislation for handicapped students is Public Law 94-142, which mandates that handicapped students be identified and educated to foster maximum personal and social growth in the least restrictive environment. The least restrictive environment, the law stipulates, is the regular classroom, unless professionals and parents judge otherwise. The law defines "handicapped children" as those who are mentally retarded, hard of hearing, deaf, speech impaired, visually handicapped, seriously emotionally disturbed, orthopedically impaired, deaf–blind, multihandicapped, or otherwise health impaired. We will revisit Public Law 94–142, with its update and legal implications, in later chapters.

You may have in your classroom an orthopedically impaired student who has a clubfoot, muscular dystrophy, or an amputated limb. Slow and mentally retarded learners will be in your class from time to time. They tend to manifest short attention spans, limited ability to process ideas, difficulty in dealing with abstractions, a tendency to forget recently learned material, and low self-concepts.

Hard-of-hearing students, deaf students, and speech-impaired students have difficulty pronouncing words accurately, or they stutter or speak in a halting manner. Blind or visually handicapped students usually squint at the chalkboard, hold books close to or far from their eyes, hold their heads at odd angles, and show unusual sensitivity to light.

Learning-disabled students have difficulties in speaking, writing, or reading. Problems vary from child to child but include inability to separate figure and ground, jumping over words, skipping lines in a paragraph, and failing to focus on a single object in a group of objects. These children do not sequence a story properly, reverse letters and words, and readily forget simple information. Their attention spans are short, they are easily distracted, and they become confused when asked a direct question.

Standing back, you will discover that handicapped children can add a special dimension to your classroom. More similarities than differences exist between these children and your other students. Modern teachers are not setting these students apart in any discriminatory way. They continue to teach in a normal fashion while marshalling resources for extra help and attention.

## Gifted Students

Traditionally, "giftedness" has been defined as possessing high intellectual ability as measured on standardized intelligence tests. Gifted students have exceptional retention in long- and short-term memory. They are quick to pick out similarities and differences and identify cause-and-effect relationships. They reason abstractly, understand complex concepts, learn new information rapidly, and separate relevant from irrelevant information. Gifted students are highly creative, widely read, and insatiably interested in the world and events around them. They pursue hobbies and well-defined interests with considerable intensity. They may be talented in music or art, or

© *David Grossman/Photo Researchers, Inc.*

show extraordinary ability in math, science, or gymnastics. Among the gifted, one finds students who are highly motivated to try new endeavors, tend to be altruistic (showing unusual sensitivity to the needs of others), possess boundless energy, relate easily to adults, and are intensely curious, well organized, and goal directed.

Gifted students bring to your classroom unique challenges and rewards. They challenge you to be well prepared, to think carefully and deeply about your subject. They question your understandings and opinions. Their keen powers of observation pick up inconsistencies and irrelevancies, and they contribute new insights during your presentations. You are prepared to offer special opportunities to your gifted and talented students. For example, you provide an expansion unit in anthropology, additional readings about *King Lear,* a research report on laser technology, and additional assignments in the computer lab.

## Multicultural Students

A wide variety of cultural and language groups enrich the fabric of the United States. In the mid-1980s the composition of sixty-four high schools in the Los Angeles area attested to this variety: 41 percent Hispanic, 29 percent white, 16 percent black, and 11 percent Asian. Other areas show similar diversity: in Dade County, Florida, 27 percent white, 32 percent black,

*Alan Carey/The Image Works*

47 percent Hispanic, and 1 percent Native American; in New Mexico: 47 percent Anglo, 41 percent Hispanic, and 9 percent Native American.

What is it like for the minority child who comes into your classroom? Joseph H. Suina, a Native American, reminisces on differences between his home and school:

> The winter months are among my fondest recollections. A warm fire crackled and danced brightly in the fireplace and the aroma of delicious stew filled our one-room house. To me the house was just right. The thick adobe walls wrapped around the two of us protectingly during the long, freezing nights. Grandmother's affection completed the warmth and security I will always remember. . . . Her shower of praises made me feel like the Indian Superman of all times. At age five, I suppose I was as close to that concept of myself as anyone. . . .
>
> And then I went to school. . . .The classroom . . . had its odd characteristics. It was terribly huge and smelled of medicine like the village clinic I feared so much. The walls and ceiling . . . were too far from me and I felt naked. The fluorescent light tubes were eerie and blinked suspiciously above me. . . .
>
> School was a painful experience during those early years. The English language and the new set of values caused me much anxiety and embarrassment.[2]

*Recent interest in ethnic and cultural differences suggests that multiculturalism is a new phenomenon in this country. However, the United States has been a multicultural country from its beginnings. Many believe that it is precisely this variety that gives the country its strength and vitality.—Ursula Casanova*

You are likely to stumble once in a while in developing an awareness of cultural differences. Miss Tanner affectionately pats Mi-Li on her head. But Mi-Li has been taught that her head is sacred and must not be touched. Despite Miss Tanner's good intentions, "cultural dissonance" is created. Had she known about Mi-Li's culture, this dissonance could have been avoided.

José-Angel consistently comes late to school and seems to take forever to complete his work. Mr. Markel soon labels him "lazy." In actuality, time is unimportant to the Ortez family, and therefore punctuality is meaningless. Besides, there is no clock in his small apartment.

Cultures differ in their expectations. One culture requires and reinforces silence, sitting quietly, and listening. Another rewards children for verbalizing ideas and feelings and for asking questions. While one culture encourages competition, singling out high performers, another discourages—even punishes—children for being competitive. In some cultures, children assume adult roles early in life, and in other cultures adulthood comes late. In one culture students learn to "look the teacher in the eye when she talks to you," whereas in another, students are taught to lower their heads in respect when spoken to by an adult. Cultures differ in their conventions: how children take turns, greet each other, participate in conversation—and even the words they use.

In reality, many students in your class may be culturally different—from the other students and from you. You not only accommodate their needs but capitalize on their cultural contributions to your classroom. You become helpful by learning what life is like in the student's home, what she values and does not value, and what conventions she follows (her ways of doing things). Additionally, you are aware of the cultural differences that impede her learning: misinterpreting word meanings, being hesitant to compete or participate in a group project, and being unaware of customs that are carried into the classroom. An important quality, however, is being patient with your mistakes as you come to respect these differences.

## Bilingual Students

Large numbers of American schoolchildren come from homes in which a language other than English is spoken. The non–English-language-background (NELB) population will have grown from 30 million in 1980 to 39.5 million in the year 2000.[3] The two largest non–English-language groups in the United States are speakers of Spanish and the various Chinese languages. Although California, Texas, and New York have the heaviest concentra-

© Elizabeth Crews/The Image Works

tions, all fifty states will continue to have large numbers of non-English speakers.

In the past, if these students had any English training at all, they were periodically pulled from their regular classrooms and placed in special English-language classes. Although they did learn English, they lost valuable time in the content areas, and many fell behind academically. To remedy the situation, "bilingual" education was developed. This educational program consisted of teaching subject matter in the students' native languages while concurrently teaching them English.

Your students function more effectively in the larger culture when they are proficient in English. Though you may not be trained to teach English as a second language, there are ways you can help: skillfully paraphrase statements and questions; talk at different levels of sophistication; use synonyms to help clarify concepts; select texts that do not overstretch the students' vocabularies; create a safe atmosphere that permits a student to stammer in English without fear of ridicule; learn enough non-English words to help clarify your English presentations; and above all, gather patience so you can reteach continually.

## Drug-Abusing Students

Drug abuse is not only increasing among teenagers but moving down into the elementary grades. No longer are drug abusers seen as sleazy teenagers hanging around back alleys and living in government housing. Drug and alcohol abuse cut across all segments of the student body: the affluent student, the class officer, the cheerleader, the popular student, the loner, the star athlete, the dropout, and the trombone player. Research shows that drug-abusing students skip classes, devalue schoolwork, work or steal to support their habit, become physically ill, withdraw emotionally, experience difficulty concentrating on schoolwork, and drop out of school.

## Unwed Mothers

Teenage pregnancy, like drug abuse, is on the rise. Four out of ten girls who are now 15 will become pregnant sometime during their remaining teenage years. Nearly three-fourths of all pregnancies among 15- to 19-year-olds occur out of wedlock; 80 percent of these are "unintended," and 90 percent of the mothers keep their babies.[4] Becoming pregnant during teenage years and while trying to complete high school places young women at risk: they are likely to drop out of school to earn money to support the baby, miss class because of morning sickness and other physical problems associated with pregnancy, become drained emotionally and psychologically, and lose enthusiasm for and commitment to schoolwork.

An "at-risk" student is virtually any student who appears to be headed for learning difficulty down the road. Special thought and attention need to

© *Rohn Engh/Photo Researchers, Inc.*

be given to at-risk students, including latchkey children, abused children (to be discussed in Chapter 7), drug abusers, and unwed mothers. You and the student sit down and work out arrangements during the earliest stages of the problem. You talk with the principal and counselors to open new avenues for the disheartened student. Still within your teaching role, you extend special consideration, such as allowing extra time to complete an assignment, creating special homework for a despondent girl who refuses to leave her home, and working with your principal to trigger counseling for the sexually abused girl. You work with the parent to introduce your latchkey boy to the nearby children's recreation center. Most of all, you are flexible.

# STUDENT DIFFERENCES IMPORTANT TO LEARNING

We have introduced you to the astonishing variety of students in your classes, and especially to atypical students. Now we turn to differences among students that have important effects on their learning.

Which differences should you concentrate on in trying to maximize your teaching effectiveness? Let's start by imagining a very small class—only two students. As you come to know these students, their differences open up before you. Charlie is muscular and athletic, whereas Dave is overweight and uncoordinated. Charlie loves skiing and soccer; Dave, photography and beachcombing. Charlie is lazy and erratic, but Dave is conscientious and consistent. Charlie enjoys fiction filled with gripping adventure; Dave is into biography and history. Charlie is stronger in art, and Dave in math. Charlie needs direct instruction in a well-ordered classroom, whereas Dave can learn through many different teaching formats.

With only two students, you can afford the luxury of exploring a wide range of differences. You note that some are nice to know and others are crucial to know. That Charlie likes to ski and Dave enjoys beachcombing is interesting, but knowing that Charlie needs direct instruction while Dave learns from a variety of formats is important. What follows is a sample of student differences that markedly affect learning.

## Engaged Time

Students differ in their ability to become involved in a learning task and stay with it until completion. Reading a short story in class and then writing a paragraph about its major theme can be surprisingly time consuming. Stephanie stays with the assignment straight through to completion. Martha works for a few minutes, breaks off into a conversation, then returns, only to be distracted by the sound of students giggling in the hall.

*We must demand the best effort and performance from all students, whether they are gifted or less able, affluent or disadvantaged, whether destined for college, the farm or industry.*—A Nation at Risk

## Time Required to Learn

From kindergarten through high school, clear differences emerge among students in the time they require to learn a given concept. At the middle school level, for example, Brandon quickly grasps the concepts behind quadratic equations, whereas Jeff requires several weeks of demonstration and guided practice, and still only partially understands the concepts.

## Social Behavior

Working cooperatively on a group project, being able to communicate with the teacher, and finding appropriate ways to be recognized are examples of social skills involved in many kinds of classroom learning. Sean works easily with three other second-graders on a map of the community. Derrick makes fun of other students in his reading group, habitually shows off, and refuses to follow directions from the teacher.

## Work Habits

Students differ in their neatness, planning, organization, and ability to get things done. Jordan has selected as her research project "Greek Influences on Modern Theatre." She conducts her library research, taking careful notes, then develops an outline, writes drafts, and completes the final phase well in advance of the due date. In contrast, Darrel waits until the draft deadline to even think about a topic. The night before the due date, he frantically leafs through the encyclopedia searching for a topic he can copy into a research format.

## Interest in Learning

Every seasoned teacher can place his students along an interest continuum for most topics taught in class. Gretchen is interested in art, anthropology, psychology, and biology—and is willing to delve into chemistry and photography as well. Even though she is not attracted to fencing, the challenge to become interested is always there. Erica shows little interest in any kind of learning and grumbles when each new topic is introduced. Only music appeals to her.

© *Wendy Malecki*

## Investing in the Future

In addressing a joint session of Congress on February 9, 1989, President George Bush called on the Congress and all Americans to invest in the nation's future by rewarding successful schools and getting involved in the education of youth. "In education we cannot condone mediocrity," he stated. "The dropout rate must be cut, and we must make America a real democracy."

President Bush proposed providing $500 million in grants to reward merit schools. Pointing out that excellence should be rewarded, he proposed that the best schools in every state be singled out. Another proposal called for the establishment of a new group of National Science Scholars. Other recommendations included creating presidential awards for the best teachers and expanding the Head Start program. The president called for expanded use of magnet schools to give families and children a real choice in education.

Announcing the formation of a new task force on competitiveness, chaired by Vice-President Dan Quayle, President Bush stated,

"The most important competitiveness of all is one that improves education in America." The president announced a new program called YES, Youth Entering Service to America. To the Congress, the president challenged, "I have said I'd like to be 'the education president.' Tonight, I ask you to join me by becoming 'the education Congress.'" President Bush asked parents to get involved in their children's schooling. He asked them to go to schools and meet the teachers, pointing out the importance of this not only to their children but to the United States. "To kids in our cities," he said, "don't give up hope. Say no to drugs. Stay in school. And yes, keep hope alive." In the president's words, "The longer our graduation lines are today, the shorter our unemployment lines will be tomorrow."

(President Bush's remarks are from a talk to the joint session of Congress, February 9, 1989, which we followed on a television broadcast. Parts were also quoted in the *Provo Herald*, February 10, 1989.)

# IMPACT OF THE HOME ON CLASSROOM LEARNING

Our discussion about student differences and their impact on learning leads us, inevitably, to the home. The home lives of students create differences that affect their learning once they enter the classroom.

Teachers cannot hope to fulfill adequately all the needs their students bring to class. For example, there are needs to communicate better with parents, learn about human sexuality, build better relationships with siblings, be loved, feel part of a family unit, and have a home life free from contention. Both the family and society continue to push the fulfillment of such needs onto the school.

Teachers feel pressure to satisfy student needs and usually respond—on an individual basis—as time and strength allow. But survival demands that you compartmentalize, as this teacher tried to do:

> It's not my job to teach students how to get along with their parents. Nor is it my job to tell them how much television to watch—but I'd give anything if I could! My job is to teach them how to read and write, and, I hope, to love learning. But I won't fool anybody. I won't take a back seat when it comes to making a difference. I'm romantic enough to believe my kids carry what I teach them into their homes.

But turn this assertion around. How will your students' home life influence their learning? What will they bring that facilitates—or impedes—your influence? How will wearing stereo headphones into class affect Gene's ability to hear once he takes them off? How will Vera's parents' divorce affect her ability to concentrate on your lesson? Following are factors in the home that influence your students' learning.

## Television and Home Videos

Research suggests that your students are watching several hours of regular television and home videos each day. Consider how your students' classroom behavior might be affected by themes like these:

- Adults do dumb things, and therefore their authority is suspect.
- Violence and sexual permissiveness are commonplace, so they must be normal behavior.
- Unending entertainment is a high-priority pursuit.
- The art of consuming goods and services should be cultivated.
- Becoming a blue-chip athlete opens the way to money and status.
- Ongoing conflict between parents and children is society's expected pattern of behavior.
- Keeping up on current events is expected.

- Exposure to other cultures and unique adventures broadens one's outlook on life.

Young people absorb these themes, and you see the results in your classroom. Students show less respect for teachers' authority, the rights of others, and private property. School vandalism, violence, and sexual activity are on the rise. Teachers feel they must compete with the slickness of television in commanding the attention of their students. Students expect learning to be entertaining, painless, and fun, saying by their attitude, "I'm doing you a favor by sitting in this class. Make it fun, or I'm liable to be bored." Consumer satisfaction! The focus is on "me." Personal success eclipses group success—getting over giving.

Identifying with the superstar athlete, students of both sexes start competing early, and with fierce intensity. For the budding young athlete (and his or her parents), pressure to excel is enormous, showing itself in sleeplessness, nail biting, nervous stomachs, headaches, inability to concentrate, and low grades. Viewing perpetual conflicts among people on television predisposes students to classroom conflicts: they expect to be involved in conflicts, often initiate them, and use them to gain recognition.

Your students may have viewed a multitude of *Discovery, National Geographic,* and special news report shows. They may have had opportunities to witness the climbing of Everest, exploration of the ocean floor, religious rites of African groups, family life of the Alaskan fishermen, a bloody coup in Central America, poverty in the Sudan, and terrorist activities in international airports. As a result, today's students come into your classroom with a developing knowledge of worldwide events and a beginning social conscience. They are armed with questions and issues, fully expecting you to provide satisfying answers.

## Single-Parent Families

Because of the rise in divorce rate and numbers of unwed mothers, the percentage of your students who come from single-parent homes is greater than ever. By the mid-1980s, 15 percent of white children and more than 40 percent of black children lived with only their mothers. The female-headed family has become the centerpiece of the "family crisis" of the 1980s. The single parent is pulled out of the home to become the breadwinner. The student comes home to an empty house and is deprived of parental companionship and an adult role model during crucial periods of the day.

Countless students coming from divorced or single-parent homes suffer few or no ill effects. For many, however, debilitating symptoms appear: resentment, insecurity, hostility toward both you and their peers, disruptive behavior, anxiety, hyperactivity, unwillingness to cooperate, exaggerated needs for acceptance, withdrawal, extreme dependency, and attention-getting behavior.

## Poverty

Increasing poverty is a major problem in American life. Nearly half of American black children live in poverty; one in five of all American children are poor. Poverty precipitates a host of school problems, including low motivation, truancy, and dropping out. Ernest Boyer, president of the Carnegie Foundation for the Advancement of Teaching, foresaw a crisis in American education:

> If failure is not to become a way of life for many urban youths, we must recognize that poverty and schooling are connected. . . .To achieve excellence in education we must confront the problems of poor children, give priority to early education, affirm the centrality of language, provide enrichment programs that reflect the changing work and family patterns of the nation, and learn more about how children learn.[5]

## Material Success

American families place a high value on material success. A father says, "I want my children to have college educations and the good things in life. My wife and I want them too. We're both willing to work long hours at two jobs so we can enjoy nicer things." A high school senior says, "Why do I want to become a lawyer? I want to serve people, but I also want to make money and be successful. Then I can do some of the things I want to do in life, like own a fancy home, have a boat, and travel." A corporate executive says, "I wanted an MBA as a ticket into corporate management. This kind of position allowed me the flexibility to move with my husband's changing jobs. But also we wanted financial freedom to come and go and to be able to afford homes in Florida and San Francisco."

How does material success as a value show itself in the classroom? For one thing, it means pressure from peers. Students from affluent homes unintentionally place the average student under duress: to wear name-brand clothing, to own an expensive skateboard, to insist on a Disneyland vacation, to upgrade a stereo system, and to buy school lunch on a regular basis. For another, it means pressure from parents to be upwardly mobile. Regardless of socioeconomic status or the student's interest, she is pushed to earn A's, to be accepted into a prestigious university, and to select early a lucrative profession.

## Emphasis on Leisure

Leisure is a priority in our society. Holidays are consolidated to provide long weekends. Employers are moving toward a four-day work week. Supersaver vacation packages are available at every travel agency. Fun-filled retirement complexes dot the landscape. Working families board planes bound for cities and resorts abroad.

Understandably, your students come into the classroom placing a high premium on leisure. Parents pull students out of class for a five-day vacation trip during the school year. Assignments are hurriedly completed to make way for goofing off. Students work hard to earn points for "free time." Homework is seen as a pesky intrusion into the evening. Our society's preoccupation with leisure deprives students of experiencing the satisfaction of schoolwork.

The home first creates and then amplifies differences among your students. These differences are double edged. They are the variety, spice, and excitement of your teaching and at the same time the vexation of your days.

# CONCLUSION

You need to know your students. This is the central message of the chapter. Understanding what makes students tick—what is going on inside their minds and hearts—opens the door to greater effectiveness on your part. When the school year begins, you are confronted with a tangle of overwhelming, seemingly unmanageable differences among a new crop of students—differences that expand over the school year. The challenge is to focus on each student. Poke around until you find the characteristics that make a difference in how each one learns. Then try to accommodate your instruction to those characteristics. Productively exploiting student differences is an immensely satisfying aspect of teaching. Work toward it.

## Expansions

1. You will undoubtedly be drawn to some students more than to others. What types of student characteristics would most attract you, and what types would most turn you away? Explain.

2. How will knowing about student differences facilitate your ability to help them learn?

3. Write down your thoughts about working with latchkey students, handicapped students, unwed mothers, drug abusers.

4. Visit with two experienced teachers. With what types of students do they experience their greatest difficulty? Which types are "a joy to work with"? Do the two teachers differ in their selections?

5. Suppose three of your students were incessant television watchers. What challenges might they present? How would you go about meeting these challenges?

6. Describe how you think the influences of your own home will affect your teaching.

7. What rewards can you predict as a result of working with a room full of diverse students?

## Notes

1. K. Devaney, "Sketches toward a Profile of a Professional Teacher," *Education and Urban Society* (May 1985), pp. 269–283.

2. U. Casanova, "Ethnic and Cultural Differences," in V. Richardson-Koehler (Ed.), *Educators' Handbook: A Research Perspective* (New York: Longman, 1987), p. 391.

3. R. Oxford-Carpenter, *Demographic Projections of Non–English-Language-Background and Limited-English-Proficient Persons in the United States to the Year 2000 by State, Age, and Language Group* (Rosslyn, Va.: Inter-American Research Associates, National Clearinghouse for Bilingual Education, 1980).

4. C. Ascher, *Pregnant and Parenting Teens: Statistics, Characteristics, and School-Based Support Services* (ERIC Document Reproduction Service No. ED 267 150, 1985).

5. E. L. Boyer, "Early Schooling and the Nation's Future," *Educational Leadership* 44(6) (1987) pp. 4–7.

# CHAPTER 3

# YOUR RELATIONSHIPS

*The relations that teachers establish with fellow teachers or with other adults will—and must—be judged by their ability to make teachers' relations with students more productive and satisfying.—Judith Warren Little*

**MAIN IDEAS**

- No aspect of your teaching means so much to your success or contributes so decisively to your failure as your teaching relationships.

- You cannot fail in relationships with students and still be successful as a teacher. Productive relationships place you in a position to escalate student learning.

- Your relationships with other adults in a school strongly affect the school's quality and character, the accomplishment of your students, and your own professionalism.

- Your principal has considerable impact on your teaching life. He or she is your instructional leader, facilitator, crisis manager, reward dispenser, helper, evaluator, and therapist.

- Take time to develop good relationships. They change, grow in complexity, and are forever modulated by your personal values and the moods of a larger society.

# INTRODUCTION

Let's listen in as Mr. Cohen, a high school principal, discusses three of his teachers with the district personnel director:

> It looked for all the world as if Becky would develop into one of my top teachers. She walked through my door well groomed, masters degree in hand, and carrying a folder full of glowing recommendations. Unfortunately, credentials can be deceiving. Things turned sour. We all quickly found she could not get along with her students and the other teachers. During this last month alone, I've had three students in my office complaining about Becky's style of teaching. They claim she is harsh and unbending. She embarrasses them and is unapproachable. She is out of touch with teenagers. Several teachers have commented on her aloofness. Few can engage her in a casual conversation. I worry about how she'll come across at back-to-school night.
>
> To put it bluntly, Cliff is an emotional drain on my staff. He's terribly dependent and requires ceaseless reassurance. Besides that, he's a worry-wart. Fuss, fuss, fuss. Every issue explodes into a major emergency. He is so easily offended, other team members have to walk on eggs. We're all getting worn out. Don't send me any more Cliffs to interview!
>
> Wes—we need more of him. What a pleasure! He's always optimistic, ready to jump in and solve the problem. He can tell you what he doesn't like without turning you off, and he's easy to work with. You don't have to tiptoe, feeling he might misinterpret something you say, and he'll give you the benefit of the doubt. He's mature enough to give others credit, and you don't feel he's always competing.

Relationships! No other aspect of your teaching means so much to your success or contributes so decisively to your failure. Skill in developing and maintaining relationships characterizes every good teacher. Your training is important, as are your daily preparations, unit plans, teaching strategies, and diagnostic abilities. But without adequate interpersonal skills, other strengths go flat. In becoming a teacher, you enter a host of relationships: with students, other teachers, the principal, parents, counselors, and custodians. Will these turn out to be productive, damaging, renewing, draining, helpful, or frightening?

## YOUR RELATIONSHIPS WITH STUDENTS

Your bread-and-butter relationships are those between you and your students. You simply cannot fail in these relationships and still be successful as a teacher. They take time, involvement, and sacrifice to develop. They can

© *Elizabeth Crews/Stock, Boston*

be easily damaged through demeaning interchanges or firmly bonded through careful cultivation. Taking the time to reexplain an assignment quietly, show interest in a student's hobby, or carry out fair discipline all bond you more closely to a student. Although some research suggests that students can learn under a variety of conditions, including from teachers they dislike, much more research supports the claim that students learn better when they have good relationships with their teachers. Here is a sample of the types of relationships teachers become involved in as they work with their students.

Teacher A writes:

> Sixth-graders—I just love them. Especially in Phys. Ed. There were a couple of boys that were kind of trouble makers, kind of loud mouths—showing off. In the gym, we played a game called "war ball," and I started playing. And those boys could not believe that a teacher could play so well—especially a woman teacher. Now they always want me on their team. It's gotten me a lot closer to the boys because of my athletic ability. That has helped me a lot. They both talk to me about sports. It's exciting to have something in common with the students. It builds a relationship.[1]

Teacher B recalls:

> I was standing there waiting for quiet and he was dancing around and running up and down the stairs just making a general nuisance of himself. I got so mad

*The classroom has all the elements of theater, and the observant,*
*self-examining teacher will not need a drama critic to uncover character,*
*plot, and meaning. We are, all of us, the actors trying to find the meaning of*
*the scenes in which we find ourselves. The scripts are not yet fully written, so*
*we must listen with curiosity and great care to the main characters who are,*
*of course, the children.— Vivian Gussin Paley*

at him at that moment! I've never really gotten as mad as I did that time. I grabbed him by the tie to make him stand still and he said, "Man, let go! Man, don't do that!" I just held his tie. I think I probably might have even choked him but he kept on saying, "Go ahead! Choke me, man! I don't care. I don't care."

Finally I said, "When you stand still, I'll let you go." He wouldn't, just in spite! He just kept pulling away and leaning back. Oh, I was so mad! Finally he just loosened his tie and took it off his head and I was left standing there with his tie in my hand.[2]

Teacher C uses a double standard:

"I promise to have your papers corrected and back by Thursday—this time without fail."

"Okay, this means no recess for you today, Teach," Charles banters.

"Yeah, Mr. Barnes has been naughty and has to stay in," chimes in Alfredo.

"All right! I've had enough of that talk. Having fun is one thing. Impudence is something else. Whether I get your assignments back on time is my business. Your business is to turn in a short essay every Tuesday and Thursday."

Later, at lunch with Miss DeVere, Mr. Barnes is still smoldering.

"This morning, two kids had the cheek to tell me I was late in handing back papers."

"Well, were you?"

"I can't believe you! That's not the point. High school kids, still wet behind the ears, have no right telling a teacher what to do."

Teacher D says:

What I had hoped would not occur had happened before I began to teach: my students responded to me as to a cardboard figure who wore the label "English teacher." Despite their gradually increasing familiarity with me as an individual, they would still react as Lenin would have liked the proletariat to have acted in Europe—*en masse*. In short, my students—at all times objectively, and occasionally also subjectively—possessed a class consciousness, an awareness of who they were, which enabled or, more correctly, forced them to define me as an "other." . . . I too, without thinking, had acted in the same general way when I was their age. It was not until that way of behaving was directed toward me that I began to realize what is really upsetting about teaching—the indifference of one's students.[3]

## Factors Affecting Relationships with Students

A student's academic performance affects your relationship. If Olaf is failing in your class, he is uncomfortable around you—perhaps hostile, withdrawn, or blaming you for his failure. If he is doing well, he sees the two of you as "thinking along the same lines"—a perception that strengthens your relationship.

Negative characteristics of your students can keep you at a distance. If Mia chatters incessantly in the back of the room, becoming a thorn in your side, you are slow to warm to her. Doyle sits in front of you with his unwashed face and unkempt hair, an affront to your sense of cleanliness; you withhold yourself when he wants to be your special friend. Frank is loud and pushy, manipulating everything to his advantage, whereas Jaime is laid back. You feel a strained relationship with Frank but are relaxed with Jaime.

You well know that relationships have their emotional peaks and valleys. A relationship can become obstructed when you try to insulate yourself emotionally from your students. You may try to buffer yourself against overinvolvement in relationships, usually to no avail. For example, after three months in her closed world, Lynn approaches you and unfolds her story: she is failing in her schoolwork because her parents are having financial difficulties. You listen empathically for an hour, offering solace, then climb into your car, emotionally drained but soaring in spirits: "The channel is finally open."

Your own ego can get in the way of your relationships. Samuel makes fun of you in subtle ways, muttering snide remarks and shattering the mood

*Paul Conklin/Monkmeyer Press Photo Service*

*I have come to understand that child empowerment is an outcome of teacher empowerment. I have seen that children and teachers learn best when they are viewed as people rather than locked into pupil roles or teacher roles and are thus freed to bring themselves and their views to the classroom world. Teachers free to be themselves are not threatened by children; they move with, not against, the energy released when children find their own answers.—Margaret Yonemura*

of serious moments through his clowning. You retaliate by calling his bluff in front of the class and by grading him more severely than the other students. This emotional tug-of-war is painful for both of you. To break the logjam, you ask him in for a talk after school. He sits in your office in stony silence, resisting any negotiation. This day leaves you feeling wiped out.

Efforts to establish a relationship can be thwarted by the student's parents. Michael's hostility toward his harsh father spills over into your classroom. His negative feelings are transferred to you as another authority figure. All you can muster is an uneasy truce. On the other side of the coin, parents can enhance your relationships with their children. Cara's mother is your best ally. In their home, your virtues are extolled. In the classroom, Cara falls hopelessly in love with you, her new teacher. She will march to the ends of the earth for you! Your words are etched in bronze.

## Implications

As you develop productive relationships, you place yourself in a position to escalate your students' learning. Productive relationships will result more frequently when you communicate certain messages to your students: that they are respected and safe, are being treated fairly and with consistency, and are being held to high but realistic expectations. Taken as a group, your messages enhance student self-esteem.

# YOUR RELATIONSHIPS WITH OTHER TEACHERS

## Starting Out as a Sponge

Your relationships with other teachers will undoubtedly change over the years. At the beginning, you turn to experienced colleagues for emotional support, reassurance, and instructional help. Note how grateful this first-year teacher was for having a friend to whom she could turn in those early months:

> I was very frustrated and very hesitant to ask other teachers because they would think I didn't know anything. I was supposed to be a teacher and yet I

© Miriam Reinhart/Photo Researchers, Inc.

didn't know what I was supposed to be teaching. But thank goodness there were some teachers I felt close enough to, so I could go and say, "Can you tell me how this program works?" That's the way I got most of my ideas—from other teachers. They said, "Well, this has worked for me." One teacher even said, "Here's my file. Take whatever you need." After you've been teaching for a while you miss that—the opportunity to go in and see other teachers. Sometimes you get stagnant because you can't do that.[4]

In addition to emotional support, new teachers need freedom to chart their own course, receive recognition for their contributions, and feel pride and success in their work. These needs cannot be met adequately in the absence of good relationships with other teachers. Janelle's experience illustrates the unnecessary frustration experienced by a new teacher:

Janelle is a first-year teacher of American literature at Washington High School. Alan and Clare, two seasoned English instructors, worked as her teammates. They welcomed her warmly at the outset, encouraging her to share ideas and feelings as a full-fledged member of the team. But Janelle soon realized that this "warm reception" and "active involvement" were little more than a facade. She found herself saddled with all the menial tasks while also carrying more than her share of the load. Her ideas were politely ignored. She felt frustrated, used, and sabotaged in her own need for fulfillment.

## Retreating into Privateness

Throughout the first year, you adjust, settle in, and carve out your own niche within the school. Experiencing initial success (along with ample failures), you are more confident in drawing on your own resources. You still look to experienced teachers for help but are selective, choosing those suggestions that conform to your own idiosyncrasies and teaching style. But daily experience in the trenches, you believe, will best build your teaching repertoire.

The tendency for teachers to develop unique styles of teaching leads them to a private professionalism that has been likened to the "parallel play" of young children:

> Two 3-year-olds are busily engaged in opposite corners of a sandbox. One has a shovel and bucket; one has a rake and hoe. At no time do they borrow each other's toys. Although in proximity and having much to offer one another, each works and plays pretty much in isolation.[5]

Teachers see each other throughout the day, but they seldom use their encounters to exchange ideas about the craft of teaching. The prevailing posture is "hands off," and one teacher never tells another what to do. Asking assistance from other teachers is viewed as a sign of weakness. Indeed, the ideal colleague, as Lortie has suggested, is willing to help but is never pushy.[6]

The physical arrangement of the school contributes to the problem. The cellular nature of school buildings and class schedules prevents teachers from having more than superficial contact with each other during the day. Each teacher has his or her own room, which is set apart from other rooms by walls and doors. The door is closed when the bell rings. (Even in open-concept schools, which have no partitions, teachers quickly build their own little nests—walls and all—to shut themselves off from other teachers.) Between class periods there is little time for conversation, let alone serious reflection on the problems of teaching. Recess, free periods, and lunch hours are so short that teachers can barely catch their breath. At the end of the teaching day, they are correcting assignments, are scurrying off to other commitments, or are simply too tired to talk. While some privateness is vital to a teacher's well-being and continued best efforts, educational reformers are trying out new solutions to teacher isolation. These include designing buildings to facilitate teacher interchange during the day, developing varieties of teaming in teaching, and offering greater flexibility for the teacher's schedule.

## A Case for Collegiality

Do you, too, contemplate privateness in your teaching? You may want to pause when such yearnings arise. There is much to be gained from a life of collaboration, not only for you but for your students and the school. Schools are working to bolster public faith, to become more credible institutions for student learning. Public faith is elevated when high levels of professionalism exist among teachers. Even the most energetic and dedicated work by an individual teacher will not be sufficient to raise public confidence; only cohesive teams of teachers, working efficiently on well-organized projects, will get the job done.

Schools benefit in at least three ways when productive collegial ties— that is, ties binding colleagues together—are maintained among teachers. First, orchestrating the daily work of teaching across classrooms is greatly facilitated. Teachers, students, and administrators are seen as a well-oiled unit conducting the daily business of education. Second, schools that foster teacher-to-teacher work can attempt classroom innovations that would exhaust a single teacher. Third, new teachers coming into a cohesive organization are given systematic assistance and are acculturated with ease and minimal shock.

One educator comments on the importance of relationships: "The nature of the relationships among the adults who inhabit a school has more to do with a school's quality and character, the accomplishments of its pupils, and the professionalism of its teachers than does any other factor."[7]

Working cooperatively on school-wide projects is, after all, no more than working to improve your own classroom teaching. Inevitably, there are spinoffs for you personally. The modern curriculum is highly complex. Working as a team, you select textbooks, pick and choose from teachers' manuals, decide on curricular units, and hammer out supplemental activities. The individual strengths within your team are consolidated. As a result, your own lessons profit from higher-quality examples, a greater number of resource materials, and increased clarity. But there is more. Four teachers, united as a team, can flex a larger muscle in presenting their case for change in the current reading text. Large projects are divided up, saving time and energy and reducing the risk of burnout.

What about esprit de corps? Suppose that over the past three years your team has created and implemented a writing program for intermediate students in your school. The project brings all of you together, cementing your commitments and engendering group pride. Teachers from other schools come to observe, take notes, and learn. Your team is visible! Students like your program and develop commendable writing skills. Parents sit up and take notice. The result is a sense of enthusiasm and accomplishment.

## Implications

Having worked from the outset on your professional relationships, you realize with satisfaction that warm personal relationships have come along naturally.

As a neophyte, you jumped in, taking advantage of opportunities to cultivate professional relationships in faculty meetings, the faculty lounge, through the principal's advisory committee, and as a local officer in the National Education Association. You took time to talk shop. You plugged into sources of new ideas, helpful services, resource materials, and possible teaching techniques. You compared notes. You kept current.

In time, teaching becomes routinized. The immediacy of grading papers and the press of preparing exams too often take precedence over exchanging ideas. Coming to decisions through group deliberations and thoughtful reflection takes too much time. Expediency leads to educational corner cutting and, finally, to a life of private professionalism. Contrarily, the vital teacher not only resists educational stagnation but actively pursues development and renewal—with his colleagues.

# YOUR RELATIONSHIP WITH YOUR PRINCIPAL

## Both Bane and Boon

Many teachers consider principals their most important source of help in becoming effective—as well as their greatest potential hindrance. This is one teacher's reaction to the principal:

> Dr. Frost had come into my room after Freddy and Thomas had had a fierce fight in the classroom, and he asked me about Freddy's record. Now, Freddy had just been transferred into my class; he was just admitted three weeks ago. I received his records only last week and I have not had the time to go through them. I told him, also, that I didn't like to make a practice of reading records before I knew the child. He told me that I was supposed to read them and I said that I disagreed. Then he said something to me which really made me feel

© *Stan Goldblatt 1980/Photo Researchers, Inc.*

very, very bad. He said, "When you have had twenty years' experience, then, perhaps, you can disagree with me." This was the first time I had ever said I disagreed with him. I always went along with what he said because he was the principal and he had feelings and he had experience where I didn't. . . . I really feel that Dr. Frost was wrong in telling me what he did. It was sort of a slap in the face and I think I've done plenty of things for him. . . . I feel he was very wrong and I don't think I can ever forgive him for that.[8]

Here is an opposite view:

Mr. Barkley was very supportive about anything I asked for, and he didn't intervene a lot without asking me. But I knew I could go to him and ask for anything within reason, and he would try to help me.[9]

The number of administrators in elementary and secondary schools varies. At the elementary level you interact with your building principal. At the high school level you have occasional contacts with the principal but daily interaction with the vice-principal, your department chairperson, or your area coordinator. Seldom do you associate with district administrators (except in small districts, where you may even work directly with the superintendent).

Relationships between teachers and principals are ambivalent. On the one hand, teachers want little interference in their daily classroom routine, including their selection of curriculum materials and methods for teaching. On the other hand, they want the principal to serve as buffer between themselves and parents and between themselves and the district office. Further, they expect to be backed up in their teaching decisions and in maintaining discipline. In return, they willingly (or grudgingly) support the principal's school policies.

Communication between principals and teachers can be helpful—or terrible. One principal laments his inability to communicate with his teachers in what he describes as the "parking-lot syndrome":

As principal, I prepared carefully for my first faculty meeting. I arranged chairs in circles and encouraged several teachers to contribute. Yet during the meeting I found that I did most of the talking while the teachers sat quietly by. A few minutes after the meeting I looked out my office window at the school parking lot and there the *real* faculty meeting was taking place. Little clusters of teachers were abuzz, expressing their ideas about all the subjects on the agenda. In faculty rooms principals talk; in parking lots teachers talk. But seldom do teachers and principals talk openly together.[10]

Admit it or not, your principal has considerable impact on your teaching life, serving as initiator, facilitator, crisis manager, reward dispenser, helper, therapist, and evaluator. She makes quick decisions, usually based on insufficient information. She is your champion, your judge, and your ogre—and often supplies the doughnuts you enjoy. Your principal sees herself in a dual role, as instructional leader and as building administrator. As instructional leader, she assists you in clarifying and making decisions about your curriculum, obtaining resources, and reflecting on potential teaching methods. Her instructional role includes evaluating your teaching and recommending contract renewal and salary increases. As building administrator, she implements school policies on dress standards, student discipline, scheduling, and extracurricular activities. These two roles are undergirded by another role, that of "cheerleader." At their best, principals provide ample emotional support with comments like these:

"Thanks for taking Adrian's geometry class yesterday."

"That was a perceptive presentation you made last night."

"Marcelle passed me in the hall and told me how much she likes having you as a teacher."

## Implications

Support your principal. Give his or her leadership a chance. Try carrying out school policies before grumbling, ignoring, or challenging them. Bring before your principal the learning goals of students and present a sharp picture of classroom events. Provide feedback on the effectiveness of the newly adopted math text and student enthusiasm for the new "Scholar-of-the-Month" program. Bring before the principal your thoughtful and creative adaptations of the school's programs, rather than miring him or her down with procedural details.

The principal needs positive feedback as much as you do. She feels rewarded when students are successful, and only you can provide evidence of her contribution to that success. Beyond that, she needs your personal expressions of appreciation of her leadership. In short, there must be a partnership:

> The principal needs a partnership with teachers. This is so because the principal needs cooperation in extending the role from a residual one to a complementary one. Even more important, however, is the life that can be brought to school-level deliberations about instructional problems by teachers who are committed to the school as well as to their particular classroom groups. Without this life, the principal can get bogged down in abstractions and details rather than bringing personal skills to bear on the real concerns of teachers.[11]

# YOUR RELATIONSHIPS WITH PARENTS

There is an adage in the folklore of teaching: if your students like you, their parents will like you too. To the extent that this is true, you have an impact on the perceptions of parents through your work with their children. Parents tend to be satisfied with the quality of their children's education when the children bring home reports about how well they like their teachers. Further, parents acquire impressions through direct contacts with you. In dinner-table conversation, Kristan protests her "unfair" grade in U. S. history. The parents are initially persuaded of your unfairness. But at a subsequent parent–teacher conference, seeing Kristan's unit test scores, they conclude that she lucked out with her C– and that you are more than fair in your grading. Marta, in middle school, extols your virtues in the home: "Donovan is my very best teacher. He's great!" Walking into a parent–teacher conference, Marta's parents expect to see the greatest guy in the world. After five minutes at your table, they shake their heads in disillusionment: "How did this guy ever get into teaching?"

Parent–teacher relationships—what are they like? Coming away from talking with a parent, you can be on Cloud Nine or ready to turn in your teaching credential. You can feel satisfied, discouraged about your abilities, elated, emotionally drained, or frightened. A parent–teacher encounter went very poorly for this teacher of a child who was disruptive and who had a short attention span:

> I was terrified! I'll never forget the look in his eyes! It was during parent–teacher conferences. Pete's dad came into my room, and we started talking. He asked where Pete sat. I pointed to the student desk that I had placed next to mine at the front of the room. Mr. Argyle wanted to know why Pete was not sitting with the other kids. I tried, diplomatically, to explain that Pete needed special attention and I could give it to him by having him sit near me.
>
> "You mean my kid's not as good as the others! What do you think you're doing! How would you feel if you was right up under the teacher's nose and she was looking down at everything you did? How would you feel if you was the only kid in the room that wasn't with the others? No wonder Pete can't get his work done!"
>
> Mr. Argyle got more and more agitated—I mean, it wasn't normal. He wanted to know if Pete had always sat up there. "No, he's been in other desks." "Where?" he demanded. I waved my hand toward the group of student desks in the center of the room. Mr. Argyle insisted that I go show him exactly. He got up and started following me around the room.
>
> I really got frightened. I was trying to hold the tears back, but it was no use. I couldn't help it. It was just the way he looked at me. I started for the door. I wanted to get Mr. Shriver [the principal]. But Pete's dad was between me and the door. I felt caged. All I could think of was, "I've got to get out of here." Nothing I said satisfied him. He yelled that it was all my fault his kid wasn't doing well in school. I got so scared I couldn't even talk.
>
> When he finally left, I was limp with fear and relief. I sat shaking and crying until I thought he had left the building. Then I fled to Mr. Shriver's office and sobbed out what had happened. He tried soothing and reassuring me. But he was furious. I found out later that he told Mr. Argyle never to step in my room again—or the police would be there in an instant. And he told me not to worry about anything like that happening again. He really helped me. I was ready to quit teaching. But Mr. Shriver pulled me through.[12]

## Perceptions and Expectations of Teachers and Parents

Both the home and the school acknowledge their roles in the child's education; nonetheless, teachers have historically expected parents to play a non-intrusive role. One writer states this position strongly:

> Teachers . . . wish to form coalitions only with parents who are obsequious, appreciative, and uncritical, or accepting of their needs for autonomy. Most parents are viewed as a critical foe that, if permitted to interfere, would threaten the teacher's already insecure professional status and self-image.[13]

This stay-away-unless-you-can-support-me message leaks out into the community and contributes to the more general perception that "schools seem content to 'run the public's business' without bothering to involve the public."[14]

Teachers perceive that parents do not want to become involved in the teaching process within the school. Further, parents are seen as lacking the pedagogical sophistication required to make meaningful contributions. At the secondary level, neither teachers nor parents can come up with productive ways to involve the parents. Additionally, each perceives the child differently. The teacher may see the child as disruptive, whereas the parents view that same behavior as the child's normal lifestyle—and maybe even as delightfully charming!

From the other side, that of the parent, we see a different set of expec-

*Paul Conklin/Monkmeyer Press Photo Service*

tations and challenges. Parents often perceive teachers as apathetic, indifferent, or hostile to their participation. Additionally, parents operate under constraints that hamper their involvement: the impossible work schedule that already burdens the single parent, fear for personal safety when going out at night and attending parent–teacher conferences, and waiting in long lines to talk with each teacher.

Differences in social class between parent and teacher also obstruct relationships. People of unequal status feel uneasy face to face, regardless of whether parent or teacher is perceived as socially superior. Evaluation of the student's performance is yet another sore spot. Parents immediately become defensive when confronted with their child's failing work ("She's implying it's *our* fault!"). They turn around and blame the teacher. Relations are also often strained because some people feel reduced to "kid level" when confronted by a teacher's inherent authority—never seeing them as equals. Also, some parents look upon teachers as if they were paid servants—always inferior because the parents are the "employers." Finally, conflicts arise when the child shifts his allegiance from the family to the teacher. Parents can interpret this development as the demise of their authority or a diminution of their child's love.

Despite common perceptions, national surveys show high levels of parental contact with schools. For example, one study reports that up to 87 percent of parents had some contact with teachers, 70 percent meeting with or writing to a teacher, within the preceding two years. Nearly half the parents had attended a PTA meeting or volunteered aid to the school. Parents making the greatest number of contacts were more highly educated, had higher incomes, lived in rural areas, and expressed greater confidence in public school teachers.[15] Although these contacts are made, they tend to be brief. Teachers make hurried efforts to meet with all parents, holding interactions to a bare minimum. Thus, since parents are involved in the school and with you as a teacher, the challenge is to make your relationship productive.

## Implications

You are warmly professional. Parents sense your concern and, for the most part, respond promptly to your counsel. Since parents have no legal obligation to meet with you or become involved in the school's education of their children, you take the lead. Being an effective teacher, you seize every opportunity to involve parents in extending your instruction, persuading them, particularly, to structure study time at home and follow through until the homework is completed. Use a variety of devices for communicating with parents about their children's progress: parent–teacher conferences, workshops, visits to the school, phone calls, notes, and home visits.

You are a good observer of your students' daily performances and keep thorough and up-to-date records. Thus you are able to alert parents, *early,* to potential problems. Since a partnership exists between you and the parents, neither hesitates to enlist the help of the other in solving specific problems.

# YOUR RELATIONSHIPS WITH OTHERS IN THE SCHOOL

In addition to classroom teachers, you form relationships with a number of other adults in your school: custodians, secretaries, lunchroom personnel, nurse, special education teachers, counselors, psychologist, and district curriculum specialists. These relationships, as well as those with fellow teachers, play a significant part in your success. A nonproductive relationship between teacher and counselor can be worse than useless:

> All because of Terry, the whole day went wrong. I'm so mad at him. He's always talking back to me—and he steals. Well, I haven't actually seen him steal, but he has to be the one who stole the colored paper and glue. He delights in breaking rules and making things hard for me.
>
> I was pretty upset today by the time one o'clock came around. He'd been goofing off, and he deliberately knocked Kim down at recess. I was fuming when the kids came back. Then Miss Knight came by. Since she's a school counselor, she ought to know how to get this thing stopped. So I told her all about Terry. "Either he leaves or I leave!" All she said was, "He seems to be doing just fine right now." Well, what did she expect! She came in during a test. She knew I was upset and told me to go take a break while she worked with the class. I really felt put down—and I still don't know what to do with Terry![16]

## Roles

One can detect differences in perceived roles, a problem that often causes strained relationships. In the teacher's view, the counselor's role is to tell her how to halt Terry's disruptive behavior. But the counselor sees her role as diagnosing the problem and working to bring about long-term solutions.

Representing the other side, a special education teacher reflects back on her interactions with classroom teachers:

> Special education teachers used to take kids out of class and play games with them. Pretty soon, the regular teachers didn't want to let them go because they thought it was just playtime: "Well, you just pull my kids out and give them rewards. What do the other students think!"
>
> I spent a lot of time on PR work with other teachers, showing them what I was doing, going over test results, trying to work with them on modifying behavior in the classroom, trying to effect changes rather than just playing games.[17]

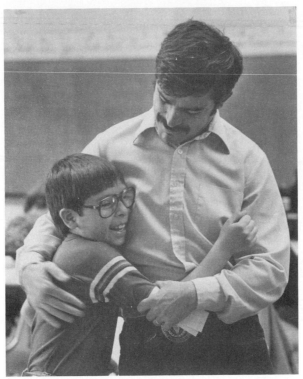

*Mimi Forsyth/Monkmeyer Press Photo Service*

Your relationship with a school nurse is also a product of interactions. During seatwork, Chelsea approaches you looking pale and sweaty, and complains of headache and nausea. You take her to the nurse, who, after a quick examination, instructs you to call the parents, saying, "I can't administer anything for her headache or upset stomach. The parents will have to do that." You are annoyed. You think to yourself, "What good's a school nurse who can't practice nursing?" But look at it from the nurse's point of view. Her commitment and training would compel her to do whatever she could to assist the child. But legal constraints often prevent her from exercising her full medical authority. Thus, you and the nurse may have a warm and friendly relationship yet feel frustrated in trying to work together to ensure the well-being of the child.

Your view of other people's roles and responsibilities affects the types of relationships you will form with them. It will help if you understand how *they* see their roles. You adjust your perception of their roles and thereby improve the productivity of the relationships.

Secretaries are inestimably important. They play crucial supporting roles in the daily drama of school life. No teacher in her right mind would offend the secretary. Secretaries coordinate supplies, tell you what to do and when to do it, buffer you from cantankerous parents, and generally keep the school running smoothly. You also want to be friends with the custodian. Smart teachers cultivate good relationships with the custodial staff, who have all the equipment at their fingertips, help solve logistical problems, take your computer in for repair, and set the tone of cleanliness and caring for the school.

## Implications

The wider your circle of constructive relationships in your school, the more effectively you can teach. Never underestimate the potential of even tangential relationships, for they will invariably find their way into your classroom. Enter into new relationships, moving outward—always.

# SOME CHARACTERISTICS OF RELATIONSHIPS

Good relationships are not developed overnight. They must be nurtured thoughtfully—here a little, there a little. Several characteristics of relationships are worth keeping in mind.

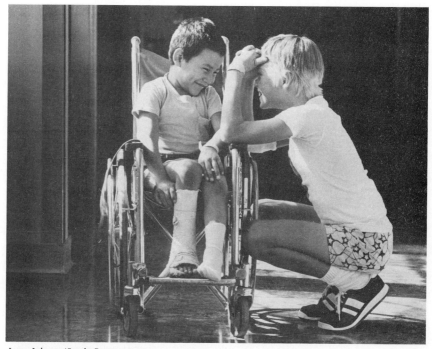

*Lynn Johnson/Stock, Boston*

*Some "psychological distance" between teacher and student is inevitable and desirable. It is a little foolish and certainly inaccurate to say that they are just friends, just equals, studying the same problem. But too often the distance between them is enormous and their voices can hardly be heard across the gulf.—Houston Peterson*

## Good Relationships Promote Learning

Young children enter the classroom picturing you as *the* authority—on everything! They fall in love with you. They turn to you for solace, recognition, direction, encouragement, and personalized attention. This loyalty, this yet-unearned veneration, is one of the rewards of teaching young children. As students mature, their dreamy identification with the teacher gives way to greater identification with the subject matter. They may develop a love for the subject matter in the midst of a strained relationship with the teacher. Indeed, students can learn from teachers they dislike. However, a wealth of research points to the following conclusion: students tend to learn more, and learn more efficiently, from teachers they like and respect. Your effectiveness increases when your students like you as a person, respect you as a teacher, are assured that you are prepared, sense your commitment to their growth, and can talk freely about what it is they are trying to learn.

Wanting to be liked can turn into a preoccupation. Teachers can become so absorbed in being seen as a friend and confidant that they blunt their effectiveness as a teacher. This misplaced priority becomes a substitute, rather than a catalyst, for student learning. New teachers lose ground by working too intensely at getting close to their students. Developing positive relationships becomes the overriding goal, displacing the learning of subject matter. Somehow you are expected to be close to your students while at the same time keeping a professional distance. A tension is created between authority and friendship. This dilemma tends to fade as the teacher learns the skillful combination of these two approaches.

## Relationships Change over Time

Your relationship with Chris at the end of the school year is quite different from what it was during the first month. Students grow and change over the school year—and so do you. Chris entered a tentative and unsure relationship with you. Bit by bit, it blossomed into one characterized by clear expectations on both sides, along with the ability to communicate them. In the same classroom, your initially close relationship with Ann waned after the first few months but is now regaining its fullness. At the beginning of the school year, you had difficulty establishing rapport with Josh. Things are even worse now; he simply goes through the motions, avoiding you.

*Elizabeth Crews/Stock, Boston*

Modifying your relationships with students to accommodate their growth contributes immensely to your effectiveness. During the year, your middle school students grow in their capacity to conceptualize rather than merely memorize, engage in thoughtful discussions, probe, reflect on their learning, consider alternative solutions to problems, and work independently. You are alert to this intellectual growth and make instructional adjustments. Watching the process causes you to *see* students differently, as the same group but with increased maturity. As your perceptions change, you automatically convey a new set of expectations, which in turn propel the students to higher performance.

But suppose that, as often happens, changes go the other way. André, characteristically a model student, is stressed by his parents' divorce. Concentration dwindles, homework is left undone, test scores plummet. How does your relationship with him change? It takes on a more patient, supportive, and understanding tone. There are other times when you need to be particularly patient and supportive, when students face unsettling events such as changing homes and neighborhoods, becoming pregnant, abusing drugs, breaking off a friendship, and failing to make the cheerleading team.

The change may be prompted by events in your own life. For instance, you are awarded a master's degree and, if nothing else, feel more confident about your abilities. Students come to see you as more relaxed and able to go with the flow of the day. Or your spouse becomes unemployed, creating a financial hardship in the home. You are seen by your students as more intense, less patient, and more standoffish.

Always be looking to change relationships in *productive* ways. "What," you ask yourself, "can I change about this relationship to facilitate Rico's growth? Does he now need me to back off a bit? Should I try to become more of a friend? Have I indulged him too much?"

## Relationships Grow in Their Complexity

Relationships can start out simple enough. But they invariably take on greater complexity as you open up to your students, and they to you. One teacher was fooled by the class's seeming tractability during the first week of school:

> The first week or two, the vast majority of my students just sat, seemed to listen attentively, and asked questions when called for. All was sweetness and light, it seemed—except that, at times, I felt like a leper. . . . As the first month passed, the routine and boredom of even this school began to set in. Many of the students did not understand why they were required to take four years of science (or English, or physical education, for that matter). The happy, relaxed, loosely disciplined class which I saw developing began to take strange and subtle turns in the wrong directions. The students were not just happy and relaxed, they were content and almost asleep. I started to get the messge: their natural curiosity had not been aroused. . . . Instead of just sitting on the tables, a few were sprawled out on them. My resolve was still not shaken. They would soon tire of such shenanigans, and I could win them back through my artfully designed presentations. . . . In reality, as far as the students were concerned, the testing period was already over, and they had won the game. I was going to be a pushover. . . . But one day when I was not mentally braced for the usual harassments, I did what came naturally and gave it to them with both barrels— a thorough chewing-out. . . . After this incident, I felt that things would simmer down, which they did for a while. But when trouble began to brew again, I asked each individual in the little core group of five to meet me after school for a five-minute conference. All agreed to come, but only one showed up. I was obviously still not a "significant other" for them, in any sense of the word.[18]

Over time, your relationship with each student takes on new dimensions. It may move toward greater empathy, stronger dislike, increased understanding, less formality, additional negotiation, shorter patience, or more affection. The result is a depletion of your energy, more worry, stronger bonding, and richer satisfactions.

## Relationships Are Affected by Society's Moods

The mood of society during any period affects your relationships with students and parents. For example, prestigious committees on education conclude that high school seniors graduate with alarming illiteracy. Parents of

## A Champion of Teachers

Albert Shanker became national president of the American Federation of Teachers (AFT) in 1974. During the succeeding ten years, the AFT's membership increased 45 percent. It now stands at 680,000, two-thirds of whom are teachers. This is still short of the 1.6 million membership in the other major teachers' association, the National Education Association (NEA). Still, throughout his presidency of the AFT, Shanker captured the attention of many millions.

In the late 1960s, Shanker and other militant leaders of teacher unionism were held in disrepute by many Americans. Over the years, however, Shanker has become a respected advocate of across-the-board reform in education. With considerable conviction and energy he calls for educational reform: making early childhood education a part of formal schooling, implementing a modified voucher system, and strengthening teacher standards.

As a vehicle for promulgating his views (and those of the AFT), Shanker instituted a long-running weekly column, "Where We Stand," in the Sunday *New York Times*. Informative, thoughtful, typically controversial, his column has frequently anticipated major movements in education and society.

Shanker continues to press for the "professionalization" of teachers. In 1985, he launched a national campaign to create a national exam for beginning teachers. His push helped the AFT to rise above its own self-interests in order to enhance the overall quality of education in the United States. In addition to pressing for teaching excellence, Shanker has promoted measures to "enrich, enhance, and empower the role and status of teachers." He feels that teachers, like doctors and lawyers, should control "the business of their business," determining their own prescriptions for professional performance.

Shanker is dedicated to what he terms the "revolution that's overdue." Everything, in his mind, ultimately affects education. A compelling and skilled communicator, he speaks out on virtually any issue. In the words of one educator, he routinely mesmerizes audiences: "He can charge an auditorium full of skeptics with an overarching vision of what it takes to make us a nation of learners." Nonetheless, he is a realist, a political operator who knows the value of compromise.

Shanker's leadership of the AFT has carried over to the National Education Association, influencing its leaders to speak out and publicize their own views on educational issues. Having earned national respect as an educational spokesman, Shanker is now being followed by a new generation of leaders. How will they now gather and disseminate a vast store of information, build networks, engage in legislative manipulation, and persuade both teachers and the public?

G. R. Kaplan, "Shining Lights in High Places: Education's Top Four Leaders and Their Heirs," *Phi Delta Kappan*, September 1985, pp. 7–16.

seniors on the road to graduation march into parent–teacher conferences with a *my*-daughter-had-better-not-be-illiterate attitude. This combative posture places you on the defensive. To assert your credibility, you start justifying the school's program. Look at the relationship—adversarial. You murmur to yourself, "It's all a media hype. Parents watch too much television. Our seniors are above the national average in literacy skills."

Or suppose there is a prevailing belief that teachers are overpaid for services rendered. At the same time, teachers are forced to strike for higher salaries. Parents are then anything but sympathetic when you cause their children to miss school: "You're overpaid as it is. You'd better make sure my child gets a darn good education!" This attitude, passed on to the child, finds expression in such comments as these:

"School's not all it's cracked up to be."

"Teachers aren't very well informed."

"I wish the teacher would take more time to help on an individual basis."

A relationship under these conditions is very different from one that is rich in mutual respect.

## Relationships Are Affected by Personal Values

Cultivating relationships with students whose values are different from your own is both demanding and rewarding. For example, feelings about classroom organization may differ. Let's say you value a relaxed atmosphere, one in which students enjoy considerable freedom. They move about, engaging in a variety of conversations, select their own projects, and work independently or in groups as their interests dictate. Your room is not terribly organized, but it nicely accommodates all sorts of student/work configurations. Fran, a compulsively organized student, is at her best in a highly structured setting. She wants the teacher at the front of the room making formal presentations and following up with clearly defined seatwork. After the first week, Fran begins complaining about "not being able to learn in this noisy room." For you, flexibility and independent learning are important; for Fran, teacher-led instruction in a well-ordered classroom is vital. Here is your challenge: facilitate Fran's learning.

## Relationships Are Affected by Personal Well-Being

Because teaching is such an intensely human experience, your emotional ups and downs are promptly revealed in your work. Periodic stressors (a death in the family, divorce, illness) as well as long-term personality needs are reflected in your teaching. Suppose you have an exaggerated need for recognition, or you are easily offended, or you are painfully shy, or you lack courage to try new ideas. These traits create anxiety and affect the nature of your teaching relationships. One teacher fears looking inferior, and therefore she cannot enter helping relationships—so she keeps her painstakingly constructed social science unit to herself. Another is so insecure in his own knowledge of the subject matter that he puts down students who challenge his ideas. A teacher who desperately wants the students to like her loses disciplinary control, enforcing rules one day and becoming a marshmallow the next.

These examples point to the importance of a foundation of emotional well-being on which to build successful relationships. When their own needs are being satisfied, teachers can achieve serenity and focus more on the needs of students than on their own.

# CONCLUSION

Less effective relationships usually result more from unwillingness than from inability. If you work at them, relationships will bear fruit. You have considerable control over how they develop and are maintained. If you start out expecting productive relationships, they tend to become so—your students and colleagues respond to your expectations. Effective teachers, as we will see in Chapter 9, exhibit a can-do attitude about their ability to breed solid learning relationships with their students. Poor relationships can improve; good ones can deepen. The possibilities abound.

## Expansions

1. Are there any aspects of your personality that might initially hinder you from developing productive relationships with your students? What aspects of your personality will probably facilitate good relationships?

2. Visit with two experienced teachers. Ask them to tell you their "secrets" for successful relationships with students, other teachers, and principals. Tuck these notes away until you have your own classroom.

3. Some teachers, as they settle into their work, tend to retreat into their own private world of teaching, not communicating much about it and not turning to other teachers to explore new ideas or receive specific help. Can you predict your own tendencies in this respect?

4. What are some advantages and disadvantages of widening your relationships within your school (with other teachers, the custodian, the department head, the assistant principals, secretaries)?

5. What will you do to form productive relationships with other teachers in your school? What are you prepared to offer?

6. Explain how you will try to relate to parents.

7. Suppose you had a strong need for recognition. How might you satisfy this need through your relationships with students? Do you see any pitfalls?

8. Explain this statement: "When a teacher fails to develop productive relationships with students, it's due more to his unwillingness than to his inability."

## Notes

1. From the journal of a first-year sixth-grade teacher (personal communication).

2. E. Fuchs, *Teachers Talk: Views from Inside City Schools* (Garden City, N. Y.: Anchor Books, Doubleday, 1969), p. 28.

3. G. Cornog, "To Care and Not to Care," in Kevin Ryan (Ed.), *Don't Smile until Christmas: Accounts of the First Year of Teaching* (Chicago: University of Chicago Press, 1970), p. 3.

4. From the journal of a second-grade teacher (personal communication).

5. R. S. Barth, "The Principal and the Profession of Teaching," *The Elementary School Journal* 86(4), (1986), p. 473.

6. D. Lortie, *Schoolteacher* (Chicago: University of Chicago Press, 1975).

7. Barth, "The Principal," p. 472.

8. Fuchs, *Teachers Talk,* pp. 65–66.

9. From the journal of a first-grade teacher (personal communication).

10. Barth, "The Principal," p. 472.

11. K. Duckworth and D. Carnine, "The Quality of Teacher–Principal Relationships," in Virginia Richardson-Koehler (Ed.), *Educators' Handbook: A Research Perspective* (New York: Longman, 1987), p. 465.

12. From the journal of a first-year second-grade teacher (personal communication).

13. S. L. Lightfoot, *Worlds Apart: Relationships between Families and Schools* (New York: Basic Books, 1978), p. 37.

14. P. O. Gonder, "Exchange School and Community Resources," in D. Davies (Ed.), *Communities and Their Schools* (New York: McGraw-Hill, 1981).

15. A. H. Cantril, *The School-Home Community Relationship: An Interpretive Summary of the Public View,* report prepared for the U.S. Office of Education (Washington, D.C.: U.S. Government Printing Office, 1979).

16. From the journal of a fourth-grade teacher (personal communication).

17. From the journal of a primary-grade resource teacher (personal communication).

18. W. Crawford, "The Other Side of the Coin," in Kevin Ryan (Ed.), *Don't Smile until Christmas: Accounts of the First Year of Teaching* (Chicago: University of Chicago Press, 1970), pp. 85–87.

# CHAPTER 4

# THE CURRICULUM

*To a person uninstructed in Natural History,*
*his country or a seaside stroll is a walk through*
*a gallery filled with wonderful works of art,*
*nine-tenths of which have their faces turned to*
*the wall.—Thomas Henry Huxley*

**MAIN IDEAS**

- Your school has both a prescribed and "hidden" curriculum which, together, create a culture for learning a wide variety of norms, behavior, attitudes, and intellectual skills.

- The curriculum you teach has been shaped by a variety of historical movements and disciplines, such as experimentalism, the behavioral objectives movement, mastery learning, programmed instruction, and educational technology.

- Curricular influences include textbooks, business corporations, research findings, government, national commissions and private foundations, school boards, parent–teacher associations, your principal, and other teachers in your school.

- Others influence the curriculum you teach, but you are the major force behind its implementation and adaptation. You enjoy ample freedom—and shoulder considerable responsibility—in shaping it to your students' needs.

# INTRODUCTION

Mr. Della Penna, sixth-grade team leader, orients Ms. Liset, a shiny new teacher, to her curriculum responsibilities:

> Here's your copy of the social studies text, and the teacher's manual that goes with it.
>
> And here's your math text. We'll probably change next year.
>
> Social studies is a mess right now. The study units were developed by the district over two years ago. Nobody in our school likes them, but the district thinks they're great. We're free to use anything better we can find, and I'm on the lookout.
>
> Science? Well, you're on your own. I've developed my own units, and you're welcome to use any that look good to you.
>
> Getting going takes almost all your first year. You'll have lots of work and worry ahead of you, but don't feel overwhelmed. It's easier once your units are in place, especially the second time around—well, until the district comes along with a different plan.

To be sure, your teacher education program exposes you to content areas such as math, reading, English, and history. But these subjects are general in nature, and your school will have its own curriculum. Naturally, teachers wonder what, precisely, they will be teaching:

"What skills and concepts will I be teaching in math?"

> "I have my own ideas about what I think kids ought to read. I wonder how much the principal will let me do on my own."

"There are parts of U.S. history I definitely want to cover. What if the adopted text leaves important topics out?"

> "I wonder what the school policy is on teaching controversial topics like AIDS and contraceptives. Kids need to know about these things."

New teachers become anxious in approaching the curriculum. They worry about their awesome responsibility, their ability to teach an assigned subject, and about having sufficient help:

"I'm coming into social studies cold. They'd better have a good teacher's manual!"

> "I feel like I'm suffocating. They teach art out of the Dark Ages—no creativity whatsoever. No wonder this stuff is deadly dull. They've programmed me into this thing and there's absolutely nothing I can do."

"They'd better understand I'll be teaching the evils of computers!"

"I've never had so much freedom! But it's a two-edged sword. I'm feeling too much pressure to come up with good material on these new units."

"The authors have done all my work. I just have to read the teacher's edition and follow along."

How do teachers feel when they first face their curriculum? Some are uneasily or defiantly negative, prepared to resign themselves to it if not to challenge it. Others are enthusiastically positive, boldly committed. In this chapter we introduce you to the curriculum, its content, and your responsibility to adapt it to your students.

# THE SCHOOL'S HIDDEN CURRICULUM

You probably think of the curriculum as *what* will be taught—the content of your day-to-day teaching: objectives, subject matter, lecture notes, assignments, tests, textbooks, teacher's manual, and content units. At first glance, the "curriculum" seems to be anything a teacher teaches in his classroom.

But there is often more teaching going on than a teacher plans, much of it unintentional. Further, more learning is occurring than the teacher can control or hope to harness. Not only do your students learn about the inter-

© George Mars Cassidy/The Picture Cube

*As with all great teachers, his curriculum was an insignificant part of what
he communicated. From him you didn't learn a subject, but life. The best
teacher made his students think and he opened windows and he pointed to
the horizon beyond.*—Houston Peterson

nal organs of a frog through dissection but they simultaneously acquire attitudes during the process. ("I'd hate to operate on animals. I get sick every
time I think about cutting up those poor things. I can't get over what amaz-
ing machines living creatures are.")

Many definitions of "curriculum" are limited to those experiences for
which the school can take responsibility. Helping the student learn to read,
develop computational skills, appreciate history, and type is the school's
function and the teacher's responsibility.

However, there is another curriculum at work in the school, a *hidden*
curriculum, which plays a major role in the overall development of your students. In addition to academic learning, the hidden curriculum includes the
learning of attitudes and social behaviors: attitudes toward bullies, preferences for hairstyles, ways to become a leader, unwritten rules for becoming
a member of the "in" group, and ways to apple-polish the teacher. Some
writers suggest that this hidden curriculum, because of its social nature, provides the most critical training students receive in school. For example,
on the playground a second-grade boy soon finds out what it feels like to
be chosen last on a kickball team. An eighth-grade girl discovers how to
get attention from boys by wearing "hot" clothes. A senior boy learns, too
late, that his three years of varsity football have cost him entrance to the
university.

Often the goals of the hidden curriculum are different from those the
school hopes to achieve in its *manifest* curriculum. Being accepted by the
"in" group may be far more significant to a student than receiving an A in
French. Being seen as a person who wears neat clothes may be more important than being "Scholar of the Month." Note how the hidden curriculum is
operating in this group of young learners:

"There! I didn't understand that, but I got it done."

"I'm almost through—just two more."

"How far are you?"

These comments reveal a hidden curriculum goal on the part of the children:
completing the assignment rather than comprehending the task. They are
more concerned with the progress in completing the task and receiving approval than in performing accurately.[1]

From the hidden curriculum, the student can learn how to gain the respect of a social group. The football player enjoys rewards from his team-

mates for fair and valiant play on the field. The gymnast is acclaimed by her teammates for giving it her all in the floor exercises.

The hidden curriculum also transmits covert messages to the student—messages about social groups and social roles valued by students (for instance, cheerleaders, athletes), behaviors valued by the school (such as getting to class punctually, not being disruptive in the halls, completing assignments on time), and types of people that are excluded from the most influential social groups (for example, minority students, "nerds," "fringies").

The school would like to take credit for some aspects of this hidden curriculum and deny responsibility for others. For example, after being excluded from the "in" group, Mary learns that she can gain recognition through high achievement. Although the school cannot be responsible for fostering "in" groups (so students can learn to deal with acceptance and rejection), Mary's outcome is a positive one for which the school would like to take credit. In contrast, Jim, through a social group at school, starts experimenting with drugs and becomes a frequent user. The school would not claim responsibility for a hidden curriculum that encouraged his drug abuse.

The school curriculum, manifest and hidden, creates a culture in which the student engages in a wide range of activities that generate learning: seatwork, homework, class discussions, lunch period, recess, casual conversations in the halls, and reviewing for tests. The curriculum also includes sitting through boring lunch-hour films, operating a sewing machine, typing on a computer, being sent to the school counselor, becoming hoarse from yelling during a pep assembly, learning songs for a special program, playing on the soccer team, being a member of the marching band, working on the yearbook, trying out for cheerleader, being cut from the golf team, going on tour with the madrigals, being called into the principal's office, witnessing a fight on the playground, not having a date for the prom, and being laughed at for wearing braces.

# YOUR CURRICULUM

## History of Your Curriculum

The major historical movements summarized in Chapter 1 shape much of today's curriculum. We briefly review these movements from a curricular point of view. Then, as we address the question "What will your curriculum be like?" you will recognize its historical underpinnings and understand, in part, what makes it the way it is today.

From the 1600s well into the 1800s, the curriculum for children was intensively religious. Over time, religious subject matter was replaced by academic content, which in time was infused with vocational content. In each case, these shifts were a response to the values of a rapidly changing society.

Young children learned to read so they could study the Bible, which

*Education is life, not subject matter.—John Dewey*

included principles valued by a developing country. Soon, however, reading and writing became essential for children to master the increasingly complex crafts of their parents. Somewhat later, leaders and visionaries realized that only a society with an informed citizenry could succeed. So the curriculum was adapted for the masses. The ensuing Industrial Revolution demanded a practical curriculum.

Dewey's experimentalism moved schools toward a life-centered curriculum designed to prepare students to live effectively in a society. The force of the testing movement prodded teachers to prepare students to perform well on standardized tests measuring various kinds of cognitive skills. This reaction drove teachers toward a drill-and-practice curriculum. Later, life-centered movements pulled the curriculum back toward social interaction, communication, and helping students cope with the problems of a complex society.

Sputnik drove us back to hard-headed subjects such as math and science and to the development of tougher technical skills. The federal government moved into schools for the first time, funding large curriculum projects in the hard sciences. The War on Poverty turned the curriculum back again to social needs. Vocational, handicapped, socially disadvantaged, and ethnic programs were funded. The Vietnam War inspired a cry for relevance that found its way into the curriculum: "Is it good or right? If not, throw it out!"

The behavioral objectives movement was a thrust to make the curriculum specific and precise, to render learning measurable. Teachers were pushed toward greater accountability and toward focusing on quantifiable outcomes for their students. This shift brought about an emphasis on piecemeal information and low-level mental skills such as memorizing and recalling. Today, teachers are expected to list specific objectives at the beginning of each lesson plan.

The concept of mastery learning, based on the behavioral objectives movement, placed an emphasis on individual differences. Individual pacing and tailored learning activities were generated to meet the needs of each student. Programmed instruction moved us in the direction of "packaging" the curriculum and paved the way for an exploding technology to enter education. Technology focused us on the need for a potent vehicle to design and carry the instructional message. The curriculum took on greater structure and was broken down into precise concepts and step-by-step procedures for learning them.

The computer opened the way for startling versatility in presenting instructional material and in allowing students to interact with subject matter in order to learn. Cognitive psychology has provided knowledge about student thought processes, including how students think, reason, and solve problems. The 1983 report *A Nation at Risk,* from the National Commission on Excellence in Education, asserted that our country was suffering from an alarming rate of illiteracy. This and other similar reports accelerated the curriculum's movement once again back to the basics—math, science, reading, and other traditional subjects—an emphasis that had begun as early as the mid-1970s.

Although concerns about teaching "thinking" are not new, having been in and out of fashion under such labels as "inquiry," "inductive teaching," "discovery," and "learning styles," the period from the latter 1970s into the 1980s brought a rediscovery of this emphasis. Teachers and administrators were presented with many programs designed to train students to think. Most were aimed at upper elementary, middle school, and secondary school students.

One highly successful example of these programs is DeBono's CoRT thinking program. CoRT stands for Cognitive Research Thrust and represents a series of lessons for directly teaching thinking skills as a curriculum subject in schools. The first of the sixty lessons is the PMI (plus, minus, interesting) scanning program. PMI is a thinking tool students are taught to use when confronted with a particular situation. For example, if students are asked to react to the idea of receiving $5 a week for attending school, they might think of all the pluses, minuses, and interesting possibilities with such a reward system.[2]

Another example of a learning-to-think program was developed by Perkins, who stressed that understanding any knowledge or any object involves viewing it as a design, a structure shaped to a purpose. In particular, understanding involves exploring four questions: What is its purpose? What is its structure? What are model cases? What arguments explain and evaluate the knowledge or the object?

In one of Perkin's lessons on "inventive thinking," students are taught strategies for analyzing everyday designs like chairs and tacks. They evaluate these designs, plan improvements on them, and use them to invent original gadgets. Another series of lessons, building on the same approach, helps these students view daily activities such as shopping in terms of design. After learning this approach, students include in their designs more features to help solve a given problem, describe their designs in much more detail, and include more detail in their sketches. Apparently, students learn patterns of creative thinking as they apply these simple design tasks.[3]

Cutting across the curriculum, flashy programs such as these attempt to train students to think critically and reflectively, reason logically, make inferences, organize ideas, and solve problems. Strategies used to teach thinking skills have been dressed up in such labels as *schema* (using prior knowledge, relating ideas to experience, integrating the old and the new), *focus* (breaking things down, analyzing, encoding, representing, deciding what is relevant and what are the key units to focus on), *pattern* (combining, putting together, synthesizing, seeing patterns, forming concepts, conceiving

*Merely having an open mind is nothing. The object of opening the mind,*
*as of opening the mouth, is to shut it again on something solid.*
—Lord P. D. Chesterfield

the whole entity), *extension* (using what is known to understand and act upon increasingly complex problems and situations), *projection* (diverging from the known to create new and different understandings or forms), and *metacognition* (thinking about one's own thinking; using executive/control processes).[4]

These and other contributors have advanced the curriculum along its evolutionary path.

## Nature of Your Curriculum

What will your curriculum be like? If you teach at the elementary level, what math book will you use and what mathematical operations will you teach? If you teach in a middle school, what will your general science course be like? What English literature will you cover at your high school? Clearly, we cannot answer these questions specifically, since even within a particular district, schools show differences in their curricula. When you arrive at your own school you will learn the particulars soon enough.

© Rick Mansfield/The Image Works

GOALS   Are there some national objectives, some universal subjects taught to all students at a given age level across the country? Yes. National educational goals have been with us for many years. Here is an example: "A purpose of the school is to produce good citizens." Such general goals provide little direction to a teacher attempting to generate specific instructional objectives in her building. Time and energy are required to translate national goals into specific goals for a particular set of students. For example, an elementary teacher may define her huge "citizenship" goal as including the principle "All students will respect the personal belongings of others." A high school may define this same universal "citizenship" goal as including a policy like this: "Students will take part in at least one community service project, such as assisting in voter registration, joining a work project to clean a public park, or distributing flyers for city officials." Large goals, when translated into specific instructional objectives, become unique to a given district, school, or even classroom.

The standard curriculum also includes specified general subject areas. States and districts provide textbooks and curriculum guides that are major sources of your academic curriculum. Following is a sample recommended by one state curriculum guide. It shows what subjects are taught statewide and how those subjects change or reappear in more expanded form over the course of the student's educational career.

Elementary (grades K–6)
  *Core areas:*
  Language arts (reading, writing, speaking, listening)
  Mathematics
  Science
  Social studies (introductory citizenship, principles and practices)
  Arts (music, dance, art)
  Healthy lifestyles
  Information technology
  *Options:*
  Foreign language
Middle school (grades 7–8)
  Language arts
  Math (algebra)
  Science (physical science, earth/space, life science)
  Social studies (U.S. history, state history)
  The arts (visual arts, music, chorus, band, orchestra, dance, drama)
  Information technology
  Healthy lifestyles (beginning and intermediate fitness, team sport skills, dance, personal health)
  Prevocational exploration

High school (grades 9–12)

> Language arts
>
> Math (algebra, geometry, trigonometry, analytic geometry, calculus)
>
> Science (physics, chemistry, biology, biological earth science, physical earth science)
>
> Information technology
>
> Social studies (economics, psychology, sociology, U.S. government, world cultural geography, ancient world civilizations, world cultural geography, U.S. history, state history)
>
> Arts (music theory, chorus, band, orchestra, dance, theater)
>
> Healthy lifestyles (consumer health, participation skills and techniques, fitness for life, advanced individualized lifetime activities)[5]

## What does this sample of subjects tell us?

1.    Students are exposed to the same subjects repeatedly over the course of their schooling. This pattern attests to the importance of basic subjects such as math, science, social studies, and language arts.

2.    At higher grade levels, the same subject is covered with increasing sophistication and detail. For example, social studies in the elementary grades consists of introductory citizenship; in the middle school, of U.S. and state government; and in senior high, of economics, psychology, sociology, and a host of other subjects. Topics in psychology are mentioned from time to time in elementary grades; they form a week-long unit in the middle school; and they constitute a semester's class in high school.

3.    Students have greater freedom to choose which subjects they take as they move up through the grades. At the elementary level, art is an integral part of the curriculum for all students; in high school, it is an elective.

4.    New options for subject matter become available in later grades. For example, high school students can enroll in theater, consumer health, or fitness for life.

5.    The subjects you teach will, in all likelihood, have been taught at an earlier stage to your students, and they will receive instruction in your subject after they leave you. Thus, you are either creating a foundation or building on one, teaching material for the first time or reteaching it. Realizing that you are a link in the chain tends to engender a feeling of responsibility to those teachers who will pick up where you leave off. Suppose you are helping first-graders build their repertoire of words that can be recognized by sight. You realize that their subsequent success in reading comprehension will depend, in part, on the groundwork you provide. Or you are a third-grade teacher drilling students on their multiplication tables. Tiring as these drill-and-practice exercises seem now, you know that automaticity of multiplication facts is essential to all subsequent work in mathematics.

## A Changing Curriculum

The curriculum is a mirror that reflects America's dreams for its next generation. It is through the school curriculum that Americans attempt to translate their values into reality. Therefore, no area of this nation's schooling has such a difficult, complicated, and dramatic history as the school curriculum.

The term *curriculum* is derived from the Latin word *currere,* which, in its most literal interpretation, means a running course. In recent years, as our society has placed increasing responsibility on its schools, the image of the running course has become less appropriate. The curriculum of the American school has come more to resemble a labyrinth, replete with serpentine twists and turns, and less a well-designed track.

This transformation of the American school curriculum can be attributed to two general sets of factors. The first of these is the increase in the complexity of society, requiring that individuals know more to serve in a technologically sophisticated environment. Second, in the last half of the twentieth century a tide of rising expectations has swept over all aspects of our country's life, necessitating that the schools and their curricula be more elaborate and accountable with each passing year. Each of these sets of factors has made the curriculum much more involved than it has been in the past.

A. K. Ellis, J. A. Mackey, and A. D. Glenn, *The School Curriculum* (Boston: Allyn and Bacon, 1988), p. 3.

OBJECTIVES   Each course in a given subject is described by a set of instructional objectives sometimes defined in the curriculum guide but often defined by the teacher. The objectives are distinct from the subject matter itself: an objective is a statement of the student's expected behavior with respect to some subject. For example, if your subject is English literature—specifically, the short story—then an objective for your students might be "The student will be able to describe the characteristics of short stories." Objectives can be used to help you plan your instruction and your evaluations.

The following sample of objectives is probably representative of what you will find in your own classroom curriculum guide.

EXAMPLE 1   Taken from a visual arts curriculum, grades 7–8

*General objective:* The students will develop skills vital to making art by rendering structure, value, scale, shapes, texture, depth, and color in a picture.

*Specific objectives:* The students will be able to

1.   draw objects as variations of the circle, square, and triangle.
2.   render variations of darkness and lightness in a drawing.
3.   use structural lines to define the planes or surfaces of objects.

© Elizabeth Crews/The Image Works

**EXAMPLE 2** Taken from a mathematics curriculum, grades 9–12

*General objective:* The students will demonstrate knowledge of a mathematical system.

*Specific objectives:* The students will

1. be able to define the Trichotomy Principle.
2. know that if unequals are added to unequals in the same sense, the results are unequal in the same sense.
3. know that if $a$, $b$, $c$, and $d$ are positive and $a > b$ and $c > d$, then $ac > bd$.

**EXAMPLE 3** Taken from a social studies curriculum, grade 1

*General objective:* The students will understand that individuals need rules to govern group behavior.

*Specific objectives:* The students will be able to

1. identify the reasons for authority and rules.
2. make classroom rules with other class members.
3. explain how orderly classrooms depend on cooperation.[6]

# MAJOR SUBJECT AREAS IN THE CURRICULUM

The subject matter taught in today's curriculum is rather consistent at both the elementary and secondary levels and from state to state. Typical subjects are language arts, science, mathematics, foreign languages, social studies, the arts, and physical and health education.

## Language Arts

Language arts hold a preeminent position in the curriculum, since language skills are necessary not only for communicating but for studying almost any subject. Language arts include reading, writing, speaking, and listening. These four communications skills emphasize the use of language symbols (words, letters, and sounds).

READING   Reformers and critics are of one voice in emphasizing the importance of reading, from the youngest levels on up. United States Secretary of Education William J. Bennett said,

> The elementary school must assume as its sublime and most solemn responsibility the task of teaching every child in it to read. Any school that does

© Paul Conklin/Monkmeyer Press Photo

© Elizabeth Hamlin/Stock, Boston

not accomplish this has failed. There is no excuse for the illiteracy and semi-literacy we are finding in our high schools and colleges, though there is a powerful explanation for this lamentable situation. The explanation, simply stated, is that some elementary schools—and responsible adults in other settings—have failed in their most basic responsibility: to send children forth into junior high, high school, and the adult world, reading fluently. . . . It is not as if we do not know how to achieve universal literacy among our young people. . . . According to *Becoming a Nation of Readers,* the report of the Commission on Reading: "The last decade has witnessed unprecedented advances in knowledge about the basic processes involved in reading, teaching and learning. The knowledge is now available to make worthwhile improvements in reading throughout the United States.". . . With all we know, we must not accept failure.[7]

Just what is reading? The exact nature of the reading process is the subject of ongoing debate; how you view the process will influence how you teach reading. Some teachers emphasize decoding (translating printed letters into speech sounds) more than comprehension (skills that enable the reader to recognize the meanings of words and sentences and to think about what the author is saying). They are less concerned with the author's message than with word accuracy. Other teachers stress getting the message more than the practicing of subskills and word-by-word accuracy.

However one views it, reading is a complex undertaking: "Reading is an interactive process, involving the interplay of several thought processes at the same time and making use of our incredibly complex brain."[8]

The skills and habits practiced by good readers reveal much about the act of reading in general. These are things that good readers have in common:[9]

- Good readers view reading as a process of communication between reader and author.

- Good readers score high on reading comprehension (though often making meaningful substitutions, self-corrections, omissions, and insertions).

- Good readers make use of
  1. syntax cues (context cues provided by word type; for example, noun, verb, and word order)
  2. semantic cues (content cues provided by the meaning of surrounding words)
  3. graphophonic cues (cues provided by single letters or groups of letters, such as -ing)
  4. background cues (cues provided through memories, mental images, or association, that facilitate understanding).

- Good readers make better use of decoding skills than poor readers (for example, sight vocabulary, phonics, and suffixes).

- Good readers use comprehension monitoring while reading (for example, recognizing that they have not understood what they read and going back to reread it).

WRITING  Writing is a communications skill that has been seriously neglected. Evidence is found in the weak writing ability of high school students and the embarrassing lack of skill among college students. College freshmen flock to remedial writing classes. University officials are pressuring high schools and elementary schools to teach these skills thoroughly and at earlier ages.

Renewed interest in teaching writing skills has resulted from (1) an increasing number of low-income and minority students entering college and seeking middle-class occupations requiring writing skill and (2) the need in many occupations for information-processing skills requiring the ability to write.

Much of a student's writing in school is incidental to some other purpose, such as recalling and writing down answers on a test measuring his academic achievement. But focusing on writing itself, for its intrinsic value, has been stressed recently by educators. The major aim of "expressive" writing, such as personal journals and self-descriptions, is to bring satisfaction to the student, and only secondarily to develop writing skills. Composition, spelling drills, sentence combining, punctuation drills, and proper formatting are exercises intended for the express purpose of developing writing skill.

The advent of the word processor and a growing body of research on the teaching of writing suggest the value of a coaching-while-writing approach.[10] While the student is considering a topic, outlining an approach,

*Education is not something that is done for a student or to a student. It is what the student does for himself in developing his own powers. Teachers can help; so can a curriculum and an atmosphere of devotion to things of the mind. But ultimately the problem is utterly the student's.—Charles W. Cols*

and writing sections of a paper, the teacher stands by as coach. Traditionally the teacher has been a judge, waiting until the student has completed the entire writing process before providing corrective feedback. Accumulated research suggests that whatever approach is used, the most effective results come when students write regularly and receive guided feedback along the way. Therefore, effective teachers establish a "culture of writing" in their classrooms, where writing occurs on a daily basis.

Recent research has shown the power of direct teaching of writing skills. Programs for teaching expository writing in high school teach students how to analyze, organize, and write clearly. For example, students are asked to arrange jumbled sentences into logical order and form them into an essay. Exercises of this type force students to see relationships among sentences and discover the logic inherent in different writing patterns. At the elementary level, programs are appearing that teach children how to process information, coordinate ideas, and write them clearly.

Recent years have brought an increasing urgency to teach middle and high school students the basic writing skills needed for employment. Particularly concerned about those who are functionally illiterate, teachers are turning back to the teaching of basic skills:

> The basic skills movement in English is seen in the demand for more history of classical literature, more traditional grammar, and a greater emphasis on formal rather than personal writing. There is a return to the workbook and hard cover anthology. Elective programs are being dismantled (they are accused of fragmenting and diminishing the goals of an integrated approach to English); the new linguistics is gone; 'personal growth' and 'creativity' are disparaged.[11]

SPEAKING AND LISTENING  Developing students' speaking and listening skills is a major task of the schools. Listening forms the basis of the language arts curriculum; indeed, in many classrooms, students are required to listen more than half of every school day. Research has shown that a good foundation in speaking and listening helps students become better readers: "When children learn to read, they are making a transition from spoken to written language. Reading instruction builds on conversational skills, and the better children are at using spoken language, the more successfully they will learn to read written language."[12]

Teachers can do much to facilitate development of speaking and listening skills, engaging their students in thoughtful discussions about a wide variety of subjects, conversing with them about their world, and helping them reflect on past experiences and those yet to come. Children develop speaking and listening skills through a wide range of school experiences: listening to and telling about sounds, words, and sentences; participating in group speech and dramatic activities (including storytelling and puppetry); creating art projects and describing them; and making up words for songs.

There is a strong connection between reading and listening. Good listeners can repeat instructions, remember details, retell stories, and exhibit many of the qualities possessed by good readers.

## Science

Today's push for a strong science curriculum had its origins in the late 1950s, when the Soviet's launching of *Sputnik* put a burr under our technological saddle. A number of large science curriculum projects emerged in the early 1960s, including the Elementary Science Study, the Science Curriculum Improvement Study, the Physical Sciences Study Committee, the Biological Science Curriculum Study, and Science—A Process Approach. Private and government monies were poured into the development of modern science courses "which were discipline centered, laboratory based, and founded upon an inductive problem-solving philosophy designed to encourage students to behave 'like practicing scientists.'"[13]

Today, the ideal elementary school science curriculum is characterized as follows:

1.  It is taught as a unified subject, not as separate sciences (that is, as "science" rather than physics, chemistry, biology).

© Spencer Grant/The Picture Cube

2. It involves children in direct experiences with living and nonliving objects and materials.

3. Its goal is to focus on the development of mental and physical skills, attitudes, and concepts rather than on merely learning facts and principles.

4. It takes its subject matter from the child's immediate surroundings.[14]

But despite ambitious goals and urgings from various groups, science instruction in most courses at all grade levels follows a rather traditional pattern: the teacher is in control, lecturing about scientific facts, occasionally supplementing the textbook with this or that piece of information.

In a typical classroom, science teaching suffers in quantity as well as quality. The Association for Supervision and Curriculum Development found, for example, that fourth graders have only twenty-eight minutes per day allocated to science. (This is merely the amount of time allocated, not the actual instructional time, which might be considerably less.)[15] Further, teachers tend to use discretionary time (that is, time to be used as they choose) for subjects with which they have greater familiarity, typically reading and language arts.

At the secondary level, science is characteristically taught as separate subjects: biology, physics, and chemistry. Here is a lofty and comprehensive science goal for college-bound students: "Students will develop the ability to understand the unifying concepts of the life and physical sciences, such as cell theory, geological evolution, organic evolution, atomic structure, chemical bonding, and transformation of energy."[16]

The laboratory part of the course, that student hands-on activity where "discovery" takes place, is currently undergoing scrutiny. Investigations of the efficacy of this traditional and highly valued experience are producing some surprising results. For one thing, many students perform experiments in the absence of any sense of their purpose. They are asked to breed fruit flies, red-eyed long wings with black-eyed short wings. The experiment is inevitably a success, but students often fail to recognize that they are learning the principle of genetic dominance. While teachers may be clear in their own minds about what is to be learned from such experiments, some of their students get sidetracked in the mechanics. Others, however, acquire the underlying concepts and a lifelong passion for science.[17]

## Mathematics

Mathematics is an indispensable tool in business, engineering, and the natural sciences. Along with language arts, it continues to occupy center stage in both elementary and secondary curricula. In the 1970s, the typical math program looked like this:

> The "median" classroom is self-contained. The mathematics period is about 43 minutes long, and about half of this time is written work. A single text is

*The smallest fact is a window through which the infinite may be seen.*
*—Thomas Henry Huxley*

used in whole-class instruction. The text is followed fairly closely, but students are likely to read at most one or two pages out of five pages of textual materials other than problems. It seems likely that the text, at least as far as the students are concerned, is primarily a source of problem lists. Teachers are essentially teaching the same way they were taught in school. Almost none of the concepts, methods, or big ideas of modern mathematics programs have appeared in this median classroom.[18]

Following is a summary report from one observer in a study commissioned by the National Science Foundation in the late 1970s:

In all math classes I visited, the sequence of activities was the same. First, answers were given for the previous day's assignment. The more difficult problems were worked by the teacher or a student at the chalkboard. A brief explanation, sometimes none at all, was given of the new material, and problems were assigned for the next day. The remainder of the class was devoted to working on the homework while the teacher moved about the room answering questions. The most noticeable thing about math classes was the repetition of this outline.[19]

We have already seen how the "new math" movement, beginning in the 1960s, shifted focus from mere calculating to understanding math concepts. But by the 1970s teachers were reacting negatively to these programs. Originally, the intent of the new math curriculum was to present math concepts through "discovery" methods. But this approach broke down (or never really got started) and teachers reverted to their old patterns of teaching calculation skills. Subsequent research on "new math" programs showed that students were not learning the concepts well, that the emphasis was on mechanical repetition, and that students were not able to solve real-life math problems. This disillusionment carried on into the 1980s and has, in part, led educators to develop a "back to basics" movement in math.

## Foreign Languages

As early as six years before Sputnik, the Modern Language Association of America was deploring the lack of foreign language instruction in our schools. There was, by the late 1950s, major concern in the United States about not doing more to advance scientific and technological research. This concern led to an accelerated program of foreign language study, designed to prepare students for an international exchange of knowledge. Schools responded. One and even two foreign languages became graduation requirements in many secondary schools and universities. More than 8000 elementary schools began offering instruction in foreign languages.

However, interest in foreign languages had waned by the mid-1960s. Reversing themselves, high schools and colleges started eliminating foreign-language requirements. Course enrollments fell, since most students signed up only to meet graduation requirements. In 1976, a presidential commission reported that only 4 percent of the nation's high school graduates had studied a foreign language for as long as two years. By 1980, only 15 percent of America's high school students were enrolled in foreign language courses, and one-fifth of the public high schools offered no courses at all. Among those that did, Spanish, French, and German were most frequently offered, in that order.

In the late 1980s, interest in foreign language instruction once again went on the upswing. This time, the emphasis was on making foreign language instruction more relevant to the student's current and future needs: to be able to work in firms with international clients, to travel and reside in foreign countries, and to expand personal interest in worldwide events. *What Works,* a 1986 U.S. Department of Education pamphlet presenting recent research on teaching and learning, reported, "The best way to learn a foreign language in school is to start early and to study it intensively over many years."[20] Further, "total immersion" language programs (teaching all subjects in the foreign language) that begin in early grades have been highly successful in teaching both language and regular academic subjects.

In secondary schools, foreign language departments are emphasizing speaking skills and striving to integrate the student's foreign language experiences into other subject areas of the curriculum:

> Subject matter integration is accomplished by introducing students to the contributions of language to all subject areas. English classes study the contribution of foreign languages to the development of American English, music classes study lyrics of foreign folk songs, and art classes share their work with those in foreign countries.[21]

## Social Studies

"Social studies" refers to that part of the school curriculum centering on human relationships, intentionally cultivating the development of good citizenship. This subject draws from history, geography, civics, economics, sociology, political science, and anthropology.

The term *social studies,* which first appeared in 1905, gained prestige in 1921 at the formation of the National Council for the Social Studies. By the 1920s, a social studies curriculum appeared in schools throughout the United States. With few exceptions, the same curricular sequence is still found in most elementary and secondary schools:

Grade 1    Families

Grade 2    Neighborhoods

Grade 3    Communities

Grade 4    State histories and geographic regions

Grade 5    American history

Grade 6    World cultures, Western Hemisphere

Grade 7    World geography or history

Grade 8    American history

Grade 9    Civics or world cultures

Grade 10   World history

Grade 11   American history

Grade 12   American government

Over the years, a central purpose of social studies has remained the same: to educate for good citizenship, particularly at the elementary level. Along the way, a number of societal factors have fortified this emphasis: (1) a need to socialize the flood of immigrants coming to the United States before and after the turn of the twentieth century, (2) an increased need to commit the nation's students to civic responsibility, and (3) heightened patriotism growing out of the two world wars.

Along with other aspects of the curriculum, social studies underwent revisions in the 1960s. More than forty curriculum projects produced the "new social studies." These projects made an important impact on education through influencing commercial publishers to develop instructional materials.[22] In this reform, heavy emphasis was placed on inductive teaching. One skill that students learned was to draw accurate conclusions from factual information.

Neither the earlier curriculum nor the revised model has succeeded notably in its basic purposes. Courses today represent a hodgepodge of unrelated learning activities. As one Secretary of Education has lamented, students "pick up bits of these lessons from an odd, amorphous grab-bag called 'social studies.'"[23] Nonetheless, educators continue forging ahead on the road of reform.

Social studies courses such as economics, sociology, psychology, and, to a lesser extent, geography and anthropology have found their way into seconday schools as electives. With popular concern about social issues such as racial and sexual equality, social studies is stoking its flickering fire.

## The Arts

The area of the curriculum known as "the arts" includes visual arts (for example, painting), music, dance, drama, and aesthetics (the appreciation of things that are beautiful). A director of the National Gallery of Art heralded the central role of art in our world: "The texts of man's achievements are not written exclusively in words. They are written, as well, in architecture, paintings, sculpture, drawings, photography, and in urban, graphic, landscape, and industrial design."[24]

© Dan Chidester/The Image Works

Historically, the arts have been shortchanged in the curriculum. In 1985, the Council of Chief State School Officers reported that in only thirteen states did boards of education include the arts in their formal statements of educational goals.[25] Another study found that elementary schools commit only 4 percent of their school week to art instruction, with only a quarter of that provided by trained art teachers.[26]

Responding to this lack of attention to the arts, the Getty Foundation has established a program called Beyond Creating to promote the arts in U.S. elementary schools. The assumption underlying this program is that art education must include not only art activities but instruction in the historical and critical understanding of art. One leading art educator has argued the impact of art on other academic areas:

> We should all benefit by seeing arts education in a larger context. For one thing, the arts can give coherence, depth, and resonance to other academic subjects. . . . Intellectual skills cultivated by art education not only represent the mind operating in its finest hour but are precisely the skills that characterize our most complex adult life tasks.[27]

In this section, we introduce you to only two of the major arts, those with which you are most likely to be involved: music and art.

MUSIC  The overall goal of music education is to develop children's musicality; that is, to increase their sensitivity and responsiveness to music. The curriculum consists of a variety of activities: listening to music, singing,

© Paul Conklin/Monkmeyer Press Photo Service

playing instruments, participating in rythmic activities and expressive bodily movements, and creating compositions. Here is an example of general goals for music education:

Students will

1. develop skill in music (including listening and performance)
2. become intelligent critics of major types of serious music
3. acquire knowledge of music (i.e., history of music, form and design)
4. recognize music as an international language and vehicle of international goodwill.[28]

Instrumental music instruction (for example, playing in the band or orchestra) is available in many schools, beginning in middle elementary grades. Objectives include achieving the highest possible performance standards and providing opportunities for students to perform. Most music teachers endeavor to expose their students to a wide range of types and styles of music. Students can participate in a variety of musical performing groups or ensembles. Depending on size, funds, and priorities of the school, high school students can become involved in string quartets, brass and woodwind quintets, wind ensemble and chamber orchestras, symphonic bands, madrigal groups, and jazz, show, and concert choirs.

Through the years, music curricula have been heavily weighted toward the development of performance skills. In the early 1960s, however, music educators began stressing the importance of music as an academic discipline with its own structure and content. More recently, the "comprehensive musicianship movement" has attempted to balance music instruction more evenly among music analysis, the creation of music, and musical performance. The "aesthetic education movement," also recent, helps students appreciate the contributions of composers, performers, music historians, and critics. Going further, students themselves participate in the various processes of composing, performing, and criticizing. This movement also emphasizes an integrated approach (for instance, integrating music, dance, and drama). Today, your own district's music specialist, if there is one, is likely to take an eclectic approach. If there isn't one, you are on your own. You can count on a decided involvement in the experience, regardless of your musical background.

ART   The art curriculum encourages self-expression and appreciation. Art is placed in the curriculum because of its intellectual content, historical significance, and intrinsic value. One philosopher argues for the importance of art in developing the intellect: through art education, students become sensitive to the appearance of things and become aware of the expressive properties of color, sound, texture, and movement organized into aesthetic objects.[29]

© Peter Vandermark/Stock, Boston

During the 1940s and 1950s, curricular activities in art included painting, sculpting, and other artistic productions. Although students gained creative pleasure through their inventive activities, few learned the fundamental concepts underlying art. Gradually, this type of curriculum shifted. Students were now taught the vocabulary, structure, and aesthetic underpinnings of the discipline itself. Educators had finally come to believe that art education required both the creative process and the formal study of good art. Teachers realized that they had to do more than hand out paper and crayons and turn their students loose. A fundamental grasp of art theory and an adeptness in conveying this knowledge to their students became important. One art curriculum specialist articulated this view: "Simple exposure to good painting, good music, good dance, and so on is not enough. Instruction will need to go beyond exposure, to the cultivation of artistic values, the development of artistic sense, and a basic familiarity with the artistic process itself."[30]

Sensing the need to enrich the artistic experience of students, private foundations and other organizations joined the act. Among them, the Rockefeller Brothers Fund, the Getty Foundation, the National Endowment for the Humanities, and the Alliance for Arts Education have all fostered new programs. Through programs such as Education for Aesthetic Awareness, Arts in Education, Comprehensive Art Program, and Artists in Schools, professional artists come into schools and share their talents and commitments with young students.

## Physical and Health Education

Physical education aims not only at an overall development of the body but at a feeling of mental and emotional well-being. The early movements cultivated in elementary school—running, climbing, jumping, and swinging—serve as the foundation for sports, dance, and games in later years. Physical education received a shot in the arm in the 1960s when President Kennedy proposed a national standard of physical fitness. Soon thereafter, most students in elementary and secondary schools were required to participate in annual assessments of physical fitness. When the fitness tests became too competitive, physical education offerings were expanded to include noncompetitive activities, with a new emphasis on life-long sports such as scuba diving, bicycling, running, and golf. Additionally, girls were given greater opportunity to participate in traditionally male sports.

Because of recent budgetary cuts and a national back-to-basics movement, physical education programs have fallen on hard times. In some schools, students participate in physical education for brief periods, sometimes only twice a week. This decline in the school's fitness programs, together with a leisure-oriented lifestyle in which we may sit for three hours a day in front of television, has contributed to an alarming unfitness among American students. In the late 1980s, the President's Council on Physical Fitness and Sports reported that American children are in remarkably bad shape. Forty percent of boys age 6 to 12 cannot do more than one pull-up (one in four cannot do any). Seventy percent of girls age 6 to 12 cannot do more than one pull-up (55 percent cannot do any). In a fifty-yard dash, today's 10-year-old girls are "significantly" slower than those tested ten years ago. According to the council chairman, most of today's adults had a taste of fitness from their physical education classes in school before phys-ed was dropped. But today's kids don't get that taste of fitness now when they're young.[31]

Responding to this need for better fitness, physical education curricula have shifted. They emphasize "fitness for life." Individuals establish their own programs, evaluate and adjust their eating, exercising, and living habits, and learn about drug abuse, alcohol, stress, and human sexuality.

# WHO DETERMINES WHAT YOU TEACH?

For better or worse, your curriculum is more than just a list of subject areas and instructional objectives. It is also the product of influences of individuals, groups, and agencies who all have something to say about what you teach.

When you're starting out, the matter of who has a say in what you teach may seem maddeningly irrelevant in your frantic preparations for the next day's class. "Who cares!" you exclaim. "How can you worry about draining the swamp when you're up to your cars in alligators? I haven't time or energy to worry about who decides what I teach."

Fair enough. But as the dust settles and you survive the first months (with success), you start to notice what you are being asked to teach. And you look more closely. Student feedback, along with your own impressions, tells you that some of your curriculum is inappropriate, uninteresting, and unimportant. The question of who is responsible now becomes relevant.

## Textbooks

More than any other factor, the text currently in use influences what you teach. Textbooks enjoy high credibility in teachers' minds; they are the authority to which both teacher and student turn. Teachers both new and experienced assume that texts have been carefully selected and are the best source available for teaching social studies or math or French. By and large, texts are thoughtfully written and represent an orderly approach to the subject area. Texts are ready guides. They are easy to use. They contain an exposition of the subject matter, organized under general and specific headings. Contents include study questions (designed to provoke thought and assess understanding), related references, and other learning helps. Texts are frequently accompanied by a teacher's edition or a teacher's manual, leading you step by step through the presentation of information. New teachers, especially, appreciate this structuring of their curriculum.

## Corporate Influences

Corporate America undeniably finds its way into your classroom by several avenues. Suppose you have three distinctly slow learners in your fourth-grade class. They require large amounts of drill and practice to grasp even simple math concepts. (The demands of the rest of your students prevent you from offering individualized tutoring, painstakingly drilling to the point of overlearning.) Enter computers from the world of technology and business. You are grateful not only for the computer in your room but for software that helps students practice partially learned math skills. These three students can take turns, during class time, being drilled by the computer.

Business enters from another door as well. It needs to hire graduates who have been well trained in the educational system, individuals who can function effectively in all positions including salespersons, heavy equipment operators, computer programmers, word processing experts, and accountants. Swift, thorough, and effective training translates into higher profits.

For their part, educators increasingly draw on business know-how to improve educational programs. For years, companies have studied—and perfected—the most effective ways to train people in a variety of skills. For the most part, these training techniques are sophisticated and well proven. They have been used successfully in training people to use time effectively, manage human conflicts, delegate responsibility, create and use visual aids to optimize learning (such as overhead projectors, special handouts, colored graphics), work productively in small groups, learn quickly, listen effectively, present ideas clearly, and complete assigned work on time. These and similar skills, with useful classroom application, are increasingly borrowed from industry by educators.

Interchange between education and corporate America is on the increase. Educational partnerships are being formed. For example, a large computer corporation may "adopt" a school, providing instructional software in math and science. Personnel from the company come in and help teachers implement the instruction on their existing computers. After a testing-out period, students are invited into the corporation to offer feedback and suggestions about the learnability of the software and, in the process, learn about the computer industry. Through practices such as these, both business and education benefit.

## Research on Effective Teaching

Since the early 1970s, a stockpile of convincing research on effective teaching has been accumulating. A consistent body of information now identifies factors that improve classroom learning. Research-based principles have been formulated on classroom management, student-engaged time (amount of time student is actually engaged in the learning activity), teacher wait time (time teacher waits for students to respond after asking a question or making a statement), disruptive behavior, guided practice (students working on problems under teacher guidance), and teacher questioning (when teacher asks questions). School districts are relying more than ever on research-based information in crafting their curricula. For example, the research literature shows that whole-class instruction (a style of presentation with you as the teacher standing in the front of the room conducting instruction) is effective in helping students learn large amounts of factual material quickly. Application of this finding helps you know when to use whole-class instruction and allows coverage of more material. (Chapter 9 takes a closer look at this research.)

## Federal Government

From 1960 onward, the federal government's influence on your curriculum has escalated. Money is provided to ensure opportunities for target groups such as handicapped children, minority students, and children of lower socioeconomic groups. The announcement of allocation of federal monies for multicultural education, AIDS education, giving minority children a "head start," sex education programs at the elementary level, and drug abuse programs for high school students prompts a flood of requests from schools. Pressed for funds, schools are more than willing to generate such programs in order to receive federal monies. New classes are plugged into the curriculum, special training is provided, and new facilities are made available.

## National Commissions, Private Foundations

Congress, the president, and the Department of Education periodically create commissions to assess the quality of education in this country, to identify needs, and to extend challenges to schools. The National Commission on Excellence in Education offered in 1983 its report, *A Nation at Risk.* The National Commission on Excellence in Teacher Education published in 1985 *A Call for Change in Teacher Education.* The Secretary of Education, under sponsorship of the U.S. Department of Education, in 1986 produced *What Works,* a summary of research about teaching and learning. The Carnegie Forum on Education and the Economy in 1986 issued *A Nation Prepared: Teachers for the 21st Century.* A number of foundations provided funding for the Holmes Group, a select consortium of colleges of education across the country. Published in 1986, its *Tomorrow's Teachers* set forth a commitment to the improvement of teacher education in America.

These reports call for educational reform, both in America's schools and in the institutions that train public school teachers. Because these reports disclose, for example, serious weaknesses in the academic preparation of graduating high school seniors, schools return to an emphasis on basics such as reading, writing, math, and science. Reforms generated by these reports press for emphasis on some subjects at the expense of others. In an era of basics, classes in building interpersonal relationships take a back seat to chemistry.

## State Government

State governments are charged with the responsibility of educating the state's students, a responsibility typically delegated to local districts. Nevertheless, state legislatures pass statutes ensuring quality education and equal opportunity for all students. Budget shortfalls require cutbacks in certain curricular programs; for example, Spanish-immersion programs, programs for the gifted, and physical education. State finances affect physical facilities, which also have an impact on your curriculum. Year-round schools, implemented as cost-effective measures, affect the amount of time available for instruction in various subject areas. Graduation requirements, stipulated by the state department of education, force you to teach some units and set aside others. For example, if the state requires for graduation an additional unit in English, enrollment in your senior photography course declines, and eventually the course may have to be canceled.

## Local School Boards

Local school boards likewise affect what you teach. Members of the board feel pressured by national calls for reform and by demands from the local citizenry to upgrade the quality of education. For example, your school district encompasses a high-tech area. Parents employed in high-tech occupations pressure the board to beef up the physics, math, and computer training their children receive. Responding, the school board and district provide new offerings in the curriculum. Or parents with axes to grind push the school board to ban suggestive books, to include consumer education at the middle school level, and to include more electives in high school. The impact of these various decisions is quickly felt in your classroom.

## The PTA

The Parent–Teacher Association jumps in too. For example, suppose this organized group of parents, wanting their children to become more computer literate, conducts a fund-raising project for the purchase of six computers and a small library of software. The hardware is installed, and one of the classrooms is converted into a computer lab. As a seventh-grade math teacher, you are naturally a part of this enterprise. You face decisions: Should I develop a computer literacy unit? Where in my general math class would it fit? Would I have to start from scratch in teaching the computer?

## Your Principal and Colleagues

More than any other entity, the individual school—your own school—determines what you teach. Your building principal plays a key role in emphasizing various aspects of the curriculum. Most principals are far from overbearing in their curricular expectations, yet teachers clearly understand a principal's "leanings" and are either sensitive to them in developing their curriculum or move to another school where the principal's philosophy is more similar to their own.

Suppose, for example, that your high school principal, Dr. Sawyer, is a staunch advocate of "preparing students to live in society." She turns on to the state's programs in career education, work experience, and vocational counseling. In her charge to the school curriculum committee, the principal urges the inclusion of work experience in the senior year and asks the staff to flesh out the current vocational education program. In faculty meetings over the year, Dr. Sawyer waves her banner devotedly. The vocational education faculty pick up on her expectations and try to respond to them. In hiring, Dr. Sawyer tries to bring on board new people who are at least warm to her commitment to vocational education and other life-related training.

Curriculum committees, composed of teachers in the school, make decisions about which textbooks to adopt, which social studies materials to purchase, which algebra sequence to follow, and what electives to include in the curriculum. Faculty groups, working in earnest, wield considerable influence as they deliberate about the curriculum. More than one principal has voiced a lament like this: "I want to experiment with the social studies program Lakeview uses, but my teachers want to stay with what we've got. So I guess we will, for a while." Principals try to stay in step with their teachers. More often than not they accept recommendations from duly constituted committees within the school.

## Your Influence on Your Curriculum

It turns out, then, that it is hard to think about what you teach without thinking about who is behind it. One teacher breathes a sigh of relief: "Who can go wrong in teaching, with all those people to tell you what to do?" Another teacher pauses to speculate: "I've assumed I'd be in charge of what I teach, but maybe I'm wrong. Maybe I can't throw things out when I don't like them—or add things on my own." Still another teacher feels closed in and combative: "All the decisions have been made! I walk in, somebody hands me a book and says, 'Teach this.' For this they need somebody who's trained in education?"

How much control *do* you have over what you teach? The results of one massive survey of nearly 22,000 teachers across the country give some indication. Seventy-nine percent said they helped choose textbooks and sixty-three percent said they were involved in curricular decisions. But fewer than half said they participated in formulating standards for student behavior or setting promotion and retention policies. Only one in five said they helped determine school budgets, and ten percent said they helped evaluate the performance of other teachers or select new teachers and administrators.[32] Still, within the classroom itself, you have considerable freedom, sometimes more than you bargain for. But to worry about how much freedom

*Some educational scholars reject this image of the teacher as a "black box"*
*through which researchers' knowledge passes into the classroom. In their*
*view, the teacher has an active role in deciding how to teach.*
—Magdalene Lampert

you have is not very productive. Shift gears. Spend that same energy trying
to adapt your curriculum optimally to the needs of your students.

# ADAPTING YOUR CURRICULUM

You have a good deal of latitude in adapting your curriculum, even in a
highly bureaucratic school and even when you are at the low end of the
totem pole. One new teacher observed:

> I think the curriculum is fine. We have a curriculum which teaches each subject
> matter, science and health, reading and language, math and social studies. But
> how you handle this is your particular job and concern. There are objectives
> they want us to cover. Okay, this has to be done, but how we do it or how
> much importance we give to certain areas is left up to the teacher's judg-
> ment. . . . In reading, for example, I try to touch on all the skills but stress and
> focus more on the ones that I think are extremely important. I think the skills
> of drawing conclusions and inferences are tough ones for the children, and I
> don't hesitate to make one of these reading skills a part of math. . . . Also the
> textbooks today are well chosen. . . . There are too many of them, but here
> again . . . we can select.[33]

## Reasons for Adaptation

You constantly feel the need to adapt your curriculum: add a new unit, delete a less relevant one, make up more interesting practice exercises, create
culturally relevant illustrations, update a history unit, and introduce two additional experiments in psychology. Your sixth graders are a little behind, so
you simplify the unit on mixed fractions.

Teachers adapt their curricula for a variety of reasons. Most important, they want instruction to be interesting and understandable to their
students. Good teachers become restless quickly when their subject matter
misses the students:

"I can't stand having bored students."

"When my kids can't understand what's going on, we're all wasting time."

A teacher's background and personal interests prompt some adaptations. Suppose, over the years, you have become an ardent leather crafter.

Predictably, you expand your art program to include a unit on leathercraft. Your principal, aware of your keen interest, allocates a section of the custodian's workroom for your students' leathercraft work. At Christmas time, your leathercraft unit is in full bloom. Students are completing their wallets, purses, belts, and bookmarks. Other teachers include in their curriculum special units on bird watching, fishing, mountain climbing, speleology, cooking, Eskimo culture, volcanoes, fairy tales, and the history of magic.

Teachers also adapt their curriculum by playing to their strengths and compensating for their weaknesses. Every teacher wants to be seen as an expert in some area and, conversely, no teacher wants to appear as a bungling incompetent in front of the class. Thus, one area is emphasized while another is downplayed—for psychological survival! Suppose grammar has always been your nemesis. Your dreadfully low language grades so deflated your confidence that you can't pump it up even today. You are forced to teach grammar. But you allocate as little time as possible to it, stay close to the manual, and promise more interesting topics "once we get our grammar out of the way." Math? A different matter. Here you shine. You are confident, relaxed, well informed, ready to roam widely. You average twenty minutes per day for grammar and more than an hour and a half for math—regardless of what the curriculum calls for!

Another factor inviting teachers to adapt their curricula is expediency. Suppose, in teaching ninth-graders, you face five sections per day with two different preparations. At the beginning of the year, you assigned each student to write a theme a week. During those first weeks you were valiant, even heroic, in reading and writing comments on every paper. But you went under from having to read night after night and on weekends. Burnout was just around the corner. You were forced to be more realistic. Unable to come up with other plausible solutions, you reluctantly decided to cut back on theme writing and have students spend more time reading short stories—a compromise in your curriculum.

Expediency becomes a factor as a result of your outside commitments, too. You purchase a horse and, in addition to underestimating the time required to care for it, you simply cannot stay away from it—too much fun! By the time 3:30 rolls around, you are flying out of the building to ride your new responsibility. Your preparation nowadays is confined to in-school hours. You look for shortcuts, like having students correct each other's papers and reusing units that require minimal preparation. You no longer take time to build on already existing units. Administrative paperwork is done during recess and student library time. You "get everything down to a science" and shy away from accepting additional committee responsibilities.

## Methods of Adaptation

**ADAPTATION THROUGH SUBJECT EMPHASIS**  One way teachers adapt their curricula is through emphasizing some subjects and barely touching on others. You enter your teaching career strong in some areas and weak in

*The lesson plan that goes in well organized often comes back out fifteen minutes or an hour later disjointed and beaten out of shape.—Daniel Meier*

others. A natural unevenness shows itself in your expertise and preparation. Without even being aware of it, you emphasize certain subjects and soft-pedal others. Ample research shows that teachers make inequitable allocations of time to various subjects. For example, one fourth-grade teacher may allow fifteen minutes per day for math and an hour and fifteen minutes to reading, whereas another may do the opposite. Over a nine-month period, the first teacher's students receive 45 hours of math instruction and 225 hours of reading! Clearly, the verbal skills of these students will be more advanced than their math skills. The second teacher's class will show an imbalance in the opposite direction.

When a teacher emphasizes a particular aspect of the curriculum, the students may gain something extra, though perhaps at the expense of some other aspect:

> Ms. Washington, a black high school teacher, having experienced discrimination in her growing-up years, feels strongly about discussing civil rights issues in her U.S. history course.
>
> Mrs. Ruano, whose family comes from Italy, flies to Europe each summer. She uses artifacts gathered from her travels to enrich a month-long study of Italy in her "Cultures of the World" unit, which was scheduled to last only two weeks.
>
> Miss Parker, who minored in physical education, runs five miles each morning and enjoys running marathons. She incorporates an extra unit on lifelong benefits of exercise into her ninth-grade health class.

Teachers emphasize areas in which they are strong or have avid interest. Their strengths increase and have school-wide results, contributing to better overall instruction. Some teachers strive to overcome their weak areas; others merely slide along.

**ADAPTATION THROUGH ADDITION AND OMISSION**   Curriculum guides are a composite of units and subunits and/or topics. Here are samples from curriculum guides:

Language, grade 2
  Nouns
    Definition
    Types of nouns
      Singular and plural nouns
      Common and proper nouns
      Possessive nouns
    Using nouns correctly

Health, grade 4
    Body systems
        General structure of the body
            Cells
            Tissues
            Organs
        Functions of body systems
        Skeletal systems
            Function of the skeletal system
            Parts of the skeletal system
Mathematics, grade 6
    Multiplication and division of decimals
        Multiplication by a whole number
        Multiplication of decimals
        Division of decimals
            Division by tenths
Literature, grade 12
    The Romantic Age
        William Wordsworth
            "The World Is Too Much with Us"
        Samuel Taylor Coleridge
            *The Rime of the Ancient Mariner*
        Percy Bysshe Shelley
            "Ode to the West Wind"
            "To a Skylark"

Because of time constraints, insufficient resources, and oversized classes, teachers are compelled to pick and choose among units, at times omitting completely rather than deemphasizing. Suppose you were teaching the following high school unit in biology:

Classification of plants
    Nonvascular plants
        Mosses
        Liverworts
    Vascular plants
        Club mosses
        Horsetails

> Ferns
>
> Gymnosperms
>
>> Cycads
>>
>> Ginkgoes
>>
>> Conifers
>
> Angiosperms
>
>> Monocotyledons
>>
>> Dicotyledons

You might decide to omit the entire topic "Horsetails" and the subtopic "Ginkgoes" freeing up more time for "Angiosperms."

Your shop curriculum calls for a unit on oxyacetylene welding. You elect to take up butt and fillet welds under the subtopic "Fusion Welding," but omit "Bronze Welding."

In your U.S. history class, there is a unit on labor workers who came from the ranks to lead the revolution of labor unions; you choose to talk about Samuel Gompers and John L. Lewis, while omitting Eugene Debs and Uriah Stevens.

In teaching tennis to girls, you decide to concentrate on grip, stroke, volley, and footwork, omitting the history of tennis.

**ADAPTATION THROUGH MODIFYING OBJECTIVES**    Whether sitting quietly in the back of your mind or written boldly in black and white, objectives provide direction and impetus in your curriculum. Many curriculum guides present predefined objectives—packaged, ready to be used. In reviewing them, you decide they need to be modified. For instance, you are teaching in a community where the majority of families work in the lumbering business, or in a community where the students come predominantly from lower socioeconomic families. In either case, you tailor at least some of your objectives so as to accommodate these cultures. In the first instance, you include objectives, say, on ecological principles such as selective cutting, reforestation, and water conservation. In the second, you emphasize objectives designed to strengthen verbal skills, functional writing, and overlearning of arithmetic operations.

Through working with your objectives you can effect substantial changes in your curriculum. You can alter their type, level, comprehensiveness, and relevance in meeting the needs of your students.

**ADAPTATION THROUGH MODIFYING TEACHING**    Adaptation occurs through changing not only the "what" of teaching but the "how" as well. Endless combinations of teaching methods and classroom activities await your discovery. Varying one or more of the many components produces kaleidoscopic possibilities; for example,

1. type of presentation (e.g., lecture, demonstration)

2. mode of presentation (e.g., teacher talk, classroom texts and workbooks, films, computers, readings from the library, small-group reports to the class)

3. type of student practice (e.g., whole class engages in review games, students work independently at their desks, students complete homework exercises, teacher conducts a recitation with the students, pairs of students engage in peer review)

4. type of student assessment (e.g., paper-and-pencil tests, in-class worksheets, computer testing, whole-class question-and-answer sessions, independent homework assignments).

In adapting your curriculum, remember that you can make changes in both the "what" and the "how" of your teaching. Too often, teachers circumscribe their effectiveness, assuming that they have control over only the "how." Don't place artificial restrictions on yourself. Use the power you have to emphasize and delete topics and reshape your objectives. In choosing your learning activities, the sky's the limit. You may be bound to serve the curriculum, but you don't have to be its slave.

# CONCLUSION

This chapter has introduced you to your curriculum, its roots, and forces that influence it. Whereas others influence your curriculum, you remain the key player in its adaptation and implementation. You have ample freedom—and considerable responsibility.

Effective teachers seldom allow themselves merely to go through the motions of teaching, presenting irrelevant or incomprehensible subject matter just to fill up the day. Good teachers quickly become restive. They aggressively revise and mold the curriculum until it becomes a potent tool in accomplishing their purpose—to bring about student growth.

Teachers who feel at home with a creatively adapted curriculum enjoy teaching it. They have a sense of confidence, and their students benefit by its relevance. Eagerly anticipate receiving your curriculum, and accept the challenge of adapting it.

## Expansions

1. Suppose, after a year of using the school's adopted list of readings, you concluded that many of the listings fall short of your purposes. Write down some actions you might try.

2. Talk with a principal in an elementary or high school. Find how much freedom he or she has in making decisions about the school's curriculum. Are you surprised at any of the responses?

3. Describe any feelings of anxiety and/or excitement you have about the subject(s) you plan to teach.

4. This chapter discusses the "hidden" curriculum. What learning do you hope will result from the hidden curriculum in your class? What learning do you wish you could prevent?

5. Explain what it means to be a link in the chain in teaching the school's or department's overall curriculum.

6. In adapting the curriculum to the needs of your students, how much freedom do you anticipate having? Suppose you had total freedom. Can you think of any disadvantages?

## Notes

1. L. Anderson, "The Environment of Instruction: The Function of Seatwork in a Commercially Developed Curriculum," in G. Duffy, L. Roehler, and J. Mason (Eds.), *Comprehension Instruction: Perspectives and Suggestions* (New York: Longman, 1984).

2. E. DeBono, *Creative and Lateral Thinking,* paper presented at Conference on Thinking for a Change (Edmonton, Canada, August, 1988); idem, "The CoRT Thinking Program," in A. L. Costa (Ed.), *Developing Minds: A Resource Book for Teaching Thinking* (Alexandria, Va.: Association for Supervision and Curriculum Development, 1985), pp. 203–209; idem, *DeBono's Thinking Course* (New York: Facts on File Publications, 1982).

3. D. N. Perkins, "Creativity by Design," in A. L. Costa (Ed.), *Developing Minds: A Resource Book for Teaching Thinking* (Alexandria, Va.: Association for Supervision and Curriculum Development, 1985), pp. 172–174; idem, "Knowledge as Design: Teaching Thinking Through Content," in J. B. Baron and R. J. Sternberg (Eds.), *Teaching Thinking Skills: Theory and Practice* (New York: W. H. Freeman, 1987), pp. 62–85.

4. A. A. Hyde and M. Bizar, *Thinking in Context: Teaching Cognitive Processes Across the Elementary School Curriculum* (New York: Longman, 1989), pp. 1–56.

5. Utah State Board of Education, *Elementary and Secondary Core Curriculum* (1987).

6. Ibid.

7. W. J. Bennett, *First Lessons: A Report on Elementary Education in America* (Washington, D.C.: U.S. Government Printing Office, 1986), pp. 21–22.

8. F. B. May, *Reading as Communication: An Interactive Approach,* 2nd ed. (Columbus, Ohio: Merrill, 1986), p. 29.

9. Ibid, pp. 28–51.

10. M. Scardamalia and C. Bereiter, "Research on Written Composition," in M. C. Wittrock (Ed.), *Handbook of Research on Teaching,* 3rd Ed. (New York: Macmillan, 1986), pp. 778–803.

11. J. D. McNeil, *Curriculum: A Comprehensive Introduction,* 3rd ed. (Boston: Little, Brown, 1985), p. 307.

12. W. J. Bennett, *What Works: Research about Teaching and Learning* (Washington, D.C.: U.S. Department of Education, 1986), p. 15.

13. E. W. Jenkins, "History of Science Education," in T. Husen and T. N. Postlethwaite (Eds.), *International Encyclopedia of Education* (Oxford: Pergamon, 1985), 8:4454.

14. W. Harlen, "Science Education: Primary-School Programmes," in T. Husen and T. N. Postlethwaite (Eds.), *International Encyclopedia of Education* (Oxford: Pergamon, 1985), 8:4456–4457.

15. G. Catwelti and J. Adkisson, "ASCD Study Reveals Elementary School Time Allocations for Subject Area; Other Trends Noted," *Curriculum Update* (Association for Supervision and Curriculum Development, April 1985).

16. College Board, *Academic Preparation for College—What Students Need to Know and Be Able to Do* (New York: College Board, 1983).

17. R. T. White and R. P. Tisher, "Research on Natural Sciences," in M. C. Wittrock (Ed.), *Handbook of Research on Teaching,* 3rd Ed. (New York: Macmillan, 1986), p. 882.

18. Conference Board of Mathematical Sciences, *Overview and Analysis of School Mathematics, Grades K–12* (Washington, D.C.: Author, 1975), p. 77.

19. W. Welch, "Science Education in Urbanville: A Case Study," in R. Stake and J. Easley (Eds.), *Case Studies in Science Education* (Urbana: University of Illinois, 1978), p. 6.

20. Bennett, p. 57.

21. NcNeil, *Curriculum,* p. 317.

22. "Pre-College Science Curriculum Activities of the National Science Foundation," in *National Science Foundation Curriculum Development and Implementation for Pre-College Science Education,* a report prepared for the Committee on Science and Technology, U.S. House of Representatives Ninety-Fourth Congress, First Session (Washington, D.C.: U.S. Government Printing Office, 1975), pp. 166–167.

23. Bennett, *First Lessons,* p. 29.

24. J. C. Brown, "Excellence and the Problem of Visual Literacy," *Design for Arts in Education* (November/December 1983).

25. Council of Chief State School Officers, *Arts, Education and the States: A Survey of State Education Policies* (Washington, D.C.: Department of Education and National Endowment for the Arts, September 1985). (ED 287 749)

26. G. Hardiman and A. Johnson, "The Condition of Art Education," *Art Education* 36(1) (1983), 23–27.

27. E. W. Eisner, "Why Art in Education and Why Art Education?" *Beyond Creating: The Place for Art in America's Schools* (Los Angeles: The J. Paul Getty Trust, Getty Center for Education in the Arts, 1985).

28. E. L. Dejnozka and D. E. Kapel, "Music Education," *American Educator's Encyclopedia* (Westport, Conn.: Greenwood Press, 1982), p. 335.

29. H. S. Broudy, "Some Reactions to a Concept of Aesthetic Education," in S. Madeja (Ed.), *Arts and Aesthetics: An Agenda for the Future* (St. Louis: CEMREL, 1977), pp. 250–261.

30.   L. Rubin, *Curriculum Handbook: The Disciplines, Current Movements, and Instructional Methodology* (Boston: Allyn & Bacon, 1977), p. 18.

31.   G. Allen, "This, Too, Is Sports," *New York Times,* May 17, 1986.

32.   E. L. Boyer, "Teacher Involvement in Decision Making: A State-by-State Profile," *The New York Times,* September 14, 1988, p. B8.

33.   M. M. Cohn, R. B. Kottkamp, and E. F. Provenz, Jr., *To Be a Teacher: Cases, Concepts, Observation Guides* (New York: Random House, 1987), p. 254.

# CHAPTER 5

# GOVERNING YOUR SCHOOL

*Treating all students the same is not a formula for equity or excellence.—Charles Nevi*

**MAIN IDEAS**

- You are involved daily in issues of school governance and finance. Understand the concepts involved and wisely exploit the opportunities.

- The governance of schools is affected by the U.S. Constitution, the federal government, individual states, corporate America, local districts, and local schools.

- Local control of education by lay citizens is being eroded as state governments increasingly take over decision-making power.

- Your school has its own governing rules, which largely determine your patterns of conduct. Learn them.

# INTRODUCTION

We are now ready to look at the system in which you work; specifically, how it is governed. "Why?" you ask. "What has this to do with me? My job is to teach. I'll let my principal worry about that sort of thing."

Unfortunately, a teacher's role in today's schools is no longer either as circumscribed or as simple as that. Consider four examples:

Miss Ruiz, teaching sixth grade at Jefferson Elementary, was ecstatic at the success of her "Marathon Reading Week," then in its last day. The students had surprised themselves with their volume of reading over the preceding four days. At 11:30, Miss Ruiz said, "Students, you've performed a colossal feat. I think you deserve a significant reward. Class dismissed for the rest of the day!"

Mr. Price, no longer able to tolerate the district-prescribed social studies text, was ready for action. After a two-week search, he had uncovered a lively, well-illustrated, flexibly written text. So he mailed off his order for twenty copies.

Mrs. Chen, faculty sponsor of the high school newspaper, was in the hot seat. Her editor had been about to run a student article on the anguish of teen-age pregnancy, but Mr. Bruen, the principal, got wind of the article, read it, and yanked it. Her staff was furious. "Our First Amendment rights are being violated by disallowing the publication of this article!" The staff, with other students rallying around, hired an attorney, who calmly announced, "A First Amendment case like this could end up in the Supreme Court." Mrs. Chen supported the position of her staff, yet felt a responsibility to her principal.

Three parents, one of them a college math professor, approached the PTA president with charges that the math text used in the fifth grade was miserably out of date and that no teacher should be allowed to be so far out of touch. The PTA president, pushed by their argument, met with your principal, who, in turn, brought in your fifth-grade team. You were all a little miffed. "Who runs our classes—teachers or parents? Does their expertise extend to making decisions about a math text?"

These four examples—all issues of school governance—portend what you will meet on a daily basis. Does Miss Ruiz have the legal right to dismiss her class during a calendared school day? Does her principal? Is Mr. Price free to change his textbook in midyear? If not, why not? Who governs what student newspapers can print? Could Mrs. Chen overrule the principal's authority, since she is the faculty sponsor of the newspaper and therefore legally accountable? How much curricular decision-making power do parents or the PTA have? They are, after all, the public, and schools belong to the public.

Most new teachers expect or at least hope to be issued a handy guide titled *Rules about Your School—Simplified*. School governance, and your involvement with it, is complex. It surely deserves more than a slick list of dos and don'ts.

There are fundamental reasons for studying school governance. First, most teachers are perfectly willing to be governed by the rules and policies of the school. As professionals, they realize that orderliness and predictability facilitate their effectiveness and contribute to a comfortable working atmosphere. Knowing this allows them to fit in, to adjust to a system of routines (even though they may have every intention of changing the routines later).

Second, understanding the governance of your school alleviates personal stress. Several sources of stress arise when teachers are confronted with rules and regulations:

1.   The frustration and conflict of trying to work at cross-purposes with school policy. Suppose your middle school has the policy of adopting textbooks upon recommendation from the Teacher Curriculum Committee. Once a textbook is adopted, all teachers at each grade level use the same series of texts. In this setting, for you, a seventh-grade teacher, to set aside the current text and adopt one you find more pleasing without committee approval is not a matter of personal choice. Pedagogically, it throws your class out of sync with the curriculum that was presented in the sixth grade and that will be presented in the eighth grade. And past experience has shown your principal that textbooks adopted individually— either by whim or after studied effort—soon disrupt the curriculum's continuity. Even though you resign yourself to the current text, at least for now, you simmer with resistance—which produces stress. In this situation, stress is unnecessary, but it is there, and it grinds away at you each semester you are forced to use the text.

2.   Ignorance of the freedoms available within a school. For teachers, questions like these represent the unknown: "Am I free to call a special parent night for my class?" "Do I need to inform anyone when I drop three major units and add my own?" "I've kicked Nathan out of class for a week. Surely I don't need permission to remove a student for disruptive behavior!" The best-kept secret in education is that teachers have far more freedom than they suppose. Teachers err more often when they conclude, "I could never get away with doing that," than when they think, "I'm free to do whatever I need to do that's in the best interest of my students."

3.   The pressure of trying too hard to live up to every rule. Teachers who are trying too hard focus on their own anxieties rather than on student learning. They are so tense with fear of making mistakes that they are stilted and unable to relax, enjoy the students, and participate in productive give-and-take learning experiences.

The third reason for learning about school governance is certainly the most important: the knowledge empowers you to carry out your own teaching goals more effectively. Governance is, after all, well intentioned. At its best, governance provides resources, opens doors, and gives help, support, and ready direction. Unfortunately, our systems of school governance and their implementation and workings sometimes curtail, stifle, and impede, well intentioned though they may be. Whatever the case, your responsibility is to marshal these rules and regulations, making them work *for* you to the fullest extent possible. And the greater your understanding of governance, the greater your freedom—and control. In this spirit, a teacher approaches her principal soon after arriving and asks, "Would you show me all the doors [the freedoms] that are open to me as a teacher in this school? I plan to go through them all in accomplishing my purposes."

Inevitably, you will feel hemmed in by the "must do" parts of the system: filling out attendance rosters, collecting lunch money, issuing hall passes, completing the district questionnaire, writing out suggestions of new texts, signing up for in-service training, taking playground duty, monitoring the lunchroom, and computing grades. Try to burst through this, and use your school governance as an avenue for your own accomplishment.

# THE GOVERNMENT AND GOVERNANCE

## School Governance and the Constitution

The Constitution protects individual rights and freedoms and provides the foundation for our legal system. Historically, the Constitution has also served as the basis of our educational system, even though it makes no mention of education. Let's look briefly at how sections of the Constitution have been interpreted to reflect upon public education.

The First Amendment reads as follows:

> Congress shall make no law respecting an establishment of religion, or prohibiting the free exercise thereof; or abridging the freedom of speech, or of the press; or the right of the people peaceably to assemble, and to petition the Government for a redress of grievances.

Over the years, this amendment has been interpreted to mean that religion is not a mandatory subject matter of public education. Further, religion and religious organizations are not to control public education. Even more forcefully, this statement ensures the separation of church and public education. So although this amendment does not speak of education, it does state what *cannot* happen to or be done with public education.

The Fourth Amendment reads as follows:

> The right of the people to be secure in their persons, houses, papers, and effects, against unreasonable searches and seizures, shall not be violated, and no warrants shall issue, but upon probable cause, supported by oath or affirmation, and particularly describing the place to be searched, and the persons or things to be seized.

This amendment has come into play in education during recent years and has served as the basis for interpreting students' and teachers' rights to privacy (for example, in cases involving searches of student lockers or purses and dismissal of tenured teachers for privately practicing homosexuality).

The Tenth Amendment reads as follows:

> The powers not delegated to the United States by the Constitution, nor prohibited by it to the States, are reserved to the States respectively, or to the people.

For years this amendment has been interpreted to mean that since public education is not a power of the Constitution, it is therefore a power of the state or, more liberally, it is a state responsibility, not a federal responsibility. This being the case, the state has the power to formulate educational policy and conduct its public education.

The Fourteenth Amendment reads as follows:

> All persons born or naturalized in the United States, and subject to the jurisdiction thereof, are citizens of the United States and of the State wherein they reside. No State shall make or enforce any law which shall abridge the privileges or immunities of citizens of the United States; nor shall any State deprive any person of life, liberty, or property, without due process of law; nor deny to any person within its jurisdiction the equal protection of the laws.

This amendment is the basis for ensuring a free public education for all citizens. No American child should be denied the privilege of an education. Further, equality of educational opportunity must be guaranteed for all. The states (on the basis of the Tenth Amendment) are responsible for providing for this free and universal education. Interpreting these seemingly simple statements about freedom and equality has led to considerable controversy. For example, what about allowing children with AIDS to attend school? What about teachers' strikes that close schools? Further, what about variation in educational quality within and among states? (The legal issues surrounding these questions will be addressed in Chapter 7.)

Article I, Section 8, of the Constitution reads in part as follows:

> The Congress shall have power to lay and collect taxes, duties, imposts and excises, to pay the debts and provide for the common defense and general welfare of the United States; but all duties, imposts and excises shall be uniform throughout the United States.

Some believe that Article I, Section 8, gives the federal government an entree into education, because it stipulates that Congress shall provide for the general welfare of the United States. Certainly education is part of this general welfare. Thus, many subscribe to the legitimacy of a federal interest in education, coupled with a state responsibility for education.

*The perpetuation of the American form of government is dependent upon an
informed citizenry, and that can only be attained by the operation of free
public schools.—P. E. Burrup, V. Brimley, and R. R. Garfield*

These constitutional amendments, and the "general welfare" mandate,
have affected the governing of our schools; from them have arisen educational policies, practices, and initiatives, as well as legislative statutes and
reform movements. The federal government's interest in and commitment to
public education has been impressive indeed. We'll take a closer look.

## The Federal Government's Role in School Governance

The federal government's interest in education predates the Constitution,
with the passage of the Northwest Ordinances of 1785 and 1787. The Ordi-
nance of 1785 divided the Northwest Territory into townships and required
the reservation of the sixteenth section of each township for the maintenance of schools. Congress has a long history of enacting laws to support
education. Examples are the Morrill Land Grant Act of 1862, the Hatch Act
of 1887, the Smith-Hughes Vocational Act of 1917, the National Defense
Education Act of 1958 (triggered by Sputnik), and the Elementary and Secondary Education Act of 1965. The Morrill and Hatch Acts encouraged expanded agricultural, mechanical, and scientific education in institutions of
higher education. The Smith-Hughes Act represented the first partnership in
education between the federal government and the state, with the former
matching every state dollar put toward education. The George-Reed Act of
1929 and the George-Dean Act of 1936 provided supplemental monies for
vocational education programs: agriculture, home economics, and distribu-
tive education (process of marketing goods and services).

**EQUALITY OF EDUCATIONAL OPPORTUNITY**   The National Defense Education Act gave $15 million annually to postsecondary vocational programs,
strengthening occupations that would contribute to our national defense.
Later, in 1968, Congress amended the act, earmarking money for disadvantaged children, mentally and physically handicapped children, and students
desiring education beyond high school. The Elementary and Secondary Education Act poured $1.3 billion into a number of areas, among them pro-
grams to help children from low-income families. This act sought to provide
better educational opportunities for the educationally underprivileged. One
year earlier, Title IV of the Civil Rights Act of 1964 had stated, "No person
in the United States shall, on the grounds of race, color, or national origin,
be excluded from participation in, be denied the benefits of, or be subject to
discrimination under any program or activity receiving Federal financial assistance." This act resounded with far-reaching implications: any program

© W. B. Finch/Stock, Boston

that discriminated against students on the basis of color, race, or origin would suffer the withdrawal of federal funds.

On March 1, 1867, the country was introduced to its first Department of Education, which had the purpose

> of collecting such statistics and facts as shall show the condition and progress of education in the several states and territories, and of diffusing such information respecting the organization and management of schools and school systems, and methods of teaching, as shall aid the people of the United States in the establishment and maintenance of efficient school systems, and otherwise promote the cause of education throughout the country.

What an inglorious role—a bureau of statistics for the country! But slowly the status of this national agency was elevated as education moved into the national limelight. After being jostled about for years, education became a part of the Department of Health, Education and Welfare in 1953.

Its latest promotion (in 1979) was to Department of Education, headed by a Secretary of Education who is a member of the president's Cabinet. Its career has been uneven and its success not unqualified. Pressure groups have worked to dissolve the department; others have pressed for more clout. Currently, the Department of Education spearheads only a fraction of the educational activities affected in some way by the federal government.

You will undoubtedly have some contact with federal programs that find their way into your school. Here are three separate examples:

> The federal government sends Chapter I monies to your state (in accordance with the Elementary and Secondary Education Act). Your district, through a grant application, receives some of this money. You are teaching in a school where a large number of students are on the free lunch program, are on welfare, or come from foster homes. These criteria were used in selecting your school to receive compensatory funds. Chapter I teachers, hired to work in your school, teach three low-achieving students in your class, pulled out for one hour each day. These students receive instructional "boosting" through supplemental reading instruction and one-to-one tutoring. You are obligated to coordinate your reading units to "fit" those being used by the Chapter I teachers.
>
> Chapter II monies come into your school to be used for programs designed for gifted and talented students. You are asked to serve on a district committee to help develop curricula for these students, and you are released from regular duties one half day each week.
>
> A Title IV Indian Grant has been awarded to your district to supplement the education of its 280 Native American children. Two Native American students are in your ninth-grade class. Twice each week, a traveling aide pulls these students out for one hour of specialized reading instruction and one hour of Native American cultural heritage. Your task is to pick up on this cultural enrichment in your social studies unit on Native Americans.

**EDUCATION FOR THE HANDICAPPED**   Let us look at one illustration of how the federal government governs in a very direct way. Growing out of the Fourteenth Amendment is the assurance of due process for all students. "Due process," in this context, means a student cannot be deprived of his or her rights. Prior to the 1970s, segments of our society felt that students of a certain type—namely, the handicapped—were not being awarded due process; that is, they were not receiving the same educational opportunities as nonhandicapped children. In fact, early estimates indicated that half the handicapped children in the United States were being denied adequate educational opportunities.

On November 29, 1975, President Ford signed into law the Education for all Handicapped Children Act (PL 94-142). This legislation, which finally went into effect for all states in 1978, provided assistance to the states in the initiation, expansion, and improvement of programs for the education of the handicapped. The federal government said, in effect, "Every state must abide by this law. We will provide excess funds for educating handicapped children."

This law requires that all students, regardless of their handicaps, receive a free, appropriate public education in the least restrictive environment consistent with their handicaps. The "least restrictive environment" has been interpreted to mean that the student will, insofar as possible, be assigned to a regular classroom, or "mainstreamed" or "integrated." When students are suspected of having a handicapping condition, they are tested and diagnosed by an elaborate process in which parents are intimately involved. At that point, an individual educational program is prepared, describing in detail the objectives of the program and stipulating the instruction the child will receive. This individualized program is reviewed at least once every three years.

On October 8, 1986, the act was amended (PL 99-457) to include programs for handicapped (1) infants and toddlers, (2) children 3 to 5 years old, and (3) high school and post–high school students. Thus, eleven years following its enactment, the act included an even wider range of handicapped programs.

**WHAT THE GOVERNMENT HAS LEARNED** What is to be said about the federal government's involvement in education? First, and certainly foremost, the government continues to be vitally interested in education. Its style of "getting involved" is to gather large sums of money, announce what programs will be funded if implemented at the state or local level, and then tightly monitor the funds. Historically, the government has championed the cause of the poor and underprivileged.

Throughout this journey of giving, the government has learned important lessons. First, a top-down system of management is insufficient to ensure change. Sitting in Washington, an administrator is a long way from, for example, the implementation of a bilingual reading program in a fourth-grade classroom in south Chicago. Too many layers come between the federal administrator and the child in the classroom. Sometimes the money is spent more for overhead expenses and indirect costs than for the benefit of students. The goals, so lucid on Washington letterhead, become diffuse and unclear by the time they reach the teacher's desk.

A second lesson is that funds must be targeted specifically. Money that was first earmarked to help the educationally deprived was spent on things not even remotely resembling education for underprivileged. For example, some school districts used the money to buy themselves airplanes.

Finally, the federal government has learned that the nation's educators have improved their ability to teach the disadvantaged child. Evaluations of the early compensatory programs showed those programs were falling short in their effectiveness. But later programs have improved. Secretary of Education T. H. Bell remarked, "After being away [from Washington, D.C.] for five years and coming back, I can tell you that American education has learned how to educate disadvantaged children."

What of today and the future? The federal government will continue to have strong goals for education and assume responsibility for reaching those goals. Congress, as it has done for the past sixty years, will act as watchdog, ensuring that civil rights, defense, the economy, and alleviation of poverty—all national priorities—are inextricably linked to education. While different administrations load down or buoy up the federal education budget, Congress steadies the ship.

## The State's Responsibility for School Governance

State responsibility for education derives primarily from the interpretation of the Tenth Amendment: "The powers not delegated to the United States by the Constitution, nor prohibited by it to the States, are reserved to the States respectively, or to the people." The states, not the federal government, are legally responsible for educating the youth of the United States.

States have constitutions that provide for the establishment and operation of education within the state. For example, Article VIII, Section 2, of the Constitution of the State of Michigan reads: "The Legislature shall maintain and support a system of free public elementary and secondary schools as defined by law. Each school district shall provide for the education of its pupils without discrimination as to religion, creed, race, color, or national origin."[1] State legislatures pass enabling legislation to actually carry out these constitutional mandates. This legislation, consisting of statutes, is bound in a volume and becomes the School Code or the State Law of Education.

Most states have a state board of education that oversees all education within the state. The board is made up of a group of citizens who are elected by the people or are representatives of the people, appointed by the governor, or serve by virtue of another office held. Their functions are (1) to make policies (for example, establish the number of mandatory school days in a year), (2) to regulate (for example, ensure that standards for teacher certification are carried out), and (3) to advise (for example, recommend a budget increase to the governor and the legislature).[2]

The day-to-day running of the education in the state is carried out by the state office of public instruction. This office is headed by an executive officer, often called the state superintendent of instruction. The superintendent and his or her staff are assigned supervisory responsibility for carrying out the policies established by the state board of education. These include providing help for local school districts that are implementing state-established policies. Here is a sample of responsibilities assigned to the state office of public instruction:

1.  Enforce compulsory attendance laws, see that schools operate the required number of days, and enforce the general state laws relating to education.

2.  Assume responsibility for certifying teachers and ensure their tenure and their welfare.

*State responsibility for education includes the right of the state to require compulsory attendance of those it deems wise to education.—P. E. Burrup, V. Brimley, and R. R. Garfield*

3.  Distribute funds for all state and federal programs, striving to achieve equal educational opportunity across the state.

4.  Collect and tabulate statistical information about the state's education programs.

5.  Approve building plans, sites, and equipment.

Although it is true that states have turned over much of the responsibility for education to local school districts, there are those who argue that better education would result from keeping control at the state level. These proponents argue for state selection of textbooks and curriculum. For example, one spokesman said, "It makes more sense for the state of California to review materials for alignment with curriculum requirements than it does to ask over 1,000 districts to select from over 1,300 state-approved textbooks."[3]

## CORPORATE AMERICA'S POTENTIAL ROLE IN GOVERNANCE

There is a new kid on the educational block. Big and powerful, this newcomer is clearly making his presence known. Private industry, flourishing its profit motives and new technology and operating with enormous efficiency in the open market, promises to affect educational reform in bold and exciting ways—far more powerfully than an awkward federal government or a bureaucratically hobbled state government. Picture a school in the sky, delivered by satellite to subscribing homes throughout the country, beginning in late afternoon. Currently, 43 million homes are wired for cable. If cable subscriptions did cost about $20.00 per month, consider how quickly vast sums of money could be generated for curriculum development.

Corporate America will certainly not stop to ask permission of state and local offices of education. It will move aggressively in developing an "after-school" curriculum. Some of the brightest and most experienced teachers in the nation will be hired away to develop this curriculum—slick, effective, and easily accessed. Parents can view, on a trial basis, foreign language instruction (taught on videotape from the foreign country itself), math, science, literature, and reading—all available for about $20.00 a month. The finest teachers using the latest technology will be teaching students how to read, compute, and write. The curriculum will be forward looking and fast paced and will reflect the latest research and training techniques from industry.

But what if students are in the habit of coming home and flopping down in front of their favorite television show? How could middle school students be persuaded to switch channels for another hour of math and science instruction, especially after sitting through an hour of "ho-hum" math in school? Well, the best and most expensive minds in business—with large profit potentials gleaming on the horizon—can surely solve *that* problem! Education is a large account for corporate America. Unlike the public schools, business does not need to operate on tax dollars. Business goes straight to parents and sells them on the advantages of high-tech education for their children (an age-old winner). This "personalized" education, within their own homes, is far more attractive to parents than an increase in property tax to fund local education.[4]

# LOCAL CONTROL

An assumption embedded in American education is that schools are established to serve the needs of society. Through the years, Americans have viewed education as a major means of fulfilling both societal and individual needs—so much so that current educational systems provide formal instruction for nearly 60 million students, ranging from preschoolers to postgraduates, with an annual expense of more than $328 billion. Indeed, only defense and health/medical spending equal or exceed what our nation spends on education each year, a clear evidence of our country's commitment to education. Yet despite its magnitude, education is traditionally seen as a local enterprise. The original school boards were school committees composed of parents. The feeling was that patrons should have the ability to govern what went on in their schools, making sure professionals were hired who would provide the best education possible for their children. The nature of local control has been modified over the years, but the spirit of local control is still strong:

> The approximately 15,000 local school districts in the United States and their nearly 90,000 individual schools comprise the fundamental operational units of American education. It is at the local level that the overwhelming majority of educational professionals are employed. This is the locus of curriculum planning and instruction. It is here that most school administrators receive their initial and probably more formative professional experiences. It is at this level that America's educational systems are the most visible, and it is here that the public frames its views regarding the success or failure of schools.[5]

Beginning in the 1950s, the conventional decision-making prerogatives of local school officials began eroding. Today, state legislatures, state agencies, and the federal government exert a substantial policy-making influence on American education.

*Public instruction should be the first object of government.*
—*Napoleon Bonaparte*

## School and Community

Still, local education agencies continue to play a significant role in the larger society. If society has high-technology needs, schools should provide students with advanced computer and electronics training. If society needs more food to feed a burgeoning population, schools should teach scientific agriculture. Obviously, "society's" needs depend on where you live. The American society is a composite of minisocieties, each working to satisfy its own needs. If a rural community is supported by the mining industry, the local high school, responding to these needs, offers classes in chemistry, metallurgy, and geology and provides credit for early work experiences. In a large suburban area, with more diversified needs, students plan to become bus drivers, city managers, attorneys, construction engineers, and urban planners. So the suburban high school provides a smorgasbord of curricular offerings: prelegal and premedical training, merchandising, business, finance, city planning, and sociology.

But we oversimplify. No section of the country can totally satisfy its own needs any more. High-level communication and jet-age travel shrink the country, making its parts complexly interdependent. If the Wheat Belt underproduces, reverberations are felt in supermarkets throughout the country. If the northwestern lumber industry slides, furniture stores in New York feel the pinch. If the winter is harsh in Texas, the price of beef rises in San Francisco. Add to this delicate balance the shifting of values, increase in socially transmitted diseases, ups and downs of the economy, increasing isolationism within large cities, and breakdown of the family as the basic unit of society—all these forces make it difficult for local school boards to identify and assign priorities to local school needs. Local needs cannot be addressed independently of the needs of the larger, interdependent society.

## School Boards and Superintendents

Legally, the schools belong to the people of the state, not to a local community. This means that local school board members are actually state officers, representing the state as a whole but working on local problems. Realistically, however, their loyalties are riveted to immediate problems facing their own district.

The school board itself is a unique American invention, linking the school with the community. Local school boards are constitutionally and statutorily empowered to make significant decisions. Powers typically granted local school boards include these:

© Spencer Grant/Photo Researchers, Inc.

1. selecting the superintendent (chief executive officer)
2. approving budgets
3. determining school sites and attendance boundaries
4. entering into contracts for goods and services
5. negotiating collective bargaining agreements or contracts with employees, as agents of the district
6. establishing criteria for employing school district personnel
7. determining curriculum
8. establishing codes for student conduct.[6]

The board's most important responsibility is the selection of the superintendent, since this selection has far-reaching implications for the district. The superintendent keeps the board informed about problems and accomplishments in the district, as well as plans for building new schools. A major responsibility is to prepare and submit the district's annual budget. Further, the superintendent represents the district and school board to the public, often in the role of negotiator. The overwhelming proportion of his time is devoted to budgetary and finance matters, personnel, facilities, and public relations work. Indeed, only one-fifth to one-fourth of his time is spent on matters relating to instruction or students.[7]

Another major responsibility of the school board is to approve a budget, generally by mid-June, and to hold public hearings. During the year, the board plays watchdog over budget expenditures and adjusts the budget as needed. Legally, a person cannot be hired or fired by a school district without the approval of the school board. The board also approves salary and benefit contracts negotiated with teachers' associations. Decisions about buying and selling property are made by the board, including where and when to build school buildings and what to include in them. Further, the board is legally responsible for formulating policy for the district. It establishes goals for the curriculum and spearheads evaluations of school programs. For example, the board decides that all report cards from grade six on up will show letter grades, and it brings in professional evaluators to determine the effectiveness of the district's cultural arts program.

Many feel that school boards spend too much time on trivia and not enough on substantive policies involving the curriculum. This tendency is partly the result of organizational and environmental constraints such as state statutes, insufficient information, and limited resources. Still, the board's influence is considerable. Capable and committed members must serve. Members are elected or appointed from the community and usually serve from three to six years. School board members must

1. be nonpartisan
2. demonstrate a genuine interest in and devotion to the cause of public education
3. possess more than average intellectual ability
4. be both broad-minded and open-minded
5. be able to accept criticism without becoming upset
6. be willing to give devotion to a cause or program directed by the superintendent
7. possess a sense of humor and a capacity for human understanding
8. have a genuine interest in civic and government problems, an average (or better) education, plenty of common sense, and some degree of imagination and enthusiasm.

A governing interplay takes place between the school board and the superintendent, varying immensely within a state. In one district, the board legislates a policy and the superintendent oversees its implementation in the district's schools. In another district within the same state, the superintendent hands the board a list of recommendations, which they adopt without question. In both cases, final authority lies with the board, not the superintendent. However, any seasoned superintendent knows better than to take a combative stance in dealing with the board. Both know the value of a productive working relationship—or the hopeless results of an adversarial standoff.

The superintendent together with staff members in the district office and in conjunction with the school board have considerable governing power over their schools:

*Personnel administration is the real core of successful school administration.*—B. J. Chandler and Paul V. Petty

*Principals.* School buildings are operationally under the control of building principals. Principals have control and responsibility for the buildings and grounds, for all supplies and equipment housed at the building, for all school-related activities carried on there, and for all pupils, teachers, and other employees assigned to the building.

*Handling of supplies.* Each building will be provided an annual supply budget based on a formula that takes into account the number of students to be served and the supply costs of the programs in which the students will engage. Principals, in consultation with their staffs, are responsible for the requisitioning, management, distribution, and utilization of supplies within the building. The Office of Business Services is responsible for the actual purchasing, warehousing, and distribution of supplies to buildings and for providing the necessary forms and establishing efficient procedures to facilitate the process.

*Equipment budgets.* Principals, in consultation with their staffs, are authorized, when necessary, to spend equipment allocation funds for supplies or supply allocation funds for equipment. Funds unexpended in either account at the end of the budget year are carried over and added to the allocation for the ensuing budget year.

*Selection of staff.* The personnel office is responsible for conducting an initial screening of all applicants and keeping a current list of all candidates meeting district standards for employability. Principals will recommend from the approved list appointments to fill their vacancies.

*Courses of study.* To assist the school staff and to provide some degree of coordination among schools, the district provides a written curriculum in each subject area. This curriculum specifies goals, includes teaching plans, and identifies recommended materials. In most cases, schools may use methods or materials other than the recommended ones, provided they have the written permission of the associate superintendent for instruction.

*School hours.* The amount of instructional time will be essentially the same for all buildings at each instructional level, but starting and dismissal times may vary to meet individual building conditions.[8]

## Erosion of Lay Control

Our discussion of federal, state, and local influences on school governance is accurate as far as it goes. But the picture is incomplete. Americans have always thought of education as an enterprise belonging to the people and controlled at the local level. But the power structure at the local level has gone topsy-turvy, with erosion of the lay citizen's governing power. Here, briefly, are some of the reasons for the weakening of this authority.

Over the past seventy years, there has been a movement toward the consolidation of many rural and small school districts into larger units. The number of local school districts reached its peak in the 1920s, when nearly

130,000 were in existence. By 1950 the number of districts had been reduced to 80,000, and by 1984 the number had dwindled to fewer than 15,000. Small districts were being gathered together into larger districts in order to save money and increase efficiency of school operation. Arguments arose for and against these consolidations. Whereas large districts appear to be more economical in such respects as utility costs, transporting students to a central site increases fuel costs. Districts with larger enrollments can afford to offer more specialized courses, such as advanced science, math, and foreign languages, but they also give rise to problems of student alienation and indifference. Bigger is not necessarily educationally better.

The centralizing of schools fostered complexity and bureaucracy. Greater numbers of professional educators were required to handle large and sprawling school operations. Cities added these administrative and supervisory personnel under the direction of the superintendent to relieve board members of what had become overwhelming "professional" responsibilities. Not only were lay citizens feeling overloaded with supervision of large districts but they were becoming awestruck by the increasingly esoteric nature of running the schools, as well as buffaloed by the large cadre of career administrators. Their traditional authority was being drained away into the hands of educational pros.

Other factors, some of which will be discussed in later chapters, have contributed to a weakening of local control: courts are frequent participants in educational policy making; teachers are demanding increased decision-making power; special interest groups bring pressure to bear on educational policy; and apathy is pervasive among the citizenry.

Citizen apathy can be explained in part by the fact that many feel they have little say in how schools are run. In 1900, the ratio of school board members to citizens was one board member for every 138 citizens. This relatively small ratio provided opportunity for close contact between school board members and citizens. Disagreements could be handled on a personal basis. By the mid-1970s, the ratio had risen to approximately one in every 2470, and by the 1980s, even higher. To many citizens it seems hopeless to try to gain a voice in local school policy. As a result, they give up and hope their case will be argued by pressure groups and lobbyists.

During recent years, efforts have been made to restore policy-making power to local citizens. Some of these efforts are aimed at breaking up large city districts and returning to smaller, locally run districts whose boards receive grass-roots input in reestablishing local policy.

## Local versus State Control

Some look upon the erosion of local control as a loss. But others consider it a favorable development. They argue that local control *should* be relinquished—to the state. Here is a sample of statements made by proponents of state control:

"From our experience in California, we contend that states should take the lead in defining and controlling educational content."

"School improvement efforts need not focus on the local school; decisions about curriculum content, textbooks, and testing should be made at the state level."

"If there is a state-determined content, as we recommend, the alignment of the curriculum materials and programs with that content can also be handled most readily at the state level."[9]

# GOVERNANCE IN YOUR SCHOOL

Federal, state, and local influences on school governance are all felt in your particular school, regardless of its grade level. What is the value of having multiple influences governing your school? Are there any safeguards in such an arrangement? Yes. Like the Constitution, this arrangement is an example of federalism, a system in which some responsibilities rest with the federal government, some with the states, and some with local districts. The Constitution's founders felt that citizens (and teachers are citizens) could be freer under this system than under a unitary system in which all power belongs to the central government. In keeping with that philosophy, it will be helpful for you to view your own school's governance as involving (1) federal *interest,* (2) state *responsibility,* and (3) local *control.* It is the third, the local control, that you face on a daily basis.

"That's all fine and good. I can appreciate the fact that my school is

© Vivienne della Grotta/Photo Researchers, Inc.

affected by all three groups, but I'm a teacher. What I need is to find out from the principal what the policies are for me, and follow them. That's my job." Such is the reaction of a pragmatic teacher who senses the beat of the drummer to which she must march.

You can look at the governance of your school from a number of perspectives. You might look at it from a management perspective, focusing on regulatory practices, goals and objectives, and ways of exercising administrative authority. Or you might view it in terms of how decisions are made and carried out, how the leaders behave, and what motivates and satisfies the people in the school. For our purposes, we simply describe what you are likely to walk into and what you might expect to find.

Your school is a miniature society, with its own norms, values, patterns of behavior, customs, traditions, expectations, and, generally, "ways of doing things." For example, at the elementary level, one expected pattern of behavior is walking, not running, in the halls. At the high school level, sports are valued, and dismissing classes on the day of homecoming is a tradition. One expectation at all levels is that teachers will not verbally abuse students.

Every school, and yours will be no exception, initiates you into expected patterns of conduct. During your first interview, the principal hands you *Policies of Central Junior High*. Browsing through its pages, you see statements like these:

"Teachers are expected to be at school one-half hour before opening and remain one-half hour after closing."

"Teachers are expected to be in attendance at all faculty meetings."

"No classes are to be dismissed prior to the ending of the school day."

These are formal school policies (and often district policies as well). You learn them quickly and unambiguously.

But many expectations, policies, and rules are unwritten; they are learned from living in the culture. Mr. Chavez helps Mr. Singleton, a transfer teacher, learn the ropes at Rivermount Middle School: "You can use the supplies in the workroom, up to a point. You'd better not miss more than two faculty meetings. Scheduling the gym can be a hassle; make sure you do it well ahead. You can excuse kids early—but not *too* early. Some kids you send to the principal's office, some you don't. Ask Candy Rogers for help, but stay clear of Bulldog Barker!"

Those who have gone before you have learned the pattern of governance in your school. Most will offer help and support when you come along. The process of becoming acculturated into a school is, to a great extent, the process of learning how to fit into the governing structure. Both your colleagues and the principal will be surprisingly facilitative—if you decide to enlist their help.

In Chapter 3, we discussed your principal's relationship with you and explained how you can enter a productive partnership. Here we focus on the principal's leadership and governing role. For better or worse, the principal is a powerful governing force in your teaching life. Every principal has a unique style of leadership. One is authoritative, highly regimented, caught up with rules and regulations, hovering, lost in minutiae, and worried about

---

## Getting Tough

Joe Clark, principal of Eastside High in Paterson, New Jersey, is known for his "get tough" approach to discipline. In Principal Clark's view, if something is wrong, school administrators and teachers should get tough about it—now. "Discipline is the ultimate tenet of education," says Clark. "Discipline establishes the format, the environment for academic achievement to occur."

A rash of controversy has surrounded the high-handed approach of Joe Clark and other administrators who have adopted tough, often harsh discipline. On a single day in his first year, Clark threw out 300 students for being tardy or absent and, he said, for disrupting the school. Problems of due process and school board approval have been cited, and questions about how best to approach discipline problems have been debated. In the words of George McKenna, a Los Angeles principal, "We want to fix the schools, but you don't do that by seeing the kids as the enemy. Our role is to rescue and to be responsible." Thomas P. O'Neill, Jr., a Boston principal, says, "Clark's use of force may rid the school of unwanted students, but he also may be losing kids who might succeed." Albert Shanker, President of the American Federation of Teachers, agrees: "Paterson, N.J., school principal Joe Clark grabs headlines by illegally expelling 60 'troublemakers' and, to keep out drug pushers and other thugs, chaining shut school fire exits. The issue was real: Too many school boards are reluctant to remove youths who terrorize our classrooms. But Clark's bullhorn-bellowing, bat-brandish-

ing style probably did less to convince kids that schools are for learning than it did to convince them that schools are prisons."

Others feel that Clark's tough methods are justified because of the difficult problems he faces. Kenneth Tewel, a former New York high school principal who now teaches school administration, says, "You cannot use a democratic and collaborative style when crisis is rampant and disorder reigns." Odette Dunn Harris, principal of William Penn High School in Philadelphia, citing her own experiences of confiscating crack bags from student pushers, handling riots in the lunchroom, and dealing with students who carry knives and guns as casually as pocket combs, says of Clark: "Here is a principal with principles. He is trying to develop strong, independent, law-abiding citizens and is trying to provide the students with a safe, secure place to learn, and for this he is going to be nailed to the wall."

Joe Clark's methods have had mixed results. Math scores are up 6 percent, reading scores remain the same, and dropouts have increased from 13 to 21 percent. Observers have pointed out that other principals have accomplished important results using *different* methods.

How does one deal with the realities of teaching good behavior while teaching the subject matter?

*Time,* February 1, 1988, pp. 52–58; *New York Times,* January 1, 1989, p. E-7; *New York Times,* March 14, 1989, p. A-18.

friends and enemies. Another is relaxed, overly democratic, committed to teachers' comfort and satisfaction. One is goal oriented, full of expectations, respectful of teachers, forceful, and energetic. Yet another is quiet, avoids confrontations, and is seldom around.

Part of the excitement (and challenge) of teaching is being exposed to varying styles of leadership. Research has shown that the effective principal possesses personal vision, takes initiative for change, handles routine tasks efficiently, is committed to quality and personal persuasiveness, does not dictate, maintains a sense of control over what happens in the school, can focus his or her involvement, and maintains a clear set of goals for the school.

What if your principal is deficient in *most* of these characteristics? What if your principal is painfully ineffective? You have two options: either work around this person's style of leadership, accomplishing your goals with skill and effectiveness, or apply for a transfer. Both are reasonably good solutions.

Being a principal is no trivial assignment. Most feel they are unable to "keep up" with their stewardship. One study of the busy life of principals found that variety, brevity, and fragmentation characterize their work. More than 80 percent of the principals' activities take from one to four minutes to accomplish. Interruptions occur during 50 percent of all their activities. On the average, they work fifty hours per week, and their number of tasks per hour exceeds seventeen. Verbal interaction marks nearly 85 percent of all activities and occupies 64 percent of time expended. They prefer live action to reflective activity. Although their responsibilities extend beyond the school, more than 90 percent of all contacts occur with people in their school.[10]

Principals are busy, and they occupy a focal governing position in your school. These are but a sample of a high school principal's specific duties:

1. Administers the school's budgeted allocations and takes responsibility for all the financial affairs of the school. Prepares department chairpersons' and faculty meeting agendas, and conducts staff meetings to keep members informed of policy, changes, and new programs.

2. Supervises the school's teaching process. Plans, implements, and supervises the course of study, registration of students, student records, parent–community relations, and region interschool activities and relations.

3. Supervises the development and implementation of special programs and administers such programs according to district, state, and federal guidelines.[11]

What follows is a real-life view of school governance at work in several critical areas of governance. The areas in which governance is occurring are in boldface type.

In Lincoln Elementary there is give and take, but if a **problem** arises that can't be resolved among team members or between grade-level teams, then the principal, Mr. Black, makes the decision. It's important for teachers to feel they are having their needs met. For this reason, Mr. Black prefers to use a democratic approach to running the school, and he encourages teachers to work out problems at the lowest possible level rather than appealing to higher authorities.

Major areas of concern for Mr. Black are curriculum and instruction, faculty relations, discipline, and scheduling. He explains that teachers were on their own in **curriculum** until the district came up with a district-wide curriculum program. He thinks the program is helpful and has led to more direction, accountability, and positive student outcomes. The district program has clearly defined objectives for student learning in the basic areas. There is a prescribed set of **textbooks** that teachers in the district have accepted. Teams of teachers at the various grade levels decided on two to four textbooks in each subject area for their grade level. Teachers within a school can choose which of these textbooks to buy. They are free to use additional money in the textbook fund to purchase supplementary texts beyond the adopted texts.

During orientation at the beginning of the school year, Mr. Black discussed duties such as **lunchroom supervision** with his teachers. One of them questioned how much additional pay would be given for **nonteaching duties** and whether teachers should be required to perform such tasks. Mr. Black replied that he understood the faculty member's concerns and agreed with his position. He went on to explain that he wanted the school to operate on a harmonious rather than an adversarial basis and that he would try to work out procedures that would be fair for everyone, but that he hoped teachers would be willing to give a little **extra time** or effort beyond the contractual agreements. A procedure for supervision was worked out, involving paid supervisors supplemented by assistance from teachers on a rotating, voluntary basis. Some teachers willingly put in extra time to help with supervision when asked; others complained or refused. Yet these same teachers, on their own initiative, devoted extra time to their instructional programs. Mr. Black is lenient in making requests of teachers or holding them to task, even on contractual agreements, expressing his policy thus:

> The superintendent has to be rigid about **contract requirements,** or he would have all kinds of exceptions. But I leave it to the teachers. They are professionals, and I see no reason why they should punch time clocks. I prefer trust and leeway for flexibility. Actually, my teachers are very dedicated. But when there is an emergency and they need to be away from the school, I try to facilitate it. It's important to me that my teachers know I care about them and how they feel about their work.

Mr. Black acknowledges that sometimes a **teacher falls short** of what should be expected of a professional educator. When this happens, it helps relationships if Mr. Black is open and up front, so the teacher concerned senses that the principal is being honest and fair. Mr. Black explains:

Whenever there is a **problem,** I try to document it and write it up if it is serious. In the write-up I tell the direction I gave the teacher and have the teacher sign it. I indicate the deficient areas and what I think the teacher needs to do to improve. I do this to protect both myself and the teacher. I do the same if there is a parent complaint. I go to the teacher and hear his or her side. For some teachers this is a problem because they are sensitive and don't want criticism.

**Discipline** is a concern for all administrators. Regulations about how a school is run affect the type of discipline developed and maintained. Mr. Black learned that he had to exercise greater control over the school's discipline. During his first year as principal at Lincoln Elementary, he had two or three students in his office every day because of disciplinary problems. So the second year he worked with the teachers at the beginning of school orientation. Together they produced a **school-wide discipline plan,** which was carefully explained to students, parents, and all school personnel. The plan presents in writing the school's basic philosophy, its "super citizen" and monthly "good citizen" assembly, "reward" slips and "reminder" slips, classroom offenses (both minor and major), strikes given for rule infractions (three strikes and you're out), and expected procedures in the school. If a classroom offense occurs, the teacher writes down the problem behavior, the warning given (in which the problem was explained and correction was requested), the disciplinary action taken, the contact with parents, and action taken by the principal. Mr. Black says that discipline has been much better as a result of this school-wide policy. Besides enforcing this policy, Mr. Black counsels his teachers about the **use of punishment.** He advises them to refrain from corporal punishment and spontaneous acts carried out in anger, to give sufficient warning, to document any disciplinary action, and to avoid repeating mistakes.

# CONCLUSION

As quickly as possible, learn how your school is run. It is important to have a confidant, a person to whom you can turn with questions—lots of them, serious ones and silly ones. Never be apprehensive about asking questions.

Be clear on your personal accountability. Know to whom and for what you are being held accountable. Minimize surprises.

Know, clearly, your school's policy on inappropriate student behavior: the policy on cheating, fighting in class, drug use, smoking in the halls—and whether it's okay to ignore kissing in the back of the room.

Recognize your responsibilities to the entire school, not just your classroom. You are a model to all students in your school. Misbehaving seniors, as well as your own sophomores, need your help.

Be well organized, fully intending to stay on course, but also be flexible about including unplanned stops on your itinerary. Special programs, school assemblies, and football games are part of your curriculum. Smart teachers plan for intrusions. Rather than merely "rolling with the punches," they capitalize on invasions whenever possible. For the astute teacher, every event represents a potential teaching moment.

## Expansions

1. What advantages result from knowing how your particular school or department is governed?

2. Suppose you find yourself in a school or department you like, but in which your decision-making power appears curtailed. Can you think of any options, short of seeking a transfer?

3. What are some advantages and disadvantages of PL 94-142 to both you and the handicapped students?

4. Talk with a principal who receives federal money for a program in her school. What advantages and drawbacks does she see with this type of funding?

5. Some people want the state to assume greater control of education; others argue that local school boards should be in the driver's seat. After reading this chapter, what are your ideas?

6. What are the responsibilities of a local school board? Can you identify some ways a school board affects your role as a teacher?

7. What factors tend to erode the local school board's control over schooling?

## Notes

1. J. H. Johansen, H. W. Collins, and J. A. Johnson, *American Education: An Introduction to Teaching,* 4th ed. (Dubuque, Iowa: Wm. C. Brown, 1982), p. 376.

2. Ibid., pp. 376–378.

3. J. Murphy, R. P. Mesa, and P. A. Hallinger, "A Stronger Role in School Reform," *Educational Leadership* (October, 1984), pp. 20–26.

4. D. Mann, "Galapagos on the Potomac, or the Evolution of Federal Policy," *Educational Leadership* (October 1984), pp. 31–33.

5. J. W. Guthrie and R. J. Reed, *Educational Administration and Policy: Effective Leadership for American Education* (Englewood Cliffs, N.J.: Prentice-Hall, 1986), p. 42.

6. Ibid., pp. 50–51.

7. R. F. Campbell, L. L. Cunningham, R. O. Nystrand, and M. D. Usdan, *The Organization and Control of American Schools* (Columbus: Charles E. Merrill, 1980), p. 235.

8. J. C. Prasch, "Reversing the Trend toward Centralization," *Educational Leadership* (October 1984), pp. 27–29.

9. Murphy, Mesa, and Hallinger, "Stronger Role," pp. 20–26.

10. W. J. Martin and D. J. Willower, "The Managerial Behavior of High-School Principals, *Educational Administration Quarterly* 17 (1981), pp. 69–90.

11. Guidelines prepared for principals by the Provo School District, Provo, Utah.

# CHAPTER 6

# FINANCING YOUR SCHOOL

*The number of dollars spent on education should be based on the educational needs of the children rather than the wealth of the school district.—National Educational Finance Project, Gainesville, Florida*

**MAIN IDEAS**

- Public education in your state is financed by a combination of local school district taxes, state grants, and federal aid.

- With fewer dollars in local coffers, the slack in financial support for your school is being taken up by your state government.

- Even though you may have too little money for what you want to do, there is, nonetheless, some budget that can be wisely stretched.

# INTRODUCTION

Like school governance, school financing may seem to be a concern very remote from your classroom—another aspect of the system best left to the principal. But, like governance, finance is very much a part of your teaching life, as the following scenarios illustrate:

> You are faculty advisor for the *Eagle,* your high school yearbook. In spite of your careful planning and subsequent monitoring of expenses, the project faces a cost overrun of $600. Your principal tries valiantly, but unsuccessfully, to bleed funds from a nearly depleted budget. "Our only recourse is to bring in outside money," you announce at an emergency meeting of the *Eagle*'s staff. You negotiate a contract with a large plastics company to sell trash bags door to door for 25 percent of the gross revenues. Two weeks later, your staff of twelve students is out knocking on doors, trying to raise funds to complete the yearbook.
>
> During this past school year, you have scrimped on your materials budget. Your plan is to apply unused monies toward the purchase of an air conditioner for your classroom. Your principal, though sympathetic, informs you that (1) money from a materials budget cannot be transferred to a capital equipment budget, and (2) money from your materials budget cannot be carried over from one year to the next.
>
> You are faced with four different chemistry lab preparations each day. Trying to read 150 lab reports a week has become an overwhelming task. Still, students need written feedback—how else will they learn to write? Each faculty member is awarded sufficient funds for attending one professional conference per year. Thinking you have a solution to your problem, you approach the principal. "Marin, I'm burning out, fast! Can I use this year's travel money to hire a part-time aide to help me correct my chemistry lab reports?"

Making financial decisions is part of your teaching life:

"Do I spend my remaining budget on scissors and poster paper or on shelving for the reading area?"

> "Do I ask students to help pay for the paperbacks I want to use to supplement my literature program?"

"I'd like to join the National Education Association, but will the school pay my dues? If not, can I afford it?"

> Where can I get the money to take my advanced placement class to see *Macbeth?*"

"How much extra pay can I get by attending Saturday workshops? I wonder if my principal would be willing to take the money I receive and apply it to a new lathe for our woodworking shop."

School finance is a complex, gigantic enterprise. In all states except Hawaii, public education is financed by a combination of state grants, local school district taxes, and federal aid. (Hawaii, having only one school district, is financed totally by the state legislature.) State legislatures control state budgets, carving out major portions for education.

These sources of funding are shifting, becoming intertwined, diffuse, and sometimes obscure. In states where local-level funding is drying up, state and federal dollars are being called upon in order for the schools to survive. This "outside" money can be both a blessing and a curse: a blessing in providing educational opportunities not otherwise available; a curse in occasioning a loss of local control. Outside agencies can exert influence on what you teach, how you teach it, and whom you teach. For example, the federal government announces a special humanities and arts program, offering money to states willing to implement the program in schools heavily populated with disadvantaged children. Your school adopts the program (that is, your district superintendent, after study, identifies your school for a pilot program). After brief discussion, your school faculty decides to participate: third-, fourth-, and fifth-grade classes will go on the program. Quickly you find yourself immersed in the new program. On the minus side, you give up one hour three days a week from your planned curriculum; on the plus side, an aide is hired to help develop materials.

Some of the same benefits of knowing about governance apply to a knowledge of school finance. It helps alleviate anxieties and frustration and opens up opportunities. For example, you understand the source of your $500 materials budget, what it can and cannot be used for, and whether supplemental monies are available. You know how to apply for federal grants through your district and how to obtain help from the PTA to raise additional funds for classroom needs. You do not sit and grumble. Rather, you take the time to open up new and creative funding sources. Armed with knowledge about funding sources—along with a little ingenuity—you can conquer more territory.

# TAXES: THE FUNDING FOR EDUCATION

The public schools are public because they are paid for by public funds. This fact—so simple, so obvious, so fundamental—is often overlooked; its implications not well understood. Yet local, state, and national controversies erupt because of our frequent failure to grasp its stunning impact.

Look at the concept again: public funds come from taxes. Taxes are levied on *all* the people and *all* must pay. Rich and poor, the God-fearing and the godless, single and aged citizens without children in school, and childless businesses—*all* must pay taxes. These dollars are eventually, in one form or another, channeled to support the schools. It is taxation which gives meaning to the word "public" and to the phrase, "the schools belong to all the people."[1]

The theme running through this chapter is that schools belong to the people. No single segment of society can dictate control of programs or direction of the curriculum. Because of constitutional guarantees, the majority of the people cannot say, "We pay most of the taxes, so we should control the schools." The courts would not uphold their claim. The minority's rights are also guaranteed by the Constitution.

## Property Tax

In the early days of our country, local schools were supported in haphazard ways: tuition charges, endowments, compulsory as well as voluntary contributions, gifts, and land grants. Early on, the basic principle was that children should pay according to the benefits they received. As time went on, it became apparent that the "benefits received" principle would not work because education was being priced beyond the ability of low-income families. So alternatives were considered. Taxation based on a person's assets seemed more fair. Since the possession of property was a reasonably good measure of a person's assets (and therefore tax-paying ability), property tax became the standard local source for school funds.

Property tax is the workhorse tax, and it is raised exclusively at the local level. Approximately 98 percent of the local money required to run schools comes from the property tax. The process of collecting this tax is relatively simple. The county assessor places an assessed value on a family's property—a market or "fair" value during that particular year. (The voters have already determined what percentage of that assessed value can be taxed.) For illustrative purposes, let us assume that the amount is 60 percent. If the market value of the home is $100,000, then $60,000 is taxable. Suppose it is determined that the family owning this home owes $900 in property taxes for the current year. Some of these property taxes are earmarked for the city, the county, and the water district. But the lion's share goes to the local school district. In this case, let's say $560 goes to the local school district this year. Once property taxes have been collected and the portion going to the district has been computed, the county assessor makes out a check and mails it to the treasurer of the school district.

Property taxes have several advantages as sources for educational funding. They do tend to go up a little each year, but in general they are stable. Further, most homeowners find it difficult to evade this type of tax. Most important, the benefits from the tax go directly to the residents of the district. (We will later discuss disadvantages of this tax—and the resulting court battles over "unequal opportunity" that property taxes have fostered.)

## Other Taxes

In addition to educational funding through property taxes, a variety of other tax revenues find their way into education. These include state sales tax, federal personal income tax, corporate tax and excise, severance, and inheritance and estate taxes.

States levy sales taxes, then send the revenues to the local districts in the form of grants. In most states, about 30 percent of the total taxes are derived from sales tax. This tax has the advantage of being easy to collect, and it increases revenue as the income increases.

The federal government levies a personal income tax, as do some states. This tax has several advantages: it is directly related to the income of the taxpayer; it can be adjusted to take into account special circumstances such as hardships or illnesses; and it increases as personal income increases.

Many states levy an income tax on corporations, thus providing an additional source of revenue. Corporate tax also has several advantages: revenue increases as corporate income increases, the tax can be equitably applied, and it can be structured to hold administrative costs to a minimum.

There are other, smaller taxes. Excise taxes are collected on motor fuel, tobacco, and liquor. These revenues, collected by federal and state governments, have limited use at the local level. Estate and inheritance taxes are levied at the state level and are also of limited use at the local level, as are severance taxes on minerals and oil.

In most states, income tax is earmarked for education. General sales taxes and smaller taxes usually flow into a general fund, some of which may be used for specific educational purposes. For example, in one state, taxes from the sale of liquor help underwrite school lunch programs. Money for education comes from other state sources as well. In twenty-six states, for example, revenue from state lotteries goes toward educational needs.

# THE MYTH OF EQUAL EDUCATION

Let us examine the natural consequences of a system of funding based on local property taxes. Suppose that within the same state there are two school districts that vary greatly. One comprises an older, urban area whose families are large and poor and whose properties have decreased in value over the years. The other, predominantly suburban, is filled with high-income families who enjoy luxurious homes. If the state levies a property tax of, say, 14 percent on all taxable property, the suburban district will yield a huge sum of money, and the urban district only a small sum.

In the affluent district, it may mean that $5000 can be spent on each student (per-pupil expenditure); in the poor district, only $1200 per pupil. Suppose that, in an attempt to equalize the per-pupil expenditures, the urban district were taxed at a higher percentage. Even then, the per-pupil expenditure would remain small. A higher percentage of a small amount of money is still small when compared with money from the suburban district. Yet the suburban district could raise large sums of money (high per-pupil expenditure) even while paying a smaller percentage property tax.

Now the educational question arises. Does the child who attends a school in a district that spends $1200 per pupil per year have the same edu-

© Cary Wolinsky/Stock, Boston

cational opportunities as one who attends school in a district spending $5000 per pupil? Certainly not. The more affluent district can spend more on teachers' salaries, sometimes twice as much. With such attractive salaries, the competition for jobs is much greater in the affluent district, and administrators have the luxury of selecting the cream of the crop. In addition to generally high-quality teachers, affluent districts can spend more on instructional services, textbooks, supplies, supplementary workbooks, guidance counselors, teacher aides, specialists, administrative services, computers, software, and physical facilities. The bottom line is that wealthy school districts spend more money on education than nonwealthy districts.

## The Tarnished American Dream

For a long time, Americans have believed that all children should have a free public education. But embedded in this belief is an assumption: a universal free education is synonymous with an equal education. From this assumption has arisen a second assumption in educational funding: the educational opportunity of every student should be a function of the total taxable wealth of the state and therefore should *not* be limited to the taxing ability of a particular school district.

As it turns out, universal education is not the same as equal education. Whereas *all* children in a state may have a free education, the quality of education varies greatly, largely because of the practice of funding through property taxes. Some families, observing the poignant effects of this inequity in the lives of their own children, have taken legal action.

In 1971 a class action suit, *Serrano* v. *Priest*, was filed by poor parents and their children against the state of California. They challenged the California law that called for financing schools with local property taxes. The California Supreme Court ruled in favor of the parents, stating that the system of financing education violated the "equal protection" clause of the Fourteenth Amendment of the Constitution; that is, a child from a poor home and a child from a wealthy home are not receiving equal "protection" against a weak education. One is protected (by virtue of where he or she lives) and the other is left unprotected. The court declared that the state's school financing system was discriminatory since it "makes the quality of a child's education a function of the wealth of his parents and his neighbors." The court concluded that proper education was a "fundamental right" and that this fundamental right could not be conditioned on wealth. (In 1973, the *Cahill* v. *New Jersey* decision provided a further impetus toward the elimination of massive interdistrict inequities in educational funding.)

In March of 1973 the United States Supreme Court handed down its

© Frank Siteman/Stock, Boston

*Does the child who attends a school in a district that manages to raise $500 per pupil per year through struggle and sacrifice have the same opportunity as the child who attends a school that raises $1,200 or more per pupil per year with a lower level of effort?—National Educational Finance Project, Gainesville, Florida*

decision in the *San Antonio Independent School District* v. *Rodriguez* case. The Supreme Court, reversing a lower court decision, found that the system of school finance did *not* discriminate against any class of persons considered "suspect," since the case did not present a definable class of poor persons (as opposed to poor districts). Furthermore, education was not a fundamental right, since it was neither explicitly nor implicitly guaranteed by the Constitution. The result of this ruling was that states are not required by law to equalize funding across districts in the state.

*Serrano* and *Rodriguez* were landmark cases. One ruled that financing by property tax was unconstitutional and the other ruled it constitutional. These cases are significant in that they were two of the first suits filed against a long-standing system of school financing. From them have flowed a wide variety of court actions challenging "equality" of educational opportunity. These cases continue to appear regularly in courts across the country.

The court decisions of *Serrano, Rodriguez,* and related cases that followed have seemed to agree, with only minor exceptions, with the following general principles or conclusions about school finance:

1. Education is considered to be a fundamental interest of the state.

2. Since educational needs vary from district to district, the state does not have to require all its school districts to spend the same amount of money or offer identical educational programs.

3. Although local property taxes discriminate against the poor, state legislatures are not required to eliminate this type of tax in favor of other sources of revenue.

4. Additional expenditures may be made by schools for programs for exceptional children and compensatory programs for culturally disadvantaged children, and also for other educational needs of children that are significant and worthy of special treatment.

5. No specific plans have been mandated to achieve equitability in school finance formulas; states are allowed to establish their own system if an adequate minimum education offering exists.[2]

## Attempts to Equalize the Quality of Education

The local school districts, struggling as they are to equalize quality, can never be accused of ill intentions—nor, frankly, can the state or federal government. All three continually wrestle with the problem in the midst of the harsh reality of property taxation. All three are committed to the American dream, but the problem is complex and knotty.

Many states have been working on some variation of an "equalization principle." Simply stated, it is the practice of taxing the wealth of the state, regardless of where its source is located within the state, to educate all the children in the state, regardless of where they live. For the taxpayer, the principle means sharing equally the burden of educating the children within the state. Equalization programs intend to provide equality of education regardless of race, religion, or any other physical or socioeconomic conditions (can you detect the guiding spirit of the Constitution?). In practice, this does not necessarily mean an identical education for all, but rather, a minimally adequate education for all. Since equalization programs not only support but insist on preserving local initiative, once each district has achieved this minimal level, it is free to go on to a level limited only by its resources and imagination.

Here is a description of one type of equalization program (considerable variety exists among states). On the basis of the average daily attendance and other criteria, the district determines how much money per pupil will be required to conduct a minimum school program. The district is not allowed to operate on less than this minimal amount, once it has been established. The district is then required to conduct a levy against the taxable property in the district. If this amount falls short of the minimum funding level required, as it often does, the state guarantees to make up the difference. For every district, then, a minimum program is ensured. If, in its levy, the district brings in money above what is required for a minimal program, that money is turned over to the state to be used by other districts having difficulty reaching the required funding level.

What if a district wants to bring in more tax dollars to benefit its own program? Some equalization formulas allow and even encourage this initiative, matching additional funds brought in by the district.

# GOVERNMENT'S ROLE IN SCHOOL FINANCE

## State's Role

Attempts to equalize the quality of education are one way that states become involved with the funding of education. This is an example of the Big Brotherism (a benevolent Big Brother) that exists in most states. States are committed to the proposition that every child, regardless of the economic condition of the school district in which he or she lives, should receive an adequate education. The state announces to each child, "I may not be able to provide you with the best education available, but be assured that you will have an adequate one."

Equalization programs are only part of a state's overall commitment to education. Education is high on the state's list of priorities. The large goal of

*The whole people must be willing to take upon themselves the education of the whole people and must be willing to bear the expense of it.—John Adams*

state legislatures and state departments of education is to improve the quality of education within the state—not just to provide each child a "minimal" education. But, as any legislator can attest, this is no easy task.

States are exerting more control over local education now because they are paying more of the bills. In recent years, money from property taxes has been dwindling in many areas. States have had to step in with compensating dollars. Anxious that their monies be wisely spent, state officials look over shoulders. States are acting more like the federal government—identifying programs they feel ought to be implemented, then earmarking monies for them. Well-intentioned legislators, working on their own brand of educational reform, enact legislation that often increases state control over local school districts. For example, as a result of reviewing state-wide high school achievement scores in math and reading, a state legislature passes a bill requiring all students to take two years of math and two years of English prior to graduation.

From the local school district come both protests and thanks. Many superintendents feel that their curricula are inflated with state-mandated programs, arising from the whims of well-intentioned but ill-informed do-gooders. At the same time, local boards realize their increasing dependence on state coffers: "We need state funds to augment our resources, but we don't need legislators' uninformed attempts to overhaul education."

Voucher plans and tuition tax-credit plans represent current, aggressive attempts to reform the financing of public education. However, they also raise issues relating to school finance.

A voucher plan is a financing method whereby funds are allocated to students' parents, who then purchase education for their children in a public or private school. The parents are given a voucher worth a certain amount of money, generally the actual per-pupil cost of educating one child in the district for one year. If the cost of attending the school selected by the parents and student exceeds the amount of the voucher, the parents or student make up the difference.

A tuition tax credit differs from a voucher system in that the voucher system allocates funds to parents, whereas the tuition tax-credit plan provides a tax credit for the parents. A broad tuition tax-credit program was proposed at the federal level in 1978, when Senators Packwood of Oregon and Moynihan of New York introduced a bill that would give parents a $500 tax credit on their federal income taxes for each child they enrolled in a private school. A system of tuition tax credit is available in some states (Minnesota, for one), and the United States Supreme Court has ruled it constitutional:

In June, 1983 the Supreme Court handed down its opinion in *Mueller* v. *Allen*. In a 5 to 4 vote it approved a Minnesota law that permits taxpayers to deduct from their state income taxes expenses for tuition, textbooks, and transportation. The deduction is neutrally available to every family with children of school age, but is especially beneficial for parents who send their children to private school.[3]

These voucher and tuition tax-credit systems are the focus of considerable debate. Advocates say that systems such as these promote competition in education, much as the profit motive spurs competition in business, and that competition among schools will produce higher-quality education for less money. Opponents argue that public schools will continue to be full of students unable to afford the additional cost of attending a private or parochial school and that the private or parochial schools will continue to be full of children from well-to-do homes. Further, they contend that public monies will be used to support parochial schools, which they see as a violation of the First and Fourteenth Amendments.

For years to come, states will be hammering away at school reform. The row is tough to hoe, even with the best minds working on the problems. There is the ever-present and nagging problem of finding fair ways to distribute the financial burden. Further, as some states find it necessary to shoulder more of the funding responsibilities, there is a tendency for local districts to sit back and pick up the phone each time they need help. State legislators see that solution as unrealistic: "Local districts *must* continue raising revenue to help in the task," they say. In other states, a partnership between the state and the local district has emerged, with each carrying a fair share of the financial load. In still other states, the local district remains the primary funding agent.

The following statistics for 1985 illustrate the great disparity found among states in state funding ratios: in Oregon, the state contributed 27.8 percent to the total cost of education; in New Hampshire, 5 percent; in West Virginia, 66 percent; in Washington, 74.2 percent. Nationwide, the average contributed by states was 48.8. (The average contributed by the federal government was 6.5 percent, and the average contributed by local sources was 44.7 percent.) These state monies are not coming from local property taxes. Their sources are mostly income and franchise taxes on individuals and businesses, sales taxes, and gasoline, alcohol, and tobacco taxes.[4]

## Federal Government's Role

The level of federal support for education depends to a large extent on the incumbent administration's commitment to education and its budget priorities. Thus, there is an ebb and flow of support for education. Still, through the years, priorities for spending the educational dollar have not changed. The federal government has assumed the posture of providing support in both geographic and subject areas where states and local districts lack resources. For example, if schools in Miami, Dade County, lack resources for Cuban refugees, the federal government will supply. Likewise, if schools are weak in providing for compensatory needs, the federal government will help. Further, the federal government has been consistent in boldly declaring *its* goals and how education can further them. Finally, the federal government has been prescriptive in its educational funding. In declaring goals, mandating programs to meet the goals, and outlining specific procedures to be followed, the federal government is most influential. Given the massive bureaucracy that exists, this prescriptive posture maximizes the federal government's impact on education.

Among the federal government's priorities, providing money for educational programs that bolster national defense has long been high on the list. Recently Congress targeted improved instruction in science, math, foreign languages, and computers and other high technology that give the country a competitive edge.

Fighting poverty in its multiple forms is another priority. Compensatory programs abound. Students of all ages with serious learning problems, emotional difficulties, and social maladjustments often require specialized tutoring and remedial education. Perhaps the most far-reaching of these programs to date has been Chapter I of the Elementary and Secondary Education Act of 1965. The act provides grants to local districts that have large concentrations of families with poor children. In recent years, new programs have appeared, including help for delinquents, school dropouts, unmarried pregnant students, and drug abusers. "Alternative" schools designed to reach out to students with special needs can be found in most school districts.

Federal attention is given not only to compensatory programs, trying to remedy problems students bring with them, but to boosting or "head start" programs as well. Increased monies spent on early childhood education, including kindergarten, are evidence of this federal thrust. The federal government traditionally gives money for food and transportation. Monies are earmarked for school breakfasts and lunches, milk programs, busing, and special vehicles. Transporting students to the school and feeding them once there is a direct way of contributing to their education.

Likewise, vocational training programs continue to receive monies. Vocational exploration has moved down to upper elementary grades and follows through into middle school and high school. Work-experience programs are a regular part of many high school curricula. At the college level, many students would have dropped out and gone into the labor market had they not received low-interest government loans.

Federal dollars are also being channeled into adult education and career-change programs. Older Americans have opportunities to develop new leisure-time activities, engage in self-improvement programs, and train for midlife career change.

Money influences the curriculum. It hums an alluring tune to a faculty, who chorus "We can receive a federal grant if we include metrics in our curriculum." But the jingle of money on the table of a financially strapped state or district can sound both sweet notes and sour. To illustrate, we use the mandated Public Law 94-142, introduced in Chapter 2.

PL 94-142 requires free and equal educational opportunity for all handicapped children in the least restrictive environment, generally interpreted as the regular classroom. In one state, $240 was allocated by the federal government for each handicapped child. This sum covered but a small fraction of the total amount spent on each child, thus burdening even further the state's already strained resources. Numerous services were provided for handicapped children. They were picked up at their doorsteps, a service requiring prolonged busing time during the school day. Extra bus drivers were hired. Since many children lived in difficult-to-reach areas, small multiple-passenger vans, capable of navigating tight places, had to be purchased. To construct a lift on a bus (for bringing wheelchair users aboard), the district paid from $3,000 to $10,000. In order to transport wheelchairs in regular buses, seats had to be removed, precluding the transport of a full load of able-bodied students. Once in school, some handicapped children required regular attention. Aides were hired to provide help, costing the district from $5,000 to $10,000 per child per year.

Classroom teachers of handicapped students attempt to comply with the law, yet few see themselves as qualified to deal with mainstreamed or integrated students. Even when qualified, teachers worry about the additional time they have to spend with a handicapped student—more than they can spare. Teachers worry as well about being evaluated on how well their handicapped students learn. Many teachers request special aides to help with the task, thus bringing in another hidden expense.

With biting candor, one teacher assesses the impact of federal funding for disadvantaged children in his school:

> Those teachers in the federal programs like Chapter I have bucks—big bucks! They have their own typewriters, telephones, counselors, computers. It depends on the teacher. Some will work with the regular classroom teacher and share. But others say, "That's been purchased with federal money, so you can't use it." When you want to use their telephone they won't let you. It's even getting to be that way in the lunchroom. For example, I wanted a cup of powdered milk. It wasn't just for my class. It was for all the fourth grades. Do you know how many pounds of powdered milk they go through? But the lunchroom supervisor said she couldn't give out any food. I think it's good to account for your money, but that was ridiculous! Over at Monroe Elementary, the PTA decided not to use any kitchen equipment for Halloween because of the flack—the lunch workers say federal funds bought that equipment and it can only be used for school lunch. Then, too, there are feelings about those programs. When those Chapter I kids finally show some improvement, they're rewarded by going on a field trip. What about the high achievers and the middle kids in the regular classrooms without federal bucks? Chapter I students are given a big splash—field trips, special performers, anything, you name it. Other teachers wonder. We have to sit back and do our best on our own.[5]

At the classroom level, well-intentioned federal programs are sometimes implemented at enormous financial and emotional cost. Some teachers, exhausted by their efforts at complying with federal programs, conclude that fewer cooks would make a better broth: "If I had the money they spend on this handicapped child—with no strings—I could take her a lot further."

# DISTRICT'S ROLE IN SCHOOL FINANCE

The school district's budget is a marvelous medium through which the school board can express its concerns and interests to the district. More forcefully, it is a mechanism for control, determining which programs are emphasized and which are phased out, whether new books or new computers are purchased, whether girls' athletics becomes coequal with the boys', whether new vocational equipment becomes available, or whether the counseling staff is cut back.

In most cases, the budget covers a twelve-month year, usually from July 1 to June 30. Budgets are always in process. Teachers make lists of needed supplies for the coming year. Principals review the lists and add or cut back. Assistant superintendents prepare lists of new texts to be ordered. Maintenance people assess the needs for resurfacing the gym floor and purchasing a new vacuum cleaner.

The superintendent, along with his staff, prepares the budget. It is then submitted to the school board for review and revision. Finally, in open meeting, it is placed before the voters of the district. Vested interests of various groups significantly affect the budget. If, for example, two board members are staunch sports fans, then the request for new football uniforms stays in the budget. If the superintendent is opposed to alternative schools, less funding shows up for that item. Concerned parents bring pressure to update the science curriculum; their demand is reflected in a new budget item for science-teacher workshops. If teachers in the district insist on more supplies, this category of the budget shows a substantial increase.

School budgets include several major categories, such as (1) maintenance and operation, (2) capital equipment and debt services, (3) transportation, (4) school food, (5) recreation, and (6) agency fund (which allows for some discretionary use). Many school district boards authorize the transfer and investment of surplus funds, which are usually put into short-term bonds or notes guaranteed by the state or federal government. Earnings from the investments then become part of the school fund.

The superintendent submits his draft of the budget to the school board, in effect announcing, "Here is a categorical breakdown of monies required by the district to operate for the coming year." The board, after deliberating and receiving input from the general public, accepts or modifies the budget. When there is a shortfall in funds, the school board must ask the public if it will approve a tax increase or, in the case of construction of a new school, pass a bond issue. The district is "referring" to the voters its proposal to raise taxes. Thus, we have a "referendum."

Districts are forever trying to cut costs. Cost-cutting activities take place at all levels. Here is a sample of procedures that one district asked all principals to enact:

1.  Analyze the pattern of teacher absenteeism. Call in for conferences teachers who appear to be abusing their privileges.

2.  To save energy costs, have custodians turn off fresh air intake fans and monitor heating and lighting in unused or partially used school space.

3.  Establish a tight control and scheduling system for use of the school computer.

4.  Set up new controls for use of office photocopiers.

5.  Train all custodians to make minor repairs.

6.  Set up a schedule for hiring temporary clerical help.

7.  Buy all possible items in larger lots. Investigate cooperative or joint purchasing procedures with other school districts.

8.  Examine the use of paraprofessionals: Where and how can they be used to save teacher time and salaries?[6]

## Your Salary

The item in the district budget most important to you is your salary. Although "salary schedules," or their equivalent, differ from state to state and among districts, they have some commonalities. Table 6-1 is an example of a *single* salary schedule, meaning that it applies to all teachers in the district, new and experienced, men and women, elementary and secondary. Although the figures are fictitious, they approximate a national average for the late 1980s. The seven columns are different "lanes" available to a teacher. Over the course of their careers, the vast majority of teachers move from Lane I through at least Lane IV or V. Moves can be accomplished through (1) taking additional hours of college credit (after graduation with a teaching certificate), (2) accumulating in-service hours, and (3) obtaining an advanced degree.

A beginning teacher in this fictitious district starts out at Step 1, Lane I (upper left-hand corner). His starting salary is $17,500 (the national average in 1987). Each year in the district, he moves up a step (down the column) to a slightly higher salary. At the same time, he may be working to move across lanes by taking additional college courses and pursuing an advanced degree. A teacher is enticed by the prospect of a higher salary to change lanes while building up longevity. After twelve years of teaching, and having earned a Ph.D. (or, in some districts, Ed.D.) along the way, a teacher earns the highest salary possible in this district ($34,993, bottom right). In some districts,

**Table 6-1  Example of a teacher salary schedule**

| Lane I<br>B.S.<br>Degree | Lane II<br>B.S.<br>Degree<br>+ 30<br>Hours* | Lane III<br>B.S.<br>Degree<br>+ 55<br>Hours* | Lane IV<br>M.S.<br>Degree | Lane V<br>M.S.<br>Degree<br>+ 30<br>Hours* | Lane VI<br>M.S.<br>Degree<br>+ 55<br>Hours* | Lane VII<br>Ph.D.<br>Degree |
|---|---|---|---|---|---|---|
| $17,500 | $17,626 | $17,719 | $17,875 | $17,970 | $18,063 | $18,253 |
| $17,967 | $17,988 | $18,081 | $18,237 | $18,332 | $18,424 | $18,612 |
| $18,252 | $18,271 | $18,364 | $18,521 | $18,614 | $18,708 | $18,896 |
| $20,421 | $21,001 | $21,524 | $22,398 | $23,097 | $23,979 | $24,495 |
| $21,301 | $21,876 | $22,400 | $23,272 | $23,971 | $24,672 | $25,720 |
| $22,182 | $22,926 | $23,625 | $24,672 | $25,371 | $26,078 | $27,120 |
| $23,414 | $24,151 | $24,850 | $25,896 | $26,595 | $27,304 | $28,344 |
| $24,646 | $25,376 | $26,075 | $27,120 | $27,821 | $28,529 | $29,568 |
| $25,878 | $26,600 | $27,301 | $28,344 | $29,047 | $29,754 | $30,794 |
| $27,110 | $27,826 | $28,526 | $29,568 | $30,272 | $30,979 | $32,018 |
| $28,343 | $29,052 | $29,751 | $30,794 | $31,496 | $32,204 | $33,244 |
| $29,575 | $30,801 | $31,502 | $32,544 | $33,246 | $33,955 | $34,993 |

* Semester hours

once a person reaches the ceiling (bottom of a column without changing lanes, or bottom of the rightmost column), there is a one-time-only salary increase, usually a large bonus, designed to retain a person in the teaching profession.

Salary schedules reflect the philosophy of a district. Some districts prefer to offer high initial salaries with but small increases as time passes. This policy attracts new teachers but is not as rewarding for veteran teachers. Other districts offer small beginning salaries, then sizeable jumps later on. This policy may cause young teachers to go elsewhere, but mature teachers tend to stay in the district. Salary schedules will look somewhat different in years to come, incorporating such concepts as the career ladder (a program in which teachers progress through increasing levels of responsibility). Whatever the changes, the concept of a salary schedule has several advantages:

1. The schedule assumes equal pay for equal training and experience. Teachers are not left to wonder whether they are receiving more or less than a colleague with the same number of years' teaching experience. The disadvantage with this "equal pay" concept is that better teachers are not rewarded with higher pay. But since the criteria for "effective teaching" has been, until recent years, too slippery to be fair, teachers are more comfortable with equity than with merit differences.

2. With single salary schedules, elementary and secondary teachers with the same training and experience receive the same salary. (For years, hard-working elementary teachers complained about their lower salaries.)

*Although the economic benefits of teaching are important, working
conditions in schools and teachers' success in teaching students are
also important—if not more important—determinants of attracting and
retaining good teachers.—Allan Odden*

3.  There is no sex discrimination. Men and women receive the same pay, given comparable training and experience.

Your basic salary is not your only income. In addition, you receive health and accident insurance benefits, time off with pay, compensation for extracurricular supervision, reduced-rate loans through teachers' credit unions, early retirement, additional compensation for summer-school classes and alternative programs, and leaves of absence.

At some point in every discussion on teacher salaries, the comparison issue arises: when compared with other professions like law and medicine, teachers end up low on the totem pole! To be sure, there are considerable differences. However, here are some financial advantages of teaching:

1.  Teachers are usually employed on contracts of one year or more. During this period, their salaries are protected. They can expect to be paid each pay period without fear of job or income loss for any of the usual reasons that affect business and industry.

2.  A teacher's salary is guaranteed under all but the most drastic of circumstances. Teachers' salaries are often the last ones to be raised in a period of improving economy; but they are also the last ones reduced or seriously affected when the bottom drops out of the economy. Nobody believes teachers ought to be laid off!

3.  Teachers' salaries do not show the great variance found in other professions. Although no teacher becomes wealthy through teaching, no teacher is forced to face a starvation period while building up a clientele, like the doctor, dentist, and lawyer.

4.  The earning period of a teacher is relatively long when compared to that of movie stars, professional athletes, and other higher salaried groups with short earning periods. With the closing of tax loopholes, high taxes are now being paid on huge incomes earned during a short period of time. A teacher's low but consistent salary, by comparison, is not as meager as some would believe.

5.  The operating expenses of a teacher are usually low in comparison with other professionals. In business terms, operating investment is small.[7]

In addition to a teacher's basic salary and financial benefits, many states have a career-ladder system that provides opportunities for teacher leaders. The career ladder typically has four tracks: (1) probational, (2) professional, (3) teacher specialist, and (4) teacher leader. Along with enhanced

## Salaries and Shortages

Teacher salaries respond strongly to fluctuations in demand. Student enrollments peaked nationwide in 1971; this was also the peak period for the purchasing power of teachers' wages. During the subsequent decade, when enrollments were declining and the teacher labor pool contained many available and qualified individuals, purchasing power (teacher salaries in constant 1981 dollars) decreased 14 percent. Beginners' salaries particularly were affected negatively. The relationship between teacher supply and pay is most pronounced when the focus is on entry-level salaries. In 1975, beginning teacher salaries were $2,000 lower than entry-level salaries for all college graduates as a group. (See figure.) By 1983, beginning teacher salaries were $6,000 lower than the average entry earning for all college graduates. In comparative terms, the beginning teacher's salary was slightly over half the median entering wage of the electrical engineer.

Few school districts in the United States relate an individual's compensation to instructional ability or teacher productivity. Rather, teacher remuneration is linked almost exclusively to length of service and level of academic preparation. . . .

By his or her mid-thirties a classroom teacher's earning power has peaked. In 1987, the mean maximum salary for United States teachers approximated $34,000. In contrast, a successful medical, legal, or technical professional's salary begins to escalate rapidly at this career juncture. Small wonder that many of the most ambitious teachers, sensing this salary ceiling, either leave education altogether or pursue . . . organizational incentives to leave the classroom for more lucrative opportunities in education.

Society expects teachers to perform like professionals, but be rewarded like missionaries. The figure displays, in constant dollars, starting teacher salaries relative to beginning salaries for other professional and occupational undertakings. Two important features are presented here for the period from 1975 to 1983. First, teacher starting pay lagged behind most other occupations requiring comparable training. Hence, education starts the competition for talent at a deficit position. Also, these data make it plain that salaries in other fields far more effectively matched inflation over the eight-year period involved in this analysis than did compensation for entry-level teachers.

J. C. Clifford and J. W. Guthrie, *Ed School* (Chicago: University of Chicago Press, 1988), pp. 28–31.

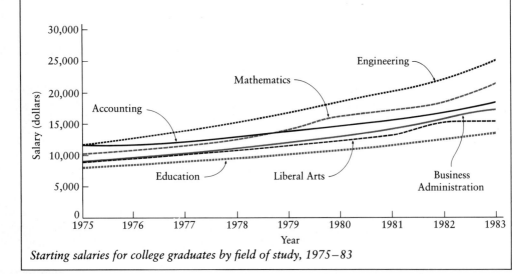

*Starting salaries for college graduates by field of study, 1975–83*

opportunities and responsibilities, teachers receive salary increases as they progress up the career ladder. We will have more to say about career ladders in Chapter 12.

## Finances and Your Classroom

Every district and every school has its own policies for distributing funds for operating individual classrooms. Perhaps the only funding characteristic common to teachers throughout the country is "too little money for what I want to do." These teachers' comments not only underscore the problem but suggest some ways of coping with it:

"We have two budgets, one for instructional supplies and one for textbooks. For each student in my class, I receive $25 per year. I can buy any supplies I want, no questions asked. Usually, it amounts to scissors, ink, cardboard storage boxes, material for making transparencies—you know, all that exciting stuff. I feel lucky though—my friend's principal controls everything that's bought in his school. In the textbook fund, I get about $40 per year per student. You have to buy a set of the district-approved textbooks. But there's still almost half left over. I use it to build up my supplemental books over the years. The other fifth grades have money left over too. We pool money and share books. By this method we've been able to purchase about 70 percent of the books we want."

"The teachers know that financing comes from the people. But there's a paradox in taxing. The polls say the majority of the people feel okay about spending more for education. But the legislators don't want to raise taxes. The money I get for running my class is fine for textbooks but not supplies. But I'm conservative—*very* conservative. I get by."

"I spend too much time dittoing. The dittoing saves the district a lot of textbook money, but it takes our valuable time. They think they pay me a lot as a teacher. But then they turn around and try to save money by having me do the job of a secretary. If they'd spend more on textbooks, I wouldn't have to stand around copying handouts. It's crazy!"

"Speaking of finances, I spend a lot personally. I'm not sure where the funds for my school come from but I want to be successful. So I decide that if I can do a better job by spending $10, I spend it. I don't mind spending my own money. But I realize everyone can't do that."

"You get a budget at the beginning of the year. If you're careful it will last. But when it's gone there's no more. I don't know many teachers who run out—they've learned."

From these comments we see that the quality of teaching is indeed affected by a teacher's finances—not only by how much he receives but by the way he uses it. For the most part, teachers deplete their budgets wisely, stretching the dollar, sensing a responsibility to students in its careful use.

# CONCLUSION

Governing and financing, the topics considered in these last two chapters, are two giant operations with which you must live every teaching day. They are as integral to your teaching life as are your blackboard and reading glasses. "But life would be so much less wearisome," says one voice, "if my only task were to teach the understanding and appreciation of Shakespeare." Yet school governance and finance are not just roadblocks. They are assets to be exploited. They open pedagogical doors, enabling you, for example, to purchase those supplemental readings, add more Erlenmeyer flasks, and secure new music for your madrigal singers.

In addition, governance and finance hold a curricular advantage. Any vocation your students choose enmeshes them in governance and finance, just as your profession has enmeshed you. In the area of governance, your students will note the way you buck the system or the way you gracefully and skillfully achieve your purposes in a less-than-optimal setting. From your example, they learn respect for authority, productive compromise, respectful confrontation, advise and consent, and quiet acquiescence. In finance, they observe your money management: frugality, fiscal priorities, planning ahead, and effective purchasing. Indeed, by example, effective teachers incorporate into the curriculum their constraints, their freedom, their impoverishment, their affluence.

## Expansions

1. What kinds of financial decisions do you anticipate being able to (or having to) make about teaching resources for your classroom?

2. Suppose your department has a book budget for the purchase of new readings. Suppose, also, it has been depleted for this year. You feel quite strongly that several new selected readings need to be made available to your students. What are some options you might try?

3. Explain how property taxes are used to fund education. Identify advantages and disadvantages of this system of financing.

4. What is the difference between a universal free education and an equal education? Why does unequal education continue to exist in this country? What attempts are being made to remedy this situation?

5. Some argue that those who hold the purse strings (that is, legislators) decide on the nature of educational reform. Describe how this could be so, and list possible disadvantages.

6. Tax-credit programs continue to be hotly debated. In one type of plan, parents would receive income tax credit for enrolling their children in private schools. The parents would pay the tuition and the government

would cut their income taxes. List some arguments for and against a tax-credit system in our public schools.

7.   In recent years, a greater percentage of the total funding for education has come from state and federal governments. Offer some advantages and disadvantages of removing support from the local school district level.

8.   What are some advantages and weaknesses of a single salary schedule (equal pay for teachers who have equal training and experience)?

## Notes

1.   National School Boards Association, *Becoming a Better Board Member: A Guide to Effective School Board Service.* (Washington, D.C.: Author, 1982), p. 176.

2.   P. E. Burrup, V. Brimley, Jr., and R. R. Garfield, *Financing Education in a Climate of Change,* 4th ed. (Newton, Mass.: Allyn & Bacon, 1988), p. 258.

3.   Ibid., pp. 320–321.

4.   T. D. Snyder, *Digest of Education Statistics* (Washington, D.C.: U.S. Government Printing Office, 1987), p. 106.

5.   From an interview with a fourth-grade teacher.

6.   National School Boards Association, *Becoming a Better Board Member,* p. 193.

7.   D. Andersen, C. Hungerford, D. Wasden, and R. Garfield, *Becoming a Professional Teacher* (Provo, Utah: Brigham Young University, 1987).

# CHAPTER 7

# YOU AND THE LAW

*A knowledge of the law is useful, but it is not a substitute in any sense for an understanding of the educational responsibility of our profession.*
—Ryan L. Thomas

**MAIN IDEAS**

- Educators are becoming preoccupied with the law through fear of lawsuits and the growing frequency of litigation in schools.

- Your rights as a teacher are ensured and protected. Thus, you are freer to focus on your responsibilities as a teacher—to yourself, your students, and your school.

- Your teaching is affected by federal legislation, court cases, and local school district policy. The issues at stake concern the family, the student, you the teacher, and your school.

- The students' rights movement has prompted legal disputes in a variety of areas, including speech and expression, dress and grooming, physical protection and privacy, suspension and expulsion, and equal opportunity.

- Under the law, you have rights of expression, privacy, dress and grooming, tenure, and personal protection. Your responsibilities include reporting child abuse and being free from malpractice or incompetence.

# INTRODUCTION

We embark upon an exciting chapter! When you read the Constitution, you come away feeling its strength. That document, the charter of our federal government, also deals with assurances of personal freedoms, liberties, and rights. This chapter introduces you to the impact of the law on education and shows you how the law can and does affect your teaching in the classroom. It deals with court decisions, civil rights movements, and protests, many of which focus on ensuring and protecting individual rights. Upon completion of this chapter, you will feel considerable assurance that your rights as a teacher will be protected. This is as it should be. At the same time, we hope you will also feel that you have certain responsibilities as a teacher. Some teachers spend so much time worrying about their rights that they forget their responsibilities—to themselves, their students, and their school.

With this caution, let us jump into the fascinating world of the law in education. You will be helped in your reading if you realize that a major responsibility of the law is to implement and help interpret the Constitution. Virtually every topic we cover in this chapter can, in some way, be traced back to rights and protections guaranteed by the Constitution.

As we commence a discussion of the law in education, you might ask, "Why study educational law?" There are numerous reasons for knowing potential legal consequences of your teaching; we offer two. First, you are less likely to make mistakes of the sort that lead to legal action because you are sensitized to what could happen. Let's look at several examples of how the law comes into play in daily teaching life:

*Example 1.* "I know I shouldn't have slapped him, but his defiant attitude—standing there, baiting me, daring me to do something. Then, when he started attacking me personally—as a woman—using such foul-mouthed language, I blew my stack! All fear left me—I let him have it. It caught us both completely off guard. I about knocked him over the desk. I don't know how I hit him because I've never done anything like that before. He was as shocked as I. I didn't know whether he would hit me back, but I didn't care. He just glared at me, then turned around deliberately and walked out of the room. I don't know what to do."

*Example 2.* "This whole thing has been blown out of proportion. I had the kids in the gym for P.E. I haven't been trained in gymnastics, but neither have the other teachers. We all lead kids through these exercises almost every day. Three weeks ago we were doing tumbling—flips and cartwheels. Some of the boys wanted to try backward somersaults. I got Eric and James to help me as spotters and everything was going fine. Then Jeremy landed improperly and apparently hurt his back. It didn't look too serious at the time. Well, two days later he shows up in a partial back cast. Then, last week, I'm approached by some attorney representing Jeremy's parents, informing me they're bringing suit for 'negligent conduct.'"

*Example 3.* A few weeks after Mr. Cowin was hired at Buscher High School, he was observed going into the school with three female seniors between 8:00 and 9:00 at night and remaining in the building from forty-five minutes to an hour without turning on any lights. The four of them continued this conduct for two more nights. Evidence gathered by the custodian following these evening sessions clearly indicated that someone had been in the building. No evidence of immoral conduct was produced, but the school board sued to break the teacher's contract and dismiss him from employment by the district.

> *Example 4.* The principal of an elementary school discovered that one of his teachers belonged to a spouse-swapping club. When questioned, she freely acknowledged her membership. Shortly thereafter her teaching credential was revoked by the state board of education. She sued the board, insisting that her credential be reinstated, claiming that her private life was her own business and no concern of the state board of education.

Imagine that you face a confrontation like the one in Example 1. Suppose you know that striking a student under *any* conditions can lead to legal action against you. Suppose you know, too, that telling a student to stop talking *never* leads to legal action. Consequently you avoid escalating confrontations with students that might cause you to lose composure and perhaps do something regrettable. When you cannot handle the situation in a professional manner, and your emotions start running awry, your automatic response is to walk away—straight to the principals' office (or the teachers' lounge, where you can gather your wits and plan something rational).

What about risks in performing backward somersaults? Unlike the teacher in Example 2, you are aware that parents might bring suit against the school district for a disabling neck injury to a child. But you have played out these possibilities far earlier. On the school liability forms signed by parents at the first of the year, you made certain that activities like "tumbling" were covered. Then, in the gym, you remind yourself to take precautions when engaging in high-risk stunts. To be sure, accidents happen even with careful planning and forethought—but you change the odds.

Example 3 is another instance of lack of forethought. Say you are a male teacher serving as faculty advisor for the high school newspaper. The publication deadline is upon you and extra work time is required. Three of your staff, senior girls, need a boost to meet the deadline. So a three-night work session is planned. You are aware of cases in which charges of immoral conduct were filed against teachers. You are aware, also, of what others, including your principal, might think, even though you are certain that no improper conduct will occur. The problem is easily sidestepped by including male staff members and scheduling the extra work periods immediately after school.

*An educator who understands what the real legal ramifications of a course of action are will view the law to be more of a protection than an infringement on his or her education endeavors.—Ryan L. Thomas*

In Example 4, membership in a private spouse-swapping group makes things a bit more complex. As a "public" school teacher you are well aware that your private life can be brought into public view—and scrutinized. You weigh potential legal consequences of such scrutiny and act with your eyes open.

There is a second important reason for knowing about the law. Becoming familiar with that part of the law that deals with your teaching frees you to focus on your teaching responsibilities rather than your legal liabilities. It is a teacher's *ignorance* of the law more than his or her knowledge of the law that leads to a preoccupation with legal consequences. And that preoccupation, with its accompanying uncertainties, draws the teacher away from his or her primary responsibility, that of being a good teacher.

A teacher may experience unwarranted concern about being sued for educational malpractice. However, by law, before the courts will hear such a case, stringent conditions must be met: (1) there must exist a clear and standard definition of what the student will look like once the teacher has completed her work with him—a definition of successful learning (few such definitions exist); (2) even if the teacher's "product" has been well described, only the teacher's *behavior,* not her product, can be assessed. This is because the student's agency is at work and he may choose not to become a successful "product." Thus, on the one hand, the teacher does not exercise total control over his learning. On the other hand, a teacher may be held liable for not performing her proper duty for the student; that is, not doing some things that ought to be done in the best interest of the student. Clearly, it would be very difficult for a teacher to be sued for educational malpractice—yet more and more teachers worry about it.

Assuming your responsibility, in full view of potential liabilities, you are much like a physician coming upon the scene of a horrible accident. His training and experience call him to render immediate aid. If the victim dies in the process, there is always the possibility that the family may call an attorney, rather than expressing thanks. To be sure, the Hippocratic Oath and threat of lawsuits are both fixed firmly in his mind. But in desperate moments, he thinks about neither—only the life to be saved. Effective teachers, too, are aware of legal consequences, but are undeterred from doing what needs to be done during important teaching moments.

# AN INTRODUCTION TO THE LAW

To facilitate your understanding of concepts in this chapter, we provide a short and simplified description of how our legal system works.

## Sources of the Law

There are four main sources of law in this country: constitutions, statutes, court cases, and administrative rules and regulations. The fundamental source of law is a constitution. We have a United States constitution and, in addition, each state has its own state constitution. A constitution is a written charter, adopted by the people, that establishes the structure and power of the federal or state government and ensures the personal rights of individual citizens, their property rights, and their political rights. For example, the First Amendment of the U.S. Constitution states:

> Congress shall make no law respecting an establishment of religion, or prohibiting the free exercise thereof; or abridging the freedom of speech, or of the press; or the right of the people to peaceably assemble, and to petition the Government for redress of grievances.

Pursuant to the authorities granted by the federal Constitution and state constitutions, Congress and state legislatures pass statutes (laws) designed to regulate the offices of government and citizens. New statutes are passed from time to time and old ones are repealed or changed. Here is an example of a federal statute, part of the Civil Rights Act of 1964, to be discussed later:

> No person in the United States shall, on the ground of race, color, or national origin, be excluded from participation in, be denied the benefits of, or be subjected to discrimination under any program or activity receiving Federal financial assistance.[1]

And here is part of a state statute regulating education:

> Any person having control of a minor between six and eighteen years of age is required to send the minor to a public or regularly established private school during the school year of the district in which the minor resides.[2]

Through a group of statutes, a state legislature creates a public system of education, describing how it will be organized and operated. These statutes, as a group, are called the State Education Code or State School Laws. The state board of education and the state superintendent are responsible for making certain that local school districts comply with these statutes. State and federal courts are often called upon to review statutes to determine whether they are in harmony with or in violation of the state or federal Constitution.

The third source of law is decisions made by courts. Constitutions and statutes affect all citizens. The responsibility of the courts is to apply and interpret these laws when solving problems brought forward by individual citizens. The decision rendered in one case typically becomes a "rule of law" in a later case with similar conditions. This is the doctrine of "precedent." The *Tinker* v. *Des Moines Independent Community School District*[3] (to be discussed later) is an example of a precedent-setting case.

A lower court decision can be reversed by a higher court that has jurisdiction (authority to act) in that particular case. For example, the U.S. Supreme Court can overturn a state supreme court's decision in a case involving the violation in school of a student's civil rights, which are protected by the U.S. Constitution.

A fourth source of law is administrative rules and regulations developed by state departments of education and local school districts, which have authority to formulate those rules. The rules must be consistent with the U.S. Constitution, the state constitution, statutes, and court decisions. Here is an example of an administrative regulation:

> Age seventy (70) has been established as the mandatory age for all District personnel to retire. The termination date shall be at the end of the contract year in which educators have their 70th birthday.[4]

## Structure of the Courts

In the United States there are two court systems, federal and state. These two systems operate concurrently, and usually without conflict. Most states have three or four tiers of courts:

1.   courts of special jurisdiction (juvenile, probate, divorce, and small claims courts)

2.   district or circuit courts, where criminal and civil cases are tried

3.   appellate courts, usually called supreme courts, where the appeals from the trial court cases are heard.

Teacher disputes involving contracts are tried in a district court. Also, a school district would go to this court to obtain an injunction ordering teachers off the picket lines and back into the classrooms.

In the federal system, there are three tiers of courts:

1.   district courts (several within each circuit, totaling 92 in all), where trials are conducted; an appeal may be taken from a district court to a circuit court and, finally, to the Supreme Court

2.   circuit courts of appeal (thirteen covering the territory of the United States), which hear appeals from the district courts

3.   The United States Supreme Court (the final court of appeal on federal disputes).

The federal system of courts handles only two types of cases: suits that involve citizens of different states (for instance, a dispute between a teacher from Oklahoma and one from Florida) and those that deal with federal law and the U.S. Constitution (for example, the claim of a student and his parents that the school district is violating the student's freedom of expression).

## Tort Law

There are two major types of law, criminal and civil. Criminal law protects the rights of society. A person who commits a crime (for example, a teacher who steals one of the computers from the business lab) violates a law enacted by Congress or the state. A person accused of committing a crime is "charged" with the crime by the state or federal prosecutor, and the government prosecutes the case. If the accused is determined to be guilty of the crime, he or she will be punished by fine, imprisonment, or some form of probation, or a combination.

Civil law is designed to protect the rights of individuals and organizations. For example, civil law is concerned with (1) disputes between individuals (for instance, a student claims that her right to free speech is being violated by the principal), (2) disputes between an individual and an organization (for instance, a tenured teacher brings suit against a school district for her dismissal), and (3) disputes between organizations (for instance, a local school district brings suit against the state department of education because it mandates the district's textbooks). Some typical areas of civil law are contracts, real estate, divorce, wills, estates, and torts.

Tort law is a most important area of civil law in our discussion of teachers and the law. A tort occurs when a teacher is accused of causing an injury to one of his or her students. The key factor in a tort case is neglect of duty: the teacher is at fault when a student, in the care of the teacher, is injured as a result of the teacher's negligence. The teacher is then answerable to the injured student in money damages. Applications of tort law that will most interest you as a teacher are administration of corporal punishment (physically striking a student), negligence during supervision of student activities (on the playground or in extracurricular sports), and educational malpractice (being accused of incompetence). A court, in considering tort suits, is concerned primarily with several questions:

1. What duty of care does the teacher have in a particular situation? (Did the teacher take reasonable precaution to ensure the safety of the students?)

2. Was this duty met or was it breached? (Did the teacher take the precautions that should have been taken or was the teacher negligent?)

3. If the duty was breached, was the breach the cause of the claimed injury? (Did the teacher's negligence of duty actually contribute to or cause the injury?)

4. What special immunities or privileges exist that would make the teacher not liable? (Did the teacher have the legal privilege of administering corporal punishment at the time during which the injury occurred?)[5]

# EDUCATORS' GROWING PREOCCUPATION
# WITH THE LAW

## Fear of Lawsuits

Superintendents, principals, and teachers are all pausing these days, eyeing possible "legal ramifications" of their actions. As a result, there is a growing tentativeness among some teachers and administrators, a reluctance—even an unwillingness—to engage in actions that have been routine for many years. Too often, school people back off to safer ground. Extracurricular sports are cut back or eliminated because of the inevitable injuries, which, if serious, can prompt court action by parents seeking, for example, compensation for a nonhealing knee injury. An innovative program is tabled for fear of reverberations among parents in the community. Novels traditionally made available are pulled from library shelves to head off growing concern among parents about "sexually explicit" material. A civil rights suit against your district prompts your school's curriculum committee to bolster its units on minority cultures. Counselors hesitate to exert authority, not only for fear of being sued but because they are no longer certain what is morally right, or whether they are free to impose it. Alert to the growth in acceptance of the creationist philosophy, a teacher softens her unit called "The Evolution of Man" and even retitles it "Man's Cultural Heritage."

The fear of even the possibility of a lawsuit makes some teachers timid. The actual number of lawsuits brought against teachers, though on the increase, is rather small. There might as well be a large number of cases, however, since the effect is the same: fear, hesitancy, overcautiousness—stopping short of doing what might have been done.

## Litigation in the Schools

Some of the fear is justified. Lawsuits filed against school districts and teachers are gaining in frequency. Students, or more often their parents, are suing for teacher negligence resulting in a student's injury, violation of a student's rights of privacy, curtailment of students' freedom of speech, suspension of students from athletics, teacher malpractice, injury resulting from corporal punishment, and lack of protection of students while on school grounds.

Teachers themselves are suing for being fired while tenured, violation of rights to privacy, denial of equal opportunity for employment, cruelty by a principal, denial of employment for failure to take a loyalty oath, and being terminated for incompetence.

Parents, for their own purposes, are suing for being refused access to student records, school encroachment into the privacy of the family, disruption of vacation time as a result of year-round schooling, defamation of character by the principal, the school's conspiring with the divorced mate about the welfare of a child, changing school-district boundaries, and causing transportation hardships.

## Explanations for the Increase in Litigation

Why is the teacher being drawn more deeply into the legal aspects of teaching? We offer several explanations.

"Common law" is law developed through court decisions. "Sovereign immunity" is a common-law principle that protects state employees (including teachers) from lawsuits resulting from the performance of their duties. When a teacher is engaged in the normal performance of her duty and a student receives an injury, the teacher has been "immune" to prosecution. Suppose you are a fifth-grade teacher on playground duty. A first-grader falls off the jungle gym, incurring a spinal injury of serious magnitude. If parents bring suit against you, they will have difficulty winning, since you are "insured" by the immunity clause. However, since 1980, state legislatures have increasingly abrogated this protection. At least twenty-eight states have now removed this immunity, with the rest likely to follow by the turn of the century.

A second force drawing teachers into the legal arena is the parent. Parents have the legal right and responsibility for the upbringing of their children. They therefore have a "legal standing" (that is, their lawsuits are recognized by the courts) to challenge decisions or actions by the public schools, especially those that adversely affect the legal rights of their children (involving, for example, issues of religion, curriculum, health, safety, and racial and sexual equality). Parents are simply less willing to live with what they perceive to be social injustice and inequality of opportunity these days, and they are exercising their legal standing. In earlier times, parents would only lament the lack of bilingual education for their child; now they do something about it. Formerly, they moved to a new district when their persuasion failed. Now, they hire an attorney—a new combat weapon, the forger of lawsuits (or at least the threat of one). Action! Ten years ago, parents would work through the PTA, holding conversations with the principal, persuading, and arguing passionately. Now, a shortcut is an attorney's phone call to the principal. So an intolerance for perceived injustice, coupled with the power of a threatened lawsuit, propels parents into action—a quicker, often more painful, and certainly more expensive attempt to resolve their problem.

A third factor precipitating legal action is the periodic aftershock of the now-quiet students' rights movement, so vocal in the 1960s and 1970s. Newspapers, television, and national periodicals continue to give visibility to lawsuits involving students' rights. Although this movement has tapered off during the 1980s, equal educational opportunity, freedom of expression, and student privacy are causes so fundamental that lawsuits will continue coming to the courts.

Fourth, teachers are more assertive about their professional rights,

*A parent may delegate part of his parental authority, during his life, to the
tutor or schoolmaster of his child; who is then in loco parentis, and has such
a portion of the power of the parent committed to his charge, viz. that is
restraint and correction, as may be necessary to answer the purposes for
which he is employed.—William Blackstone*

particularly in the area of contracts. An ever-rising cost of living forces
teachers to stretch the salary dollar. Teachers are taking tough stands on
contract negotiations and are entering collective bargaining with a more
militant posture. These negotiations involve not only strikes but lawsuits as
well. Conflicts between a teacher's regular teaching duties and an outside
second job sometimes result in legal action. Vacation time, health insurance,
and retirement benefits are further areas for dispute.

Legal issues surrounding the *personal* rights of teachers are emerging
for the first time in history. In some sections of the country, teachers struggle
with issues related to personal safety and protection against verbal abuse.
Some states compel teachers to take and pass competency exams, a threatening experience for many. Some districts require teachers to sign loyalty oaths
and disclose activities in their personal lives. Both of these requirements
stoke the fires of litigation. Still, by comparison with parents and students,
teachers are slow to initiate lawsuits. They tend to be noncombative and to
look for less aggressive ways to resolve difficulties in their teaching lives.

A fifth factor involving schools in litigation is the proliferation of
broken families. When single parents, unable to provide adequate financial
support for their children, turn to the state, the school is brought in to help
make decisions about the child's educational needs. Further, children from
some broken homes are being turned over to schools in hopes of achieving
emotional stability, socialization training, and good work habits—characteristics often difficult to cultivate in rocky marriages. Because the roots of
education originate in the family, the public schools have felt a sense of accountability toward parents. Schools have, at times, followed the doctrine of
*in loco parentis* ("in place of parents"). When parents are ruled by the
courts as unfit to care for their children, the state steps in and takes custody.
The state then turns to the school to ensure adequate education for the child.
In deciding what is best for the family, teachers are often summoned to provide information about the child to facilitate the court's deliberation about
custody.

Finally, there is a growing sense of isolationism in society; people turn
away from each other into their own private worlds. Impersonalization is
cultivated through modern urbanization: living in compacted apartments,
commuting long distances, rushing to meet overlapping schedules, gulping a
deli sandwich, and watching cable television. Personal negotiations and

agreements are giving way to legal arbitration. Nowadays, calling an attorney is an easy way to bypass emotionally draining personal confrontations.

# THE FAMILY AND THE LAW

To prepare for a discussion of the law itself, we have suggested why knowing about the law is important to you as a teacher, introduced you to the basic structure of our legal system, and offered reasons why teachers and administrators are concentrating more on the legal aspects of education. We look now into four areas: the family and the law, the student and the law, the teacher and the law, and the school and the law. Our purpose will be to acquaint you with some of the major legislation, court cases, and policies in these areas, all of which can and probably will affect you in some way during your teaching career. Along the way, we introduce you to issues, many unresolved, and to implications for your teaching. Finally, in explaining rights we will, where possible, suggest responsibilities as well.

In Chapter 1, we learned that early education was conducted in the home, which became the first schoolhouse for neighboring children. As time passed, education grew "public," and responsibility shifted from parents to the state and the local school districts.

Today, in homes where parents have failed in their responsibility to care for their children, the state steps in, attempting to ensure the general welfare of the child. Preventing parental child abuse (to be discussed later in the chapter) is one example of state intervention into the family; compulsory education is another. The Supreme Court case of *Pierce* v. *Society of Sisters* articulates the state's power to require children to attend school:

> No question is raised concerning the power of the state to regulate all schools, to inspect, supervise and examine them, their teachers and pupils; *to require that all children of proper age attend some school,* that teachers shall be of good moral character and patriotic disposition, that certain studies plainly essential to good citizenship must be taught, and that nothing be taught which is manifestly inimical to the public welfare.

Despite this language, the U.S. Supreme Court has been unwilling to allow the state to intrude *too* far into life of the family. Parents' rights with respect to the education of their children have been largely protected. In this same decision the Court went on to say:

> The fundamental theory of liberty upon which all governments in this Union repose excludes any general power of the state to standardize its children by forcing them to accept instruction from public teachers only. The child is not the mere creature of the state; those who nurture him [parents] and direct his destiny have the right, coupled with the high duty, to recognize and prepare him for additional obligations.[6]

Children are especially vulnerable, and the state acts to protect the general welfare of the child—which at times means protection from the child's parents! As one writer has put it:

> Children have a special protected place in the eyes of the law and society. The focus of children's rights extends naturally from the nurturing relationship of the family. These rights are not essentially coextensive with those of adults— but originate from the child's status in the nurturing and learning environments of the home and the school. . . . Children lack the legal capacity for decision making; therefore, this role is generally left to the mature judgement of parents, teachers, and counselors.[7]

Over the years, people have tended to take extreme positions concerning children. At one extreme are the "child savers," those who would make all the decisions for the child. At the other extreme are the "child liberators," who are opposed not only to state control but also to parental control and maintain that the child should direct the course of his or her own life. Toward that end, they argue that children should be guaranteed the full range of adult legal rights, from the right to vote to the right to marry.

However, all the child cases, taken as a group, show that the courts have not significantly altered their assumptions about children as minors, nor have they departed significantly from the belief that children lack the maturity necessary to exercise constitutional rights involving free choice. Nearly all the cases are designed to *protect* children from various forms of abuse. It is precisely because of children's dependency and unique vulnerability that additional forms of protection have been developed. Thus, the argument by some that children are "innately wise and realistic" and are "capable of developing" without "adult suggestion of any kind" has not been accepted by the courts. The abortion case *Bellotti* v. *Baird*[8] contains the Court's most complete statement to date of the reasons why "the constitutional rights of children cannot be equated with those of adults"—the "peculiar vulnerability" of children, their inability to "make critical decisions in an informed, mature manner," and the importance of the parental role, which supervises children's decision making.[9]

Several conclusions can be drawn from cases of children and family rights. First, your students are still considered by the courts to be lacking the capacity to make many of the decisions that affect their general welfare (this is more so with elementary than secondary students). Second, parents have an inherent right to make welfare decisions about their children who are students in your classroom. Third, the courts are saying that students' rights are not the same as parents' rights—students lack legal capacity and therefore have more limited rights than adults.

What are the implications about your responsibilities to students and their parents? The parents are very much in the driver's seat. You are assisting them as they make decisions about the welfare of their children, both at home and at school. Further, there are many decisions you make about students' welfare during the school day, decisions for which you, as the teacher, take responsibility.

# THE STUDENT AND THE LAW

In the school system, the state must maintain a delicate balance between protecting the student and safeguarding the student's rights. This balance is revealed in various state and U.S. Supreme Court rulings. The students' rights movement has prompted legal disputes in a variety of areas related to your teaching. We will look at a sample.

## Students' Speech and Expression

The landmark case, precipitating twenty years of students' rights cases, was 1969's *Tinker* v. *Des Moines Independent Community School District*.[10] A high school principal suspended two students for wearing black armbands as a silent protest against the Vietnam War. The U.S. Supreme Court upheld the right of the students to wear black armbands in a peaceful protest so long as their symbolic expression did not create a disruption in the school. This decision protected the free-speech interests of the students, which are guaranteed by the First Amendment to the U.S. Constitution. Although parental interests were not the focus of the opinion in the case, the trial record showed that the children had been encouraged by their parents to wear the armbands. When the trial court's decision was appealed, the U.S. Supreme Court stated, "It can hardly be argued that either students or teachers shed their constitutional rights to freedom of speech or expression at the school-house gate."[11] Further, "the record does not demonstrate any facts which

© Alan Carey/The Image Works

might reasonably have led school authorities to forecast substantial disruption of or material interference with school activities, and no disturbances or disorders on the school premises in fact occurred."[12] Justice Black of the U.S. Supreme Court cast a dissenting vote in the case. In his argument against the decision he stated:

> I think the record overwhelmingly shows that the armbands did exactly what the elected school officials and principals foresaw they would, that is, took the students' minds off their classwork and diverted them to thoughts about the highly emotional subject of the Vietnam War.
>
> And I repeat that if the time has come when pupils of state-supported schools, kindergartens, grammar schools, or high schools, can defy and flout orders of the school officials to keep their minds on their own schoolwork, it is the beginning of a new revolutionary era of permissiveness in this country fostered by the judiciary.

*Hazelwood School District* v. *Kuhlmeier*[13] dealt with a different kind of student expression, this time written material. This case represents an historically significant decision regarding students' rights of free expression in school newspapers. The Supreme Court gave school administrators broad power to censor student newspapers and other forms of student expression. By a 5-to-3 vote, the justices ruled that a Hazelwood, Missouri, high school principal did not violate students' free-speech rights by ordering two pages deleted from an issue of a student-produced newspaper. "A school need not tolerate student speech that is inconsistent with its basic educational mission even though the government could not censor similar speech outside the school," Justice White wrote for the Court. The controversy arose in the spring of 1983 when Robert Reynolds, principal of Hazelwood East High School, refused to permit publication of two articles in *Spectrum,* a school-sponsored newspaper produced by journalism students. One of the articles dealt with teen-age pregnancy and consisted of personal accounts by three Hazelwood East High students who had become pregnant. The other dealt with the effect of divorce on children, quoting interviews with students from divorced homes. Reynolds objected to the two articles, and the pages on which they appeared were deleted. The students sued, contending that their freedom of speech had been violated. Justice White ruled that educators may exert editorial control in such instances "so long as their actions are reasonably related to legitimate pedagogical concerns." Such concerns, he noted, might extend to work that is "poorly written, inadequately researched, biased or prejudiced, vulgar or profane, or unsuitable for immature audiences." He indicated that *Spectrum* was not a "public forum," saying, "School officials did not evidence . . . any intent to open the pages of *Spectrum* to indiscriminate use by its student reporters and editors, or by the student body generally."

In *Bethel School District* v. *Fraser*,[14] another freedom-of-expression case, the Supreme Court ruled that a high school administrator *may* discipline a student for a vulgar speech in a school assembly, even when the speech causes neither a material disruption nor harm to others.

*A school need not tolerate student speech that is inconsistent with its basic educational mission even though the government could not censor similar speech outside the school.—Justice White,* Hazelwood School District *v.* Kuhlmeier, *1988*

---

## Inappropriate Speech

Surely it is a highly appropriate function of public school education to prohibit the use of vulgar and offensive terms in public discourse. Indeed, the "fundamental values necessary to the maintenance of a democratic political system" disfavor the use of terms of debate highly offensive or highly threatening to others. Nothing in the Constitution prohibits the states from insisting that certain modes of expression are inappropriate and subject to sanctions. The inculcation of these values is truly the "work of the schools." The determination of what manner of speech in the classroom or in school assembly is inappropriate properly rests with the school board.

The process of educating our youth for citizenship in public schools is not confined to books, the curriculum, and the civics class; schools must teach by example the shared values of a civilized social order. Consciously or otherwise, teachers—and indeed the older students—demonstrate the appropriate form of civil discourse and political expression by their conduct and deportment in and out of class. Inescapably, like parents, they are role models. The schools, as instruments of the state, may determine that the essential lessons of civil, mature conduct cannot be conveyed in a school that tolerates lewd, indecent, or offensive speech and conduct such as that indulged in by this confused boy. The pervasive sexual innuendo in Fraser's speech was plainly offensive to both teachers and students—indeed to any mature person. [Matthew Fraser, at a school-sponsored assembly, nominated a fellow student for office, referring to his candidate in terms of an elaborate, graphic, and explicit sexual metaphor. Fraser was suspended for three days and removed from the list of candidates for graduation speaker.]

Opinion delivered by Chief Justice Burger in *Bethel School District* v. *Fraser, 1986.*

---

In these three cases, which are illustrative of the kinds of free-speech cases brought before the courts, we see both protection of the freedom and its curtailment. First, if they did it in a peaceful and orderly way, students could express themselves about a war they (or perhaps their parents) disagreed with. In the second case, students were free to print their stories in the school newspaper as long as the stories would not create disorder or harm to others—and the burden of proof that harm was being caused rested on the principal. Finally, school administrators could take disciplinary action against students using vulgar speech even when the speech was not causing harm to others if the principal felt the speech was in "bad taste."

## Students' Dress and Grooming

Students express their individualism, and often their group membership, through their clothing and hairstyles. Students have a right to dress and groom themselves according to their own taste or in accordance with that of their parents so long as they are not immodest or provocative in ways that would cause material or substantial disruption to school operations. School officials may restrict this right only if there is a legitimate health or safety reason and if less drastic measures are inadequate in protecting the health or safety of others. Furthermore, school officials may not discriminate on the basis of sex in applying the health and safety restrictions.[15]

In *Karr* v. *Schmidt*,[16] the school district's rights and policies regulating student dress and grooming came face to face with students' rights of self-expression. The district had a rule prohibiting boys from wearing their hair hanging over their collars or obstructing their view. Several students were suspended for refusing to cut their long hair. Students brought suit, claiming their constitutional right of expression had been violated. The Supreme Court ruled for the school administrators, indicating that states (and therefore school districts) were to be left free to set policies about such nonessential matters as hair length.

## Students' Physical Protection

In recent years, in both rural and metropolitan areas, the physical safety of students and teachers has become a widespread problem. In several cases, schools have been accused of not providing adequate protection for students in the school and on its grounds.

In the following examples, the issue in the case is whether the student has protection against physical injury while involved with schooling. In *Fazzolari* v. *Portland School District*,[17] a student at Franklin High School in Portland, Oregon, was assaulted and raped on the school grounds shortly after she had been dropped off by her mother at 6:50 A.M. The student sued the school district for damages resulting from her rape. Only fifteen days before the student rape occurred, a newspaper delivery woman was attacked and raped on the school grounds at 4:30 A.M. Although school officials had knowledge of the previous early-morning assault, they failed to warn the student population of the danger. The Oregon Supreme Court held that the student was entitled to collect damages from the school because the school had neglected to give the students in the school reasonable warning after the earlier assault had occurred.

In *Broward County School Board* v. *Ruiz*,[18] a student was severely beaten by three other students as he waited for his father to pick him up after school. The school had an extensive supervision program but had failed to assign anyone to watch the students who regularly waited in a certain area for rides after school. A jury awarded the student $30,000 for his injuries. On appeal, the district court affirmed the trial court's decision, ruling that a school may be held liable for foreseeable injuries to students while at school, even if the harm occurs after school hours.

Personal physical injury occurred in both cases. Although students have a responsibility for their own safety on school grounds, the school lost in the first case because it did not warn students of a known potential danger, and in the second case because it failed to provide adequate protective supervision.

## Students' Privacy

SEARCH AND SEIZURE   Students have long felt that school officials have no right to examine their personal belongings kept at school. The issue of students' privacy has taken on much intensity in recent years, primarily because of increased drug use in the schools. In *New Jersey* v. *T.L.O.*[19] a teacher reported T.L.O., a high school student, to the vice-principal for smoking in the restroom in violation of school rules. After T.L.O. denied she had been smoking, the vice-principal asked to see her purse. Upon searching the purse, the vice-principal discovered cigarette wrapping papers in "clear

© Peter Meuzel/Stock, Boston

view." The presence of wrapping papers gave the vice-principal "reasonable cause" to search the remaining contents of the purse for contraband. He discovered marijuana, a bundle of small bills, a list with persons' names who owed money, and two notes implicating T.L.O. in the selling of drugs. The court ruled that the rights of students are not necessarily "co-extensive with those of adults" and that the vice-principal's initial search was reasonable. Reasonable cause does not require "actual knowledge," the court said, but only requires a "reasonable probability" that the evidence exists. Since the vice-principal had reasonable cause to conduct the search, it did not violate T.L.O.'s Fourteenth Amendment rights under the Constitution; and, since the search was legal, the evidence gathered by the school official was admissible in a court of law.

In *Doe* v. *Renfrow*,[20] police and school administrators, using drug-detecting dogs, walked through all the classrooms on an organized search for drugs. During the process, if a dog went on alert, students were asked to empty their pockets and purses. A body search was conducted on eleven students when dogs continued on alert. One student was strip-searched by female teachers, but no drugs were found. That morning the girl had played with her own dog, who was in heat (which brought the drug-detecting dogs to alert as they approached her and caught the scent). When legal action was brought against the school by the girl, the court ruled for the school administrators, indicating that the search was legal. Since the school administrators acted in good faith, the court said they were immune to liability for violating students' rights of privacy.

In these two search cases, we note that school officials are given considerable latitude in searching a student's personal belongings when they have a reasonable suspicion of contraband. The courts offer this latitude, assuming that principals are not interested in rummaging around in a student's purse or locker unless they are reasonably sure that something is awry. It is the responsibility of students to obey the law and avoid having illegal materials on their person or in their lockers.

RECORDS  In recent years, courts have been faced with an increasing number of cases relating to privacy of student records. School records contain information about a student's academic performance, and they may also provide data in such areas as student aptitude, attitude, ability to get along with others, perceived learning potential, and behavioral strengths and problems. Infrequently, there may be medical and psychological information resulting from professional assessments. These records are regularly used by guidance counselors, teachers, and administrators in making educational decisions about the student.

During recent years the following question has surfaced with considerable regularity: who has the right to examine a student's school records? Elementary students might never ask such a question, but some high school students and many college students are vitally interested in it.

Generally it is parents rather than children who express concerns about the privacy of school records; they want nothing in their children's records that reflects negatively on their child. For example, they may not want their child's new teacher or a school counselor to be privy to past low performance because they fear the child will be labeled "learning disabled"; or a mother is reluctant to have her former husband see the drop in the child's grades since the divorce.

The Family Educational Rights and Privacy Act of 1974 represents a milestone in protecting rights of students and parents. The act governs policies about students' records for any school that receives federal financial assistance. It gives students of 18 or over and custodial parent(s) of younger students the right to examine official school records kept in the student's personal file. Students 18 or over or those with legal custody of younger students can inspect, reproduce, and challenge the accuracy of their educational records and can control who receives information personally identifying the student. Major provisions of the act are as follows:

1.  Parents have the right to inspect and review the educational records of their children. The school should respond to the request within a reasonable time, in no case more than 45 days after the request has been made.

2.  Parents have a right to have records explained and interpreted by school officials.

3.  Schools may not destroy any records if there is an outstanding request to inspect and review them.

4.  Parents who believe that information contained in the education record of their child is inaccurate, misleading, or violates any rights of the child may request that the records be amended.

5.  If the school decides the records should not be amended, the parent shall be advised of the right to a hearing.

6.  Parent consent is required before the school can disclose personal information from education records to other agencies or individuals.

7.  A log containing information regarding requests for records should be maintained in the students' files. This information can be inspected by parents.[21]

Notice that eligibility is a condition of access. An area of recent concern is the rights of separated or divorced parents to their child's records. Sometimes a parent deprived of custody goes to the school seeking access to the child's records in order to locate the child's new address. Does a noncustodial parent have access to his or her child's school records? The Family Educational Rights and Privacy Act permits school authorities to allow a natural parent (regardless of whether or not the parent has custody) access to the school records unless state law or court order limits that right. State statutes and case law governing noncustodial parents' rights to their child's records vary greatly and are often determined on a case-by-case basis.

What are the implications for you, the teacher? Know for certain what information should be placed in a student's file. Whatever information you include must be accurate. In trying to interpret test scores and other objective information, stick to the facts—refrain from going out on a limb. Avoid giving information that stereotypes a student. In preparing written assessments, be alert to who might read them and how they might be misinterpreted.

## Suspension and Expulsion of Students

The courts have ruled that before any student is suspended or expelled from school the student is entitled to due process. The "due process" clause of the Fourteenth Amendment of the U.S. Constitution protects a person from *unjustified* deprivation of his rights. What process is due a student charged with a wrongful act or some other violation that may result in suspension or expulsion from school? The following basic elements have been stressed by the courts:

1.  The party must be given a fair and reasonable notice of the charges.
2.  The party must be afforded a hearing.
3.  The hearing should be set far enough in advance to allow the party to prepare for it.
4.  The party is accorded the right of legal counsel.
5.  The party is permitted to present oral and written evidence at the hearing.
6.  The party and his counsel are allowed to confront and challenge all the evidence against him.
7.  The hearing must be conducted by an impartial tribunal.
8.  The party is entitled to have an official record, a transcript, of the hearing.
9.  The party is allowed to appeal to a higher legal authority, including access to courts to redress legal errors.[22]

The importance of due process is evident in the *Goss* v. *Lopez*[23] case. A group of high school students were suspended from the Columbus Ohio Public School System for ten days. One incident involved disruptive behavior in the school lunchroom in which property damage occurred. The students were suspended without a hearing. The U.S. Supreme Court ruled that under the "due process" clause of the Fourteenth Amendment, students had a legitimate property and liberty interest that entitled them to an education and to due process before being suspended. The court held that the "due process" procedures to which schools must adhere for a suspension of ten days or less are as follows: the student must be (1) informed orally or in writing of charges levied against him or her, (2) given an explanation of the basis upon which these charges are made if they are denied by the student, and (3) be provided an opportunity to present his or her interpretation of the occurrence.

In every case of suspension, teachers and principals must provide, at a minimum, some kind of notice and hearing. This is the constitutional "due process" guarantee in action. A "hearing" in the principal's office, with a fair discussion of grounds for a short suspension, usually meets the legal requirements. However, due process can be set aside when the student's actions constitute an immediate danger to person or property or threaten disruption of school operations. This provision means that the principal can remove the student from the school—immediately—in cases of imminent danger to others. When this happens, an appropriate hearing takes place at a later time.

## Equal Opportunity for Students

The school desegregation movement has been society's attempt to resolve its most serious discrimination practice, the historical separation of black and white students. Black students and their advocates have fought to gain the same educational opportunities enjoyed by other students in society. Besides racial discrimination, students have also been subject to discrimination on the basis of sex, religion, nationality, and school achievement. The legal system, through legislative enactments and court decisions, continues to try to eliminate all types of discrimination.

SCHOOL DESEGREGATION   Historically, racially segregated schools had been the rule in many parts of the United States, even after the Civil War. But in 1954 the United States Supreme Court, in one of the most momentous and far-reaching decisions in its history, struck down state laws that allowed racially segregated schools. In *Brown* v. *Board of Education of Topeka*[24] the Court overturned the "separate but equal" doctrine that had permitted states to operate racially segregated schools so long as the education provided to each race was substantially equal.[25] Segregation of this type is referred to as *de jure segregation* because the policy of the schools intentionally accomplishes racial segregation. The *Brown* case challenged a Kansas law by which school districts maintained segregated schools under the "separate but equal" doctrine. Reverend Oliver Brown of Topeka, Kansas, challenged the legality of the busing of his daughter across town to an all-black school when there was an all-white school in his neighborhood. The trial court found that the curriculum, buildings, teacher qualifications, and salaries in the Topeka schools were equal and that the district had not violated students' constitutional rights in providing segregated schools. The U.S. Supreme Court ruled, however, that even though the schools were "outwardly" equal, they were inherently unequal in the actual education the children received. The quality of education in the black schools was not as high as the quality in the white schools; therefore, students in the black schools were not receiving an equal education as required under the "equal protection" clause of the Fourteenth Amendment to the Constitution. As a result of the *Brown* ruling, schools throughout the United States could no longer be legally segregated by race.

Following the *Brown* decision, parents successfully brought suit against school districts to eliminate another type of racial segregation, called *de facto segregation*. De facto segregation occurs when (1) a school district boundary is established without regard to the racial mix of the students, but the boundary (usually drawn by neighborhoods) includes only, or mostly, students of one race, or (2) the school boundary is drawn in such a way as to provide a proper mix of races, but over time, population patterns change and the established boundaries no longer provide an adequate racial mix of students in a school.

In 1955 the Supreme Court said that school districts should "proceed [with the integration of their schools] with all deliberate speed."[26] But progress in integrating schools after the *Brown* cases was slow because school districts were reluctant to implement policies to accomplish integration. Their reluctance was based on a variety of reasons, but expense, fear, and bigotry kept integration moving at a snail's pace. Finally in 1964 the Supreme Court, in *Griffin* v. *The School Board*,[27] declared that "the time for mere 'deliberate speed' has run out and that schools [can] no longer justify denying children their constitutional rights."

A variety of integration procedures have been implemented since *Brown,* including busing of students, district reorganization, and interdistrict transfers. These attempts at integration have met with both success and failure. For example, in *Goss* v. *Knoxville Board of Education*,[28] black students claimed that the transfer policy of the school board perpetuated a segregated system by permitting a student to transfer freely from a school where he was in a racial minority to a school where he would be in a racial majority, but requiring that transfers to a school where the student would be in a racial minority be for "good cause." Thus, a white student attending a largely black school could freely transfer to a predominantly white school, but a black student attending a largely black school would have to show "good cause" to transfer into a predominantly white school. The U.S. Supreme Court ruled that the transfer policy violated the "equal protection" clause of the Fourteenth Amendment.

Today, in hundreds of school districts across the country, schools are racially integrated. But the future is unclear, especially with competing priorities: should monies be spent on programs for academic reform or on programs that ensure greater equality of educational opportunities for minority students?

MINORITY STUDENTS   Black students no longer qualify as "the minority" in many sections of the country. White, Chicano, Asian, and European students are now the minority in many large city school districts. Indeed, schools in America are emerging from minority/majority groupings to "multiethnic"

© David M. Grossman/Photo Researchers, Inc.

blends. Although classrooms increasingly reflect ethnic diversity, there continue to be claims of discrimination against "minority" students.

In a 1974 case,[29] non–English-speaking Chinese students filed suit against the school district, claiming they were being discriminated against because California laws required that all students be proficient in English, but the schools provided little bilingual education so the students could learn the required English. The Court ruled that the school district was not required to provide any specific type of bilingual education but that by offering no bilingual training the district was unlawfully discriminating against non–English-speaking students.

In *Keyes* v. *School District No. 1*,[30] Hispanic parents living in Denver claimed the school district was discriminating against their children who had limited English proficiency by failing to provide sufficient bilingual instruction. The U.S. Supreme Court ruled that deficiencies in the school district's bilingual program violated the Equal Educational Opportunities Act of 1975.

DISCRIMINATION BY GROUPING   Discrimination against students can be based not only on race and culture but also on academic performance. The practice of grouping students on the basis of their standardized test scores deprives many students of a diversity of educational experiences and peers. Parents have disputed the legality of "lanes" and other methods of homogeneous grouping based on test scores, claiming these tests are unreliable, invalid, and culturally biased. The courts have pointed out the problems of measuring ability through language skills and social perspectives that disadvantaged children lack: "If a student has had little or no opportunity to acquire and develop the requisite verbal and nonverbal skills, he obviously cannot score well on the tests." [31]

Grouping students according to their performance levels is instructionally helpful in a variety of situations. However, when students are discriminated against because of their lack of ability, the resulting feelings of low self-worth are too high a price for the small instructional gains.

SEXUAL DISCRIMINATION   Schools that segregate students on the basis of sex are constitutionally vulnerable. Title IX of the Education Amendments of 1972, Section 901, provides in part: "No person in the United States shall, on the basis of sex, be excluded from participation in, be denied the benefits of, or be subjected to discrimination under any education program or activity receiving Federal financial assistance." [32]

Schools receiving federal funding cannot discriminate between male and female students or teachers. Sexual discrimination is particularly evident in nonacademic activities, especially contact sports. Schools are thus faced with the dilemma of being charged with sex discrimination, on the one hand, and the possibility of tort liability for injury to females participating in contact sports, on the other hand. Schools are struggling with this dilemma on a case-by-case basis, and there are no easy solutions in sight.

HANDICAPPED STUDENTS   In Chapter 6 we discussed discrimination against handicapped students along with the handicapped antidiscrimination legislation, PL 94-142 and its sequel. Here is one example of a court case testing that law. In *Irving Independent School District* v. *Tatro,* [33] a child with spina bifida was not allowed to go to school because she required intermittent catheterization. The school claimed that catheterization was a medical service that did not fall under the normal responsibility of the school, and that it was therefore not obligated to provide the service. The parents contended that it should be part of the regular service of the school in providing free and appropriate education for a handicapped child. The court ruled that the district had to provide the service.

In Chapters 2 and 3, we discussed the importance of knowing your students and developing productive relationships with them. In this section we have discussed legal ramifications of discriminating against students. A common thread runs through these three chapters: students have a right *not* to be discriminated against. What, then, are the implications for you as a classroom teacher? Capitalize on the multiethnic nature of your classroom— and help your students to appreciate it. Search out and, to the extent you can, uproot your own discriminatory tendencies. We have learned in earlier chapters that a change in a teacher's perception about differences among students requires time and effort. But the rewards are worth it, especially in the area of discrimination.

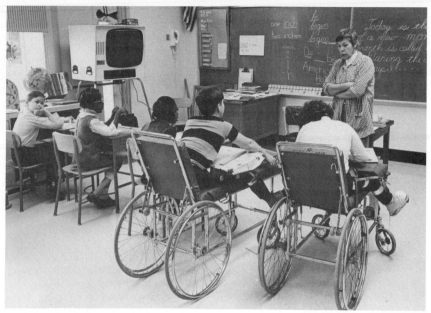

© Marion H. Levy/Photo Researchers, Inc.

# THE TEACHER AND THE LAW

Knowing about families' and students' rights and responsibilities is part of your education as a teacher. What are your own rights and responsibilities under the law? We have been selective in our discussion, choosing legal areas of particular importance to the new teacher. Some of the areas we have omitted will be introduced in other contexts in later chapters.

## Teachers' Rights of Expression

As a teacher, you express yourself continuously in one way or another. The way you dress, talk, and move, what you say (how, when, and to whom you say it), how you act—all are on display as you express yourself.

The courts have stated the general rules regarding teachers' freedom of expression:

1. No teacher can press his or her constitutional right of freedom of expression to the point that it disrupts the operation of the school.

2. A teacher cannot be forced into making expressions against his or her will. For example, a teacher cannot be compelled to cancel class (upon the urging of other teachers) and take his students to a demonstration rally. Nor can a teacher be forced to pledge allegiance to the flag if to do so would violate her personal beliefs.

*Freedom of speech includes the right to criticize and protest school policies in a nondisruptive manner, but it does not include the use of "fighting" words or the abuse of school superiors with profane and vulgar speech.*
—Scoville *v.* Board of Education, *1970*

3.  A teacher cannot be suppressed from speaking out on public (as opposed to private) issues. For example, a teacher can speak out on what he perceives to be the weaknesses of the social studies curriculum in the district. But a teacher is not free to use class time to promote his own political opinions and impose them on his students.

When a teacher criticizes the principal in such a way that her expression becomes disruptive, she loses her constitutional protection of free expression. However, the courts have protected private speech that has *not* been disruptive. In *Givhan* v. *Western Line Consolidated School District*,[34] a junior high teacher allegedly made petty and unreasonable demands to her principal in a manner described by her principal as insulting, hostile, loud, and arrogant. In addition, she criticized the policies and practices of the school district. Her employment contract was not renewed. The school district held that her private speech was not protected by the First Amendment, and she was fired. The U.S. Supreme Court ruled that the teacher's termination violated her First Amendment rights, and she was reinstated with back pay.

## Teachers' Privacy

Historically, educators and parents have expected teachers to live exemplary lives outside as well as inside the classroom. But some teachers have balked at society's demands of them, claiming that school officials have no right to intrude into their private lives. This resistance is evidenced by the increasing number of court cases involving teachers' rights of privacy.

The Supreme Court upholds the states' long-recognized authority to consider moral fitness of public school professionals, stating, "We are, therefore, in full agreement . . . that there is a legitimate and substantial interest in promoting . . . traditional values, be they social, moral or political."[35]

Teachers' sexual conduct has become a much more disputed issue in recent years. School boards who discipline or fire a teacher for sexual misconduct—in school or out of school—must show a connection between a teacher's inappropriate behavior and his or her teaching in the classroom; that is, the misconduct must in some way be detrimental to the teacher's effectiveness in working with students. For example, in one case a teacher was not discharged for engaging in consensual sexual acts with a former student in her home since the school could not prove that the behavior was a continuation of activity started while he was her student. In another case, a Tacoma high school teacher admitted to his vice-principal that he was a homosexual, and he was subsequently dismissed by the school board for that reason. The Washington Supreme Court ruled in favor of the board on the basis that knowledge about the teacher's homosexuality would cause disruption in the school and adversely affect his teaching. Similarly, a teacher was dismissed for openly engaging in sexual acts with men other than her husband at a swinger's club. She contested the dismissal. The court upheld the school board's decision, explaining that her actions rendered her unfit to be a public school teacher.[36]

The sexual revolution, together with new constitutional rights of privacy, has prompted changes in the law regarding unmarried teachers who have children or are pregnant. The growing number of teachers acknowledging homosexual lifestyles poses even more complex legal issues because some teachers openly practice homosexual living and others, not practicing it, defend those who are attacked for their homosexuality.

Whenever a school board intrudes into the private conduct of a teacher, it must be careful to focus only on conduct that affects that person's teaching or the ongoing operation of the school. The difficulty arises in determining what type of private misconduct might, ultimately, affect the teacher's teaching.

## Teachers' Health

The majority of states require a teacher to supply proof of good health from a physician at the time of employment. Historically, courts have upheld decisions by districts to dismiss teachers whose poor health would endanger the health and well-being of their students. But this tradition is becoming more complex as AIDS and other social diseases are carried into classrooms by teachers. Counterbalanced with the fear of spreading disease is the protection of the teacher's civil rights. For example, in November 1987 the 9th U.S. Circuit Court of Appeals ordered the reinstatement of a San Francisco teacher with AIDS who had been dismissed by the school district. The court ruled, for the first time ever, that discrimination against AIDS victims is barred under civil rights laws protecting the handicapped. The court interpreted AIDS to be a handicap: "Although handicapped, he [the teacher] is otherwise qualified to perform his job within the meaning of the Rehabilitation Act of 1973," which prohibits job discrimination against the physically handicapped. The court explained that medical evidence "overwhelmingly indicates that the casual contact incident to the performance of teaching duties in the classroom presents no significant risk or harm to others."[37]

## Loyalty of Teachers

Some teachers are reluctant to sign oaths of loyalty when they are hired by a school district. Generally a loyalty oath is a signed statement by the teacher that he or she is not planning to overthrow the government by force. Some oaths are simply a signed assurance that the teacher will not act in any way that will place the state in clear danger. Some teachers feel that signing an oath of allegiance to the state is professionally demeaning and claim that the school district has no business asking them about their loyalty in the first place. Since the teacher is a public employee, however, the state has a right to refuse a contract to a teacher who is planning to overthrow the government by force. Beyond this, the courts have consistently ruled against oaths that appear to suppress individual teachers' rights. Courts have ruled that teachers cannot be denied employment for refusing to disavow, in writing, any association with a "subversive organization."

The case of *Shelton* v. *Tucker*[38] illustrates the refusal by teachers to divulge certain personal background information. A state statute required teachers to file lists of all organizations to which they had belonged or had contributed funds during the preceding five years. Certain teachers refused to list any organizations and were denied employment. The Court ruled that the statute that required the list was neither clear nor specific enough and that to deny teachers employment through its use was unconstitutional. The state violated the guarantees of free speech and freedom of association under the First Amendment.

## Teachers' Dress and Grooming

Teachers are free to dress according to their own tastes as long as their dress does not disrupt normal school operation and they do not continually violate the school district's dress and grooming policy. Violation of a district dress policy may not be disruptive to normal school operation, but simply be in "poor taste" as far as the school district is concerned. A female teacher who refuses to lengthen her short skirt and a male teacher who will not wear a jacket and tie when required place themselves in a position of liability to dismissal for failure to abide by the district's dress code.

## Teachers' Tenure

Upon reaching a tenured status, a teacher has the right of employment for an indefinite period of time and can be removed only under conditions prescribed by law; for example, mandatory retirement, professional unfitness, or necessary reductions in school staff. The primary reason for offering tenure is to provide job security, thereby attracting and holding good teachers, protecting them from unlawful types of dismissal such as being caught in a power struggle with a difficult principal. Teachers are often required to move through a probationary period of regular and continuous service before, by law, they can become tenured. The following example involves a policy that provoked claims of reverse discrimination.

In *Wygant* v. *Jackson Board of Education*,[39] the U.S. Supreme Court found unconstitutional an agreement by the board of education and a teachers' union that protected minority groups against layoffs. Under the agreement, if teacher layoffs were necessary, those teachers with the most seniority would be retained, but at no time would a greater percentage of minority personnel be laid off than the current percentage of minority personnel employed at the time of the layoff. The effect of this provision was that race rather than seniority determined layoffs: some nonminority teachers with more seniority had to go so that minority teachers with less seniority could stay. The Supreme Court held that, absent a history of discrimination against a particular class of employees, the layoff agreement violated the Fourteenth Amendment rights of senior nonminority employees.

## Corporal Punishment of Students

Corporal punishment, a school practice with a long history, became one of the early targets for litigation. Most state courts have adopted the federal view that corporal punishment does not per se violate rights to bodily security and is not a form of "cruel and unusual" punishment. School authorities agree that public school students are entitled to be free from arbitrary or excessive punishment.

One of the more famous cases involving this issue was *Ingraham* v. *Wright*.[40] The U.S. Supreme Court upheld a school official's right to administer corporal punishment, even without parental approval. Students claimed that paddling as a disciplinary procedure was cruel and unusual punishment and that even if it was constitutional, there still needed to be "due process" before they could be disciplined. The Court ruled that corporal punishment was not cruel and unusual punishment and that no hearing was required before such punishment could be administered. Further, the Court said that students and/or parents could go to court for relief only if corporal punishment went beyond reasonable limits.

This case established that states may authorize corporal punishment without prior notice or hearing and without consent of the student's parents. The rule still applies in most states: teachers and educators have a legal privilege of administering *reasonable* corporal punishment. However, in view of the trend supporting students' rights, corporal punishment by the *in loco parentis* privilege of teachers is being used less and less. Districts are now much more specific about the occasions, the nature, and the manner of administering corporal punishment. Many districts authorize only the principal to administer corporal punishment. In any event, corporal punishment must be reasonable in purpose served, methods employed, and degree of force. (Courts have disapproved use of cattle prods and blows severe enough to break paddles!) The burden of establishing the unjustifiableness or excessiveness of the punishment rests on the student and his or her parents.

## Teachers' Physical Protection

Teachers themselves are afforded the privilege of defense from personal injury by students. When attacked, they may react with reasonable force in defending themselves. (Even the use of a "sneeze gun," which shoots a chemical, causing the attacker to start sneezing uncontrollably, was consid-

*The duty of public school authorities to educate and protect the children placed in their charge gives them the authority to adopt rules of conduct necessary to carry out that duty even though a parent may object to the application of a particular rule to his child.—Justice Goldstein*

ered justified when a teacher was warding off a student attack.) In all cases, the circumstances surrounding the teacher's act of self-defense are taken into account, including the student's age, sex, and physical condition and the means of defense used by the teacher.

## Nonteaching Duties of Teachers

Teachers are forever being asked to take on nonteaching duties such as supervising of study halls and cafeterias, serving as linesmen at football games, and attending teacher workshops. Many of these duties fall within regular teaching hours; others occur after working hours with no extra financial compensation. By and large, teachers have willingly accepted such duties, reasoning, "They are simply part of my overall load and I ought to support my students and principal." Increasingly, however, teachers are pointing to clauses in their contracts, insisting they are not under obligation to perform any duties not expressly described in the contract. As a result, more contracts are now clearly spelling out heretofore "implied duties." The courts have ruled that any duties, including nonteaching assignments, that are reasonable adjuncts to the normal school activities may be required of teachers, provided that they are not professionally demeaning, unreasonably burdensome, or discriminatory.[41]

## Child Abuse

Child abuse problems have exploded within our society during recent years. You will no doubt encounter victims of child abuse. Here is a case example:

> One day, while teaching her class, Mrs. W. noticed some nasty, reddish marks on the neck of one of her pupils. During a free period, she took the student to the school district's child development specialist. When asked about the marks, the child first said that a cat had scratched him. When questioned further, the child stated that his mother had choked him, as she had done on other occasions.
>
> The Division of Youth Services acted on her report of suspected abuse, temporarily placed the child in a foster home, and initiated proceedings against the parents. At a later hearing, Mrs. W.'s suspicions that the mother had physically abused the child were not substantiated by a physician's examination, or the child's own testimony.
>
> The parents of the child then brought action against the teacher, the principal, the child development specialist, and the school district, to recover dam-

ages claimed to have been caused by their reporting the alleged abuse to Youth Services.

The trial court ruled in favor of the teacher and principal. The parents appealed, but the Court of Appeals affirmed that the teacher and principal were immune from liability, because they acted pursuant to an Oregon State statute providing immunity for persons who make such reports in good faith and who have reasonable grounds for making the report.[42]

During recent years, the incidence of reported cases of child abuse has risen dramatically. An estimated one to two million cases of child abuse occur each year in the United States. This trend has been accompanied by a flurry of court cases. In the 1980s state legislatures acted with vigor to protect children from abuse, including sexual abuse. Child abuse is a growing concern among all who work with children. However, a major problem is that teachers are uninformed about what to do when they suspect a child has been abused or neglected, and consequently many suspected cases go unreported. One study found that, although two-thirds of the child abuse victims are of school age, educators reported fewer than one-third.[43]

In response to the growing crisis, Congress passed the Child Abuse Prevention and Treatment Act[44] and established the National Center of Child Abuse and Neglect. The act defines child abuse and neglect, but it provides only funding and registry assistance, not legal sanctions.

The traditional view of child abuse—excessive physical punishment—has been expanded to include a greater range of indicators:

1. nonaccidental injury or pattern of injuries without reasonable explanations, such as burns, bites, or beatings

2. neglect in regard to food, clothing, shelter, or medical care

3. sexual molestation of a child for the gratification of an adult, such as rape, incest, fondling of the genitals, or exhibitionism

4. aggressive or excessive emotional deprivation or abuse, or verbal assault to force the child to meet unreasonable demands.[45]

Since 1964, all states have enacted laws that require the reporting of suspected child abuse. Originally those laws were directed solely at physicians, who were required to report serious physical injuries or nonaccidental injuries. Now, in at least nineteen states, laws require *all* citizens, regardless of their professional status, to report suspected abuse. In all states, any person is legally permitted to make a report.

Following is an example of a state's Child Abuse Reporting Act. The language of the act makes it mandatory for any person, regardless of profession or position, to report *immediately* to a law enforcement agency or the Division of Family Services his or her suspicions or observations of child abuse or neglect. Part of this act is as follows:

Whenever any person including, but not limited to, persons licensed under the Medical Practice Act or the Nurse Practice Act, has reason to believe that a child has been subjected to incest, molestation, sexual exploitation, sexual abuse, physical abuse, or neglect, or who observes a child being subjected to conditions or circumstances which would reasonably result in sexual abuse, physical abuse, or neglect, he shall immediately notify the nearest peace officer, law enforcement agency, or office of the division.[46]

This state's attorney general, issuing an opinion to the state superintendent of instruction, emphasized the role of the teacher (rather than the principal) in reporting abuse. He scolded some districts for their requirement that the teacher go through an intermediary, the principal. He argued that the teacher should report "immediately" to the nearest law enforcement officer. Even if the teacher did go first to the principal, he or she was not relieved of the mandatory obligation to report directly to the nearest authorities.[47]

Are there clues to which you should be alert in keeping a lookout for abused children in your classroom? Here is a list of possibilities:

1.  a fearful or withdrawn manner
2.  evidence of unusual bruising, lacerations, or fractures
3.  frequent "accidental" injuries
4.  looking to strangers randomly for attention
5.  indifference to parents in regard to relief from discomfort
6.  excessive anxiety
7.  truant or runaway behavior
8.  inconsistency between observed injury and its causation as expressed by the parent
9.  denial by child that any problems exist
10. self-deprecating comments by the child
11. destructive or cruel behavior on the part of the child.[48]

Child abusers are not just people in the home and on the street. Upwards of 16 percent of the reported child abuse cases in the United States involve teachers, administrators, and other adults working in the schools. The myths about child molesters are gradually being abandoned in the face of statistical reality. The myth that child molesters are single, antisocial, or sexual misfits is untrue. They tend to be in their midthirties, male or female, married, holding positions of trust in the community and church, are known as excellent teachers, and are good with children.[49]

The educational profession has established policies for removing teachers from the classrooms who are found guilty of child molestation. The protection of children must remain the primary concern of educators, and those who violate the trust of children, parents, and society should be denied the privilege of teaching.

## Teachers' Malpractice and Incompetence

Most malpractice suits are brought against the schools for misclassification of students, for failure to bring students up to an acceptable level of learning, or for failure to warn students of grave threats against their safety. Malpractice suits are filed against schools and school districts more often than against individual teachers. Those that are filed against teachers usually involve teacher negligence during supervisory activities in settings such as playground, lunchroom, or woodshop. "Negligence" involves conduct falling below an established standard of care that results in an injury to another person or persons. The courts require only that the teacher do whatever is reasonable and practical to ensure the safety of the students.

A school may be charged for failing to exercise due care in testing and evaluating a student and then placing the student in a class that subsequently produces intellectual or emotional damage. A school may also be charged for not bringing a student up to a satisfactory level of achievement in basic skill areas such as English and math.

In neither of the following two cases of malpractice suits did the courts find malpractice. Nonetheless, both schools and teachers need to be constantly alert to ensure not only student safety but high-quality education. In *Paulsen* v. *Unified School District No. 368,*[50] a student received lacerations to several of his fingers while using a school table saw. Twenty minutes earlier the instructor had replaced the saw's blade and left the safety guard lying on the floor. The student had received instruction on proper operation of the saw and had passed a safety test prior to using it. In an action for damages against the school, the Kansas Supreme Court ruled that the student had been given proper instruction and supervision. Since the school had met its duty to the student, the court ruled in behalf of the school.

In *Peter W.* v. *San Francisco,*[51] a student claimed the school district was liable for educational malpractice because he could not read or write upon graduating from high school. The school district claimed that his charge did not meet standards of negligence. The court ruled that the student had not shown (1) what duty of care was owed by the district, (2) that willful negligence had occurred, (3) that his inability to read and write was directly due to the school's failure to teach properly, or (4) the extent of his reading and writing injury.

We turn now to teacher incompetence and termination. The most frequent reasons for termination of teachers include consolidations of schools, reductions in staff, and closing out areas of the curriculum. One other reason for discharging a teacher is lack of "fitness." States have created statutes that school districts can use as yardsticks when the need arises to possibly terminate a teacher's contract. Job termination may result from application of these statutes by a school district. If a teacher files suit in the courts for re-

*It is manifestly true that students may or may not choose to learn, and the law in recognition of the student's role in the process, will not hold us accountable for a student's lack of knowledge acquisition. But we can and should be held educationally accountable for our accomplishment of that which we are trained to do.—Ryan L. Thomas*

instatement, these statutes are considered by the courts in rendering a decision. The following are examples of state statutes describing teacher fitness:

*Incompetency:* physical or mental incapacity, lack of knowledge or ability to impart knowledge, failure to adapt to new teaching methods, physical mistreatment of students, violation of school rules, violation of duties to superiors or co-workers, lack of cooperation, persistent negligence, failure to maintain discipline, and personal misconduct in or out of school

*Incapacity:* physical, mental or emotional illness or disability that is permanent and incapacitating

*Insubordination:* taking time off work without official authority, encouraging students to disobey or disrespect school authorities, disrupting school harmony by untoward criticism of school superiors

*Unprofessional conduct:* offensive language in dealing with students, threatening and insulting a fellow teacher in the presence of students, using class time to promote political causes, distributing poems that proclaim the joys of marijuana, beckoning students to throw off family morals and enter a new world of freedom, inspiring disloyalty

*Immorality:* dishonesty, sexual misconduct, or criminal action.[52]

What is the likelihood a teacher will be involved in a court case, say, during a twenty-year career? In your role as a teacher, you will undoubtedly encounter plenty of problems that could lead to legal difficulties, but your chances of ending up in court are rather slim. Should you be pulled into a family squabble or be confronted by a student who is bound and determined to discredit you as a teacher, there are sources of immediate help long before a court hearing. Your fellow teachers, your principal, and your superintendent are ready to help you work through difficult circumstances. To merit their support, your own teaching life should be free from unlawful and unethical practices.

# THE SCHOOL AND THE LAW

Beyond individual families, students, and teachers, the law has something to say about the schools themselves. What are the rights and responsibilities of the school, the school district, and the school system? Our sampling introduces important—and controversial—areas.

## Compulsory Education

Are children under 18 required by law to attend public or private schools? Can parents pull their children out of school when they disagree with the subjects being taught or take issue with the quality of the teaching?

Jonas Yoder and Adin Yutzy and their families withdrew their children from school after the children had completed the eighth grade. By this act, the parents violated Wisconsin's compulsory school attendance law requiring students to stay in school until age 16. The parents were tried, convicted, and fined $5 each. They defended their position on the ground that the compulsory attendance law violated their freedom-of-religion rights under the Constitution. Testimony at the trial showed that the families believed, in accordance with the tenets of Old Amish communities, that their children's attendance at high school, public or private, was contrary to the Amish religion and way of life. They believed that by sending their children to high school they not only would expose themselves to danger of church community censure but would endanger their own salvation and that of their children. The U.S. Supreme Court ruled that the state's compulsory attendance law impinged on the families' religious beliefs, and ruled in favor of the families.[53]

Although that case was decided on religious grounds and cannot be taken as a precedent for whimsically violating compulsory attendance laws, it has awakened in parents a hope for legal alternatives to public education, such as home and private schools.

The Fourteenth Amendment gives parents the fundamental right to direct the upbringing of their children. This amendment prohibits the state from requiring all children to be educated *only* in the public schools. Also, the "free exercise" clause of the First Amendment limits the state from imposing educational requirements that force parents to act against their religious beliefs. But, aside from these two liberties, parents can be prosecuted criminally for violation of state compulsory education laws—and even be deprived of their child's custody in cases of extreme neglect. However, the U.S. Supreme Court, in more recent years, is requiring greater proof of child neglect, which makes enforcement of compulsory attendance laws more difficult.

There is an increasing tendency for parents in some areas of the country to defy attendance laws, arguing that a particular school environment exposes their children to unreasonable risks of physical and emotional harm due to unruly school conditions. Further, the courts are generally sympathetic when parents remove a child from a particular *activity* within the school that, in their minds, goes against the child's religious training. They are less so when the parents want to remove their child altogether.

As a result of parental dissatisfaction, there has been an increase in the number of "home schools" around the country. Thirty-eight states have allowed home instruction; the remaining states have no such legal provision. Reasons cited by proponents of home schools include overburdened classrooms, increased student dropout rates, and exploding technology, which permits the curriculum to be channeled into the home. Home schools are an alternative to both public and private schools. Many school districts, in an effort to free up overburdened classrooms and respond to a more pluralistic society, support the home-school concept. They make available free materials such as textbooks and study guides. They also provide opportunities to consult with regular teachers and to have children participate in district-wide testing programs. Home-school students may take part in special events such as field trips and sports events.

Home-school students often enroll part time in a public school for core subjects, to broaden their curriculum, and to increase their social experiences—without losing the benefits of their home education. Dual enrollment permits them to earn state-recognized credit for graduation, and it allows the school district to collect state money by counting them as regular students. Among states recognizing home education, requirements vary. Here is an example of requirements for receiving a high school diploma:

1. Parents who conduct the teaching must possess a teaching certificate.
2. The child must perform at a passing level on standard achievement tests administered by the district for all students.
3. The home school must be accredited by the State Department of Education.
4. Students must enroll in some of the required classes for graduation in a regular school setting, or take equivalent instruction elsewhere.

Figure 7-1 is an example of an agreement form for parents wishing to educate their child through home schooling.

## Textbooks

Academic freedom is the freedom to teach and the freedom to learn. The issue of academic freedom is most often encountered at the university level; however, even the public schools may become involved in disputes in this area. Educators have wrestled with textbook selection for years. Most states allow local school districts the freedom to select their own texts from state-approved lists. Some states recommend books to the districts; others, offering no recommendations, simply prohibit the use of subversive books. In recent years, students, exercising their First Amendment rights, have challenged school boards' decisions to remove certain books from classroom use. Some teachers, exercising their academic freedom, stubbornly resist using district-mandated texts, and substitute their own selections of supplemental readings.

Blacks have challenged state-approved textbooks for insufficient attention to their culture. Ethnic groups complain of cultural stereotypes portrayed in textbooks. Religious and fundamentalist groups object that some content is subversive or socially immoral. These and other challenges have

Date _____

Board of Education
Alpine School District
50 North Center
American Fork, UT 84003

Dear Board of Education:

   I, the undersigned, hereby request that my
child, _____ who attends _____ School and
would be in the ____ grade, be excused from attendance at school and
be taught at home.

   I am aware of the state requirements listed as follows:

Elementary School Requirements K-6 grades
   Reading, Mathematics, Writing, Science, Speaking, Listening,
   Problem Solving, Social Studies, Introductory Citizenship Prin-
   ciples & Practices, Arts, Movement, Fitness & Health, Computer
   Literacy

                    State Board Minimum Requirements

| Middle School Requirements (7-8) | Units | High School Requirements (9-12) | Units |
|---|---|---|---|
| English | 2.0 | English | 3.0 |
| Math | 2.0 | Math | 2.0 |
| Science | 1.5 | Science | 2.0 |
| Social Studies | 1.5 | Computer Studies | .5 |
| The Arts | 1.0 | Social Studies | 3.0 |
| Computer Literacy* | .5 | Arts | 1.5 |
| Movement/Fitness/Health | 1.5 | Healthy Lifestyle | 2.0 |
| Prevocational Exploration | 1.0 | Vocational Education | 1.0 |
| Local District Option | 1.0 | | |

State Board of Education Time Requirements for School Attendance:
   The State Board of Education requires school to be held 180 days
   each year.
   Time requirements are as follows:
   One-half day for Kindergarten
   Four and one-half hours per day or 22.5 hrs. per week for grade
   one
   Five and one-half hours per day or 27.5 hrs. per week for grades
   two through twelve.

Credit
Only credit given from a state accredited school can be applied toward high school graduation. If the home school has not been accredited by the State Department of Education of the State of Utah,
the credit received from the home school cannot be applied toward
high school graduation in the Alpine School District.

   I would appreciate receiving an attendance exemption certificate
for my child, _____ , so that we will be in compliance
with the law.

                         Sincerely,


                         _____

                         Parent's Signature

                         _____

                         _____

                         Address

*Figure 7-1   Parental agreement form for home schooling*

rendered textbook and curriculum content selection increasingly complex. Add to this the fact that there has been an historical unevenness in court rulings regarding textbooks and other reading materials, and schools are left in a rather confused state. In one classic court case, *Island Trees Board of Education* v. *Pico,*[54] students rebelled against the school's removal of library books. The school board had removed nine books from the high school library, claiming they were "educationally unsuitable." The books were *Slaughterhouse Five, The Naked Ape, Down These Mean Streets, Best Short Stories of Negro Writers, Go Ask Alice, Laughing Boy, Black Boy, A Hero Ain't Nothin' But a Sandwich,* and *Soul on Ice.* Students in the school brought suit against the school board, claiming violation of their right to receive information, as guaranteed by the First Amendment to the Constitution. The Supreme Court upheld the students' claim that their First Amendment rights had been violated. The different opinions authored by justices of the Supreme Court in this case highlighted the difference of opinion that exists in this area. On the one hand, school boards have been granted discretionary powers to control the curriculum; on the other hand, students do have the right to receive information.

## Teaching Religion in the School

The issues surrounding religion and the schools continue to be cloudy and emotionally charged. Many grow out of the interpretation and application of the religion clauses in the First Amendment: "Congress shall make no law respecting establishment of religion, or prohibiting the free exercise thereof." The Constitution neither favors nor abridges the practice of religion, and local school policies regarding religion are unsure and often murky. In the historic case of *Wallace* v. *Jaffree,*[55] the Supreme Court struck down the Alabama "moment of silence" statute, which endorsed silent prayer in public school classrooms. The statute had authorized a daily period of silence in the public schools for meditation and voluntary prayer. Some parents did not want their children to participate in religious exercises, claiming that the practice violated the "establishment" clause of the First Amendment. The Supreme Court ruled the statute to be a violation of that amendment and therefore unconstitutional. The "moment of silence" statutes in other states continue to be challenged,[56] and the entire issue of "prayer" in the classrooms is not likely to be resolved in the foreseeable future.

What about being excused from school for religious purposes? In 1948 the Supreme Court struck down a school program excusing students from regular classes to attend religious activities on school premises. In 1952 the Court allowed students to be dismissed from school to engage in religious activities outside the school premises. Closing schools for religious holidays and excusing teachers to observe special religious days are practices still unresolved in the courts.

Reciting a school-sponsored prayer, even though voluntary and non-denominational, has been considered a religious activity and therefore unconstitutional, as has voluntary reading from the Bible and recitation of the Lord's prayer. However, as part of the curriculum, schools can use the Bible to teach *about* religion as if it were a secular subject in the curriculum. Taken as a group, the rulings of the courts on this issue suggest that any activity (such as meditation or observance of a moment of silence) whose *purpose* is to promote prayer is unconstitutional; any similar activity that is expressly educational and secular is not in violation of the First Amendment. Still, the issues remain difficult.[57]

There is a dilemma of neutrality in teaching religious and scientific viewpoints. Some parents are offended when a subject such as the origin of life is taught from a religious point of view. Other parents are offended when it is taught from an evolutionary point of view. Cases have come before the courts, which have ruled that a particular practice is not unconstitutional even though parents may find it offensive. The courts, in general, have taken the position that "the [First] Amendment does *not* guarantee that nothing about religion will be taught in the schools, nor that nothing offensive to any religion will be taught in the schools."[58] These are the difficulties inherent in this double-protection clause of the First Amendment.

The courts have not been against religion, as we see, for example, in Justice Black's opinion in the famous *Engle* v. *Vitale* case. Justice Black stressed that prohibiting prayer does not signal an attack on religion:

> Doesn't prohibiting school prayer indicate a hostility toward religion? "Nothing," wrote Justice Black, "could be more wrong." The Bill of Rights, explained the Justice, tried to put an end to government control of religion and prayer, but it "was not written to destroy either." The Court concluded that "it is neither sacrilegious nor anti-religious to say that each separate government in this country should stay out of the business of writing or sanctioning official prayers and leave that purely religious function to the people themselves."[59]

## Teaching Sex Education in the School

In the area of sex education, courts have upheld the state legislatures' control of the curriculum, even in delicate, sex-related areas. The courts neither forbid nor authorize sex education courses. Usually, parents with religious objections to such courses (containing sensitive subjects like venereal disease, AIDS, contraception, and abortion) have met with little success in the courts—but some success in arguing before school boards. Many states have statutes that allow parents to remove their children from sex education classes (or other "offensive" classes) if they have religious or moral objections to them. But the recourse of excusing a student from such a class is filled with issues certainly not as yet resolved. Consider this passage of a court opinion on the issue: "If the course is taught within constitutional limits, every student should be required to attend. If the course is necessary to the education of one child, it is equally necessary to the education of all students."[60]

# CONCLUSION

Knowing about the law, not as an attorney but as a teacher, helps you understand your rights and responsibilities within the school setting. Take assurance from this chapter. You have ample rights, and they are protected by statutes and the Constitution. You have the right to express yourself, to make decisions about your students and what they learn, and to enjoy privacy in your professional life. The law, as you have seen, paves the way; it does not constrict you. Nor does it force you to assume your responsibility; rather, it facilitates your taking it.

## Expansions

1. Discuss this statement: "Some teachers spend so much time worrying about their rights, they forget their responsibilities."

2. Explain why teachers are being increasingly drawn into the legal aspects of their teaching.

3. Visit with a department head or a principal. What are some of his or her legal worries?

4. Write a list of what you think your rights are as a teacher.

5. The courts still see children—and to some extent adolescents—as lacking the maturity to exercise their full constitutional rights. They focus on protecting the child (and often the adolescent) from various forms of abuse. Can you see any implications for your role as a teacher?

6. Courts are stressing the importance of the parental role in supervising children's decision making. Can you see any implications for your role as a teacher?

7. Suppose a girl in your third period regularly came to class dressed immodestly. What might you do? Are there any legal implications of some options you list?

8. Suppose, during a parent/teacher conference, a father demanded access to his teenage son's school records. You are not sure whether he has legal custody of the son. What might you do?

9. From a legal standpoint, how free are you to express your own political and religious views to your class?

10. Suppose, in applying for a teaching position, you were asked to sign a loyalty oath (that you are not planning to overthrow the government by force). What would be your reaction?

11. Should teachers be paid extra for taking on nonteaching duties, such as faculty sponsorship of cheerleaders or serving as linesman at the football games? Explain.

12. Discuss your feelings about a school policy that permits a teacher to be fired for incompetence—as judged by the principal and a committee of teachers.

## Notes

1. Title VI, §601, Civil Rights Act of 1964, 42 U.S.C. §2000 (d).

2. Utah Code Ann. §53-24-1 (1987).

3. *Tinker* v. *Des Moines Independent Community School District,* 393 U.S. 503, 89 S.Ct. 733; 21 L.Ed. 2d 731 (1969).

4. Negotiated Agreement between the Board of Education of Alpine School District and Alpine Education Association, 1986–1987 School Year.

5. E. C. Bolmeier, *The School in the Legal Structure* (Cincinnati: W. H. Anderson, 1968); P. D. Travers and R. W. Rebore, *Foundations of Education: Becoming a Teacher* (Englewood Cliffs, N.J.: Prentice-Hall 1987), chap. 16; W. D. Valente, *Law in the Schools,* 2nd ed. (Columbus: Merrill, 1987), chap. 8.

6. *Pierce* v. *Society of Sisters,* 268 U.S. 510, 45 S.Ct. 571, 69 L.Ed. 1070 (1925).

7. J. H. Jolley, "The Legal Rights of Children," *Education and Law Perspectives* 1(3) (1987), p. 4.

8. *Bellotti* v. *Baird,* 439 U.S. 925 (1979).

9. B. Hafen, "Developing Student Expression through Institutional Authority: Public Schools as Mediating Structures," 48 Ohio St. L.J. 1(1987); B. Hafen, review of F. E. Zimring, *The Changing Legal World of Adolescence,* 81 Mich. L. Rev., 1045 (1983).

10. Note *3 supra.*

11. *Id.* at 506, 89 S.Ct. at 736, 21 L.Ed. 2d at 737.

12. *Id.* at 514, 89 S.Ct. at 740, 21 L.Ed. at 742.

13. *Hazelwood School District* v. *Kuhlmeier,* 56 U.S.L.W. 4079 S.Ct. (1988).

14. *Bethel School District* v. *Fraser,* 106 S.Ct. 3159, 54 U.S.L.W. 5054, 92 L.Ed. 549 (1986).

15. Travers and Rebore, *Foundations of Education,* pp. 355–356.

16. *Karr* v. *Schmidt,* 401 U.S. 1201, 91 S.Ct. 592, 27 L.Ed. 2d 797 (1971).

17. *Fazzolari* v. *Portland School District,* 303 Or. 1, 734 P. 2d 1326 (1987).

18. *Broward County School Board* v. *Ruiz,* 493 So. 2d 474 (Fla. 4th Dist. Ct. App. 1986).

19. *New Jersey* v. *T.L.O.,* 469 U.S. 325, 105 S.Ct. 733, 83 L.Ed. 720 (1985).

20. *Doe* v. *Renfro,* 475 F.Supp. 1012 (N.D.Ind. 1979), *reh'g. denied,* 631 F.2d 91 (7th Cir. 1980).

21. National Association for Retarded Citizens, Research and Demonstration Institute, *The Right to Education: Where Are We and How Did We Get Here?,* Book 1 (Author, 1977), pp. 18–19.

22. *S.* v. *Board of Education,* 20 Cal. App. 3d 83, 97 Cal. Rptr. 422, 425 (Cal. App. 1st Dist 1971). *Appeal denied,* 405 U.S. 1005, 92 S.Ct. 1297, 31 L.Ed. 2d 472 (1972).

23. *Goss* v. *Lopez,* 419 U.S. 565, 573, 95 S.Ct. 729, 42 L.Ed. 2d 725 (1975).

24. *Brown* v. *Board of Education of Topeka,* 347 US. 483, 74 S.Ct. 686, 98 L.Ed. 873 (1954).

25. *Plessy* v. *Ferguson,* 163 U.S. 537 (1896).

26. *Brown* v. *Board of Education of Topeka,* 349 U.S. 294, 301, 75 S.Ct. 753, 757 (1955).

27. *Griffin* v. *The School Board,* 377 U.W. 218, 234, 84 S.Ct. 1226, 12 L.Ed. 2d 256 (1964).

28. *Goss* v. *Knoxville Board of Education,* 373 U.S. 683, 83 S.Ct. 1405, 10 L.Ed. 2d 632 (1963).

29. *Lau* v. *Nichols,* 414 U.S. 563, 94 S.Ct. 786, 39 L.Ed. 2d (1974).

30. *Keyes* v. *School District No. 1,* 670 F. Supp. 1513 (1987).

31. *Smuck* v. *Hobson,* 408 F. 2d 175 D.C. Cir. (1969).

32. 20 U.S.C. §1681—Education Amendments of 1972, Title IX.

33. *Irving Independent School District* v. *Tatro,* 468 U.S. 883, 104 S.Ct. 3371, 82 L.Ed. 2d 664 (1984).

34. *Givhan* v. *Western Line Consolidated School District,* 439 U.S. 410, 99 S.Ct. 693, 58 L.Ed. 2d 619 (1979).

35. *Island Trees Board of Education* v. *Pico,* 457 U.S. 853, 102 S.Ct. 2799, 79 L.Ed. 2d 435 (1982).

36. *Pettit* v. *State Board of Education,* 10 Cal. 3d 29, 513 P. 2d 889, 109 Cal. Rptr. 665, (1973).

37. Associated Press release, November 1987.

38. *Shelton* v. *Tucker,* 364 U.E. 479, 81 S.Ct. 247 (1960).

39. *Wygant* v. *Jackson Board of Education,* 476 U.S. 267, 106 S.Ct. 1842 (1986).

40. *Ingraham* v. *Wright,* 430 U.E. 651, 97 S.Ct. 1401, 51 L.Ed. 2d 711 (1977).

41. *District 300 Education Association* v. *Bd. of Education,* 31 Ill. App. 3d 550, 334 N.E. 2d 165, 176 (Ill. App.Ct. 2nd Dist., 1975).

42. *McDonald* v. *Children's Services Division,* 71 Or. App. 751, 694 P. 2d 569, 22 Ed. Law Rep. 1001 (Or. App., Jan 23, 1985) (No. 63-3-324, CA A30126).

43. B. Beezer, "Reporting Child Abuse and Neglect: Your Responsibility and Your Protection," *Phi Delta Kappan* 66 (February 1985), p. 435.

44. Public Law 93-247.

45. National Committee for Prevention of Child Abuse, *Questions and Answers on Child Abuse* (Chicago: Author, 1977), p. 1.

46. Utah Code Ann. §78-36-3 (1985).

47. Unpublished letter to State Superintendent of Public Instruction from Utah Attorney General David L. Wilkinson, June 18, 1986.

48.  Parents Anonymous, Inc., *Child Abuse Is Scary* (Redondo Beach, Calif.: Author, 1977), p. 4.

49.  *McDonald* v. *Children's Services Division,* 71 Or.App. 751, 755, 694 P. 2d 569, 571–72 (Or.Ct. App. 1985); *Summary Reports of Cases Heard by the Utah Professional Practices Advisory Commission 1974–86* and *Summary Reports of Cases of Sexual Abuse of Children 1974–86,* Gloria Thomas, Executive Secretary, Utah Professional Advisory Commission (1987).

50.  *Paulsen* v. *Unified School District No. 368,* 239 Kan. 180, 717 P. 2d 1051 (1986).

51.  *Peter W.* v. *San Francisco,* 60 Cal. App. 3d 814, 131 Cal. Rptr. 854 (Cal. Ct. App. 1st Dist. 1976).

52.  Valente, *Law,* pp. 210–213.

53.  *Wisconsin* v. *Yoder,* 406, U.S. 205 (1972).

54.  *Island Trees Board of Education* v. *Pico,* 457 US. 853, 102 S.Ct. 2799, 73 L.Ed. 2d 435 (1982).

55.  *Wallace* v. *Jaffree,* 472 U. S. 38, 105 S.Ct. 2479, 86 L.Ed. 2d 29 (1985).

56.  *Karcher* v. *May,* argued Oct. 6, 1987, U.S. S.Ct. case no. 85-1551.

57.  Valente, 124–129.

58.  *Williams* v. *Board of Education,* 388 F. Supp. 93 (S.D. W. Va. 1975), *aff'd,* 530 F. 2d 972 (4th Cir. 1975).

59.  *Engle* v. *Vitale,* 370 U.S. 421, 82 S.Ct. 1261 (1962).

60.  *Vaughn* v. *Reed,* 313 F.Supp. 431, 433–34 (W.D. W.Va. 1970).

# SECTION THREE

# THE GROWING KNOWLEDGE ABOUT TEACHING

# CHAPTER 8

# EFFECTIVE SCHOOLS

*A good school does not emerge like a prepackaged frozen dinner stuck for 15 seconds in a radar range; it develops from the slow simmering of carefully blended ingredients.*
—*Theodore Sizer*

**MAIN IDEAS**

- Contrary to early reports, later research shows that schools do make a difference in student achievement—a difference over and above that contributed by students' backgrounds.

- Two major forces have helped create the effective schools movement: research on schools and school reform reports.

- An effective school produces higher achievement, deeper knowledge of subject matter, less truancy, better jobs upon graduation, and increased interpersonal skills.

- Effective schools are characterized by strong leaders; a climate fostering support and a strong sense of community; teachers with a mission and with high academic expectations; and a tightly integrated, academically-oriented curriculum.

- Achieving success in your classroom is difficult within the context of an ineffective school; therefore, assume responsibility to help create an effective school environment.

- Though your principal gets the ball rolling, you and your colleagues are key players in creating an effective school.

# INTRODUCTION

Right off the bat! What if, for your first teaching position, you were hired to teach in your dream school? From your vantage point, what would that perfect school be like?

Suppose you were an elementary teacher. Would you walk into a spacious, cupboard-filled, multiwindowed room? Would there be cubbyholes brimming with construction paper, scissors, pencils, crayons? Would there be textbooks for every child and a refreshing supply of playground equipment? Would there be fifteen eager, well-behaved students sitting before you each day, ready to recite yesterday's homework assignment accurately? Would they all enjoy reading, math, writing, and learning from the new computer programs? Would your teaching team be composed of three likable, energetic teachers united in purpose and agreeing on methods? Would your newly adapted science and social studies units be breathtakingly interesting, filled with enabling visual aids and exciting expansions? And would your principal be instruction minded, eminently supportive, your champion with parents?

If you were a high school English teacher, would you walk into your own private office, adjacent to but isolated from your classroom? Would the school enjoy a warm, supportive climate, with high expectations for learning? Would your students come from predominantly high socioeconomic homes where parents are academically nurturing? Would you have a healthy budget for purchasing supplemental readings to place in the hands of your bright, uncommonly responsible learners? Could you purchase tape recordings of the biographies of great writers and poets and the music of eminent composers, and could you obtain tickets for museum visits? Would your modern building, staffed by well-trained and experienced teachers, boast the latest technology and learning systems? Would the district furnish ample funds to support your ambitious educational ventures—as well as a complete sports program? Would parents be standing by, responsive to your request to form a committee for reviewing new novels? Would they agree to offer book reports and sponsor a community literature fair?

Seasoned and new teachers alike dream of life in a truly effective school, one where significant learning takes place among *all* students in *all* areas of the curriculum. This chapter is about "effective" schools, how they become so, and what characteristics they possess. It provides insights that will help you answer important questions, such as how much difference schools make in the lives of students.

These are the words of one teacher who became serious about creating an atmosphere that fostered effectiveness:

In this school the professional staff help each other. We have similar challenges and needs and different talents and knowledge. When I was having problems with cliquishness among the girls, I brought it up at lunch and got some excellent ideas from the other teachers. I wasn't afraid to bring it up because I know people here are on my side. If someone thinks they hear a strong noise coming from my room, they'll stop to check it out. It isn't everyone for themselves and just mind your own business.

I think these people are darn good at what they do. I know I can learn from them, and believe I have things to offer in return. Sometimes we evaluate and develop curriculum and plan special projects together—like Esther, Lorrie, and Allen doing the one-week SCIS workshop for all of us this summer. Teaching each other sometimes requires more time to plan than "expert-led" workshops, but it allows us to work together on a significant project. Similarly, our study groups—organized around topics such as cooperative learning, thinking skills, and involving senior citizens—allow us to exchange ideas. In this school we resist the notion that teaching is our "second most private activity."[1]

Here, Sara Ingrassia reports on her acceptance of a challenge to become part of a school effectiveness program:

What if you're an elementary teacher, and a second-year principal challenges you to join the staff of a school smirkingly referred to as the armpit of the district? You could smile, say "No, thank you," and opt to stay in your pleasant position as teacher of gifted students. Or you could get caught up in his energy, his enthusiasm, his plans—and accept the challenge. So, challenge it was: become involved in improving the effectiveness of an inner-city school that suffered from sagging plaster and sagging spirit. Kishwaukee, in Rockford, Illinois, serves about 500 K–6 students, mostly poor, many transient, and approximately 50 percent minority (Spanish-speaking, black, Laotian, Native American).[2]

Making the choice between personal comfort and the unsettledness that accompanies change caused a struggle for this teacher:

Garrett Franklin, a sparkling new teacher, was offered a position at a large suburban high school in a wealthy section of Seattle. After several months of working with students and the staff, his once-glowing impression began to tarnish. The high school was amply funded, but student test scores at all three grade levels were disappointingly below national norms in science and math. Too few of the school's seniors were being accepted to colleges and universities. Too many were giving up and dropping out before graduation. Teacher morale, appearing strong on the surface, was discouragingly low. Undercurrents of backbiting and bickering ran among the faculty and spilled over into the classrooms.

Mr. Santiago, the principal, nearing retirement, had grown apathetic about the school's downward spiral. A school climate of indifference affected both teachers and students. The school lacked a unifying cause—a banner to march under. Football and basketball seasons were dismal. Few students attended the games and fewer cared if the school won. Frustrated and apprehensive, parents pulled out their high-achieving children, enrolling them in private schools. As a result, the school's composition began changing to a low-achieving student body. Increasingly dissatisfied with school conditions and the lack of able students, teachers began transferring to other schools. In desperation, the superintendent took aggressive action. Mr. Santiago was replaced by Ms. Molina, a woman whose intensely energetic leadership infused new life into the school—and she promised to turn the tide.

Garrett was torn. Should he transfer to a comfortably successful school, or roll up his sleeves for what would surely be a convulsive improvement effort—one that might not succeed?

In a school where teachers and the local PTA decided to create a solution to disciplinary problems, real change resulted:

Mr. Tobler, the principal, explained, "Things went pretty well at the school for its first year. But we had to work out some bugs. Our main problem was discipline. I had students in my office all year long—had to suspend thirteen during the year. But I think we're down the road now. I haven't suspended anyone this year."

Everyone had been frustrated with the discipline problem. Too many kids were sitting in the principal's office. PTA and parents to the rescue! Based on a simple needs assessment conducted by the PTA president, a school-wide disciplinary program was conceived and initiated. It featured Super Citizen Awards, monthly Good Citizen Assemblies, and Best Citizen pictures plastered on the wall in the main entrance. "Oops" and "Wow" slips were freely passed out to remind students about proper student behavior. Beaming children deposited their "Wow" slips in the Wow Box, winning the recognition of the principal and secretary. The most important thing about this change in emphasis was that everyone now began to value good citizenship.

# DO SCHOOLS MAKE A DIFFERENCE?

## Early Studies

Until the mid-1960s, confidence in the ability of schools to educate children was high. As we have observed in Chapters 5 and 6, the government believed in the power of schools to bring about learning in children and teenagers. The Elementary and Secondary Education Act of 1965, and its near-universal support by educators and society, attested to this belief in the efficacy of America's schools.

But from the mid-1960s into the 1970s, confidence eroded, mainly on account of the results of several large-scale studies. Most influential was the now-famous Coleman Report,[3] a popular title for the study *Equality of Educational Opportunity,* published in 1966 by sociologist James S. Coleman, of Johns Hopkins University, Ernest Q. Campbell, of Vanderbilt University, and others. Many school districts during that period still allowed (even supported) segregated schools. The government suspected that black

© Elizabeth Crews/Stock, Boston

minority students and poor students were attending schools that lacked the quality and resources to raise student achievement. The Department of Justice wanted to document this widespread discrimination. It sought information "concerning the lack of availability of equal educational opportunities for individuals by reason of race, color, religion, or national origin in public educational institutions at all levels."

The Coleman study identified the distribution of educational resources within the United States by race, socioeconomic status (the social and economic level of the family), and ethnic background. Data were gathered on more than one-half million students in grades one, three, six, nine, and twelve in 3000 schools.

The way the study was designed revealed an underlying belief by legislators and the public at that time: if you want to improve student achievement (the "outcome" of the educational process), pour more resources into the school (the "input" of the educational process). It seems that people had a mental model of education as an "assembly line." In effect, this model said, "What takes place during the *process* of education is not most important; it's what you pour in at the outset that counts." It seemed reasonable to allocate more money for newer buildings, better equipment, and more highly trained teachers—all those things ought to produce higher student achievement. "Indeed," the reasoning went, "we can equalize educational opportunities for minority children and poor children—and increase their achievement—by putting more resources into the school!"

*The "good old days" are long gone when an educator's best judgment constituted sufficient proof of learning outcomes.—L. W. Lezotte and B. A. Bancroft*

The erroneousness of these assumptions was exposed by the major findings of the Coleman study:

1.  Dramatic differences in achievement were found in average classroom scores within the same school, in average school scores in the same district, and in average district scores (that is, the average verbal score would be high in one classroom and low in another classroom across the hall; high for one school and low for a neighboring school; high in one district and low in another). This has been a consistent finding in virtually all the research on effective schools. The major question, of course, is, "What factors are causing these differences?"

2.  School resources (e.g., physical facilities, the operating budget of the school, years of teaching experience of the teachers) showed almost no relationship to student achievement as measured by verbal ability on standardized tests (that is, sometimes the average score for students in brand-new buildings with plenty of resources was high—and sometimes it was low; sometimes the school average for students in old, run-down facilities was high—and sometimes it was low).

3.  Family background and socioeconomic status correlated highly with student achievement, much more so than did school resources (that is, students from low socioeconomic homes tended to have low achievement scores; students from high socioeconomic homes showed high achievement).

4.  The relationship between socioeconomic status and achievement did not diminish over the school years but remained strong (that is, in high school, students from low socioeconomic homes still tended to show low achievement, and students from high socioeconomic homes showed high achievement).

From these findings, most people concluded that (1) schools are not very effective, (2) teachers have little impact on student learning, and (3) a student's family background primarily determines how much he or she will achieve in school.

In another large study conducted during that period, the investigators found that only about 2 percent of the differences ("variance") among achievement scores could be attributed to schooling, whereas almost 50 percent were attributable to family background. For example, 2 percent of the differences among Jamie's score of 92, Antonio's score of 73, and Dylan's score of 51 is due to schooling—while a whopping 50 percent is due to family background. Thus, these researchers echoed the Coleman Report as they concluded pessimistically, "Our research suggests . . . that the characteristics of a school's output depend largely on a single input, namely, the characteristics of the entering children. Everything else—the school budget, its policies, the characteristics of the teachers—is either secondary or completely irrelevant."[4]

To add to this dismal state of affairs, the Rand Corporation, reporting to the President's Commission on School Finance, reviewed these and other studies and concluded that nothing in schools unambiguously made a difference in student learning.[5]

## Later Studies

Predictably, these early studies evoked a rash of controversy:

"It can't possibly be the case that teachers make no difference—utter nonsense!"

"If the research says that schools have no effect on student learning, why don't we just junk our teacher training programs!"

"Everyone knows the home is important—but that doesn't mean schools don't make a contribution. Suppose a school teaches Sanskrit and there is no other place kids can learn it. Sure, kids will differ in how well they learn it—due to their heredity and family background. But if the school didn't teach Sanskrit in the first place, the kids would never learn it. How can you say that schools don't make a difference?"

CRITICISMS OF THE COLEMAN REPORT   The Coleman Report was criticized on a number of fronts. Researchers, for example, attacked the methods and conclusions. Discussion of most of their criticisms is beyond the scope of this book, but we offer several in simplified form.

First, Coleman used a single score to represent the student performance for an entire school—an average. This one score did not provide a representative picture of how different students within the school performed. For example, some of the students in a low-achieving school had to be achieving very well.

Second, it was not clear why some "resources" were included and others omitted. The quality of a school building may not correlate positively with student achievement, but the number of worksheets per school might. Thus, the type of resource determined whether or not it would be correlated with achievement.

Third, a positive correlation between family background and student achievement does not necessarily mean that family background *causes* high or low student achievement. (Just because there is a correlation between number of ice cream cones sold and number of drownings at the beach does not mean that ice cream causes drownings. Rather, they both follow from hot weather, an unnamed third factor.)

The next criticism of the Coleman Report is most important to our discussion on effective schools. This study (as well as others of the time) reflected an "input/output" way of thinking about schools and student achievement. By focusing on the input, the researchers ignored (or at least downplayed) the contribution of *what goes on during the process of schooling*. Pouring in resources at the front and then running around to see what comes out at the back is a way of ignoring what happens in between—the effect of the teacher and the schooling process itself!

STUDIES OF THE PROCESS   Realizing this, educators and researchers began turning their attention to the process of schooling (that activity between the input and output). During the 1970s and early 1980s, there was a flurry of "process–product" studies. Rather than asking, "Are school resources related to school achievement?" these studies asked a different question: "What takes place during the process of schooling that affects student achievement?" More specifically, "What teacher behaviors are associated with various types of student outcomes?" For example, if a teacher waits after asking a question before accepting a reply, is this practice related to the quality of student answers?

In these later studies, researchers began to broaden out. They soon recognized that the behavior of teachers was only one of many influences at work in the process of schooling. The school's climate, values, norms, and social groups are all important factors that affect student achievement. Researchers expanded their range in another direction as well. Thitherto, studies had focused on one narrow student outcome: a verbal score on a standardized test. However, the outcomes of education are surely more extensive than this! So researchers started looking at achievement in specific subjects like English, math, and science. They also examined the classroom behavior of students: attention, interest, engaged time, and disruptiveness. They studied students' attitudes toward learning, self-motivation, effort, leadership, and initiative. They explored character formation, absenteeism, continuation of education, and employment. And they investigated interpersonal skills, cooperativeness, creativity, curiosity, and satisfaction with learning. All these are important outcomes of an effective school.

During the late 1970s, continuing into the 1980s, another design for studying schools was emerging. Researchers selected "effective" and "ineffective" schools and compared them, asking, "What differences exist between effective and ineffective schools?" and "Which of these differences are responsible for high student achievement?" But in conducting these studies, the researchers found very few "effective" schools. For example, in one large study involving Michigan and New York school districts, only 2 to 9 percent of the schools in the sample could be labeled "effective."[6]

## Example of an Effective-School Study

In a now-classic 1979 study, Brookover and his group observed sixty-eight Michigan schools. In sixty-one of the schools, student populations were more than 50 percent white; in the remaining seven, student populations were more than 50 percent black. In effect, Brookover sorted the schools into major groups: high achieving and low achieving ("effective" and "ineffective"). Within each of these two groups there were black and white schools. He looked to see if certain factors were related to student achievement, including socioeconomic status of the students, percentage of white students in the school, degree of parental involvement in school activities, whether students were grouped according to ability, and teacher satisfaction in the school.

The results showed that the following were related to student achievement:

1.   Teachers in the high-achieving schools spent more time on instruction than did teachers in the low-achieving schools. They reviewed, presented new concepts, then moved on to other material. Students were given only small blocks of time to do independent seatwork assignments. (In low-achieving schools, on the other hand, students had a great deal of time to study, read, or play while the teacher attended to duties such as grading papers.)

2.   Teachers in the high-achieving schools "wrote off" fewer children as being destined to fail. They expected most of the children to master the curriculum. (In the low-achieving schools, on the other hand, large numbers of students were written off by the teachers. Many of these students were required to attend remedial classes, which were seen as "dumping grounds.")

3.   Teachers in the high-achieving schools expected *all* their students to work at grade level. (Teachers in low-achieving schools had much lower expectations for their students' success.)

4.   Teachers in the high-achieving schools gave more appropriate rewards; that is, they gave students rewards that were likely to increase their learning. (Teachers in low-achieving schools gave rewards that were often unrelated to student learning.)

5.   Teachers in the high-achieving schools did not group their students according to ability. (Teachers in low-achieving schools did group according to ability.)

6.   In the high-achieving schools, principals played an active role in assisting teachers with their teaching. (In the low-achieving schools, the principal was more of an administrator and less involved with instruction.)

7.   Teachers and principals in high-achieving schools were more highly committed to effective instruction than were those in low-achieving schools.[7]

This exemplary study, along with other studies conducted during the 1970s and 1980s, provides evidence that school effects are indeed real. Both teachers and schools *do* make a difference in student achievement—a difference over and above that contributed by the student's background. But *how much* difference they make and precisely what *causes* the differences are largely unknown at this point.

# WHAT IS AN "EFFECTIVE" SCHOOL?
## Definition

Think back a moment to the idea of a dream school. You can see by now that the qualities of a dream school are not necessarily those of an effective school. Shiny new buildings are more important to the teacher's morale than

© Ed Carlin/The Picture Cube

to the student's achievement. Having ample textbooks and supplies, though certainly helpful, is not as crucial to student achievement as one might think. Often, when picturing a dream school, we focus on the material aspects of the school more than on the school's ability to produce learning in students. Effective schools, on the other hand, focus foremost on the student.

"Effective schools" have been defined as those that produce in students such outcomes as higher achievement, deeper knowledge of subject matter, less truancy, better jobs upon graduation, and increased interpersonal skills. No single set of qualities characterizes an effective school. Still, almost everyone agrees that in addition to whatever else it does, an effective school brings about achievement in most of the students in a wide range of subjects.

The effective schools movement grew out of concern about possible educational discrimination against minority and poor students. Run-down facilities, lack of funds, and meager teachers' salaries *appeared* to preclude adequate education for these children. Thus, it is understandable that definitions of "effective schools" tend to focus on poor and minority learners. For example, the effective school "need not bring all students to identical levels of mastery, but it must bring an equal percentage of its highest and lowest social class to a minimum mastery."[8] To see what this definition means, suppose a school were divided into three classes of students, those from economically poor homes, those from average-income homes, and those from affluent homes. According to the definition, poor students in an effective school would show *as much* growth as affluent students. The poor students, as a group, need not be at the *same* achievement level as the affluent group at year's end, but all groups should show equivalent amounts of growth. Thus, the "lines of growth" remain parallel.

This definition of effective schools holds true for both elementary and secondary schools. The National Council for Effective Schools defines an

*Walk into a successful school, and you'll find a place that has a vision of what an educated child should be like.*—William J. Bennett

effective high school as one that has (1) high and sustained overall achievement when compared with state and national performance, and (2) no significant difference in percentage of growth in achievement of students from different socioeconomic or ethnic groups within or across schools, in reading, language arts, and mathematics.

## Characteristics of Effective Schools

The following list of characteristics represents an amalgamation of those found in schools judged to be effective during the 1970s and 1980s. In reading through this list, you might want to keep in mind that a school can be "effective" without exhibiting *all* these characteristics.

### LEADERSHIP

1. The school district supports a given school not by mandating change but by helping as the school assumes its own leadership.

2. The leaders and teachers in the school enjoy considerable autonomy in determining how they will improve student achievement. They have a strong sense of ownership of their effective-school program.

3. Administrators do not burden teachers with a lot of administrative chores; rather, they keep them free to attend to instructional responsibilities.

4. School leaders are strong, and they initiate and keep the improvement program moving within the school.

5. The principal spends considerable time in classrooms. He or she continually tries to identify and diagnose instructional problems. The principal is never satisfied with merely diagnosing, but provides alternative solutions to the teachers.

### SCHOOL CLIMATE

1. The school's climate is safe, orderly without being rigid, quiet, nonoppressive, and generally conducive to the instructional business at hand.

2. There is a strong sense of community and academic mission among the teachers and leaders. There is a "moral order" in the school that entails respect for authority, genuine and pervasive caring about individuals, respect for their feelings and attitudes, mutual trust, and consistent reinforcement of acceptable behavior. This not only increases achievement but improves student behavior and reduces delinquency.

3. Students and teachers have a strong identification with the school's goals and overall direction.

4. The informal "ways of doing things" are consistent with the formal academic goals of the school.

5. High expectations are conveyed to all students. No students, including poor and minority students, are permitted to fall below minimal levels of achievement. These minimal levels are rigorous enough so that, when attained, the students' skills will be adequate for later work. There is a school-wide academic "press" for high student achievement.

6. Teachers and students continually receive school-wide recognition for personal and academic excellence.

## TEACHERS

1. Teachers in the school tend to remain together as a cohesive group. There is little teacher turnover.

2. A high level of professional collegiality exists among teachers. They work cooperatively rather than in isolation. There is an expectation that both new and experienced teachers will continue to improve. Teachers focus more on their own impact in the classroom than on background factors of students.

3. Teachers provide good role models of punctuality, behavior, dress, and care of facilities.

4. Teachers take responsibility for *all* students everywhere in the building and on the school grounds.

5. Teacher-development programs are school-wide, involving all teachers, not just selected individuals.

## CURRICULUM

1. Unlike less effective schools, which are "loosely coupled," effective schools are "tightly coupled"; that is, a close relationship exists among goals, curriculum, and measures of student achievement throughout the school.

2. All critical subject matter is covered at each grade level, and the subject matter from one grade dovetails with that of the next grade.

3. Each grade level has its own standards and expectations in reading, math, and language, and the instruction in these subjects begins in kindergarten.

4. The school has a planned program of required courses rather than a batch of electives with only a few requirements.

## INSTRUCTION

1. Academic work is given top priority over other school activities, and large amounts of time are allocated to it.

2. Teachers have discretionary instructional time and tend to use it for individual tutoring and personal assistance.

3. Teachers establish clear goals and high expectations for their students. They focus on these important goals in their instruction and continually monitor students' progress.

4. Order and discipline characterize the school. Rules and policies are reasonable and are fairly and consistently enforced. Classrooms are orderly

and well managed, with few behavior problems, few classroom intrusions, and a low absence rate.

5.  Certain key instructional behaviors are at work in the classrooms: review and homework checks, good lesson development, actively monitored seatwork, and homework assignments that relate to course objectives.

### SUPPORT SERVICES

1.  All out-of-classroom activities (e.g., assemblies, field trips) are coordinated with what is taking place in the classroom.

2.  Pull-out instruction (e.g., going to computer lab) occurs only if it does not fragment or interfere with the classroom instructional program and does not result in lower expectations for some students.

### EVALUATION

1.  Student achievement is assessed routinely and frequently.

2.  Report cards contain precise information about the student's progress, particularly about how well the basic skills are being mastered.

3.  Students develop a serious attitude about taking tests, and they see tests as measures of their achievement.

### PARENT AND COMMUNITY SUPPORT

1.  Parents are regularly informed about the school's goals and expectations and about students' responsibilities and behavior standards.

2.  A clearly defined policy on homework is explained to both parents and students.

3.  The school emphasizes the importance of regular attendance.

4.  Parental support is present but is generally limited to areas other than instructional involvement.

5.  The school uses community services such as work experience and the public library to reinforce and extend student learning.[9]

"Anyone could have predicted all this," you may be thinking. "No surprises at all—so what else is new?" To be sure, you could have foreseen most, if not all, of these characteristics of effective schools. But, as the next chapter will confirm, these characteristics are critically important to you. The extent of their presence or absence affects your personal success in the classroom.

OTHER FINDINGS    Many findings from the effective-schools research are obvious. Others, though less obvious, also affect your success. Here are some examples:

1.  School resources, including facilities, are not related to student achievement. Factors such as the size of the school, its age, and the quality of the buildings make no significant difference in the achievement of students.

2. Teachers' salaries, years of teaching experience, and percentage of teachers with graduate degrees do not significantly affect student achievement.

3. The overall expenditure per student, the number of books in the school library, and the number of students in a class (within reason) do not significantly affect student achievement.

Be careful about how you interpret these three statements. It would be foolish to suppose that school resources are of no importance—clearly, a basic minimum is essential. A brutal cut in resources would unquestionably have an ill effect. When programs are stopped or severely curtailed, teacher and student morale suffers. Nevertheless, given the range of resources generally available to schools, the precise level seems to be unimportant. Increasing the school's resources is *not* likely to be an effective way to improve student achievement in your school.

## The Old One-Room School and the New Effective School

Increasing optimism characterizes attitudes toward today's schools as knowledge about classroom learning opens new frontiers for school effectiveness. Educators are giving less credence to the idea that some students simply cannot learn. This change of heart began as early as 1979: "If *some* schools can teach poor and minority students effectively, *all* can, if they employ the knowledge base regarding effective practices."[10]

"But," you perceive, "we have come full circle! Modern effective schools look frightfully like the old one-room schoolhouse we hear so much about."

Indeed, similarities can be found. In early schools, the schoolmaster, a strict disciplinarian, conducted daily "direct" instruction. No grouping by ability could be found. Students were expected to be orderly, silent (except during recitation), and "on task" throughout the day. The curriculum was heavy on basics such as math and reading. Daily seatwork, recitation, and drill to overlearning typified early classroom life. Today too, effective schools are task oriented. Teachers are businesslike, focus on mastery of basics, provide ample practice, and make optimal use of time allocated for instruction. But a closer look reveals a most important difference between the early school and today's effective school: in addition to being structured and task oriented, the effective school promotes student initiative, creativity, and diversity.

# CREATING AN EFFECTIVE SCHOOL

## Efforts to Improve School Effectiveness

Over the years of public education, society has maintained pressure on schools, in one form or another, to improve their effectiveness. This pressure continues at both the elementary and secondary level.

© Frank Siteman/Stock, Boston

© Jeff Albertson/Stock, Boston

Legislatures are presenting states with "effective school" bills. The very fact that these bills are being formulated and presented suggests how strong the impetus has been during the late 1980s.[11] States have played and continue to play a significant role in the creation of effective schools. As a first step, state personnel usually invite local superintendents and other administrators to participate in designing and planning an effective-school program. Later on, these local administrators are called in again and trained to implement the program in their own districts. The state provides money for hiring substitutes to cover classes while teachers undergo training. During implementation of the program, state personnel provide ongoing assistance and evaluation for the teachers.

Governors, too, are becoming strong and eager partners in school improvement. They examine areas for improvement, making numerous recommendations for reform in which they can participate. They give more discretion to educators willing to be responsible for higher levels of student achievement. They work for increased funding as long as the funds have a positive impact on student retention and achievement.[12]

Local businesses are likewise falling in step, realizing that well-educated graduates turn into more productive employees. They provide work experiences for junior and senior high school students, contribute computer hardware and software to school programs, and donate instructional materials to classrooms. Those hiring these graduates recognize that increased excellence in public education translates into higher-quality performance and products in business and industry.

Training programs for superintendents and principals are cropping up across the country. For example, The American Association of School Administrators' Assessment Center has established Centers for Educational Excellence in Superintendency to improve skills, knowledge, and attitudes of leaders so they can have a more direct and positive impact on creating effective schools.[13] Similar training programs, such as the Professional Development Institute in the District of Columbia, have been established for training principals.[14]

## Reform Reports

Two major forces have been at work creating effective schools: one is the research already discussed, and the other is reform reports. These calls to reform began appearing during the 1980s. Let's look at four of the more influential documents.

In *The Paideia Proposal: An Educational Manifesto* a group of educators and scholars, headed by Mortimer Adler, set forth a proposal "signifying the general learning that should be the possession of all human beings." This proposal, designed to reform American education, was addressed to parents, teachers, school boards, college educators, elected public officials, employers, minority groups, labor leaders, and citizens in general. Based heavily on the thinking of John Dewey, the proposal suggested that

© George W. Gardner/Stock, Boston

education is a lifelong process of which schooling is only a small but necessary part. . . . The ultimate goal of the educational process is to help human beings become educated persons. Schooling is the preparatory stage; it forms the habit of learning and provides the means for continuing to learn after all schooling is completed. . . . Basic schooling—the schooling compulsory for all—must do something other than prepare some young people for more schooling at advanced levels. It must prepare *all* of them for the continuation of learning in adult life, during their working years and beyond. How? By imparting to them the skills of learning and giving them the stimulation that will motivate them to keep their minds actively engaged in learning.[15]

The Paideia group lashed out at the discrimination of a multitrack system of schooling and advocated the same objectives for all, without exception. Their proposal set forth three common goals for students: (1) to earn a living in an intelligent and responsible fashion, (2) to function as intelligent and responsible citizens, and (3) to make the earning of a living and responsible citizenship serve the purposes of leading intelligent and responsible lives. In achieving these goals, the curriculum would be both liberal and general, the same for every child. It would include acquiring an organized body of knowledge, developing intellectual skills, and enlarging one's understanding of ideas and values.

The Adler proposal was followed by Ernest Boyer's *High School: A Report on Secondary Education in America.* This Carnegie Foundation report was based on observations of twenty-five educators, each of whom spent twenty days visiting fifteen public high schools representative of the "cross-section of American public secondary education." On the basis of data collected, the panel proposed four essential goals of a high school and means of achieving these goals. The high schools should:

1. Help all students develop the capacity to think critically and communicate effectively through a mastery of language.

2. Help all students learn about themselves, the human heritage, and the interdependent world in which they live through a core curriculum based upon consequential human experiences common to all people.

3. Prepare all students for work and further education through a program of electives that develop individual aptitudes and interests.

4. Help all students fulfill their social and civic obligations through school and community service.[16]

In *A Place Called School*, John Goodlad reported his eight-year study of American schools. His data showed that only 75 percent of class time was devoted to instruction, and the overwhelming proportion of this time consisted of teacher "telling." Only rarely were students making decisions about their learning. Tests and quizzes stressed mainly the recall of specific information and narrow mechanical skills. Where students were grouped by ability levels, he found that the upper groups were accorded a relatively rich curriculum experience, whereas the lower groups were given far more drill and rote learning. Goodlad's conclusion was that until we change the *structure* of high schools we will be cheating students, frustrating teachers, and wasting money:

> I do in fact doubt that schooling, as presently conceived and conducted, is capable of providing large segments of young people with the education they and this democracy require. . . . But far-reaching restructuring of our schools and indeed our system of education probably is required for us to come even close to the educational ideals we so regularly espouse for this nation and all its people.[17]

Goodlad recognized the need for a general education in a free society and recommended that about two-thirds of the curriculum consist of a common core of concepts, principles, skills, and ways of knowing.

Another classic report, by Theodore Sizer, was *Horace's Compromise: The Dilemma of the American High School*. This intensely personal and vivid account of Sizer's two-year journey to more than eighty high schools throughout the United States presents a revealing and troubling picture of high schools. Sizer observed that our goals have become contradictory and our teaching methods bogged down in bureaucracy. We seem to have forgotten that inspired teachers are the key to good education and that mastery of basic intellectual skills is more important than quick exposure to miscellaneous available knowledge. Sizer uses as an example Horace Smith, a veteran high school teacher who cares about his students and about learning. He knows how to teach well, but the traditional structure of the typical suburban high school where he works makes it difficult to do so. Horace has to compromise what he knows will work in order to meet the demands of the system. "Schools," the author argues, "are going to improve only after we've taken a close look at our values and priorities and recast the school structure." [18]

---

## Raising Their Sights

Good teachers focus on student achievement and work to bring about that achievement, confident that it can be done. One such teacher is Jaime Escalante, a mathematics teacher at Garfield High School in East Los Angeles. His principal, Maria Tostado, described Escalante as a "teaching genius." In the late 1970s, Garfield High, with a mostly Hispanic student population, was on the brink of losing its accreditation. By 1988, Garfield had 15 advanced-placement teachers in subjects such as calculus and physics. As of 1988, 370 students were preparing to take the advanced-placement exams for college credit. In 1989, 540 students took advance placement tests.

What brought the turnaround? Tostado credits Escalante and a mixture of rules and demanding classes with the remaking of Garfield into a scholar factory. "We phased out the bonehead courses and put in more advanced, challenging courses," she said. Escalante set about to motivate high achievers. He has been described as a showman, math scholar, father figure, and cheerleader. As his students ceremoniously drop their homework into a basket at the beginning of each period, they join in hand clapping and warm-up music (*We Will Rock You*). His advanced-placement students wear T-shirts and satin jackets signifying their membership in the college-bound elite.

With his students, Escalante cajoles, challenges, explains, and applauds. And the results of his efforts and those of fellow teachers at Garfield are impressive: in 1982, 18 of his students passed the advanced-placement calculus examination; in 1983, 31; in 1984, 63; in 1985, 77; in 1986, 78; in 1987, 87. Indeed, 70 percent of the 1987 graduating class was accepted by colleges. This was quite a turnaround for a school that a few years before had nearly lost its accreditation. Escalante's dedication to his students and their learning prompted the production of the film *Stand and Deliver.* Escalante is a teacher willing to go to just about any lengths to win the hearts and minds of his students. His greatest ambition is to see his students get ahead. To his largely Hispanic students, Escalante says, "There are some people in this world who assume you know less than you do because of your name and your complexion. But math is a great equalizer."

Tostado praises Escalante's efforts with both students and parents: "He calls parents every time someone doesn't show up in class. He visits parents when they get home from work to get them to sign his contracts pledging hours of extra homework. He spends summers poring over the school records to find recruits for his classes like he was a coach."

Jaime Escalante and others like him are showing what can be done by hard-working, dedicated teachers who believe that their students can learn and set about to see that it occurs.

Based on an article in *Time,* February 1, 1988, pp. 52–58; the film *Stand and Deliver;* and a talk given by Jaime Escalante, Utah Valley Community College, May 17, 1989.

These reports portrayed students drifting through school, unchallenged and unmotivated, getting by with as little work as possible—a highly negative picture of American high schools. Adding to this, other studies found declining test scores, attendance problems, and increasing dropout rates. Legislators asked why so many students were failing and why some schools were more consistently successful than others. The picture emerging during the mid-1980s brought a public outcry to do something about the American high school.

The educational community was stirred to action—improve the schools! Responding to these cries for reform, educators turned to the research on effective schools. By the latter part of the 1980s, clear evidence was beginning to accumulate that many schools, school districts, and state departments of education were applying the results of school-effectiveness research in hopes of increasing student performance. As far back as 1985, there were nearly 40 effective-school programs operating in 7500 schools in 1750 districts. This was double the number found two years earlier. Since the mid-1980s, every indication has been that these programs are continuing to expand and receive public approval. For example, parents generally see their children's schools as effective. In the 18th annual Gallup poll of the public's attitudes toward the public schools, parents rated the effectiveness of public schools. They were asked to indicate how accurately a set of characteristics described the school their oldest child attended. About eight out of ten parents characterized their children's schools as "effective."[19]

## Testimonials by Teachers

Teachers are saying positive things about their "effective" schools:

ABOUT EXPERIMENTING   Teaching is an intellectually exciting activity. Around here we are encouraged by administrators and colleagues to experiment with new ideas and techniques. And we can drop experiments that do not work, yet be rewarded for having tried. We are always looking for more effective ways of teaching. Just last year we published "Opening Classroom Doors," a booklet with short descriptions of new ideas tried in classrooms. One teacher, for example, shared how she used jigsaw activities to do cooperative learning in social studies.

ABOUT EXPECTATIONS   In this school the teachers and administrators are held accountable for high performance through regular evaluations. We are expected to experiment with new ideas. Our continued professional development is highly valued by the school community. While we often feel under pressure to excel, we thrive on being part of a dynamic organization.

ABOUT TEACHING SUPPORT   When I need help to improve my instruction, people extend themselves with both time and resources. Indeed, when resources become scarce, professional development remains a priority. Around here people believe that professional knowledge and skills are very important to good schooling. Despite financial constraints we still have sabbaticals, summer curriculum workshops, and funds to attend professional conferences.

**ABOUT APPRECIATION AND RECOGNITION**   Good teaching is honored in this school and community. The other day I found a short note from the principal in my mailbox: "When Todd and Charley were roughhousing in the hall, you spoke to them promptly and firmly, yet treated them maturely by explaining the 'whys' of your intervention. It really makes our talk about respect mean something when teachers take responsibility for all kids the way you do." He just observed that incident for a minute, yet took the time to give me feedback. (Somehow it had more impact in writing, too.) Things like that make me feel there is a real value placed on what I do with students.

**ABOUT INVOLVEMENT IN DECISION MAKING**   I am included in certain meaningful decision-making processes in this school, especially when they directly affect me or my kids. That doesn't mean I am consulted on all policies or decisions; but to tell you the truth, I don't want to be—I'd never get all of my own work done. But when I am consulted, it's not a phony gesture; my input is taken seriously. And there are mechanisms open for me to raise issues. Last spring I asked the faculty advisory council to look at how kids were treating each other in the halls. That led to a faculty brainstorming session on the topic of school climate. I don't always get people to buy into my issues, or even ask them to. But when I do, the issues are treated seriously, and I am esteemed for bringing them up even if my solutions do not carry the day.

**ABOUT PROTECTION OF TEACHING TIME**   My principal protects my instruction and planning time by keeping meetings and paperwork to a minimum. In fact, we don't even have faculty meetings in the usual sense—certainly not just for business and announcements. Those needs get covered by memos and word-of-mouth contact with the principal. When we do meet, it is for curriculum and instruction purposes, often in small groups like the study group on learning styles I was in last spring.[20]

# TWO EFFORTS TO CREATE EFFECTIVE SCHOOLS

How does a staff go about creating an effective school? How does it begin? At the outset, your staff starts thinking differently. Your principal, during a faculty kick-off meeting, hands you the following "launch" list:

1.  The primary purpose of our school must be teaching and learning. We must be ready to change whatever we do that doesn't move us in that direction.

2.  Our school effectiveness must be measured by what happens to our kids. The size of our budget, the age of our school, your advanced degrees—we can't measure our success by these.

3.  We must change our current expectations and ways of treating minority and poor kids. They're not getting a fair shake. We think they can't do as well—and we treat them that way.

*There are longstanding arguments in education over fidelity, although they are rarely referred to in that way. Joseph Junell points to one of these controversies when he asks, "To what part of man does public education owe its first obligation?" Junell feels that we make a great error when we give our fidelity to training the rational intellect at the expense of affect and emotion. In agreement with Junell, one might argue further that when we give our fidelity to the training of intellect, fidelity to persons once again becomes derivative. From the perspective of an ethic of caring, development of the whole person is necessarily our concern.—Nel Noddings*

4. We need to measure student outcomes that matter most. We can't keep measuring "cognitive" outcomes if we all think "affective" outcomes are the most important.

5. We must have quality and equity. *All* our kids, regardless of family, race, or status, must master the essentials of our program. And our program must be up to par.

6. Our low-achieving kids must grow as much as our high-achieving kids. Our program has to help one group as much as another.

Many school faculties have no doubt received a similar "launch" list and have plunged enthusiastically into transforming their ordinary school into an effective school. To illustrate this process, we will examine two examples, one a large-scale effort and one a single-building effort.

## Milwaukee's Project RISE (Raise Student Achievement by Systematically Implementing the Essential Elements of Effective Schooling)

In 1979, a local school board directed eighteen elementary and two middle schools in Milwaukee, Wisconsin, to improve their achievement levels in reading, math, and language to reflect city-wide or national norms.[21] These were the twenty lowest-achieving schools in the system. All were located in the central part of the city and served predominantly low-income and minority students. During the period of the project, no changes were made in the schools' administrations, teachers, or student populations, and no additional monies were allocated.

The project defined an effective school as one in which *all* students (without regard to race or social class) perform at or above specified norms in reading, math, and language arts.

Each graph in Figure 8-1 shows two lines. The top line represents students in all Milwaukee elementary schools (109 schools). The bottom line

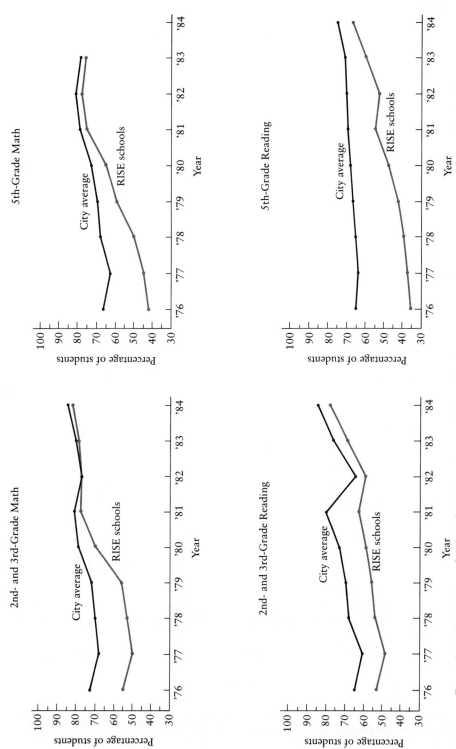

*Figure 8-1 Percentage of Milwaukee elementary students achieving average or above-average scores on standardized tests from 1975–1976 through 1983–1984 (Source: M. McCormack-Larkin, "Ingredients of a Successful School Effectiveness Project," Educational Leadership 42(6) (1985), pp. 32–33.)*

represents students in all RISE schools (18 schools). Each dot on a line represents the percentage of students who scored at or above the national average on the Metropolitan Achievement Test in math and reading. For example, in second and third grade math in 1976, 75 percent of the students in all Milwaukee elementary schools scored at or above the national average. In that same year, 55 percent of the students in the RISE schools scored at or above the national average.

By the close of the 1983–1984 school year, Project RISE (the effective-schools program) had been operating for eight years. The most significant growth occurred between 1979 and 1983, and greater growth occurred in math than in reading at all grade levels. After eight years, the performance of students in the RISE schools was near the level of students in all Milwaukee's schools in math and reading.

Within the eighteen RISE schools, several distinguished themselves by their exceptional rate of progress. The fast-improving schools had made these specific changes:

### CHANGES MADE BY TEACHERS

1. Teacher in-service training stressed the educability of *all* students. An attempt was made to refute the belief that kids cannot learn because of their home and cultural backgrounds. Teachers learned that their expectations and their classroom behavior were very powerful.

2. Teachers improved their sense of efficacy; that is, they came to feel that *they* were responsible for the growth of their students.

3. Teachers abandoned their practice of grouping students by ability level (high achievers in one group, average in another, and low in another).

4. Teachers relied upon their own expertise rather than bringing in outside consultants.

5. Both teachers and principals explained the program at professional meetings and press conferences. Those making it successful received recognition.

### CHANGES IN SCHOOL MANAGEMENT

1. Principals reinforced each other about the importance of visiting every classroom on a daily basis and about concentrating on instructional matters in faculty meetings.

2. Principals strengthened the sense of school ownership among the teachers, empowering them to be responsible for successes and failures in the school. Teachers assumed responsibility for improving the school's reading and math programs, its evaluation program, and the overall school climate.

4. The school moved away from operating as a set of separate classrooms to operating as a group where all teachers felt a unified responsibility. Each teacher was responsible for seeing that students were performing at or above grade level, and each realized the importance of bringing students to grade level before passing them on.

CHANGES IN SCHOOL PRACTICES AND POLICIES

1. A school-wide policy was adopted, protecting instructional time from unnecessary disruptions.

2. Teachers concentrated on basic reading, math, and language arts skills first. As those improved, teachers turned their attention to the development of higher-order skills.

3. Extracurricular activities emphasized academic achievement. These included such activities as reading and math Olympic teams, academic pep rallies, student recognition programs, and oratorical debates.

4. Teachers identified expected behaviors and committed themselves to enforcing them consistently.

5. For each grade level, a clear set of objectives and standards was set forth that had to be met before a student could progress to the next level. The standards were printed on "Yes I Can" sheets, reviewed with students, and distributed to parents.

6. All students were to complete daily homework assignments. Principals and teachers enforced this policy by monitoring the doors at dismissal and sending empty-handed students back to their rooms to get their homework. If students were derelict, parents were informed, and the students were detained in the "homework center" to complete missing assignments.

CHANGES IN CLASSROOM PRACTICES

1. At each grade level, the teacher taught the entire curriculum to every student. Lessons were usually taught to the whole class and supplemented with small-group corrective or enrichment instruction. Compensatory instruction was conducted within the classroom. Precautions were taken so as not to identify or label a student as "slow." To avoid embarrassing slow readers, schools prepared and distributed book covers for all students, showing only the school's name and logo.

2. Lessons were highly structured and generally included a review of the previous lesson, homework check, direct instruction, a check for understanding, actively monitored seatwork, and a related homework assignment. This teaching format minimized the opportunity for disruptive behavior and increased academic engagement of students.

These changes made by the fast-improving RISE schools suggest a different "way of doing things" from the one found in traditional schools. In our second example, a single elementary school demonstrates how a building staff can create an effective school.

# Hammond Elementary School

Hammond Elementary is in Arkansas's Acacia School District. The district serves a predominantly lower-middle-income population, about equally divided between blacks and whites. In 1979, scores in the Acacia district aver-

*The programs assume that almost all school-age children are educable and that their educability derives from the nature of the schools to which they are sent.—Ronald Edmonds*

aged at the 39th percentile on national achievement tests. Dissatisfaction was widespread, as was the desire to improve. At the recommendation of the state school officer, Hammond (and other schools within the district) adopted as its effectiveness program the nationally used Program for Effective Teaching (PET). An in-service training program for teachers and principals, PET aims to raise student achievement through improved instruction, emphasizing teaching to objectives. The program assumes that all students can learn and that schools can be improved by the existing staff.

As a first step, the district's administrators attended a state-sponsored seven-day training workshop. They were favorably impressed with the program and the manner in which they were trained. As a result of that training, they decided to implement the program.

Next, one teacher from the district was trained and certified to train other teachers. At this point, all Hammond teachers and the principal were trained together, a process that created a feeling of cooperation and respect. (The state provided grant money for hiring substitutes so teachers could be trained during the regular school day.)

Within three years of its inception, the program was completely implemented at Hammond. Every teacher had undergone at least one cycle of PET training, and the principal had changed his style of supervision from that of a bureaucrat to one that focused on improvement in teaching.

For the first time in recent years, average student achievement on national tests climbed above the 50th percentile, and no major change in the enrollment pattern had occurred to account for that improvement. Improved achievement led to higher expectations for students and teachers. Teachers reported better discipline and student self-esteem. Teachers felt they had mastered the use of instructional strategies and had gained greater self-confidence. The principal, who had previously felt uncomfortable conducting classroom observations, now carried them out with assurance. Both teachers and principal reported a greater sense of collegiality and improved public image. After five years, PET had become institutionalized at Hammond. It was no longer viewed as a special program; instead, it had been built into the organizational structure and was simply "the way things are done."[22]

The achievement levels (as measured by standardized tests) climbed in the examples of RISE and Hammond. Whether the creation of an "effective" school did in fact account for this growth is still open to question. Nonetheless, these two examples illustrate how schools move toward excellence.

# CHALLENGES FACING EFFECTIVE SCHOOLS

Attempts to turn poor and mediocre schools into effective schools will continue—some with missionary zeal, others with foot dragging. A few are
grandiose; many are small scale. An effort to create an effective school typically begins with ardor and commitment. A few efforts, through patience
and hard work, have been successful; a great many have fizzled after the first
splash. To their credit, many a school staff has rolled up its collective sleeves
and quietly gone about the business of improving its own effectiveness.

You and your colleagues will always face numerous challenges as you
work at turning your school into a more effective learning environment.
These are some of the challenges:

1. Teachers in your school may doubt their autonomy. They doubt they are
   actually empowered (or even have the ability) to make decisions and bring
   about reforms. As a result, they are reluctant to jump in and work for
   change.

2. When singled out by the district to embark on an improvement program,
   teachers in your school may think they are being seen as inadequate and
   desperately in need of help.

3. Past experience tells teachers that "community involvement" seldom
   materializes. Though parents, the business community, and the local
   chamber of commerce all promise to assist the school in reaching its new
   goals, few actually deliver.

4. Teachers at your school may resist help from outside consultants. There is a
   feeling that "It's easy for you to suggest this or that; you don't have to work
   in the trenches all day, or live with the results."

5. Thinking big—dreaming—is difficult when you are trying to stay afloat in
   your daily teaching, or even in holding onto your job.

6. Some teachers—foot draggers—spend all their time focusing on what can
   go wrong or arguing why the program will never get off the ground. The
   possibility of success is viewed pessimistically.

7. Teachers often look for quick solutions. They may feel, for example, that
   implementing the latest technology will, by itself, raise student achievement
   scores. Teachers must come to realize that in the final analysis what they do
   in their own classrooms creates the effective school.

8. At your school, teachers may lack consensus on which goals are most
   important. As a result, poor communication develops between principal and
   teachers and among teachers.

9. You may have a principal who uses a top-down approach to planning and
   decision making, one who resists involving those of you actually carrying out
   the program.

10. In its urgency to effect immediate improvement, your district may set down
    rigid policies to be followed identically in every school. This could quickly
    become a stifling move! Suppose teachers in your school have always taken

pride in the quality of education the students receive. Out of the blue, you are strapped with a uniform set of standards aimed at bringing the low-achieving schools up to par. This peculiar action soon knocks the motivational legs out from under your teachers—and their long-term commitment to their own standards begins to erode.

Finally, there are some broader unresolved issues surrounding the effective schools movement. In one form or another, they too will find their way into your school—and your classroom:

Through establishing a set of standards, state legislatures and districts often attempt to *compel* schools to improve—they mandate improvement. These frequently used strong-arm tactics seldom work because authentic change originates only as teachers themselves decide to change.

Today's effective schools are becoming proficient in raising achievement levels, but they are not very good at furnishing values, attitudes, and proper conduct that are all too often missing in the home.

Two conflicting American dreams continue to hamper the Effective Schools Movement. First, there is the egalitarian dream in which every American child attends essentially the same school, learns the same curriculum, and is held to the same standards, regardless of his or her race or family background. The rival dream is that schools should differ—the more the better. On the basis of their differences, schools compete with each other for students. One school is strong in teaching students how to read, write, and compute; another's strength is in teaching art and culture. In this second dream, the kind of education each child receives is chosen by his or her parents. Since these two dreams about what constitutes an ideal education compete with each other, there can be no one definition of an effective school.

Another problem is that, of the current teaching force, almost 40 percent were not teaching five years ago. Because of the large number of new teachers and principals coming into the system, teaching teachers how to create effective schools is a never-ending task.[23]

An "effective" school may or may not be a "good" school. Teachers can be quite effective in bringing students to a given goal, but the question remains, "Is the goal worthwhile or good?" If the school's overall achievement scores are higher because lower-achieving students have dropped out, is the press for higher achievement justified? Are higher math and reading scores good if students gain them at the expense of an appreciation of social studies, art, or music? One writer clarifies this distinction between good and effective schools:

> To be blunt, educators who care about the fate of all children must define *goodness* before they worry about *effectiveness*. There is, unfortunately, an insistence that learning must always be tightly controlled, narrowly prescribed, and clearly specified. *Some* learning fits that pattern, of course. . . . When we take an excursion into learning, we can choose to drive straight to our objective, keeping our eyes straight ahead, exerting steady pressure on the pedal, and stopping only when necessary. *Or* we can choose to make the drive part of

*Schools are full of success stories from which we must learn lessons. If we focus on failure, we might get it; if we focus on success, we might get that.*
—*William J. Bennett*

the excursion, by slowing down to admire the scenery, visiting historical and cultural sites, and dining in restaurants situated off the beaten track. If we follow the second plan, we may not arrive at our objective as quickly—but we will have learned more and spent the time more pleasantly. We are currently traveling more efficiently to a predetermined destination, but is it the *only* destination? Effective schools can be good schools, and good schools must be effective schools—but the two are not necessarily the same.[24]

# IMPLICATIONS

We can imagine the reaction of some teachers to our promotion of the idea of effective schools:

"Go for it! If you want to be teaching in an effective school, there is no choice but to dig in."

"Why me? I'm just one lone teacher in a great big school. Creating an effective school has to be a big operation. Teachers like me are hired to teach *in* effective schools, not to develop them. That's a job for principals and administrators and school districts—you know, the people who are supposed to do that sort of thing."

"Well, if your classroom could be a cocoon, placed in the middle of your building, undisturbed, that might be a legitimate position. But there is an inescapable link between what happens in your overall school and what happens in your classroom. For example, the amount of time you are able to allocate to each subject is determined, in part, by school-wide scheduling, including decisions about field trips, football games, use of the gym, and number of assemblies."

"I realize that. Anybody can see you have to be in sync with the rest of your school. But that's not the problem. My problem is just keeping my head above water with my own kids. How can I jump in and work for an effective school when I'm not even sure I can produce an effective classroom?"

Fair enough. Now may not be the right time to worry about wearing a larger hat. Working for the betterment of the entire school may be too much to think about at this point. But later, think about this: individual teachers (perhaps after they are "on top of things") are key players. We have learned in reading this chapter that gleaming new schools, carefully crafted legislative mandates, and elegantly conceived curricula are no match for an individual teacher's determination to bring about change.

But you might think modestly at this point. At the very least, let your principal find you "not guilty" on the charge of foot dragging. Even the best of programs quickly gets mired down through a teacher's unwillingness to give it a try. Without making any commitments, you can at least contribute by not throwing a wrench into the works. Acquiescing to honest and worthwhile intentions of your colleagues can be a helpful effort on your part. Of course, pitching in yourself is even better! But you may be in your first year, or you may find yourself already overcommitted. During such times, you can applaud the efforts of your colleagues, promising yourself to be more helpful when burdens are lighter.

Suppose, as is more likely the case, you do choose an active role in your school's program to increase its effectiveness. As you set sail, keep the following in mind:

1. The individual school, not the district, is the place where effectiveness begins. The district may provide impetus, rewards, and support, but you and the other teachers in your school supply the horsepower.

2. Authentic change requires time—usually several years. Patience and sustained work are virtues in cultivating an effective school.

3. The initial stages of significant change in a school involve anxiety and uncertainty. You can learn to live with this uncertainty and still carry out your normal role.

4. Trust and risk taking are critical. You must be willing to risk and to take responsibility for your successes and failures. Likewise, you do not punish colleagues or the principal for honest efforts that fail.

5. Welcome outsiders. Even though you and other teachers want and need to have ownership in the improvement program, be willing to call on outside helpers. Colleagues from the district office, parents, and consultants are valuable in helping you fully implement your program.

6. Have can-do expectations and work for a climate of success. Start by believing that all your students can reach an acceptable level of achievement. Set classroom goals, adopt a friendly but businesslike approach, work as a team member, develop a sense of personal efficacy ("What I do makes a difference"), and identify with your school.

# CONCLUSION

When your dream schools are cast in reality, they are effective schools. In a variety of areas, students in effective schools are achieving at higher levels than students in ineffective schools. Fortunately, school-improvement programs in your area will not pass you by. Some form of them is inevitable—you will be involved with renovation all the time. So don't be afraid to go to work. An enviable excitement runs through a school brewing with success.

## Expansions

1.   List the characteristics of *your* ideal school. Rank-order them in terms of importance for you. How similar are these to those characteristics found in effective schools?

2.   Visit a school. Observe everything you can and, if possible, interview several teachers. Using the criteria of an effective school set forth in this chapter, determine how this school would measure up. Explain.

3.   Which characteristics of effective schools would you be most qualified to help develop in your own school? Explain.

## Notes

1.   J. Saphier, and M. King, "Good Seeds Grow in Strong Cultures," *Educational Leadership* 42(6) (1985), pp. 67–74.

2.   S. Ingrassia, "Welcome to the Learning Castle," *Educational Leadership* 40(3) (1982), pp. 33–35.

3.   J. S. Coleman, E. Q. Campbell, C. J. Hobson, J. M. McPartland, A. M. Mood, F. D. Weinfield, and R. L. York, *Equality of Educational Opportunity* (Washington, D.C.: U.S. Government Printing Office, 1966).

4.   C. S. Jencks, M. Smith, H. Ackland, M. J. Bane, D. Cohen, H. Gintis, B. Heyns, and S. Michelson, *Inequality: A Reassessment of the Effect of Family and Schooling in America* (New York: Basic Books, 1972).

5.   H. A. Averch, et al., *How Effective is Schooling? A Critical Review and Synthesis of Research Findings,* report prepared for President's Commission on School Finance (Santa Monica: Rand Corporation, 1972).

6.   R. E. Klitgaard and G. R. Hall, "Are There Unusually Effective Schools?," *Journal of Human Resources* 74 (1974), pp. 90–106.

7.   W. B. Brookover, C. Beady, P. Flood, J. Schweitzer, and J. Wisenbaker, *School Social Systems and Student Achievement: Schools Can Make a Difference* (New York: Praeger, 1979).

8.   R. E. Edmonds, "Programs of School Improvement: An Overview," *Educational Leadership* 40(3) (1982), pp. 4–7.

9.   M. Cohen, "Improving School Effectiveness: Lessons from Research," in V. Richardson-Koehler (Ed.), *Educators' Handbook: A Research Perspective* (New York: Longman, 1987), pp. 474–490; R. Edmonds, "Effective Schools for the Urban Poor," *Educational Leadership,* 37(1) (1979), pp. 15–27; M. McCormack-Larkin, "Ingredients of a Successful School Effectiveness Project," *Educational Leadership* 42(6) (1985), pp. 31–38; J. F. Murphy, M. Weil, P. Hallinger, and A. Mitman, "Academic Press: Translating High Expectations into School Policies and Classroom Practices," *Educational Leadership* 40(3), (1982), pp. 22–26; S. C. Purkey and M. S. Smith, "Effective Schools: A Review," *The Elementary School*

*Journal* 83(4) (1983), pp. 427–452; J. Stallings and G. Mohlman, *School Policy, Leadership Style, Teacher Change and Student Behavior in Eight Secondary Schools,* National Institute of Education (Mountain View, Calif.: Stallings Teaching and Learning Institute, 1981).

10. Edmonds, "Effective Schools," pp. 15–27.

11. L. W. Lezotte and B. A. Bancroft, "Growing Use of the Effective Schools Model for School Improvement," *Educational Leadership* 42(6) (1985), pp. 23–31.

12. J. Nathan, "Implications for Educators of "Time for Results," *Phi Delta Kappan* 68(4) (1986), pp. 197–201.

13. J. Melton and R. Miller, "Assessment Project Marks Major Milestone," *The School Administrator* 44(2) (1987), pp. 15–16.

14. E. Hamilton, "Can the School System Produce Its Own Leaders?," *Negro Educational Review* 37(2) (1986), pp. 81–87.

15. M. J. Adler, *The Paideia Proposal: An Educational Manifesto* (New York: Macmillan, 1982), p. 11.

16. E. L. Boyer, *High School: A Report on Secondary Education in America* (New York: Harper & Row, 1983), pp. 66–67.

17. J. Goodlad, *A Place Called School: Prospects for the Future* (New York: McGraw-Hill, 1984), pp. 91–92.

18. T. R. Sizer, *Horace's Compromise: The Dilemma of the American High School* (New York: Houghton Mifflin, 1984), p. 34.

19. A. M. Gallup, "The 18th Annual Gallup Poll of the Public's Attitudes toward the Public Schools," *Phi Delta Kappan,* September 1986, p. 48.

20. Saphier and King, "Good Seeds," pp. 67–74.

21. McCormack-Larkin, "Ingredients," pp. 31–38.

22. A. Davis and A. Odden, "How State Instructional Improvement Programs Affect Teachers and Principals," *Phi Delta Kappan,* April 1986, pp. 590–593.

23. T. L. Good and J. E. Brophy, "School Effects," in M. C. Wittrock (Ed.), *Handbook of Research on Teaching,* 3rd ed. (New York: Macmillan, 1986), pp. 570–602.

24. C. D. Glickman, "Good and/or Effective Schools: What Do We Want?," *Phi Delta Kappan,* April 1987, p. 624. (Italics in original.)

# CHAPTER 9

# EFFECTIVE CLASSROOMS

*What more can we ask for than to have to chase our students out of the classroom because they wish to continue questioning and learning?—John E. Penick, Robert E. Yager, and Ronald Bonnstetter*

**MAIN IDEAS**

- Rapidly emerging is a systematic body of research knowledge about what takes place in effective classrooms.

- Peeking into an effective classroom, one is struck by high levels of student engagement in learning activities and low levels of disruptive behavior.

- Student learning in basic-skills areas occurs best within the context of well-managed classrooms.

- Teachers are the key figures in effective classrooms. They are capable classroom managers, have positive learning expectations, exhibit a can-do attitude, and possess a clear idea of classroom conditions and student behaviors needed for good learning.

- These same teachers plan early and thoughtfully. Their structured lessons are clearly presented and include systematic review, helpful examples, guided practice, and corrective feedback.

# INTRODUCTION

Picture it! The word is out that your classroom is alive with successful learning. Your students—the slow, the average, the quick—offer uniformly glowing reports of your teaching effectiveness: "The one class I really like is Mrs. Gomez's biology. She is *so* good." One parent talks to another, and some talk to your principal about your teaching. Other teachers in the school soon learn of your growing reputation. Students express delight in being assigned to your classes. Passing you in the hall, one or two even comment, "Everyone says you're a good teacher."

What do "good" teachers do in their classrooms? Are their classrooms different from those of "poor" and "average" teachers? In Chapter 8, we learned that schools *do* make a difference, that administrators and teachers in effective schools are doing things differently from those in less effective schools. The same holds true in classrooms. We will see in this chapter that teachers in effective classrooms behave differently from teachers in less effective classrooms.

In thinking about effective classrooms, should we focus on the behavior of teachers? Is it the teacher's behavior that determines whether or not a classroom is effective? Only partly. We define an "effective" classroom as one where students are engaged in learning activities in which high rates of learning are occurring. This definition shifts our focus to the students. We assess effectiveness in terms of student learning.

One way to study effective classrooms is to look at the *relationship* between the teacher's classroom behavior and the students' learning. Another way, less direct, is to study the teacher's thought processes as she engages in teaching, or to explore the thought processes of students as they engage in learning activities. There are many ways to approach the study of effective classrooms.

For this chapter, we focus on the relationship between teachers' behavior and students' learning. In thinking about the simplest form of this relationship, we make a distinction between the process of teaching (what the teacher does) and the product of teaching (the results in terms of student learning). It is entirely possible for the process to be quite unrelated to the product; that is, the teacher's activities may be largely *unrelated* to what the student is learning. Not liking to consider this possibility, we often conceptualize effective classrooms in terms of the product (student learning) rather than the process. Let us explain.

We peek into Ms. Yee's elementary classroom. The bulletin boards are loaded with pictures and slogans that usher in the forthcoming holiday, Thanksgiving. The chalkboard is clean, the tray dust-free. The aquarium and the hamster cage reflect constant care. Encyclopedias and reference books are in place and easily accessible. Reading tables and student desks are readied for the next day's work. The teacher's materials are catalogued by unit, signaling thoughtful organization. The inference is obvious: it doesn't take a genius to see that students in this classroom are going to be more successful than those in less well-organized classrooms.

Just now, Ms. Yee walks into her room. Neatly dressed, pleasant, and quietly confident, she engages us in productive conversation. "You can just feel kids in her class are going to come out winners," you reflect. She invites us to sit in on her upcoming social studies lesson. "What a treat," you whisper after fifteen minutes. "Did you notice her clarity in instructions? The presentation is organized, and she moves the class along at just the right pace. She uses examples very well."

In observing the characteristics of Ms. Yee's classroom, as well as of her teaching, we are focusing on the teaching process, and from it we *infer* that she is an effective teacher—surely she is bringing about much learning! But to make this inference is to stop short. Ultimately, our focus must shift to the students, and to the changes occurring in them that result from (or are at least associated with) Ms. Yee's teaching. What changes *are* occurring in her students? What student achievement is taking place as a result of her neatly arranged classroom (and attire), her clear style of expression, and her well-organized presentations? These and other student-centered questions compel us to define "effectiveness" primarily in terms of student outcomes— the *product* of the teaching.

But, you might protest, to define teaching this narrowly is too constraining. Lots of things teachers do never show up on achievement tests. What about the teacher who buoys up the sagging spirits of the girl who fails to make the drill team? What about the teacher who excites a student to design his own chemistry experiment? These outcomes of teaching won't show up on any standardized test—but oh, how important they are! How boring teaching would be if you felt everything you did for a student had to be reflected on some test. "If achievement in basic subjects is the sum total of all teaching," you say, "I'd better start looking for another career. The students *I* teach are going to learn to think, and feel, and appreciate. They will learn to relate to others—and, I suppose, do okay in basic subjects as well."

You set forth a good argument. Schooling does produce many important outcomes in addition to those in the basic skill areas: the development of positive attitudes toward study, skill in interpersonal relationships, social maturity, skill in verbal communication, and calculation skills. Optimally, schooling helps students take greater personal responsibility for learning and develop a desire for lifelong education.

Still, there is pressure to hold teachers more accountable for their students' achievement, and the pressure is increasing. Legislators, school boards, parents, the communities in which these students will someday work—all insist on literacy in math, science, reading, computers. Most important, al-

*I began to modify my 'administrator's perspective.' I stopped searching exclusively for classwide indications of successful teaching and began to concentrate on interactions with individual students.—Daniel L. Duke*

though your principal does acknowledge your attractive bulletin boards and carefully prepared lessons, she takes an exacting look at the academic growth of your students. Fortunately, most teachers *are* committed to academic achievement as a primary goal. But they have other goals as well, and this is as it should be.

Admittedly, measuring your success by your students' achievement can be frustrating, and at times threatening. Indeed, a multitude of factors compete with your best efforts to engage students in learning tasks. Often these are factors over which you have little control. For example, there is the electric anticipation surrounding today's homecoming game; Amanda is tied up in knots over tomorrow's cheerleading tryouts; Ethan is too keyed up about his opening-night performance in *Fiddler on the Roof* to concentrate on anything else; and Marianne can't keep her eyes (and chatter) off the three "hot" boys just assigned to her section of English. Or perhaps the altogether irresistible spring weather has melted the whole class into listlessness; Cheri is starting her predictable depression over end-of-term exams; Mariko, having skipped breakfast, is too hungry to focus on quadratic equations; Richard left home this morning amidst heated quarreling and sits anxiety-ridden, unable to concentrate on writing an original paragraph; Eileen is too hyped-up about her birthday party to focus on the assigned article in the *Weekly Reader;* and Brad's obsession with late-night sports programs robs him of badly needed sleep.

In spite of your best efforts, suppose your students keep scoring below their expected grade level on academic tests? What can you do? Take heart! Today, more than during any other period in educational history, you have access to solid information about how teachers can improve students' learning. Thus, while your principal holds you more accountable than ever before, you are also in a position to be more successful than ever before, using available knowledge to try out hypotheses about how to improve learning. Herein lies the challenge and excitement of teaching: there will be stronger evidence to convict you of poor-quality teaching—or establish your resounding triumph!

## SOURCES OF KNOWLEDGE ABOUT EFFECTIVE TEACHING

Many sources of knowledge about teaching are available: accumulated wisdom of experienced teachers; reflections by authorities and experts; your personal experience; and research-generated knowledge. These are all important, and each contributes uniquely to our understanding of teaching.

Sometimes knowledge from one source refutes that from another. For example, years of conventional wisdom (folklore of the culture) told us that the culprit causing lower achievement in minority children was unequal school resources. The Coleman Report, discussed in Chapter 8, showed that the major cause of lower achievement was not inadequate school resources. This report so offended the conventional wisdom of the time that for the next twenty years researchers sought evidence to refute (or verify) its findings.

Knowledge from one source may also confirm that from another. For example, research in the 1960s documented the common-sense belief that children are more likely to learn the basics (math and reading) in schools that emphasize basics than in schools that do not.

We, the authors, place high value on research-based knowledge about teaching. Accordingly, we have chosen to introduce you to the history of re-search-based knowledge.

Studies of teaching began as early as 1910. Much of the first research focused on personal characteristics of teachers: the teacher's intelligence, leadership, enthusiasm, warmth, appearance. Typically, a principal would come into the teacher's classroom and rate the teacher on those qualities. If the ratings were high, the teacher was judged to be effective. Understand-ably, this research led educators to concentrate on characteristics and virtues considered desirable in any teacher. That emphasis showed in statements like this: "Joan is warm and enthusiastic and she relates easily to people— she will make an excellent teacher."

As time passed, the focus shifted from the teacher's personal charac-teristics to the methods used. Studies during this period pitted one method of teaching against another, such as lecture versus group discussion. These horse-race studies failed to contribute much knowledge to the field of teach-ing, since in practice the methods had too much in common to produce measurably different results.

During the 1950s and 1960s, researchers began to examine the class-room climate and identify teacher behaviors that correlated with student achievement. This new area of research created a need for better ways of observing teachers at work. Systematic methods for observing classrooms began cropping up until, by 1970, more than a hundred observation systems were available.

Process—product studies were well onto the scene by the early 1970s. Using sophisticated observational techniques, researchers were looking for relationships between teacher behaviors (process) and student outcomes (product), primarily achievement in basic skills. In the early process—product research, student outcomes were evaluated chiefly by achievement in math, reading, and science among elementary-age students, as measured by achievement tests. As this research proliferated, confirming studies were conducted in other academic subjects and assessed additional student out-comes. Whereas early studies were limited to elementary-age children, later research involved middle and high school students. As we will see in Chap-ter 10, this initial process—product research has inspired a variety of different research thrusts, all in some way connected with student learning or growth.

The history of research on teaching has been prodigiously summarized in three editions of the *Handbook of Research on Teaching* (1963, 1973, and 1986). Each *Handbook* surveyed the research conducted and knowledge gathered about teaching during its particular time period. N. L. Gage, editor of the first *Handbook,* attempted for the first time to bring together and critique all previous research on teaching. He grouped the studies into such areas as teaching methods (for example, lectures versus discussions), media (for example, films), teachers' characteristics (for example, age, sex, attitude), social interaction in the classroom (for example, relationship between teacher and student), and background (for example, types of homes from which students came). In his preface he observes, "Whatever else it may be, teaching is an intriguing, important, and complex process. Because it is intriguing, it attracts scientific attention. Because it is complex, research on teaching needs many-sided preparation." [1]

R. M. W. Travers, editor of the *Second Handbook of Research on Teaching,* says in his preface:

> At the time when the original *Handbook* appeared, research on the technology of both classroom management and teaching equipment was in its infancy. Sociology had barely begun to have the impact on educational thought that it has today. The term *behavior modification* had not been introduced to educational circles. The name of Piaget was almost unknown to American psychologists. The computer had not extended its terminals to schools. The potential use of educational programs below the level of kindergarten remained largely ignored. In brief, much of what is exciting and interesting in the contemporary educational scene did not exist. [2]

Travers noted that two trends had developed: a technology of education (for instance, programmed instruction, behavioral objectives, structuring of written materials) and the application of ideas from sociology and experimental psychology to education (such as Piaget's stages of development and Skinner's operant conditioning). Many chapter authors of this *Handbook* expressed disappointment that there was not more research for them to write about and that the preceding ten years had failed to produce much knowledge about teaching.

But many changes occurred between 1973 and 1986, when the third edition of the *Handbook of Research on Teaching* appeared. M. C. Wittrock, its editor, was much more enthusiastic in reporting the results of the preceding decade:

> Research on teaching has flourished since the publication of the *Second Handbook of Research on Teaching*. Since then, traditional lines of inquiry matured and emerging areas of research evolved. These old and new areas of research led to chapters in the third edition that have no counterparts in the two earlier editions of the *Handbook*. In addition, methods for studying, observing, and analyzing teaching and thought processes of learners grew and developed.

From these areas of study and methods of research came data that added to our knowledge about teaching and to our interpretations of familiar concepts. In addition to these empirical advances, important conceptual approaches opened lines of inquiry that led to an understanding of the cognitive processes of teachers and learners that mediate the effects of teaching upon student achievement. These recent advances in empirical research, combined with improved conceptualizations, advanced our understanding of teaching and our ability to explain and to demonstrate how teaching can be improved.[3]

Unlike authors of earlier editions, contributors to this third edition had no trouble finding significant research on which to report. Much of this research was conducted in relatively new areas of teaching. For example, the chapter entitled "Teachers' Thought Processes" reported on research that had begun as recently as 1973. Another area that had cropped up since that time was discussed in "Student Thought Processes." Here, researchers started studying student motivation, attention, and comprehension as they related to such factors as time on task, teacher's praise, and reinforcement. For example, teacher's praise seems to influence the attention of many students in the class because by observing the teacher praising one student, other students learn about the teacher's intentions and objectives.

Another relatively new area appearing in the third edition was covered in the chapter "Teaching of Learning Strategies," which looked at the mental processes students go through as they remember information and attempt to understand school subjects. This edition also reported on research in full bloom in the armed services: information is emerging on intelligent computer-aided instruction in which computers try to simulate the learner's processes of responding and learning. In the area of mathematics, studies were looking at the learner's strategies of adding and subtracting. In English, new inroads were being made into the teaching of writing.

Although hundreds of studies had been conducted before 1963, they revealed little about what teachers can do to produce student learning. Over the next ten years, from 1963 to 1973, research on teaching accelerated with the promise of a systematic knowledge base about effective student learning. From 1973 to the mid-1980s, information about effective teaching exploded, propelled by several large-scale federally funded studies such as the Beginning Teacher Evaluation Study. Some researchers date the beginning of our systematic knowledge of effective teaching from Dunkin and Biddle's *The Study of Teaching,* published in 1973.

From the mid-1980s to the late 1980s, both educators and researchers stepped back, pausing to integrate and study the massive findings generated during the prolific 1970s.

# SCENE: THE CLASSROOM

What goes on in effective classrooms? Are activities there any different from those in ineffective classrooms? Are the teachers behaving differently toward their students? These questions are answered in the remaining sections of this chapter.

## Group Shots, Ineffective Classrooms

MS. SMITH   At 9:00 A.M., when the beginning-of-school bell rings, twenty-one of Ms. Smith's twenty-six fourth-grade students are in the classroom. Most are not at their desks but are milling about the room and talking noisily. Ms. Smith calls out above the din, "Everyone, sit down!" With much effort she succeeds in getting most of the children in their seats; however, three students are still standing and talking. The teacher goes to the front of the room and tries to begin a discussion of the previous day's field trip, but few children listen. A few students straggle in at 9:06. Two others leave their seats. The teacher asks the children what they liked about their field trip. Only a few students respond. Several students are not facing the teacher, and others are quietly conversing among themselves. The teacher abandons the discussion and asks a girl to pass out some papers. At 9:09, students are sitting with nothing to do while the teacher talks with some children who have walked up to her desk. At 9:10 the teacher goes to the front of the class and announces that today she will show them something new. Two students are talking loudly, but the teacher ignores them. Three other students leave their seats: one goes to the drinking fountain, one to the pencil sharpener, and one to visit with another child. The teacher displays a definition on the overhead projector and tells students to copy it. Immediately, two students leave their seats to borrow paper, and the noise level in the room increases. About half the students get paper out. The students by the far wall are quiet, but they seem to be ignoring the teacher. One student goes to the closet, another to the pencil sharpener. Ms. Smith calls out, "Everyone, be quiet and get some paper!" Several students call out, "What for?"[4]

MS. JOHNSON   Ms. Johnson carefully discusses her classroom rules and procedures each period on the first two days of class, and students are generally well behaved. However, by the beginning of the second week, problems have begun to occur. While making presentations to the class, Ms. Johnson stands at the front chalkboard to jot down important points. When she turns away from students to write on the board, students at the back of the room begin talking and passing notes. During seatwork assignments, if Ms. Johnson reprimands students for talking, they complain that they don't understand what to do and that they are just seeking help from each other. But when the teacher allows students to help each other during seatwork, by the end of the period everyone is talking, few are working, and the noise level is very high.

During discussion, students at first raise their hands to speak, as Ms. Johnson had requested, but some students occasionally call out answers and comments. Rather than ignoring these responses, Ms. Johnson begins to accept them when they are substantive. Now, as more and more students disregard the hand-raising procedure, class discussions and presentations are

*Making students sit upright in their seats does not necessarily make them*
*more responsive to learning.—Kenneth Dunn and Rita Dunn*

interrupted frequently, and some students become loud and attention seeking. Because discussion activities do not seem to work very well, Ms. Johnson has begun to reduce the amount of time spent on these activities and to
assign more seatwork.

   During seatwork activities Ms. Johnson often sits at her desk checking
papers or helping students who come up to her desk. Most of the students
work at the beginning of the activities, but when some students won't or
can't do the work, they often become noisy and distracting to others. Then
Ms. Johnson has a difficult time getting order restored and returning students to their work.[5]

## Group Shots, Effective Classrooms

MS. AVERY   Ms. Avery designates a section of the chalkboard for listing
seatwork assignments during reading-group instruction. A typical assignment consists of three parts: a reading assignment, workbook pages, and
comprehension questions and activities. At the beginning of the reading pe-

© *Paul Conklin/Monkmeyer Press Photo Service*

riod, Ms. Avery presents directions for any seatwork assignment that is common to all groups. Then she assigns the group she will meet with first a brief "get ready" activity to complete and bring to the reading circle. She gives instructions to the other groups, one at a time, for their seatwork. Each group is told when it can expect to be called and how much progress it should make. Before joining the first group, Ms. Avery quickly walks around the room to be sure each child has begun the seatwork assignment.

When she meets with each group (usually for fifteen to twenty minutes), she sits so she can see the entire class. She scans the class frequently and signals children when necessary to keep them on task. She does so by making eye contact or sometimes calling individual's names softly to prevent or stop inappropriate behavior. Because Ms. Avery does not want students coming to her for help while she is in the reading circle, she has assigned one helper for each reading group. To prevent excessive use of the helpers, Ms. Avery has taught the children to request assistance only for situations that prevent them from doing any work at all. If they can skip the problem or question and proceed with the work, they are to do so and wait for help from her.

As soon as she dismisses a reading group to begin a seatwork assignment, she circulates around the room, checking on student progress, answering questions, helping students, and making sure that students in the most recent group have started their assignment promptly. Checks between groups usually take no longer than five minutes, after which she is ready to call the next group.

If her work with one reading group lasts more than twenty minutes, Ms. Avery plans a short task for them to do independently at some point so she can leave the group to circulate among the students doing seatwork. She reminds students of how much time they have left and encourages those who are lagging behind.

After meeting with all the reading groups, Ms. Avery tells students how much more time they have to complete their seatwork activities. During those minutes, Ms. Avery again circulates, helping and prompting students who are still working and checking the work of students who have finished. By the end of the reading instruction period she has checked everyone's work. If students have not completed one or more of the seatwork assignments, Ms. Avery notes this and talks with them about when they can finish their work during the day.[6]

MR. CARL  As a springboard into a new unit, Mr. Carl decides to use a world map that shows the relative size of countries in terms of their gross national products rather than their physical areas. It is intended to stimulate higher-level thinking in his second-period economics class.

As class begins, Mr. Carl says, "Today we start a new unit, one that will require you to apply what you have learned for the past two months. We have been studying the separate parts of the economy—the roles of the consumer, producer, worker, government, corporations, and labor unions—

and how each contributes to the big picture. Now we are going to change our focus from microeconomics to macroeconomics and begin a study of the interrelationships among the sectors of the economy and the economy's performance."

He continues, "We'll start with some new ideas that contain a puzzle for you to solve." Two students at the back of the classroom glance up at the mention of a puzzle. Mr. Carl shows a transparency of the GNP map and asks, "What do you see?"

The students recognize it as a map of the world but wonder why countries are shaped differently and do not have the accustomed size relationships. Kim comments, "It doesn't make sense."

"The map does make sense if you know the key to the puzzle," replies Mr. Carl. "You can discover that key by asking me questions. But there is a hitch. I will only answer 'yes' or 'no' to your questions."

Trevor begins the questioning: "Why is the United States the largest country on this map?" Mr. Carl reminds the students of the "yes/no" requirement, so Trevor rephrases his question. As questions continue, Mike offers a hypothesis: "Does the map measure the number of cars in the world?"

"Our first proposed solution to the puzzle," comments Mr. Carl. "A good idea! Rather than answering you, I'm going to ask, what further questions could you ask me to test your guess?" Several students offer hypotheses about products such as steel, computers, and wheat. Eventually Pete hypothesizes money as the basis for each country's size. After each hypothesis is tested with more student questions, the solution to the puzzle—the depiction of GNP—is confirmed. Mr. Carl compliments the students on their perseverance and perceptive use of clues. He then defines GNP, gives examples of goods and services included in its computation, and provides statistics supporting relative sizes of countries depicted on the GNP map.

Mr. Carl explains, "We're going to spend the next several weeks on the concept of GNP because it is the most important indicator of economic growth in the United States and is directly related to how well we live." He then poses a problem: "Why are countries south of the 30-degrees-north latitude line smaller than those in the north?"

"They have smaller GNPs," several students respond.

"Right. But why are so many of the small GNP nations located south of the United States?" After a few students suggest reasons, Mr. Carl says, "You have come up with some fine ideas and possible explanations, and we will pursue our inquiry when we learn more about GNP. I have excellent sources for you to check, and I've lined up a guest speaker, an economics graduate student from Brazil, to discuss factors influencing economic growth."

Mr. Carl reviews by asking the students what they have learned about GNP. He gives Chapter 9 of the text as the reading assignment and adds, "I want you to watch or read the news tonight to find out the latest quarter's GNP figures. We will use them when we meet in small groups tomorrow to begin formalizing some possible explanations and start our search for data."[7]

## Some Differences

What are some of our initial impressions from glancing into these four classrooms? First, there *are* differences! Overall, the ineffective classrooms appear chaotic, with teachers fighting for control. Effective classrooms appear orderly, structured, and academically oriented. Teachers are in control, guiding students who are actively engaged in learning experiences. In the

---

## Flexibility

If there is any characteristic a teacher must have, it is flexibility. Beginning teachers frequently express dismay at how often they must adjust and adapt their instruction, carefully and flexibly orchestrating a multitude of classroom events. Nancy is a high school literature teacher who has mastered the ability to respond flexibly to new instructional needs. A highly active teacher, her classroom style employed substantial interaction with her students.

Nancy used a conceptual framework to help students move through several levels in their response to literature: Level 1 involved understanding the literal meaning; Level 2 involved understanding the connotative meaning; Level 3 was the level of interpretation; and Level 4 was the level of application and evaluation.

Nancy used this conceptual framework to guide her own sequencing of material and formulation of questions. She helped her students use this framework to organize their study of the texts and to monitor their thinking. With her depth of subject-matter understanding and teaching skill, Nancy capably organized the material for different levels of difficulty, different kinds of students, and different themes or emphases. Whichever work Nancy was teaching, she understood how to organize it, frame it for teaching, and divide it appropriately for assignments and activities.

One day when Nancy had laryngitis, she divided her class into discussion groups, with each group focusing on a different major character from the novel they were studying. Each group later reported to the class as a whole.

Thus she was able to change her teaching style to fit the occasion.

Nancy's flexible style was evident as she daily adapted to learners' characteristics, the complexities of subject matter, and her own physical condition. If her students experienced difficulties with the subject matter, Nancy stayed at lower levels of her reading-skills framework (for example, helping students understand denotative and connotative meanings, while emphasizing interpretation less). If her students were studying *Huckleberry Finn,* which Nancy saw as less difficult than *Moby Dick,* the students took center stage and taught each other. As Shulman observed,

> Nancy's pattern of instruction, her style of teaching, is not uniform or predictable in some simple sense. She flexibly responds to the difficulty and character of the subject matter, the capacities of the students (which can change even over the span of a single course), and her educational purposes. She can not only conduct her orchestra from the podium, she can sit back and watch it play with virtuosity by itself.

L. S. Shulman, "Knowledge and Teaching: Foundations of the New Reform," *Harvard Educational Review* 57(1) (February 1987), pp. 1–22. Also, S. Gudmundsdottir, *Knowledge Use among Experienced Teachers: Four Case Studies of High School Teaching. Dissertation Abstracts* 49 (1989), p. 3688-A.

less effective classrooms, teachers move quickly to assign students seatwork, then retire to their desks to complete paperwork. Teachers in effective classrooms continually circulate throughout the room, monitor student work, and check for understanding. They are also constantly teaching rules and acceptable classroom behavior, whereas less effective teachers allow disruptive behavior to arise before dealing with it. Teachers in effective classrooms show considerable planning and an ability to head off potential problems. They keep one jump ahead of their students, taking steps in advance to maintain the smooth flow of lessons. In contrast, less effective teachers do not evidence careful planning but appear to engage in spur-of-the-moment activities, often for the purpose of controlling student behavior. They fail to anticipate potential problems—standing around waiting for accidents to happen.

"Wait a minute," you interrupt, "what is the *real* difference between an effective and an ineffective classroom? Is it merely a difference in orderliness and control?"

No, but you are on the right track. We have already defined effective classrooms as those in which high levels of student learning are occurring. We will soon see that student learning occurs best *within the context* of well-managed classrooms. The primary goal of successful classroom managers is student learning, not tightly run classrooms—as desirable as this latter goal might be.

# CANDID CLOSEUPS

In the remaining sections of this chapter we illustrate some of the differences between effective and ineffective classrooms, provide a sample of the growing stockpile of research on teaching, and introduce you to the enormous complexity of teaching.

How can we do this without taking you into actual classrooms? We take a series of snapshots, aiming the camera at various aspects of teaching as they show up in classrooms. To introduce all the aspects of teaching that have been researched would require a great many snapshots, more than we have space for in this chapter. Any single classroom we identify as effective will not exhibit *all* the traits that the research literature has found to be characteristic of such classrooms. Some characteristics are more important at one grade level than another; some are more important for one subject than another; and some are more important for one type of learner than another. Also, our snapshot on any given day may fail to capture one or more important characteristics clearly present on another day.

Accompanying each snapshot, we provide an enlargement, introducing you to research-generated information on the aspect captured by the snapshot. For example, suppose the camera captured Mrs. Klein publicly praising Esther's neat cursive handwriting. The enlargement following this snapshot would introduce you to some of the research-generated information on classroom praise.

This sample of snapshots and enlargements offers you a glimpse of the challenging complexity of teaching. Research-based information of the sort we present can generate hypotheses to be tested in your own classroom.

## Teachers

Let's look first at the teachers themselves, the key figures in effective classrooms. They are capable classroom managers and superbly good teachers.

### SNAPSHOT

"I've got Oldroyd for AP English—didn't you have her last year?"

"Uh-huh."

"What's she like?"

"Well, you know, she's a little deceptive. She doesn't dance on the desk but she sort of gets things out of you. She's low profile, but she's tough. She goes after you. You simply have to work when you go in there. She knows what you're doing all the time. She likes being your friend but she's more interested in how well you're doing. Kids don't knock around in there. No big discipline problems. Class is always full of what she thinks are important things to do—you don't dawdle around. Actually, as I think about it, I worked pretty hard in there."

"Did you like Oldroyd?"

"Well, I guess so. But, I guess what I really liked was the way she connected me to literature. I ended up reading a *lot* of stuff—then I had to write about it."

**ENLARGEMENT** Teachers in effective classrooms are committed to teaching. They enjoy their students and their teaching roles. Reflecting a can-do attitude, they take responsibility for successes and failures in the classroom (in psychologists' terms, they exhibit high self-efficacy and high internal locus of control). Rather than giving up and making excuses for failure, these teachers redouble their efforts, giving slower students extra attention and more individualized instruction. Polite and pleasant with students, they call them by name, listen carefully to what they say, accept their statements of feeling, praise their successes, and involve them in decision making. They are unlikely to ignore, harass, or put down students.

These teachers are more concerned about their students' learning than about being liked; personal needs take a back seat to instructional goals. Though friendly, they are businesslike and task oriented, maintaining a professional teacher–student relationship. Their students are not prone to defy or manipulate. Thus these classrooms are characterized by mutual respect, as opposed to the conflict often found in ineffective classrooms.

By contrast, teachers in ineffective classrooms usually exhibit one of two contrasting orientations: (1) an overriding concern for personal relationships and affective objectives as opposed to cognitive objectives or (2) a pattern of disillusionment and bitterness about teaching, actual dislike of students, and concentration on authority and discipline.

Teachers in effective classrooms are strong managers. Walking into their classrooms, you immediately sense characteristics that tell you this is a well-managed learning environment. Everywhere, students are engaged in high levels of learning activities and low levels of disruptive behavior. Rules and procedures are established at the outset and are effectively maintained. Smoothness and momentum are evidenced in the teacher's clearly presented lessons. Lessons contain variety and challenge but are still appropriate for the students' ability levels.

The teacher consistently holds students accountable for their work; they are monitored both during the lesson presentation and in subsequent seatwork. Students are clear about where they can receive help at any time, and they know what options are available when they finish an assignment. Teachers make few errors in management, such as switching abruptly back and forth between instruction and behavior management, making illogical statements, punishing the whole class for the disruptive behavior of one student, or calling attention to themselves for no apparent reason.

Teachers in these classrooms are likewise effective instructors. They emphasize student achievement as a major part of their role. Well informed about their subject, these teachers effectively structure lesson content to enable students to move smoothly through the curriculum they are expected to master. The classroom operates as a learning environment, with the majority of time allocated to learning, not semirelevant busy work. Teachers effectively match the pace of instruction to the group's needs and respond to unforeseen events and to the needs of individuals.

Firm demands are made of students; they are to work hard and take personal responsibility for their academic progress. Students' freedom and physical movement are structured so as not to disrupt lessons. There is relatively more teacher talk than student talk; still, teachers involve all students in recitation and class discussion, and they wait for students to respond after being asked questions.

## Learning within the Context of Good Management

### SNAPSHOT

"Class, let's review yesterday's assignment—you do remember our assignment on the sonnet? Hank, why do you need to be out of your seat? The same goes for you, Jessica."

"I didn't know we were going to be reviewing that today—it's in my locker."

[*After a few moments.*] "Students, there is too much noise! All you have to do is pull out your homework. Must we make a major production out of this?

*Instruction can no longer be viewed as a static script to be prescribed in advance. Even the teacher's lesson plans are temporary documents that must be modified.*—Gerald G. Duffy and Laura R. Roehler

"Jan and Warren, will you please hold your private conversations somewhere else? Look, you are big people now—act like it.

"All right, who's with me? Let's blaze."

ENLARGEMENT    In the not-too-distant past, "disciplining students" and "controlling unruly behavior" were considered tasks quite independent of classroom instruction: "I've got to get these kids settled down before I can start teaching them anything!" Further, some teachers who considered themselves "effective" were loath to engage in such mundane activities as "running the class." Theirs was a higher and more noble calling. Our knowledge about classroom management and its connection to learning, however, has led to a more enlightened view.[8] One group of authors makes this plain:

> Good classroom management doesn't just happen. Smoothly running classrooms whose students are highly involved in learning activities and which are free from disruption and chronic misbehavior are not accidental. They exist because effective teachers have a very clear idea of the types of classroom conditions and student behaviors that are needed for good learning environments, and because those teachers work very hard to produce such behaviors and conditions.[9]

## Beginning the School Year

SNAPSHOT

"Last year at this time—oh, last year. One giant mistake! If you can believe it, I agreed to go on a camping trip one week before new-year orientation. We got home late Friday night. I could hardly face three days of orientation—meetings that ate up all my prep time. I ended up spending the whole weekend working. Monday morning I was a frazzle. I just hate going into the first week unglued!"

ENLARGEMENT    Year after year, some teachers consistently show more success in producing high student achievement than do others.[10] These teachers get a better start out of the blocks! They come into the first week of teaching on a dead run. Unlike ineffective teachers who wait till the last minute, effective teachers can be found in their classrooms several weeks early, preparing instructional units, new visual aids, and monthly and weekly schedules. When students saunter into class on the first day, the effective teacher is collected, in control, and comfortably anticipating an eventful year (rather than harried, scrambling, and weakly hopeful).

The room has been strategically arranged for smooth functioning and optimal learning:

1.  High-traffic areas are free of congestion. These include group work areas, space around the pencil sharpener and wastebasket, doorways, bookshelves, supply areas, student desks, and the teacher's desk.

2.  Students can be easily seen by the teacher. Since careful monitoring of all student work is essential, clear lines of sight are maintained to all student areas—from both the front of the room and the teacher's desk.

3.  Frequently used teaching materials and student supplies are readily accessible. Easy access to materials allows student work to begin and end on time, and it facilitates smooth transitions between activities.

4.  Students can easily see instructional presentations and displays. Seating arrangements allow all students to see the chalkboard and overhead screen without moving chairs or turning around in their desks.[11]

The first day of class! All of us as students can recall uncontrollable excitement as well as painful anxieties surrounding that first day of class. We couldn't wait to be back again with friends. And we were frightened—of failing, of not being accepted, of untold and indefinable worries. We entered both effective and ineffective classrooms. Let's have a look into an effective classroom.

From the moment students enter, "grooving" begins. Routines are established, along with rules and consequences. Students learn how to complete and turn in assignments, how they will be graded, and what materials should be brought each day. The routines for beginning and ending class periods are established from day one—the best day of the year to help students learn appropriate behavior, course requirements, and standards of work. Plenty of time is taken during these first few days to *teach* rules and procedures—as part of the curriculum!

Expectations are clear. Desirable procedures are demonstrated and rehearsed: how to check out books, participate in class, report on being absent. Course requirements and grades are discussed. Students want and need to know what is expected of them and how they can earn a good grade (or escape earning a poor one).

During the first few days of school, effective teachers plan simple lessons to ensure maximum student success. Students start off feeling optimistic about their ability to succeed. At the year's beginning, whole-class instruction (presenting the same material to all the students at one time) is the most common approach used by the teacher. Breaking down into smaller groups for project work is delayed until later. Seatwork is easy and identical for everyone. Students are kept involved: tasks are interesting and doable with little or no help, success rates are high, the teacher monitors student work, and the potential for disruptive behavior is low. No homework is assigned on the first day. Students leave the room with a feeling of safety, success, order, and predictability. They know what the teacher expects and also have a sense that "Mr. Jex is not going to let me get away with much."

## Rules and Procedures

SNAPSHOT

"Who can see what I have up here in front of me?"

"Some rules!"

"That's right. The first rule says, 'We raise our hands when we want to speak.' Now, Janice, suppose you have something to tell the class. Will you show us how you raise your hand?

"That's very good. See how she held her hand up and waited until I called on her.

"This second rules says, 'When we come into the room the first thing we do is take our seats.' I will demonstrate this rule. Let's say I'm Roger coming to school in the morning. May I be you for a moment, Roger? *[Teacher walks out of the room, then reenters, sitting down at Roger's desk.]*

"Now, I would like Bruce and Jodie to show us how they will come into the room tomorrow when they come to school." *[Class watches as the two go out, reenter, and take their seats.]*

ENLARGEMENT  What would classrooms be like without rules? Almost as calamitous as having rules without consistent consequences! Setting rules is not difficult—even in ineffective classrooms. The transcending challenge is to make certain rules are fair, clearly understood, and tied to meaningful consequences.

Effective classrooms typically have from five to eight rules, suggesting that a few well-thought-out rules are preferable to a litany of specific details. No attempt is made to cover all aspects of the student's behavior, and no unimportant or marginal rules are set forth—only those the teacher feels strongly about and considers essential in achieving his overall goals. Rules can be quite general but are always accompanied by specific examples. Mr. Svendsen posts a sign on the bulletin board in his fourth-grade class: "We do not destroy or damage the property of others." So that all students clearly understand, he walks the class through several instances:

1.  We don't get into another person's desk without that person's permission.
2.  We don't take another person's lunch or coat.
3.  We don't take anything from the teacher's desk without permission.

Notice the negative nature of this rule and its examples. Rules found in effective classrooms emphasize the positive, the "do's." For example, compare Mr. Svendsen's "don't" rule with Mr. MacCallum's "Respect the property of others," followed by applications:

1.  If you find something that has been lost, return it to the rightful owner.
2.  Return all playground equipment to the box after recess or lunch.
3.  Ask permission when you want to borrow things from others.

At the secondary level, we might find a similar set of rules:

1.  Bring all needed materials to class.
2.  Be in your seat and ready to work when the bell rings.
3.  Do not talk or leave your desk when someone else is talking.
4.  Respect other people's property.
5.  Obey all school rules.[12]

At all grade levels, effective teachers are quite explicit about *unacceptable* behaviors; for example, no gum chewing in class and no calling out. Both teachers and students save energy and embarrassment—and sometimes confrontation—by agreeing on, at the outset, what constitutes unacceptable behavior.

Some teachers invite students to participate in forming classroom rules, thereby offering them a sense of ownership and personal responsibility. However, student participation in rule making is not as important as having rules that are clearly understood, fair, and presented on the first day of class.

Procedures or "ways of doing things" are established on the first day of class also. Routines include opening the class period, getting set for work, preparing for recess, handing in assignments, taking tests, asking questions, and interacting with other students. These routines minimize the need for explanation and maximize opportunities for learning. They engender consistency and security in moving through the day's activities. Still, while providing a structure, routines are far from rigid, leaving room for the unique and unusual.

Teachers in effective classrooms give students a clear idea of what they are being required to do. In addition to giving assignments orally, these teachers write them on the board where they are in full view, and ask students to copy them into their notebooks. Grading criteria and requirements for each assignment are explained until completely understood. Due dates are set forth, with exceptions only in unusual cases. Teachers are firm about make-up work, tardy papers, and absenteeism.

Rules and procedures, then, are the avenues by which effective teachers carry out good classroom management.

## Maintaining Good Behavior

SNAPSHOT

"You want to know what Marv's problem is? He gets his kids all revved up on the first day, then peters out. He never follows through. By the third week he's lost the class. It doesn't take kids long to find out he's a patsy, all talk and no action. They run roughshod over him. By Thanksgiving he's got to start over again. Then after Christmas break, he's really got to start over. If he'd just enforce his own rules! I feel sorry for the guy. He makes it a lot harder than it needs to be."

ENLARGEMENT   Being ready at the beginning of the year is not sufficient to sustain good behavior throughout the year. Student cooperation and compliance with necessary rules and procedures must be maintained. Teachers in effective classrooms are not lulled into complacency by good behavior during the first few days of school. Problems are often gradual in their onset, developing over several weeks or months. To maintain appropriate behavior, teachers in effective classrooms monitor carefully and are consistent in following established procedures. They do not ignore inappropriate behavior; rather, they deal with it promptly.

During regular classroom activities, teachers stand or sit so they can see all the students in their classrooms. Their "active eyes" are constantly scanning as they present material and monitor seatwork. Students begin assigned seatwork tasks as whole-class activities, working on the first few problems or exercises as a group under guided practice. During seatwork,

© Alan Carey/The Image Works

the teacher circulates around to all students, not just those who raise their hands. This type of instructional strategy is crucial in letting students know they are being held accountable for good behavior.

## Managing Inappropriate Behavior

SNAPSHOT

"Chad sits in the back of the room—that's the only place I can keep him and my sanity at the same time. I used to try and cope with his uncontrollable she-nanigans, but not anymore. We have this unwritten truce. He doesn't bother me or the students with all his fussing and I don't bother him with assign-ments. It's really a baby-sitting chore at this stage."

ENLARGEMENT   Prompt management of inappropriate behavior is espe-cially important when students show lack of involvement in learning activi-ties, prolonged inattention, work avoidance, or obvious violations of rules. Successful teachers deal directly with these behaviors using low-profile inter-vention: (1) redirecting the student's off-task behavior back onto the task by calling the student by name, (2) making eye contact or moving closer to the student, (3) reminding the student of the rule by restating it, and (4) telling the student to stop the inappropriate behavior.

© R. Kopstein/Monkmeyer Press Photo Service

Inappropriate behavior should be *ignored* when (1) it is of short duration and not likely to persist or spread, (2) it is only a minor deviation, or (3) reacting to it would interrupt the class lesson or call undue attention to the behavior. Examples of behaviors which should probably be ignored are brief whispering, short periods of inattentiveness, and daydreaming.

More serious disruptive behaviors call for an immediate response and long-range strategy. Effective teachers defuse the problem, do not overreact, avoid emotional confrontations, and stay away from power struggles. Some of the more disruptive behaviors that must be dealt with include rudeness toward the teacher, chronic avoidance of work, fighting, aggressive behavior (pushing, slapping, fooling around, pulling a knife!), and defiance or hostility toward the teacher.[13]

## Explicit Instruction

### SNAPSHOT

"What an eye opener. Last year I thought seatwork was the bread-and-butter ploy for getting kids to learn. I'd talk for maybe ten or fifteen minutes, then turn them loose to learn on their own. Well, they were at my desk instantly: 'What are we supposed to be doing?' When they weren't waiting in line at my desk, they were cutting up—never would settle down and get to work. Well, I was pretty naive—no, 'lazy' is the word. I got frustrated. So I started taking charge. I spent more time explaining and then reexplaining. Lo and behold, my kids started paying attention. Now I take them farther down the road by doing most of the teaching myself. It's kind of fun seeing them understand what's going on for a change."

ENLARGEMENT   It's said that if you want someone to learn something, teach it to him—directly. "Explicit" or "direct" instruction occurs when a teacher explains exactly what students are expected to learn, demonstrates the steps necessary to attain the learning, then leads students through each step. Other labels have been attached to this procedure, including "active," "effective," "systematic," "whole-class," and "precision" instruction. Those who espouse this approach to instruction assume that knowing how to learn may not come naturally to all students, especially to beginning and low-ability pupils. Explicit instruction takes students through the steps of learning systematically, helping them see both the purpose and the result of each step.

These are the basic components of explicit instruction:

- setting clear goals for students and making sure they understand those goals
- presenting a sequence of well-organized assignments
- giving students clear, concise explanations and illustrations of the subject matter
- asking frequent questions to see if students understand the work
- giving students frequent opportunities to practice what they have learned.[14]

© *Paul Conklin/Monkmeyer Press Photo Service*

Explicit instruction has been particularly effective in teaching basic skills such as reading and math to children in elementary grades and to lower socioeconomic children who are slow learners. Later studies found explicit instruction to likewise be effective among older and higher ability students mastering complex concepts in various subject areas.[15]

Walking into an explicit-instruction classroom, you note that teachers are active in their teaching, spending time lecturing, demonstrating, or leading recitation or discussions about the lesson. Indeed, you notice considerable teacher talk. Are the teachers talking too much? Some people think so. But research has shown that higher percentages of teacher talk are correlated with higher amounts of student achievement. Even though two-thirds of the talk in the classroom is teacher talk, there is no reason to believe such talk is inappropriate or that it suggests teachers are "oppressive" or unduly dominant.

These teachers devote less time to seatwork than do teachers in less effective classrooms. Yet the effective teachers are more instructionally active during the seatwork time they do have, monitoring and assisting students rather than leaving them to work without supervision. This close supervision of independent work pays off, especially when its results are compared with results in classes in which teachers allow students freedom to meander through nonacademic activities and spend large blocks of un-supervised independent time.[16]

One original purpose of explicit instruction was to increase the amount of time students were "engaged" in learning activities (initially referred to as "time on task"). But simply to increase student "engaged time" is not enough. What students do *during* their engaged time is most critical—their "success rates." Thus, "academic learning time" was defined as that portion of the available learning time (once called "allocated time") in which students were engaged in successful learning activities.

The opportunity to learn a given subject is determined largely by the teacher's choices and by the school's constraints. Great variation exists from class to class and school to school in the amount of time the teacher actually allocates for certain subjects. For example, one teacher might allocate only fifteen minutes per day to math, while another allocates fifty minutes. Over an entire school year, this difference becomes enormous. Using nothing more than total time, we can predict that there will be large differences in math achievement between these two classrooms at the end of the school year. Further, considerable variation exists in the amount of actual engaged time that occurs in classrooms. In some classrooms, students are engaged in academic work only 50 percent of the available time; in other classrooms they are engaged as much as 90 percent.

## Heterogeneous Groups

SNAPSHOT In reviewing her plan for tomorrow's lesson, Mrs. Kumar decides to use a cooperative learning approach with her high school sophomores:

- seven students have reading skills at the fourth-grade level
- several students have excellent writing skills, but most need help with basic punctuation
- four students are social isolates; one arrived from Vietnam last week
- "socials" and "jocks" dominate class discussions while other students sit passively
- ten students seldom turn in any homework; six of these got F's last term.[17]

ENLARGEMENT If the teacher stands there teaching one big group all the time, how in the world can she accommodate individual differences? This is a fair question. Teachers in effective classrooms adjust their managerial and instructional practices to students' ages, academic abilities, and home back-grounds. Highly heterogeneous groups and low-ability groups provide plenty of challenge.

Any grade—third, sixth, eighth, twelfth—contains students with a wide range of abilities and interests. In fourth grade, for example, students often range in math achievement from second- through ninth-grade levels.

In eighth-grade English, students can range from fourth- to twelfth-grade levels in reading and language usage. Abilities in a single classroom can sprawl across five or more grade levels—a challenge to any teacher!

In attempting to meet such diverse needs, effective teachers are not likely to restructure their normal classrooms significantly. Rather, they supplement whole-class instruction with special materials, activities, assignments, and limited use of small groups. They plan a core of assignments that all students must complete, then provide optional activities for higher achievers. Class assignments are flexible and can be completed at different levels. Remedial materials are available for low-achieving students, enrichment materials for early finishers.

During discussion and recitation, *all* students are included, thus guarding against a preoccupation with only high or low achievers. Student accountability is paramount. Using daily information on students' progress, teachers make certain that low achievers work diligently and earn satisfactory grades. As soon as seatwork assignments are started, teachers give these students individual boosting, making sure they are off and running in the right direction.

Still, adaptations like these are often insufficient to handle all problems that arise in widely diverse classrooms—so the teacher engages in small-group instruction. Students are separated out into homogeneous groups representing a restricted range of talent so teachers can better instruct them. Nevertheless, there are inescapable management challenges with small groups: considerably more planning and additional materials are necessary; monitoring student work is difficult when concurrent instruction is taking place in different parts of the room; students spend less time interacting directly with the teacher; and too much time is spent in independent seatwork.

What about the low-ability students that crop up in every teacher's class? These students are typically slow in completing assignments, and they readily become discouraged. They often exhibit apathy or belligerence and engage in excessive clowning. Among these students are found poor reading skills, memory problems, inadequate study skills, and short attention spans.

While maintaining realistically high expectations for these students, effective teachers slow the pace of the lesson, use extra time for explaining, invoke more concrete illustrations, move in smaller steps, wait for students to respond (and make sure they do), and monitor ceaselessly to ensure high success rates during seatwork. Further, drill and practice become the staple of the low achievers' academic diet.

## Transitions

**SNAPSHOT**

"Class, you've had long enough on your experiments. Start putting away your equipment and cleaning your work areas. I'll come around to gather your written discoveries."

"Not fair! We're only half through. Two of us haven't even started on our unknowns."

"Some of you took too long in setting up after the bell—now you're suffering the consequences. Go ahead and clean up." *[Confusion follows: some students clean up, others try forcing their solutions, still others hurry to list properties of their unknowns.]*

"Students, turn now to Chapter 7 in preparation for tomorrow's experiment. Listen carefully. We will be distilling crude oil. You'll need to read pages 143 through 154 tonight and answer the preexperiment questions. Everyone with me? Leonard, Shon, and Michelle, you're still trying to clean up!"

"I'm confused. Are we gonna be able to finish our experiments tomorrow—or do we have to start on the oil project? What pages were those?"

ENLARGEMENT     Transitions are a shifting of gears, a movement from one activity or part of a lesson to another. For example, the teacher determines when students move from reading to social studies, when to shift from lesson presentation to independent seatwork, or when the format alters from whole-class instruction to small-group work.

Students also engage in their own transitions. They switch from engagement in the lesson to daydreaming, from reading the chapter to answering questions about the content, from listening to getting up to sharpen a pencil. By being in control of external transitions, the teacher hopes to control, in part, the student's internal transitions.

Higher levels of inappropriate and disruptive behavior tend to occur during transitions. When these happen, valuable academic time is lost. Once started, inappropriate behavior spills over into the activity following the transition.

Effective classrooms exhibit smooth transitions, with students shifting from one activity to the next with minimal disruption and loss of time. Ineffective classrooms exhibit large amounts of disruption during transitions for some of the following reasons: lack of readiness by teacher and students for the activity following the transition (the teacher starts into a math unit while trying to locate a felt pen for the overheads); unclear student expectations about appropriate behavior during transitions ("I didn't know we couldn't go get a drink!"); and faulty procedures ("I should have known better than to allow the kids to wander to the library unaccompanied—you can bet that next time they'll be marching three abreast!") [18]

## Teachers' Expectations

SNAPSHOTS

"Anton, I know you can do good work in my class. I have read over your records from the fourth and fifth grades. Your test scores show that you're very good in math and that your reading is improving. Both your teachers said you did excellent work. I'm happy to have you in my class, and I'll expect you to keep up that good work."

"I've got Donald Cascade in my sixth-period geometry. Anybody want to swap? Here we go on the roller coaster! I had his older brother, Harry, about three years ago. Talk about trouble! Every day, that kid came in sporting a different mood. One day he was sullen; the next day he was off the wall, higher than a kite. If he felt okay, you couldn't keep him quiet—Mr. All-American Student. On bad days I half expected him to pull a knife and threaten everyone. I can see it all now—Donald, the carbon copy."

ENLARGEMENT    Teachers' expectations are predictions teachers make about the future academic success (or failure) of a student. A self-fulfilling prophecy is one type of expectation. In a typical self-fulfilling prophecy, the teacher expects a student to perform in a new and uncharacteristic manner—then treats him in a way that encourages the fulfillment of that expectation. For example, Ms. Deveau expects Cameron, a very average reader, to read like a superstar by the end of the year. She places him in the accelerated reading group, provides extra reading help, and enters into a contract with Cameron to read a book every three weeks for additional credit. Cameron does not ultimately read like a superstar, but he reads at a much higher level by year's end.

At times a teacher may inadvertently engage in behavior that sustains the student's behavior at the teacher's current level of expectation. For example, Ms. Deveau expects Janet to continue with her characteristically poor performance and quite unknowingly assigns her simpler reading material and allows her to hand in shoddy assignments. Sure enough, Janet's test scores remain low.

Teachers treat their students differently according to their expectations. When interacting with students for whom they have low expectations, teachers call on them less often, wait less time for them to respond, provide them with answers more quickly, criticize them more often for failure, praise their successes less frequently, pay less attention to and interact with them less frequently, seat them farther away, and demand less of them.

Teachers' expectations do cause students to achieve at higher (or lower) levels than they might have done otherwise—but not to the outlandish extent educators once believed. Further, effects of expectations do not occur in all classrooms, and there is great variability in the size of these effects when they do occur. Whether or not they occur and how powerful they will be depends very much on the teacher.

Expectations tend to be self-sustaining; that is, they have a way of prompting teachers to be on the lookout for what they are expecting and less likely to notice what they are not expecting. For example, if Mr. Padia is expecting Mauricia to be quiet, perceptive, and supportive of his teaching approach, he will be watching for evidence to confirm his expectations. And he hardly noticed her noisy display last Thursday in the hall, her misunderstanding of yesterday's assignment, and her seeming lack of interest in playing "Superbowl." Teachers tend to act in ways that are consistent with their expectations. For example, if Randy is perceived as a low achiever, Mrs. Cume almost unconsciously acts in ways to perpetuate his low-achieving status. She may have given up on Randy and, as a consequence, accepts his failures. She and Randy become locked in a circle of futility that maintains itself: Mrs. Cume's behavior causes Randy to fall even further behind, and this in turn reinforces her already low expectations of him.

All teachers quickly form attitudes and expectations about various students at the beginning of the school year. Effective teachers have realistically high expectations for *all* their students. These expectations are based on and influenced by the student's academic performance more than by any other single factor. And these teachers remain alert, current, and flexible, allowing new information to alter their expectations when appropriate.[19]

## Lesson Planning

SNAPSHOT

[Four teachers, collaborating during an inservice workshop, engage in conversation.] "This unit on California history is incredibly out of date! I can't believe we've let it go so long. Let's divide up the chores. Two of us could pull together what's been happening in the state over the past five years; the other two could begin updating the supplemental readings. Also, we need to come up with better questions for each subunit—they're too simple for eighth- and ninth-graders. It's hard to believe teachers haven't been up in arms before now."

ENLARGEMENT   Effective instruction contributes to good classroom management. Students are kept involved in learning activities; confusion, failure, frustration, and boredom are minimized. Teachers spend considerable time thinking through and organizing their lesson materials. Information is thoughtfully sequenced, as are enabling activities such as discussions, question-and-answer sessions, seatwork, and checking for understanding. Several activities are planned for each class period and are optimally arranged for high student involvement and wise use of available time.

## Lesson Presentation

SNAPSHOT

[Mrs. Barlocker thinking to herself.] "I'll start out the 'Gas Exchange' unit with this on the board: 'People native to high altitudes have more alveoli and blood vessels in their lungs than people native to low altitudes. They also have a higher red blood cell count (70 percent of the blood volume instead of the normal 45–50 percent).'

"I think I'll start with a question to get a discussion going—something like this: 'Why do we have pressurized cabins in commercial aircraft?'

"But then where do I go from there? Shall I start talking about the relationship between breathing, respiration, and oxygen? Maybe I'd better get into examples of high-altitude mountain climbers—kids would like that—I could even talk about Sherpas."

*Colleen looked like a different teacher during that lesson. Her interactive style evaporated. In its place was a highly didactic, teacher-directed, swiftly paced combination of lecture and tightly controlled recitation: Socrates replaced by DISTAR. I sometimes refer to such teaching as the Admiral Farragut style, "Damn the questions, full speed ahead." Students were not given opportunities to raise questions or offer alternative views. After the session she confessed to the observer that she had actively avoided making eye contact with one particular student in the front row because that youngster always had good questions or ideas and in this particular lesson Colleen really didn't want to encourage either, because she wasn't sure of the answers. She was uncertain about the content and adapted her instructional style to allay her anxiety.—Pamela Grossman*

ENLARGEMENT   In effective classrooms, teachers present instruction in small installments, making certain each step is mastered before moving on to the next. They move at a brisk pace but stop frequently to assess student understanding. Key concepts, new terms, and major points are all under-

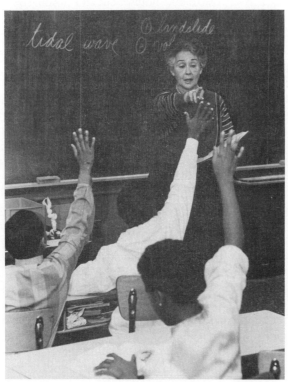

© *David M. Grossman/Photo Researchers, Inc.*

scored by being written on the board or overhead. Relevant illustrations are provided; vague expressions and verbal time fillers are avoided.

Here is an example of a general model of effective instruction:

1. Review and check of previous day's work (and reteaching, if necessary)
2. Presentation of new content/skills
3. Guided student practice (and check for understanding)
4. Feedback and correctives (and reteaching, if necessary)
5. Independent student practice
6. Weekly and monthly reviews.[20]

This sequence provides for a minimum of transitions, allows for checking of and feedback on yesterday's assignment, and includes an introduction of new material with a chance to practice it under the teacher's guidance.

In presenting new content, effective teachers often follow the rule-example-rule pattern. First they present the general rule or principle, then a series of examples of the rule, and finally a restatement of the rule. In addition to teaching the content itself, effective teachers teach accompanying study habits, such as how to take notes, read and summarize segments of the textbook, and review previously learned material.

Teachers in effective classrooms have certain dispositions as they work through a sequence resembling the one in the model. They tend to be "high structuring," "high soliciting," and "high reacting."

High structuring of lessons includes reviewing the main ideas and facts covered in the preceding lesson, stating objectives at the beginning of the new lesson, outlining lesson content, signaling transitions between lesson parts, indicating important points, and summarizing parts of the lesson as it proceeds.

A high-soliciting teacher asks approximately 60 percent higher-order questions (nonfactual questions that require something other than a memorized response) and 40 percent lower-order questions (factual questions requiring a simple memorized response). These teachers usually wait for students to respond, often up to three seconds. Low-soliciting teachers ask only about 15 percent higher-order questions and as much as 85 percent lower-order questions, and they call rather quickly on a second student to respond if the first fails to do so.

A high-reacting teacher praises correct responses, negates incorrect responses (and gives the reason for their incorrectness), prompts the student by providing hints when responses are incorrect or incomplete, and writes correct responses on the board. Conversely, a low-reacting teacher gives neutral feedback following a student's correct response, negates incorrect responses (usually without giving any reasons), and keeps repeating the same question without giving any hints.

Overall, teachers in effective classrooms structure lessons through clear presentations, systematic review, and corrective feedback to student responses.

# Recitation

SNAPSHOT

"Okay, class, put away your books. We have fifteen minutes left for review before the bell. I'll ask most of the questions that will appear on tomorrow's test. I want quick answers. If a person doesn't know, or pauses, up they stand! After someone else gives the right answer, I'll come back to the first person with the same question. Be on your toes. I want this stuff down pat!

"Ready? Who were the major leaders of the Tory Party before it became the Conservative Party?"

ENLARGEMENT    The word *recitation* conjures up images of early American one-room schoolhouses. Overall-clad students, standing before the teacher, spewed out endlessly boring bits of information. In the modern effective classroom, recitation plays a vital role in reviewing and correcting previously learned material. Teachers ask a large number of questions in a short period of time, moving from student to student for verbal replies. Students listen to other students' answers and to the teacher's acceptance or rejection of a given answer. Through this procedure, material tentatively learned is fixed correctly and firmly in the mind while material previously learned is overlearned to reduce forgetting. Not only can teachers check for student understanding in a very short period of time but they can detect weaknesses in their presentations and use of examples.

# Clarity

SNAPSHOT

"You'll love Mrs. Amada. You know what you're supposed to be doing every minute. She's easy to listen to—short and to the point. Good teachers do that—you can understand them. I get so mad when Mrs. Reuben stands there just mumbling along. I swear she thinks no one is in the classroom. We just sit there. Then there's old Willoughby in algebra. He's got this big booming voice that is totally incomprehensible! It's like he never thinks about what he's going to say before he says it. He can't explain one thing clearly. We all wait till the assignment, then read the book to see what we were supposed to be learning."

ENLARGEMENT    Clarity, more than any other factor in presentation, is responsible for student learning. Effective teachers communicate information and directions in a clear and comprehensible fashion. What factors contribute to clarity? One author lists the following:

1.   Information to be presented is organized into a coherent sequence, one that students can easily follow.

2. An adequate number of good illustrations is included in the presentation.

3. The teacher uses precise and concrete language.

4. The teacher is in touch with how well students understand the material being presented.

5. The teacher provides students with enough practice to ensure mastery.[21]

On the other side of the coin, vague language used by the teacher obstructs clarity:

> This mathematics lesson *might* enable you to understand a *little more* about *some things* we *usually* call number patterns. *Maybe* before we get to *probably* the main idea of the lesson, you should review *a few* prerequisite concepts. *Actually,* the first concept you need to review is positive integers. *As you know,* a positive integer is any whole number greater than zero.

Clarity is further impaired by use of "mazes." Mazes are false starts or halts in speech, redundantly spoken words, or tangles of words, such as the following:

> This mathematics lesson *will enab* . . . will get you to understand *number, uh* number patterns. Before we get to the *main idea of the,* main idea of the lesson, you need to review *four conce* . . . four prerequisite concepts. The first *idea,* I *mean, uh,* concept you need to review is positive integers. A positive *number* . . . integer is any whole *integer, uh,* number greater than zero.[22]

Still another impediment to clarity is discontinuity, or off-the-wallness. We have all had teachers who interrupt the flow of the lesson by interjecting (or allowing) irrelevant information or by going off on a tangent:

"We've been talking about metaphors. Recall that a metaphor is a figure of speech in which the name of an object is used in another context for comparison purposes. Yesterday I gave you several examples. Can you remember any? Okay, Beth?"

"Evening of life!"

"Well, that's pretty good."

"Yeah, it's like the night before the Superbowl!"

"Hm, an interesting application, K.C. By the way, who's everybody betting on?"

"The Broncos!"

"No chance. Washington's personnel are . . ." *[Finally, after ten minutes, the discussion comes back to metaphors.]*

Clarity is not an easy skill to develop. New teachers are forced to unlearn lazy speaking habits, replacing them with simplicity, straightforwardness, and authority. Clarity is a most critical skill—start practicing it now.

# Pacing

**SNAPSHOT**

"Oh, I'm just dying in this class! Today I almost did! Quigley was telling those jokes—those dumb jokes that nobody laughs at. I just about raised my hand and said, 'Can't we get going!' But I chickened out. You'd think we're a bunch of sixth-graders. He explains, then reexplains, then asks if there are any questions. Everybody understood the first time. Everybody's so tired of his rehash. Nobody says anything."

**ENLARGEMENT**  Teaching in America's classrooms shows immense variation. In one class, students "ho-hum" their way through the hour; in another, class members gasp at the breakneck pace of the instructor. Within a single class, fast students chafe at the bit while slow students struggle to keep up with the presentation.

"Pacing" refers to the fit between the rate of presentation of information and the students' ability to comprehend it. Teachers in well-paced classrooms work to ensure that adequate time is available for the lesson they are presenting. During the lesson, they demonstrate constant with-it-ness—an awareness of students' rate of comprehension—then adjust their rate of instruction to match it. Effective teachers tend to be brisk in their pacing, ensuring high success rates (and therefore low frustration), always pressing for continuous progress. There is an artistry in pacing. One author describes the effects of superb pacing:

> Classroom lessons "move along" more effectively when teachers and pupils are in tune with each other, in much the same way as a conductor and an orchestra, working cooperatively to interpret and perform a piece of music. Each player needs to be heard from at some point in the performance, and different sections of the orchestra are highlighted in different compositions. The music to be performed should be well within the technical capacity of the musicians, and although the tempo will vary from piece to piece, it should never be so fast that some musicians are unable to keep up, nor so slow that others become inattentive and lose their place in the score. The skillful teacher (conductor) thus leads the class (orchestra) to perform harmoniously, as well as to sharpen their skills with every performance.[23]

# Checking for Understanding

**SNAPSHOT**

"I've always found it hard to press on until the kids are with me. But I have to laugh. Last year was my first year teaching and I used to say, 'Everyone understand?' Well, when you say that, kids just sit there and look at you. How naive

© Elizabeth Hamlin/Stock, Boston

of me. I thought fourth-graders would raise their hands when they didn't understand."

ENLARGEMENT    In an effective classroom, the teacher checks her students' degree of understanding *during* a lesson presentation, knowing what is happening along the way rather than waiting until the journey is completed. She likes things zipped up as she goes. Students are usually unwilling to interrupt the lesson flow with "I don't understand" or "I'm lost!" Rather than do so, they bail out or quietly struggle on in a confused state. Then, when Mr. Lamb gives the seatwork assignment, the confused are first to his desk: "I don't understand what we're supposed to do." Translated, this means, "I got lost during your presentation."

Knowing this can happen, effective teachers constantly extend their feelers, getting inside students with short questions and strategic pauses—anything that prompts students to reveal their thought processes at a given moment. You can often observe these teachers asking students to demonstrate their understanding of the concept or skill to the class. For instance, they may follow a routine like this: "Students, I want each of you to work through this problem I have written on the board. I will be around to look at your work and your answer. Everyone begin." Not only does this process confirm the students' correct understanding of the computation skill but it unearths confusion and incorrectness. Based on her sweeping survey of the students' papers, the teacher either starts reteaching or is comfortable in assigning seatwork. She does *not* assume that stumbling through a set of practice exercises will reveal to the student the correct calculation process; rather, she takes responsibility for conveying the idea directly.

## Teachers' Questions

SNAPSHOT

"Katrina, in filing a claim against a vendor for lost or damaged merchandise, what information would you have to know?"

"I dunno."

"Come now, I mentioned it yesterday and you've read it in your chapter. You *have* read your chapter, haven't you?"

*[Before Katrina can respond, Clair blurts out.]* "Method of shipment and purchase order number!"

"Clair, surely you see I want Katrina to respond. In this class we raise our hands when we want to talk. You might as well go ahead now and finish telling us."

ENLARGEMENT   The tired controversy rages on:

"Too many teachers ask only factual questions. Students need questions that will make them think and analyze."

"Well, that's an overstatement. You can't get away from the importance of learning factual material. How would kids ever survive in the world without a repertoire of facts?"

Teachers are forever being pressed to ask "higher-order" questions—questions that require more than a factual or "yes/no" answer, questions that make students "think." In summarizing the research in the area of questioning, a U.S. Department of Education publication, *What Works,* reveals the value placed on higher-order questions:

Student achievement rises when teachers ask questions that require students to apply, analyze, synthesize, and evaluate information in addition to simply recalling facts.

But questions take different forms and place different demands on students. Some questions require only factual recall and do not provoke analysis. For example, of more than 61,000 questions found in the teacher guides, student workbooks, and tests for 9 history textbooks, more than 95 percent were devoted to factual recall. This is not to say that questions meant to elicit facts are unimportant. Students need basic information to engage in higher level thinking processes and discussions. Such questions also promote class participation and provide a high success rate in answering questions directly.

The difference between factual and thought-provoking questions is the difference between asking: "When did Lincoln deliver the Gettysburg Address?" and asking: "Why was Lincoln's Gettysburg Address an important speech?" Each kind of question has its place, but the second one intends that the student analyze the speech in terms of the issues of the Civil War.

Although both kinds of questions are important, students achieve more when teachers ask thought-provoking questions and insist on thoughtful answers. Students' answers may also improve if teachers wait longer for a response, giving students more time to think.[24]

Whether a teacher ought to be asking lower-order or higher-order questions depends primarily on the teacher's objectives for a particular unit. The most sensible answer is, "It depends on what you are trying to accomplish." If a teacher's objective is for students to know about the culture of the British Isles, then lower-order questions are appropriate. If to analyze the cultural changes in the British Isles resulting from World War II is the objective, higher-order questions are more suitable. Regardless of which side of the fence you come down on, considerable research knowledge exists about how effective teachers ask questions, a topic to which we now turn.

Teachers in effective classrooms ask more questions than teachers in ineffective classrooms. Further, fewer students fail to respond, and fewer incorrect answers are given—70 to 80 percent of the teacher's questions are correctly answered. When students do come up with incorrect answers, effective teachers are twice as likely to provide "process" feedback, as opposed to merely giving the correct answer; that is, the teacher explains *why* the answer is incorrect. Rather than, "No, that's not right, Juanita," the teacher goes on, "No, Juanita, that is incorrect; the reason the gas fails to expand is because of the pressure that compresses the gas molecules." When a student is unwilling or unable to respond, the teacher "stays with" her, providing hints and clues in order to evoke at least a partial response. Once some sort of answer is given, the teacher helps the student improve the response. Response probing is most helpful for low-achieving students who may be anxious or lacking in self-confidence, even when they know the answers. However, teachers do not keep probing high-achieving students when they are unable to answer the question. These high achievers would respond if they could, and when they cannot, pumping serves no useful purpose.

Effective teachers use a high percentage of direct and factual questions, since they are usually checking for understanding of clearly presented lessons and want high incidences of correct answers. It is important that when students are confused, teachers revert to reexplaining, rather than merely providing a correct answer to the question or continually repeating it.

Asking a large number of answerable questions to assess understanding and confirm new learning is a most important use of questions—more important than whether the teacher asks low- or high-level questions or what type of feedback she provides.

## Wait Time

SNAPSHOT

"Now, one of my favorite strategies is to throw out a question and then stand and wait. At first, it seemed like a pedagogical eternity! I thought the roof would cave in with all the silence. But you know what? Kids paid *more* attention than when I was talking."

*Whatever else the teacher may do for his students, he must first of all
awaken, arouse, startle into thought; he cannot assume that they have his
interest in the subject, or that his presence automatically eliminates boredom
and daydreaming.—Houston Peterson*

"So, what difference does it make?"

"Well, take Gerand. He gives one answer and I don't say anything. He starts
feeling like it's not good enough, so he starts justifying it. He sits there building
his own case. It's not a bad one, either."

**ENLARGEMENT**   We have seen that effective teachers ask questions as a
method of quickly reviewing previously learned material, checking student
understanding, and confirming newly learned material. For these reasons,
they tend to ask plenty of factual-type questions (lower order). But what if
they have other goals in mind, such as the development of a student's ability
to analyze, synthesize, and evaluate? Quite a different strategy of questioning is now appropriate, one that affords ample wait time. Effective teachers
are skillful users of wait time. "Wait time" refers to the interval between
when the teacher asks a question and when the student answers the question—the time that elapses while the teacher waits for something to happen
("She's just standing up there waiting for me to answer. What is she waiting
for? Why doesn't she go on—or do something!"). Another wait time is the
interval after the student's initial answer and before the teacher replies ("I

© *Steve Skloot/Photo Researchers, Inc.*

gave my best answer and she's just looking at me—I wonder if I said the right thing. I wish she'd tell me it's right or wrong!").

Wait time, at strategic points in the lesson, is one of those *seemingly* insignificant teacher actions that make a substantial difference in the classroom. Somehow students receive a special message when a teacher engages in wait time: "Looks like it's my turn to talk. I'd better get back in the ball game and come up with something profound. He's looking right at me."

The research shows that when a teacher increases her wait time from the typical one second up to three seconds or longer (a change appearing almost inconsequential), beneficial effects occur:

1. Students provide more extended responses to the teacher's question.

2. A greater number of students jump in and offer unsolicited, but appropriate, responses.

3. Fewer students who are asked to respond fail to do so—more students get into the act.

4. Students who offer responses feel more confident as they do so.

5. Students throughout the room are willing to engage in more speculation.

6. Those who offer responses tend to provide more evidence for their statements.

7. More students tend to compare their evidence against that given by a classmate.

8. The students themselves ask more questions.

9. More "slow" students get into the act.

10. Students begin to show greater variety in the kinds of responses they give.[25]

An effective teacher uses rapid-fire questions for some purposes and wait-time questions for other purposes. His effectiveness comes in knowing when to use which.

## Class Discussion

### SNAPSHOT

"I remember when I first started teaching, trying to get kids involved in discussions. What a disaster! Third-graders are 'tellers' and 'answerers' but not 'discussers.' Well, I had to get smart to survive. I learned to keep discussions very short, no more than five to seven minutes. I made sure the class was ready before turning them loose. I presented the story and talked about it myself for a while first. Then I kept my questions simple. It took a long time before those kids started listening to each other. They all wanted to carry on their private conversations with me—right in front of the class."

**ENLARGEMENT** Class discussion is that amorphous activity in which new teachers engage with abandon, and seasoned teachers with caution. Discussions usually take the form of a teacher-led whole-class activity. The stated purposes of discussion are to encourage students to clarify the basis for their judgments, to evaluate events, topics, or results, and to become aware of other points of view. In reality, discussion is often a momentary dialogue between the teacher and a single student while others wait.

There is absolutely no shooting from the hip in effective classrooms: teachers carefully plan their discussions. For these teachers, discussions are neither mere time fillers nor substitutes for thoughtful preparation. Rather, they are important vehicles to achieve objectives that can be attained only through this medium. Since discussions cannot be sustained very long, teachers plan short ones, then work to facilitate their maximum effectiveness by being nonevaluative and clarifying and by allowing students to exchange judgments and opinions in a free and safe atmosphere.

# Seatwork

**SNAPSHOT**

"I used to think seatwork was the best way students learned—dig it out for themselves. Not any more. They probably learn more when I'm talking than when they're studying at their desks. Turning students over to handouts used to help fill up the time. Now I have to work harder. Kids don't really learn that much from seatwork. The only value of seatwork is to let kids practice what they already know. If they don't understand it, they'll be hounding me at my desk. Then I have to do a replay for every student who comes to me. I always lose my slow kids during seatwork. They flit about."

**ENLARGEMENT**  Too often, seatwork has been abused and overused in classrooms. For some teachers, seatwork represents a passport to survival: "Being able to take a break at my desk while kids are working is my only respite." When used properly, seatwork serves the purpose of successfully practicing tenuously acquired skills. Seatwork is not meant to be an activity in which students chew their pencils as they struggle to learn new material on their own.

In effective classrooms, the percentage of seatwork time is usually less than 50 (whereas in ineffective classrooms it often runs as high as 90). Assignments are well matched to students' abilities, and students are not released to work on their own until they have experienced high levels of understanding. Success rates during seatwork must be very high. Research has shown that firming-up learning occurs best when seatwork success rates are 90 to 100 percent for young and low-achieving students and about 70 to 80 percent for high achievers.

During seatwork the teacher has "active feet," moving from one student to another. She accurately diagnoses stumbling blocks, offers remedial help, then moves on, spending no more than about thirty seconds with any one student. Because the material has been thoroughly explained, most students require little help. Slower learners are the first ones visited once the

© *Photo Researchers, Inc.*

assignment has been made. Everyone knows where to go for help. In this way, teachers can successfully individualize their efforts within the context of whole-class instruction.

## Homework

**SNAPSHOT**

"I never do homework for Edwards' class, because he never reads it. I used to. All I ever got was a red check on my paper. It's a farce—a bunch of busy work that means nothing. He must think he earns his money by assigning homework—probably salves his conscience. There's absolutely no rhyme or reason to what he does. He comes to class, talks for fifteen minutes, makes the assignment, then says, 'If you don't finish, take it home. Have it ready for tomorrow.' The next day he walks into class without the foggiest recollection of what he assigned the day before."

**ENLARGEMENT**   On the average, American teachers say they assign some ten hours of homework each week—about two hours per school day. But high school seniors report that they spend only four to five hours a week doing homework, and 10 percent say they do none at all or have none assigned. In contrast, students in Japan spend about twice as much time studying outside school as do American students.

Homework continues to be a grudging activity for both student and teacher. Neither welcomes the idea of extending the school day by carrying schoolwork home, either to do it or to grade it. But for all its unpopularity, carefully planned and regularly assigned homework increases student learning. When low-ability students do just one to three hours of homework a week, their grades are usually as high as those of average-ability students who do not do homework. Similarly, when average-ability students do three to five hours of homework a week, their grades usually equal those of high-ability students who do no homework.[26]

In effective classrooms, homework boosts student achievement because it increases total learning time. To be sure, time is not the only factor in learning, but little can be achieved without it. Well-designed homework does more than supplement classroom lessons; it teaches students to become independent learners. Homework gives students experience in following directions, making judgments and comparisons, analyzing material presented in class, and developing responsibility.

Effective teachers relate homework assignments directly to classwork to extend learning beyond the classroom. They carefully explain and discuss assignments, listing them on the board or overhead. Students are taught that

© *Kagan/Monkmeyer Press Photo Service*

homework is an integral part of their instruction and a significant factor in their course grade.

## Praise

SNAPSHOTS

"Good job, Javier. I like the way your paragraph shows a beginning, middle, and end, all hanging together."

"Your answer is correct, Damon."

"Class, you have done so well that I'm awarding everyone a night off from homework."

"Students, look at Melinda's paper. She always does such a neat job with her lettering. Can you all do it as she does?"

ENLARGEMENT   Times are changing, and so are praising practices. Not many years ago, teachers-to-be were taught to praise, praise, praise—if a little was helpful, more was even better. Nothing was more motivating, thought teachers, than to hold up for display the work of high achievers: "Class, I thought I'd show you how detailed this book report is that Marie

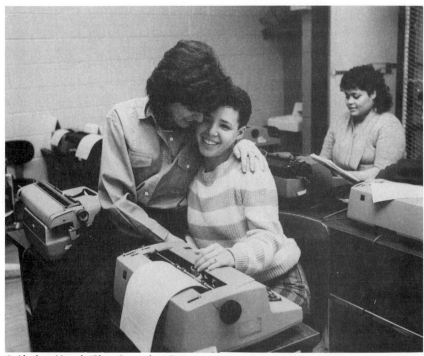

© *Abraham Menashe/Photo Researchers, Inc.*

has handed in." Horrors! Marie, whose history is one of high achievement and recognition, withers in her seat—not from pleasant embarrassment but from frustration. She has spared no effort in her quest for acceptance by the "in" group, the leaders of whom just happen to be in her section of sophomore English. High achievement, frankly, is not their bag. And now this. Mrs. Simpkin's well-intentioned accolades loom as one more hurdle for Marie to overcome.

How is praise at work in effective classrooms? Both less praise and less criticism are found in these classrooms than in ineffective classrooms. These teachers know that praise too easily earned or too difficult to earn loses its motivational effect. Praising a student in front of the class is straightforward, low key, infrequent, and aimed at the student's academic performance rather than personal qualities.

Effective teachers tend to praise elementary children somewhat differently from the way they would high school students, and high-achieving students differently from low-achieving students. With high-achieving students, effective teachers invoke challenges and high expectations, offering only occasional and symbolic rewards such as comments and marks on handed-back papers. In contrast, teachers producing the most achievement gains from low-achieving students provide gentle and positive encouragement rather than challenge or demand. Likewise, young children are praised more often and provided more concrete rewards (such as stars or tokens to be exchanged for pencils); older students are praised less frequently and, perhaps, less exuberantly.

No single praise or reward remains effective over the entire nine-month school year, so effective teachers use variety while selecting rewards that do in fact have meaning and reward value for their students. Reward procedures, at all levels, are kept simple and do not take too much time and effort to administer. The most prevalent rewards, of course, are grades. Successful teachers tie as many facets of the student's work as possible to the grade: in-class assignments, homework, extra-effort work, end-of-chapter exercises, quizzes, and attendance.

Some types of praise, though well intended, backfire. The vacuous or thoughtless "That's good" or "How nice," especially when delivered in an insincere or uninterested manner, is a way of brushing students off and is so perceived by them. Overdramatized praise is equally offensive to students. Students tend to be rather realistic about their accomplishments. They make good reality checks on their work by comparing it with that of other students. They react with skepticism when a teacher gushes with something like, "Isn't that wonderful!" Students see this as overdone and are often embarrassed by it (and embarrassed for the teacher!). Teachers offering too much praise, or overly effusive praise, may find themselves in two kinds of trouble. Students become jealous of other students and hostile toward the teacher. Or they start demanding more praise, no longer satisfied with ordinary amounts. Throughout this whole transformation, the teacher's credibility erodes.[27]

Praise given by effective teachers can show a number of important characteristics:

1. It is offered only when students do something well.

2. It specifies what, exactly, the student did well (e.g., "I like the way you brought your story to a close within the given time limit.").

3. It is spontaneous, shows variety, and is directed to the student's performance rather than to the student generally.

4. It is aimed at the student's having met the performance criteria set down by the teacher (e.g., "Camille, since you played that piece in a 'technically correct manner,' you receive the five points possible.").

5. It provides information about the value of the accomplishment (e.g., "The reason I awarded you all ten points is because you met both criteria: clarity and originality.").

6. It helps students learn to appreciate and value the behavior that earned them the praise (e.g., "I'm getting so I value the language skills I'm learning.").

7. It uses the student's prior accomplishments as a context for describing the present accomplishments (e.g., "At the beginning of the school year, you showed average coherency in your written stories; now your stories are very tight and easy to follow. You have made good progress in your ability to write with an easy-to-follow flow.").

8. It is given to recognize both effort and success in achieving difficult tasks (e.g., "Completing a two-week class project is a difficult thing to do. You have worked hard and have completed it within the time I allotted you.").

9. It honors the student's effort and ability, implying that similar success can be achieved in the future (e.g., "Being able to memorize all our vocabulary words tells me you work hard and have good ability. You should be able to do the same thing on the next unit.").

10. It makes the student believe that he has expended effort on a task because he enjoys it, or because he wants to develop the skill (e.g., "It is obvious that you have put in many hours on your table. You must enjoy woodworking.").

11. It focuses the student's attention on the behavior that was relevant to the task (e.g., "You had to have read up on human cell division in order to write such a clear explanation of the reproductive process—nice going!").

12. It fosters an appreciation of the skills acquired after the task has been completed (e.g., "I learned a few things about how to create simple computer programs from that assignment. I'm happy to have these skills, minimal as they may be.").[28]

## Criticism

**SNAPSHOT**

"Jared, you have three marks on the board. One more and you stay in for recess the rest of the week."

"Daisy, I wanted desperately to give you an A, but you blew the final. You are one of my favorite students and I know how hard you work—but that's the way the cookie crumbles."

"Nicholas, what do I have to do to get you to stop talking in class? I'm about ready to ship you out. It's one thing to sit there daydreaming, quietly, but it's another to be cutting up all the time. You're a thorn in my side. I've tried everything I can think of—time now to bring out the cannons."

ENLARGEMENT    Criticism of a student, especially in front of the class, is not often observed in effective classrooms. Teachers know that when criticism is excessively harsh or used too frequently, the teacher places herself in opposition to the students—and invites parents' criticism! In effective classrooms, criticism is more often directed at the student's misbehavior than at his academic work. For high-achieving students, private criticism of academic performance—on an occasional basis—is often motivating, but not as much as simply challenging them. Effective teachers rarely criticize low achievers for their poor academic work. Rather, they are likely to provide realistic expectations, tutorial help, and honest praise for academic progress. Effective criticizing works on the same principle as effective control of disruptive behavior: low-profile intervention. In simple terms, effective teachers do not bring out a cannon when a rifle will win the day. With misbehavior, using eye contact or moving in the proximity of the disruptive student is preferred over a public chiding. Likewise, a simple directive to improve one's neatness on written assignments is more motivating than criticizing sloppiness.[29]

## Assessing Management and Learning

SNAPSHOT

I don't like giving tests. They don't measure the important things, anyway. I can tell who's learning and who isn't. How they look during class, and what they say, and what they do on homework assignments—I know. Even after the first week I know. Sizing up students, especially after you've had considerable experience doing it, is pretty easy. Take this class, for example. I can tell you right now that Aaron, Clarice, and Justine will get the top grades. Dianne, Kevin, and Nina will be my low achievers—I can just tell.

ENLARGEMENT    We know that teachers in effective classrooms are constantly monitoring to ensure high levels of student learning and low levels of disruptive behavior. These teachers are masters at assessment, at finding out how well their management strategies are working and how well their students are learning. They gather feedback—actively.

In assessing their own management practices, these teachers key in on a number of factors, including the amount of off-task, disruptive, and cooperative behavior, the extent to which students follow (or disregard) class rules, their behavior during transitions, and their completion of assign-

*All teachers experience a moment of truth, a moment of great joy or bitter disappointment. It is the moment when teachers check their students' understanding. Did they or didn't they understand what was taught to them?*—David Berliner

ments. In assessing students' progress, they use a variety of devices, including quizzes, seatwork and homework assignments, questions, standardized tests, informal conversations, participation in class discussions, and parents' comments.

Effective teachers not only are good planners but are skillful in making midcourse adjustments. On the basis of actively acquired feedback, they make informed decisions about changes that will improve management and learning, and then they exhibit the professional security and commitment to enact the improvements.

## IMPLICATIONS FOR YOU, THE TEACHER

Our purposes in this chapter have been (1) to introduce you to effective classrooms, (2) to sample research knowledge about teaching, and (3) to acquaint you with the complexity of teaching. Considerable research has been conducted on teaching, and from that research a systematic body of knowledge is emerging. No longer can teachers say, "Well, teaching is an art, and each person has to learn to do it his own way." To be sure, some aspects of teaching are and will always be artistic. Nevertheless, a scientific basis for teaching is now developing, and we hope this chapter has given you a sense of its scope and depth.

You have the potential to tap productively into this research-based knowledge. But be forewarned. Do not falsely conclude that you can make direct and easy application to your classroom, lock, stock, and barrel. The large body of research on effective teaching, only sampled in this chapter, shows a *linkage* between certain types of teacher behavior and certain types of student achievement. These linkages are "contextual"; that is, they have been found in certain settings, such as the teaching of reading at the elementary level and the teaching of math at the junior high level. Further, there is a difference between teaching high and low achievers, and between teaching younger and older students.

Although specific findings *tend* to generalize across grade levels and subjects, we still do not have principles applicable in all settings. We suggest you view this research-based knowledge as hypotheses to try out rather than as a set of "do this" prescriptions: as a general guide to nutrition rather than a recipe book.

# CONCLUSION

Just as there are effective schools, there are effective classrooms. Teachers in these classrooms engage in activities that clearly boost student learning. But this kind of teaching, done well, is strikingly complex:

> Although it may be true that most adults could survive in the classroom, it is not true that most could teach effectively. Even trained and experienced teachers vary widely in how they organize the classroom and present instruction. Specifically, they differ in several respects: the expectations and achievement objectives they hold for themselves, their classes, and individual students; how they select and design academic tasks; and how actively they instruct and communicate with students about academic tasks. Those who do these things successfully produce significantly more achievement than those who do not, but doing them successfully demands a blend of knowledge, energy, motivation, and communication and decision-making skills that many teachers, let alone ordinary adults, do not possess.[30]

Effective classrooms are out there, waiting to be created. We invite you to the challenge.

## Expansions

1. What are advantages and limitations of defining effective teaching in terms of increased student achievement in basic skills?

2. Comment on this statement: "Besides my teaching, there are so many factors that affect how well my students learn that I don't hold myself overly responsible."

3. Visit with two experienced teachers. Ask each to describe what for him or her is an "effective classroom." Find out if their concepts of effectiveness have changed over the years. If so, why?

4. How much credence do you place on research knowledge as compared with your own experience? Explain.

5. Describe how you would set up your classroom management system to incorporate principles of "effective" classrooms.

6. Explain this statement: "Learning occurs best within the context of a well-managed classroom."

7. Can you present a case for and against ability grouping?

8. Describe methods you will use in praising students.

9. From your point of view, how could teaching be considered both a science and an art?

10. Research portrays effective classrooms as highly structured, well organized, and tightly managed. Suppose your teaching style is laid back, unstructured, and plan-as-you-go. Still, you want to run an effective classroom. How might you resolve this dilemma?

11. What do you think makes teaching such a complex activity?

## Notes

1. N. L. Gage (Ed.), *Handbook of Research on Teaching,* American Educational Research Association (Chicago: Rand McNally, 1963), p. v.

2. R. M. W. Travers (Ed.), *Second Handbook of Research on Teaching,* American Educational Research Association (Chicago: Rand McNally, 1973), p. v.

3. M. C. Wittrock (Ed.), *Handbook of Research on Teaching,* 3rd ed. (New York: Macmillan, 1986), p. ix.

4. Adapted from C. M. Evertson, E. T. Emmer, B. S. Clements, J. P. Sanford, and M. E. Worsham, *Classroom Management for Elementary Teachers* (Englewood Cliffs, N.J.: Prentice-Hall, 1984), p. 18.

5. Adapted from E. T. Emmer, C. M. Evertson, J. P. Sanford, B. S. Clements, and M. E. Worsham, *Classroom Management for Secondary Teachers* (Englewood Cliffs, N.J.: Prentice-Hall, 1984), pp. 95–96.

6. Adapted from Evertson et al., *Classroom Management,* pp. 48–49.

7. Adapted from R. Kindsvatter, W. Wilen, and M. Ishler, *Dynamics of Effective Teaching* (New York: Longman, 1988), pp. 195–199.

8. W. Doyle, "Classroom Organization and Management," in M. C. Wittrock (Ed.), *Handbook of Research on Teaching,* 3rd ed. (New York: Macmillan, 1986), pp. 392–431.

9. Emmer et al., *Classroom Management,* p. xi.

10. J. Brophy, "Stability of Teacher Effectiveness," *American Educational Research Journal* 10 (1973), pp. 245–252; T. Good and B. Grouws, *Process–Product Relationship in Fourth-Grade Mathematics Classrooms,* final report, National Institute of Education Grant NIE-G-00-3-0123 (Columbia: University of Missouri, College of Education, 1975); idem, "Teaching Effects: A Process–Product Study in Fourth-Grade Mathematics Classrooms," *Journal of Teacher Education* 28 (1977), 49–54.

11. Adapted from Emmer et al., *Classroom Management,* pp. 1–13.

12. Adapted from Emmer et al., *Classroom Management,* pp. 22–23.

13. Evertson et al., *Classroom Management,* pp. 100–106.

14. J. Brophy and T. L. Good, "Teacher Behavior and Student Achievement," in M. C. Wittrock (Ed.), *Handbook of Research on Teaching,* 3rd ed. (New York: Macmillan, 1986), pp. 328–375; B. Rosenshine and R. Stevens, "Teaching Functions," in M. C. Wittrock (Ed.), *Handbook of Research on Teaching,* 3rd ed. (New York: Macmillan, 1986), pp. 376–391.

15. W. J. Bennett, *What Works: Research about Teaching and Learning* (Washington, D.C.: U.S. Department of Education, 1986), p. 35; V. Richardson-Koehler

(Ed.), *Educators' Handbook: A Research Perspective* (New York: Longman, 1987), pp. 211–212.

16.    E. Ramp and W. Rhine, "Behavior Analysis Model," in W. R. Rhine (Ed.), *Making Schools More Effective: New Directions from Follow Through* (New York: Academic Press, 1981); J. Stallings and D. Kaskowitz, *Follow Through Classroom Observation Evaluation 1972–1973,* SRI Project URU-7370 (Stanford, Calif.: Stanford Research Institute, 1974).

17.    Adapted from Kindsvatter, Wilen and Ishler, *Dynamics,* p. 244.

18.    Adapted from Emmer et al., *Classroom Management,* pp. 117–119.

19.    T. L. Good and J. E. Brophy, *Looking in Classrooms,* 4th ed. (New York: Harper & Row, 1987), pp. 116–161.

20.    Rosenshine and Stevens, "Teaching Functions," p. 379.

21.    Adapted from Emmer et al., *Classroom Management,* p. 119.

22.    L. Smith and M. Land, "Low-Inference Verbal Behaviors Related to Teacher Clarity," *Journal of Classroom Interaction* 17 (1981), 37–42.

23.    G. Morine-Dershimer and B. Beyerbach, "Moving Right Along . . . ," in V. Richardson-Koehler (Ed.), *Educators' Handbook: A Research Perspective* (New York: Longman, 1987), p. 219.

24.    Bennett, *What Works,* p. 38.

25.    Adapted from M. B. Rowe, "Wait Time: Slowing Down May Be a Way of Speeding Up!," *Journal of Teacher Education* (January/February 1986), pp. 43–50.

26.    Bennett, *What Works,* p. 42.

27.    Adapted from Good and Brophy, *Looking,* pp. 197–198.

28.    Adapted from Good and Brophy, *Looking,* pp. 238–241.

29.    Good and Brophy, *Looking,* pp. 216–304.

30.    Brophy and Good, "Teacher Behavior," p. 370.

# CHAPTER 10

# STUDYING TEACHING

*What we learn from all this research is that teaching is enormously complex, demanding, and uniquely human.—William J. Bennett*

**MAIN IDEAS**

• The actual teaching process is being studied ever more deeply; new and provocative concepts are emerging.

• Current areas of research relating to the teacher include teachers' views about their careers, norms of acceptable behavior, and teaching frustrations and satisfactions.

• Other areas include how teachers make pedagogical decisions, relationships between teachers' thoughts and actions, teachers' planning, teachers' thoughts and decisions while interacting with students, and teachers' theories and beliefs.

• Current areas of research relating to the student include students' learning strategies, students' thought processes, and students' learning within specific subject areas.

• Other research deals with aspects of classroom life, the teaching of specific subjects, and the teaching of special learners.

• On the basis of current research findings, teachers and researchers are beginning to adapt their instruction in a wide variety of ways.

# INTRODUCTION

In Chapter 8 we introduced you to some of the research knowledge about effective schools, and in Chapter 9, about effective classrooms. In this chapter we acquaint you with other important areas in which teaching is being studied. Many fresh and provocative concepts have emerged since the mid-1970s. We regard with considerable respect the new and growing body of knowledge about the art and science of teaching. In sharing it with you, we hope you will begin to identify with the teaching profession, where deep and critical thinking is occurring and new frontiers of knowledge are being explored. We hope, too, that you will feel more responsibility to grow with the profession even more than have teachers of the past.

We'll show you some new areas of research and thought about teaching, as well as some traditional areas in which study is taking new directions. You'll see how teachers view themselves and their careers, the thought processes of teachers and students, strategies students use in their learning, aspects of classroom life, and the teaching of specific subjects and special types of learners.

# INSIDE THE TEACHER'S MIND

Research offers us a window into teachers' minds, revealing some of the views they hold about their teaching lives and the kinds of things that go through their minds when they are trying to teach.

## Teachers' Views of Teaching

Jerrett Shaughnessy, an attorney, chats with LaMar Olsen, a veteran teacher, during a parent–teacher conference:

"I've never understood why our society continues to pay teachers such poor salaries. Why don't you all just get up and walk away? That would get everybody's attention! Take up arms, or something like that. Teachers' unions could do it."

"Unions are getting pretty powerful. We've got to do something. Too many teachers are leaving the profession. But on the other hand, it's been hard for people on the outside to see how life really is for teachers. Personally, I've never had the time to try changing things. And to tell the truth, I haven't felt all that exploited anyway. I guess all these years I've seen myself as kind of a missionary—teaching young minds how to think. I like to see myself helping youngsters grow up feeling good about themselves and other people."

*Is teaching so much an art, and are classroom situations so unique and complex, that professional knowledge as we know it is useless in setting problems and designing solutions?*—*Virginia Richardson-Koehler*

There has been a major shift in the study of teachers. Historically, researchers have observed teachers in their classes doing the multitude of things they do, recording their actions and how those actions affect students. Recently, attention has turned to the private world of teachers: What is going on inside their heads and their hearts? For example, researchers are interested in such questions as these: What are teachers' beliefs about their teaching careers? What kind of knowledge do they possess about teaching? Under what conditions do they think learning best occurs? What are their values about honesty, homework, and study habits? By seeing teaching from an insider's view, researchers can tap the practical wisdom of teachers for insights that will help improve the practice of teaching.

This personal knowledge the teacher possesses, his beliefs and his values, all make up his teaching *culture*. This culture is, in a sense, the internal makeup of the teacher, and it guides what we see him doing in the classroom. Researchers are asking, What do we know about the culture of a teacher? How is this culture acquired?

Other questions related to the teacher's culture are these: From a teacher's point of view, what norms guide "proper and acceptable teaching behavior"? What do teachers see as the frustrations and satisfactions of teaching? How do teachers view their careers? How do teachers make pedagogical use of the practical knowledge they gain in the classroom?

As we discussed in Chapter 3, teachers are aware of norms for interacting with students, other teachers, principals, and parents. An example of a teaching norm is, "The teacher is an authority figure in her classroom and acts accordingly." Another norm is, "A teacher forms personal bonds with students." Here we see a possible contradiction between norms: forming personal bonds with students may conflict with being an authority figure; teachers feel a need to maintain professional distance in interacting with their students, yet find themselves drawn into close friendships.

What do teachers see as frustrations and satisfactions of teaching? On the minus side, they see a low salary, a lower status than that of other professionals, a tarnished image, and disrespectful students. On the plus side, they see students learning, gain daily satisfactions in working with students, and enjoy a comfortable work schedule.

In the area of how teachers view their careers, perceptions are changing. Historically, teachers tended to see themselves as members of an in-and-out profession; they taught for several years, then left to marry and raise a family. More recently, an image of continuity has emerged. Teachers tend to stay in the profession for a longer period of time, marrying and having children along the way. The majority do not expect vertical advancement, such as moving from the classroom into a principalship. Most continue on as generalists, but some are moving toward specialization in such areas as reading, music, and European history.

Teachers are strong on practical experience, using it to define goals, give shape and meaning to their daily teaching, structure activities, reduce tensions, simplify classroom life, and formulate "rules of practice." For example, from her experience, a teacher develops the following rule for dealing with a learning-disabled student: "He has my full attention *after* I finish all the instruction."[1] Rules of practice are formulated for the amount of unstructured talk allowed, how students are to take notes, how they are to prepare for exams, how they are to turn in homework, and what they are to do during seatwork. These and other rules emerge from a teacher's concept of how good teaching ought to be done.

What produces these norms of teaching behavior? Why do they persist from year to year? The classroom context itself determines much of a teacher's "standard" behavior. For example, the pressure of everyday teaching forces a teacher to act in certain ways in keeping attendance, evaluating students, correcting homework, starting and ending classes, and providing individual help.

The complexity of classroom life and the multitude of constantly occurring events force teachers toward simple explanations and practical solutions and invites them to resist change. The physical layout of the school and the principal's style of administration also affect a teacher's behavior. For example, the cellular construction of a school keeps the teacher working in some degree of isolation; the principal's frugal policy on use of school supplies curtails her creation of lavish bulletin boards.

As we indicated in Chapter 1, experienced colleagues and the school system itself exert a powerful socializing effect on the novice teacher, defining for him the norms of teaching behavior. Indeed, the body of research literature in this area has led educators to view the new teacher as a passive agent, buffeted by socialization forces beyond his control. But recent work suggests that this pressure may not be as strong as heretofore imagined. Apparently, new teachers *interact* with the socializing forces, not only adapting to the school but influencing the school by their presence.

Phases of change during a teacher's career have also been studied. Generally, a teacher's initial concerns revolve around sheer survival. These soon give way to concerns about being able to control the class. Finally, instruction and impact concerns take over: How is what I'm doing affecting my students? Varied models of teacher development and change have been set forth, outlining the teacher's ego, moral, and conceptual development during different phases of her career. According to one model, a mature teacher is characterized by "increased flexibility, differentiation of feelings, respect for individuality, tolerance for conflict and ambiguity, the cherishing of interpersonal ties and a broader social perspective."[2]

The teaching culture varies from school to school and is enormously powerful in shaping the teacher's life. The technical skills you learn while in your teacher education program (for instance, how to organize a classroom, how to conduct smooth transitions) will be part of your repertoire of emerging skills. The teaching culture of your school will amplify your current repertoire.[3]

## Teachers' Thought Processes

> Hmm. I'm surprised I was so defensive today. When Reba started challenging me on *King Lear,* I got a little uptight and started overstating things. Actually, I made one or two comments that weren't quite accurate—but I had to show the kids I was up on Shakespeare. I'm sure they felt I was caught a little off balance. Tomorrow, it'll be different. We have two scenes to go. This time, I'll ask for *their* interpretations first. Then maybe they won't be so quick to challenge me.

In attempting to describe the mental lives of teachers—what is going on inside as they prepare and teach—researchers have focused on teachers' thinking, planning, and decision making. *Life in Classrooms* was one of the first studies to describe the thought processes that underlie teachers' behavior.[4] This and later research has revealed the enormous complexity of teaching and the need to understand a teacher's thinking to account more fully for the happenings in a classroom. A select panel on teaching, commissioned by the National Institute of Education, emphasized the important role of teachers' thought processes in understanding teacher behavior:

> It is obvious that what teachers do is directed in no small measure by what they think. Moreover, it will be necessary for any innovations in the context, practices, and technology of teaching to be mediated through the minds and motives of teachers. . . . The question of the relationship between thought and action becomes crucial.[5]

How do researchers "get inside" teachers to "observe" their thoughts? They use various methods. In one procedure, a teacher is asked to think out loud as she plans a lesson. Another method is stimulated recall, in which each segment of a videotape of classroom interactions is played back and the teacher comments on what was in her mind during that period. Another is a journal: the teacher keeps a personal record of her planning and thoughts, writing down why she took one course of action rather than another during her teaching.

Figure 10-1 is one example of a model showing the interaction between the teacher's thoughts and his or her observable acts in the classroom. The teacher's thought processes (left circle) are broken down into three parts: (1) teacher planning (preactive and postactive thoughts), (2) teachers' interactive thoughts and decisions, and (3) teachers' theories and beliefs. Teachers' interactive thoughts and decisions occur during classroom interaction with students. Teacher planning may occur before (preactive thoughts)

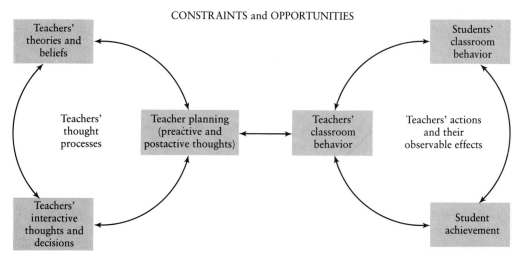

*Figure 10-1    A model of teachers' thoughts and actions* (C. M. Clark and P. L. Peterson, "Teachers' Thought Processes," in M. C. Wittrock (Ed.), *Handbook of Research on Teaching,* 3rd ed. (New York: Macmillan, 1986), p. 257.)

or after (postactive thoughts) classroom interaction. The teacher's actions (right circle) affect students' behavior and ultimately their achievement. Teachers' thoughts affect their actions, and vice versa. Likewise, both thoughts and actions are affected by the constraints and opportunities in the working environment.[6] Let's examine each aspect of the teachers' thought processes.

## Teachers' Planning

Research suggests that teachers become involved in several types of planning, including yearly, term, weekly, long-range, short-range, and unit. They spend considerable time thinking about how to organize and use time effectively; still, much planning is never written down.[7] Written lesson plans seldom reflect the teacher's entire plan, since "lesson images" reside in teachers' minds. These images usually guide the teacher, although even these are largely abandoned when activity flow is threatened with disruption. Further, teachers incorporate routines in their planning as a means of simplifying the complexity they face.[8]

Teachers give a multitude of reasons for their planning, including (1) to meet their own needs (for example, reducing anxiety, finding a sense of direction), (2) to become familiar with the material they will teach, (3) to collect and organize materials, and (4) to improve the quality of student learning.

Research reveals that teachers tend not to use those planning models learned in their preparation programs. For example, a widely described model is that developed by Ralph Tyler. This and its later versions generally consist of four planning steps: (1) specify objectives, (2) select learning activities, (3) organize learning activities, (4) specify evaluation procedures. In actual practice, teachers do not follow this pattern. They are more likely to focus heavily on learning activities; goals are less frequently included in lesson planning, and evaluation hardly at all.

Less-experienced teachers plan differently from veterans. The former are preoccupied with daily lesson plans. Experienced teachers are less systematic in their planning, and they focus on an entire week rather than on the fine details of each lesson. Also, as interactive teaching begins between the teacher and students, the teacher's previously made plans move into the background and interactive decision making takes over.

## Teachers' Interactive Thoughts and Decisions

Researchers are interested in the thinking that goes on, both while teachers interact with their students during classroom teaching and when they reflect on it afterward. Studies suggest that few teachers think about their objec-

---

### Those Who Understand, Teach

"He who can, does. He who cannot, teaches."

With these words, appended to his play *Man and Superman,* George Bernard Shaw set teaching in a dubious light. Lee Shulman questions, "Is Shaw to be treated as the last word on what teachers know and don't know, or do and can't do?" Working with colleagues on a large-scale research program called "Knowledge Growth in Teaching," Shulman says, "We reject Mr. Shaw and his calumny. With Aristotle we declare that the ultimate test of understanding rests on the ability to transform one's knowledge into teaching. Those who can, do. Those who understand, teach."

How does learning *for* teaching occur? First, Shulman is asking questions about the teacher's knowledge base: What are the sources of the teacher's knowledge? What does the teacher know and when did he or she come to know it? How is new knowledge acquired, old knowledge retrieved, and both combined to form a new knowledge?

Second, his group is asking questions about how teachers use this knowledge: How do teachers take a piece of text and transform their understanding of it into instruction that their students can comprehend? Where do teachers' explanations come from? How do teachers decide what to teach, how to represent it, how to question students about it, and how to deal with problems of misunderstanding?

Shulman and his colleagues are tracing what they call teachers' biographies—that set of understandings, conceptions, and orientations that constitutes the source of their comprehension of the subjects they teach. "We must pay as much attention," Shulman argues, "to the content aspects of teaching as we have recently devoted to the elements of teaching process. Additionally, we must learn how content knowledge and pedagogical knowledge are related."

L. S. Shulman, "Those Who Understand: Knowledge Growth in Teaching," *Educational Researcher,* February 1986, pp. 4–14.

tives, most give some thought to the subject matter being taught, and many have thoughts that center on the instructional process itself:

"After I had explained it to her, I thought, 'I didn't make that very clear.'"

"I was thinking that they needed some sort of positive reinforcement."

"At that point in the lesson I felt I was reviewing what we had already talked about yesterday."

But most teachers' thoughts focus on the learner:

"I was also thinking, 'Tricia's kind of silly right now. If I ask her, I probably won't get a straight answer.'"

"I expected him to get that."

"You can't always tell with kids whether they're truly inattentive or whether they're just mulling over what has been going on."

Teachers continually engage in interactive decision making: "They weren't too sure yesterday, and they had problems with this stuff, so I thought I would go back and ask what the problems were. So with Laura and Steve, you know, I specifically asked them a question to see if they understood what we did yesterday." [9] Figure 10-2 illustrates one kind of interactive decision-making model. It explains alternative "routes" teachers may take in making their interactive decisions. [10]

On the basis of the thoughts going through their minds, teachers make interactive decisions about every two minutes. During decision making, effective teachers seem to "chunk" information; that is, they group small bits of information into larger categories. They also differentiate among categories of information in terms of their immediate and long-term significance. Both of these activities simplify the complex classroom environment. In contrast, by not categorizing, and therefore not simplifying the information, the ineffective teacher develops a cognitive overload.

## Teachers' Theories and Beliefs

Teachers hold implicit theories about their work: what good teachers do, the role of curriculum in student learning, students' needs and feelings, classroom rules, and student involvement. We introduce, briefly, one of these implicit theories, called *attribution,* in which teachers assign *causes* to students' behavior. To what causes do teachers attribute students' behavior? [11] Teachers often ask themselves such questions as these: "Am I largely responsible for my students' failure to learn these math concepts? Are the students primarily responsible? Is our rather cryptic math text responsible? Are the students failing because we don't allocate enough time to math?"

Some teachers attribute their students' failures to themselves as teachers, and their students' successes to the efforts of the students. Conversely,

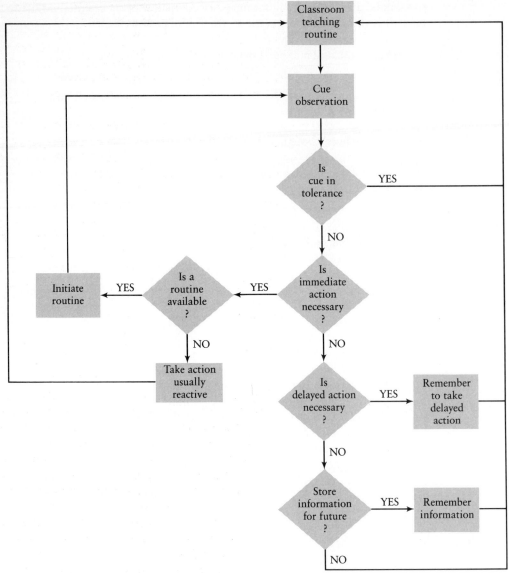

*Figure 10-2   A model of teachers' interactive decision making* (R. J. Shavelson and P. Stern, "Research on Teachers' Pedagogical Thoughts, Judgments, Decisions, and Behavior," *Review of Educational Research* 51 (1981), p. 482.)

other teachers attribute their students' successful performance to their efforts as teachers, and their students' failures to the students' own inadequacies.

Research on attribution has important implications. If teachers refuse to accept responsibility for students' successes *or* failures, seeing little relationship between their own behavior and their students' performance, they will be less likely to work to improve their teaching. Many factors, such as the student's sex, race, and social class, influence the teacher's attribution of causes. For example, a teacher might say, "All my Japanese students are tops in math—no wonder Kyoko is right up there." If a teacher holds the student responsible for his lack of learning, she tends to give him different feedback from what she would if she blamed herself or some other factor. For example, "Linc, I realize you did poorly on the test, and that's probably my fault. Your essay responses missed what I really wanted from you. But then, I'm afraid I made my questions too general."

Not surprisingly, educators and researchers are paying ever more attention to teachers' thought processes. Findings are rapidly substantiating the complexity of teaching and of the teachers' reflections about that complexity.[12]

# INSIDE THE STUDENT'S MIND

## Students' Thought Processes

Why can't I get this stuff? She's going too fast, that's why! I can't take good notes. Maybe I'll try something different. I know! I'll outline the chapter first, then take it to class. That should help me navigate a bit—at least I'll have some idea where she is. What if it doesn't work? I'm dead.

© Steve Takatsuno/The Picture Cube

In Chapter 9 we looked at the relationship between teacher behaviors and student learning. This early process–product model (teacher behavior–student learning) has turned out to be incomplete. More recent thinking has extended it by including the *mediation* that occurs between the teacher's behavior and the student's achievement. To mediate means to go between, to moderate or alter something. A student's thought processes mediate the teacher's instruction; you could say that they act as a middleman in the student's learning transaction. There are two links in the mediating process: the first link is between the teacher's behavior and the student's thought processes; the second is between the student's thought processes and the student's learning. The critical variable, then, is the student's thought processes; they determine how much learning will actually take place.

Let's look at two examples of mediation at work. Recall our discussion on the self-fulfilling prophecy. If a teacher has high expectations for a student, then acts to fulfill those expectations, that student's achievement tends to be higher than it would have been had there been no such expectations. But this result does not always happen. Why? Because the student's thought processes mediate. For example, the student may not *perceive* the teacher's expectations as actual expectations. Or she may see them as expectations, all right, but not directed toward her.

In another example, mediation operates in the area of teacher praise. Recall from our earlier discussion the common belief that praise tends to increase learning. But this is not always the case. Why? Mediation. A high-ability student, receiving praise for success on an easy task, may not see it as praise at all! But, a young, low-achieving child responds eagerly to the same praise.

Mediation also affects motivation, that process of initiating, sustaining, and directing a student's activity. We look once more at attribution, this time from the student's point of view. To what do students attribute their success or failure in school? Is it primarily their own effort that they see as responsible for their success? Or is it their inherent ability? Or is it the way their teacher taught? Students are more motivated to learn if they attribute success or failure to their own effort than to forces over which they have little control, such as luck or their teacher's teaching. If they attribute success or failure to forces outside themselves, they will be less motivated to try, because they cannot or do not see that their efforts contribute to their success. Thus, success alone is not enough to sustain motivation. Success must be perceived by the student to be caused, at least in part, by his own effort.

Your students generate their own meaning from your instruction, meaning that mediates their achievement—and this phenomenon opens up a whole new world of complexity in teaching.[13]

## Learning Strategies of Students

"Give a man a fish, and he eats for a day; teach him to fish, and he's fed for life."

For many years, teachers have entered the classroom with an overriding goal in mind: to help students learn the subject matter and teach them basic skills. Historically, society has been well served by this goal. But with the explosion of knowledge and its changing nature, teachers need a further goal: to teach their students *how* to learn. Students today must develop learning and thinking skills, in addition to knowing French, the names of the continents, how to multiply, and Boyle's gas law. One educator has described this need for students to learn how to learn:

> It is strange that we expect students to learn yet seldom teach them about learning. We expect students to solve problems yet seldom teach them about problem solving. And, similarly, we sometimes require students to remember a considerable body of material yet seldom teach them the art of memory. It is time we made up for this lack, time that we developed the applied disciplines of learning and problem solving and memory.[14]

Partly in response to this impetus, researchers have been exploring such areas as the learner's prior knowledge and what he thinks about during the learning process, or, more technically, his "cognitive processing." "Learning strategies" can be defined as the behaviors and thoughts the learner engages in during the learning process. Thus, we focus on the way he selects, acquires, organizes, and integrates new knowledge. For example, a learner may form mental linkages in memorizing the major exports of Venezuela; repeat in her mind the facts she has just read in a paragraph; fit "whales" into the larger concept "mammals"; outline on paper the major points of an essay on declining markets; reorder pieces of information about the Fall of the Roman Empire; review the mechanical steps required to "boot up" a computer system; coach herself about reading each question carefully on the test; and talk herself out of feeling anxious about taking a Spanish exam.

The cognitive approach to learning seeks to understand how incoming information is processed and structured in the memory. With the emergence of cognitive psychology, we now have a more sophisticated view of human learning:

> The cognitive approach has changed our conception of the teaching–learning process in several ways. Instead of viewing learners as passively recording the stimuli that the teacher presents, learning is viewed as an active process that occurs within the learner and which can be influenced by the learner. Instead of viewing the outcome of learning as depending mainly on what the teacher presents, the outcome of learning is supposed to depend jointly on what information is presented and on how the learner processes that information. Hence, there are two different kinds of activities that influence the encoding process: (1) teaching strategies, such as the teacher presenting certain material at a certain time in a certain way; and (2) learning strategies, such as the learner actively organizing or elaborating or predicting about the presented material.[15]

The complete teaching/learning process has many elements, some of which are these:

*Teacher characteristics,* including the teacher's background, values, beliefs about teaching, knowledge of the subject matter, and knowledge of principles related to teaching

*Teaching strategies,* including the teacher's performance as it relates to what is presented, when it is presented, and how it is presented

*Learner characteristics,* including the learner's background, values, prior knowledge of the subject matter, and his repertoire of learning strategies

*Learning strategies,* including behavior the learner engages in and his ability to select learning strategies from his repertoire and effectively use those that are most appropriate for the subject matter

*Encoding process,* including internal cognitive processes that occur during learning, such as how the learner selects, organizes, and integrates new information

*Learning outcome,* the newly acquired knowledge

*Student performance,* including performance on achievement tests and ability to apply the new knowledge and skills to in-life situations.[16]

One of these elements, student learning strategies, has received considerable attention. Here is an example of how these strategies can be classified:

REHEARSAL STRATEGIES FOR BASIC TASKS  The student repeats, over and over, information she is trying to memorize: the order of the planets from the sun; the names of the B vitamins; the order in which Shakespeare introduces the characters in *Hamlet.*

REHEARSAL STRATEGIES FOR COMPLEX TASKS  The student copies, underlines, or "shadows" (repeats aloud) the material presented in class. The strategy here is to select the material to be learned and then to learn it.

ELABORATION STRATEGIES FOR BASIC TASKS  The student forms a mental image or sentence to link together material to be committed to memory: a sentence that links the name of a state with its major agricultural products; a mental image of a scene depicted by a poem.

ELABORATION STRATEGIES FOR COMPLEX TASKS  The student paraphrases, summarizes, creates analogies, generates notes, and creates and answers his own questions. The goal is to integrate new knowledge with prior knowledge: an analogy between the operation of a computer and a post office; a relationship between the structure of simple molecules and that of complex molecules.

ORGANIZATIONAL STRATEGIES FOR BASIC TASKS  The student groups or orders items from a list or section of text: organizing foreign-language words into different parts of speech; creating a chronological list of the events leading up to the signing of the Declaration of Independence; group-ing bus, van, and truck into the category "vehicles."

ORGANIZATIONAL STRATEGIES FOR COMPLEX TASKS   The student reorga-nizes material in some meaningful way: outlines a passage of reading; cre-ates a hierarchy by pulling out main and subordinate ideas; creates a dia-gram showing the relationships among stress forces in a structural design.

COMPREHENSION-MONITORING  STRATEGIES  (METACOGNITIONS)   During the learning process, the student checks for his own failure to comprehend or his success in comprehending: using a self-questioning checklist to see if he understands the material he just read; using the questions at the begin-ning of the section to guide reading behavior.

    "Metacognition" refers to the student's own knowledge about his cog-nitive processes, and his ability to control these processes by organizing, monitoring, and modifying them. Metacognition is the process of standing back and watching oneself learn.[17]

# CLASSROOM LIFE

> "I run a tight ship, but I still feel like it's chaos—every day. Things are coming at me right and left. Something's got to give."

> > "I know the feeling. But why don't you just back off? What difference does it make in the final analysis whether you give it all you've got? Your kids won't learn that much more. I'm to the point where I roll with the punches. To my surprise, things still go pretty well."

> "Yes, but I get uptight if things are not straight and under control. What I really need to do is tighten things down more—make sure kids sit and be quiet. That's the only way to get any significant teaching done!"

What is life in classrooms like? How are the multitude of events occur-ring in the classroom handled by the teacher?—that is, how do teachers es-tablish and maintain order in their classrooms? In Chapter 9 we discussed classroom management, emphasizing that optimal learning occurs in well-organized and well-managed classrooms. Classroom "management" is an inclusive term, referring to the provisions and procedures necessary to estab-lish and maintain an environment in which learning can occur. Managing takes in a wide range of activities, including arranging the seats in the room, handing out paper and crayons for an assignment, ensuring sufficient light-ing so the students can see the board, taking roll, checking out textbooks, establishing and reinforcing rules, creating small groups for reading, moni-toring student seatwork, ordering new computer programs, and keeping the temperature from getting too high. Research has helped portray the type of life occurring in classrooms.[18]

## Type and Frequency of Events

Researchers have observed as few as eleven and as many as fifty-three classroom activities in one day. An "activity" can be defined as a relatively short block of classroom time—often ten to twenty minutes—during which students are arranged in a particular way and engage in a particular action. A sample of activities that have been identified are book reports, reading groups, silent reading, math games, creative writing, spelling bees, assemblies, field trips, gym, movies, treats, discussion, lectures, demonstrations, checking work, tests, group work, student reports, giving instructions, and tutoring.

The type of activity differs across subject matter. For example, math sessions are characterized by recitation and long seatwork segments, with an emphasis on practice. Social studies lessons have fewer recitation segments, although the duration of the recitations tends to be longer. Seatwork segments in social studies are shorter and occur less often.

In terms of time, studies show that approximately 65 percent of the total classroom time is spent in seatwork and 35 percent in whole-class presentations or recitations.[19] The teacher interacts in some way with students on an average of four times per minute; for example,

"Open your books to page 147."

"Begin cleaning your work area now."

"Who needs help?"

"Lynn, come back and talk with me for a minute."

"Robin, I would be interested in your response to that question."

## Diversity of Events

Classrooms are humming with activities, and these activities take place in small physical spaces crowded with different personalities that exhibit diverse preferences and abilities: Marchant is reading a book; Sonja is hurrying to finish yesterday's assignment; Brian is wadding up a "bullet"; Ms. Covington is writing today's assignment on the board; Jenny is passing back papers; Zachary is on his way to the bathroom; the custodian is replacing a burned-out bulb. A teacher needs to orchestrate a multitude of events involving students with diverse personalities and wide-ranging needs.

## Simultaneity of Events

Everything happens at once! Mr. Blum is at the board reexplaining the last part of the procedure; Dixie, the tutor, is coaching students at Table 3 on how to write up the experiment; students assigned to Table 1 are returning equipment to the shelves; students at Table 4 are trying to listen to Mr. Blum; and students at Table 2 are still observing their leaves and trying to classify them.

During seatwork, the teacher must help an individual while monitoring the rest of the class, acknowledge other requests for assistance, handle interruptions, and keep track of time. During discussion, she must listen to student answers, watch other students for signs of comprehension or confusion, formulate the next question, and scan the class for possible misbehavior while paying attention to pacing. When the class is divided into small groups, the number of simultaneous events increases and the teacher must monitor and regulate several different activities at once.

## Flow of Events

Classroom events occur at a rapid pace, requiring a teacher to maintain both momentum and flow: salute the flag, call roll, send in lunch money, check homework, help students correct each others' papers, demonstrate the concept, praise, reprimand, correct student responses, reexplain the concept, look up an alternate set of exercises, and listen to a tardy excuse. In addition to her rapid-fire pacing of classroom events, the typical teacher has more than 500 exchanges with individual students in a given day.

## Unpredictability of Events

Distractions and interruptions are frequent: the pep assembly has to be moved inside due to rain, and the gym is unavailable for physical education; Margeen falls from the jungle gym, opening a laceration requiring immediate attention; Derek's hyperactivity pills were left at home and you have to take him to the office; the custodian's lawnmower throws a rock through your window; the teaching aide becomes violently ill. Not only are there distractions and interruptions but it is impossible to anticipate how an activity will go on a particular day with a particular group of students.

## Living in a Fishbowl

Teachers spend their days in a fishbowl! Virtually every classroom act she performs is witnessed by her students. Everyone watches to see how she reacts to Joel's impudence and to Karen's off-color response; they see how tired she looks on Friday afternoon; they notice how she fails to take action when Brett won't stop talking; and they observe her patience when Ruby fails to understand her reexplanation of square roots. Much good modeling takes place while the teacher is acting in her fishbowl. In observing her activities and interactions, her students learn appropriate responses, procedures, work habits, and interpersonal relationships.

## Routines

In setting up his system of management, the teacher quickly establishes a set of routines to simplify classroom life and to usher students into it. They adjust to his scheme of organization and management, and he to their various habits and idiosyncrasies.

Teachers' routines have been studied by researchers. This typical routine can be observed in almost any classroom:

> Students enter the room in an orderly fashion, go to their seats, and begin to get materials ready for class. At a "switch-signal" from the teacher, the lesson phase begins. Students are now expected to pay attention and not talk to each other. The lesson typically consists of several sub-phases: teacher explanation, during which students are not to interrupt the teacher; question–answer or discussion time, during which students are expected to raise their hands and answer seriously and truthfully; and seat work, during which quiet talk is permitted. Finally, during the clearing up and exit phases, work ceases and students prepare to leave.[20]

As these routines become established, teacher and students, meeting five days a week over a period of nine months, accumulate a common set of experiences. This joint history can contribute to the smoothness of classroom life and create a bonding effect within the classroom.

## Classroom Communication

How do teachers and students communicate with each other verbally and nonverbally? How does classroom discourse affect student learning?

Verbal interchanges between teacher and students occur almost constantly within classrooms. Researchers call these interchanges *scripts*. Here are some examples:

### SHOW-AND-TELL SCRIPT

"It's time for show and tell. Who would like to be first today?"

"This is an autographed picture I got at the Jazz game last night."

"Can you read us the names of the players who signed it?"

### HEALTH SCRIPT

"Class, today we are going to talk about why water is so important to the body. Who can tell me what happens when the body goes without water for a long period of time?"

"You die."

"Well, yes. But, let's keep the person alive. What happens before death as the water in the body starts to dry up? Scott, what do you think?"

"I was on a Scout hike once and we got lost. We were tired and thirsty. My legs got cramps. Was that because we didn't have any water?"

© *Elizabeth Crews/The Image Works*

**GENETICS SCRIPT**

"Jason, why do some hemophiliacs feel they should never marry?"

"I dunno."

"Well, are they afraid their children might be born with the same problem?"

"Do both parents have to carry the gene before their child would get it?"

"Okay, let's go back to the section we have just read. Under what conditions can hemophilia be transmitted to the offspring?"

Verbal interchanges or scripts are being studied in increasingly sophisticated ways. Take the following example:

TEACHER:   "All right. Perry's ready. Who else is ready?"

ANNA:   "Me."

JIMMY:   "Not me."

PERRY:   "I'm ready."

MARIA:   "Can I go?"

ROSA:   "I don't want to read."

PERRY:   "I can't read this."

ROSA:   "I could read it."

In studying this brief verbal interchange, researchers might classify it as a "conversational act" (product answer, compliance, noncompliance, request), or as an "interactional consequence" (commitment to read, refusal to read, soliciting). Moreover, the "participation structure" of the group can be diagrammed on paper: students are shown sitting around the table, identified as primary speaker, primary attenders, secondary speakers, and secondary attenders—with the posture of each indicated.

Researchers have also studied nonverbal communication in the classroom. For example, in one study of worktime in a kindergarten/first-grade classroom, the teacher was observed giving her students certain cues whenever she wanted everyone's attention to make an announcement. She always moved to a certain area of the room and bent forward as she spoke. In this case, communicating through her body position as well as her words, she failed to be consistent in her communication:

> The teacher walked over to her instruction area, stopped, and bent forward while she was making the announcement. In the middle of the announcement, she turned away to give directions to two students standing behind her. As she did so, the rest of the students began to move around, apparently thinking the announcement was over. The teacher turned back, bent forward even more than she had done previously, and said, "Who told you to move!" The truth of the matter is that the teacher herself, by turning away, had "told" the students to move. The students had been attending to what the teacher was doing, as much as to what she was saying.[21]

Another area of research in classroom communication is *cuing,* or the techniques by which teachers prompt students. When a student is unable to answer a teacher's question, the teacher often reformulates it, leading the student toward a particular response. In the following examples, note how the teacher decreases the cognitive difficulty for her students by reformulating her questions, thereby making them more specific:

Original question:   What are those people doing?
Reformulation:   What are they planting?

    Original question:   What kind of an elephant?
    Reformulation:   Was he a very SAD elephant?

Original question:   What else did you see?
Reformulation:   Did you see a chest of drawers?

    Original question:   How did they go, Gary?
    Reformulation:   Did they go by bus or car?[22]

What teachers say to control students' behavior and their talking is known as *control talk.* These are examples:

"I can't hear you, Ian."

    "Allyson, what is our rule about going for drinks?"

"Stacy, why are you reading that book that's supposed to be read during free time?"

"C'mon, Emilio. I mean, I was looking at you when you did it. Be a little subtle."

This last comment was made by a teacher to a student who had just thrown a paper wad. The teacher was reminding Emilio about the norm of not throwing things. She was also acknowledging that he was deliberately defying her authority.[23]

The study of humor in classroom communication is a relatively recent area of inquiry. Historically, there may not have been that much humor to observe! The classic advice, "Never smile before Christmas," jokingly offered to novice teachers, may have been taken more seriously than expected. However, as one writer put it, "Jokes are part of the process of letting yourself become a person in the eyes of the pupils."[24] This research is bringing out hypotheses about the role of humor in the classroom. For example, humor can act as a social lubricant to smooth over classroom events that have the potential for friction.

Although much research on classroom communication focuses on teacher–student interaction, peer interactions are also being studied. Researchers look at how students give spontaneous help to each other (Akiko hands her felt-tip marker to Melissa, who needs something to color with); collaborate on group projects (Tamara, Royall, and Lucette are looking for library books for their fossil project); and tutor one another (Roget is helping Amy practice her Spanish vocabulary).

## Classroom Questions

"My kids ask the dumbest questions. The other day we were talking about conservation efforts in small communities. Twang! One boy wants to know if cat food is made from horse meat. I just stood there looking at him."

"I can see a connection—kind of recycling of horses once they've served well and died. His question was a bit gruesome but not too farfetched. Suppose this kid's dad works in an animal processing plant."

"But why would he even ask such a weird question in the first place? What was going through the kid's mind?"

Teachers consider questions to be an integral and important part of their teaching. Considerable research has been conducted on questioning in the classroom, seeking data on such matters as these: What types of questions do students ask in the classroom? How do high- and low-achieving students differ in the types of questions they ask? Are students' self-initiated questions different from those that are prompted by the teacher? What types of questions do teachers ask in the classroom? How do we train students to ask higher-level questions? How does the teacher promote question asking in an English as a second language (ESL) classroom?

A growing body of research knowledge on classroom questions will help teachers decide what questions to ask for what purposes, how to se-

Practical *does not mean telling people what to do. Research cannot*
*provide prescriptions for practice applicable to all settings and all*
*situations. Research can, however, provide alternative ways of thinking*
*and alternative practices that can be considered and tested by practitioners.*
*—Virginia Richardson-Koehler*

quence questions, how to classify questions according to the level of thought
they produce, how to use probes and wait time, and how to phrase questions appropriately for high- and low-achieving students.

Of particular interest to teachers is the frequency of use of lower-level
and higher-level questions, both by themselves and by their students. These
are examples of lower-level questions asked by teachers:

"What were the three major causes of the Korean War?" (Student is to recall
and write down three previously memorized bits of information.)

"Is Alcatraz still being used as a prison?" (Student is to recall one bit of previously memorized information.)

"Which president was responsible for initiation of the War on Poverty?" (Student again recalls one bit of information recently memorized.)

Following are examples of higher-level questions asked by teachers:

"What is the relationship between the two types of cell division?" (Student is
to compare one with another and point out differences and similarities.)

"How can the concept of homogenizing be applied in scientific farming?"
(Student is to take the critical properties of the concept of homogenizing
learned in one context and apply them in another context.)

"How would you evaluate the impact of the Civil Rights Movement in the
1960s on educational policy in the late 1980s?" (Student is to review the
qualities of the movement, look at decisions being made in education in
the 1980s, and look for cause-and-effect relationships over time.)

Teachers work to engage students in higher-level thinking through asking
higher-level questions. As the reasoning goes, students ask higher-level questions as a result of modeling their teacher's questions, thereby triggering
their own higher mental processes.

Teachers use questions for different purposes. Some questions inform
the teacher about students' understanding of class presentations and homework assignments. Others help students review for tests. Sometimes teachers use questions to pull students back on task. A teacher asks a "convergent"
question when she is interested in eliciting a single correct response, or a
limited number of alternative responses; for example, "What is the capital of
New Hampshire?" "Divergent" questions are asked when the teacher invites a broad range of acceptable responses; for example, "What did you

like about *Stand and Deliver?*" Although both convergent and divergent questions have right and wrong answers, divergent questions may have many right answers and therefore a much broader range of acceptable responses.

We now know more about the types of questions teachers ask and their impact upon student thinking and learning. Likewise, there is a growing knowledge about questions students ask and the effectiveness of teachers' responses to those questions.

# STUDY OF TEACHING IN SPECIFIC SUBJECT AREAS

Considerable research has been carried out on the teaching of specific subjects such as reading and mathematics. In a sample of subject areas, we identify some of the questions asked and the knowledge that is emerging from addressing these questions.

## Reading

A relentless demand for excellence in reading has challenged educators for many years. Reading scores on standardized tests were on the decline from the mid-1960s through the late 1980s. Now there is an opportunity to step back and see how American schools have responded to this problem: certainly more time has been devoted to reading instruction; reading activities have been defined with greater precision; students' reading performance is being monitored more carefully; and much greater attention is being focused on reading comprehension.

In 1986, nearly 36,000 American school children in grades three, seven, and eleven participated in reading tests conducted by the National Assessment of Educational Progress (NAEP). Among the results were the following:

1. Students at all three grade levels had particular difficulty with tasks that required them to defend their interpretations of what they had read.

2. Poor readers spent less time reading on their own than did good readers. Even in school, they read less than good readers.

3. Teachers used a smaller number of teaching strategies with poor readers than with better readers, focusing primarily on decoding rather than on comprehension and critical thinking.

4. Poor readers used a narrower range of strategies to guide their own reading. There was not much change in their strategies from grade three to grade eleven.

5. In comparison with poor readers, good readers tended to have more home support for reading, be enrolled in academically oriented programs, and spend regular amounts of time on homework each day.[25]

From these results, NAEP recommended that reading programs in the schools (1) move from an overwhelming emphasis on basal readers and workbooks toward a greater emphasis on comprehension strategies, (2) move to a wider range of higher-quality reading materials, (3) involve children in more independent reading, and (4) create more opportunities for combining reading and writing activities.

The age-old question continues to be asked, but researchers are coming up with increasingly sophisticated answers: how does a child learn to read? One point is clear: exposure to the printed page does not guarantee that a child will learn to read. What, then, are some explanations? At least four possibilities have been posed: (1) reading is acquired naturally, like learning to speak, (2) reading is acquired through a series of stages, (3) reading is learned through the mastery of a set of specific skills, and (4) reading is learned by formal instruction in a new domain of knowledge.

Those who give the first explanation, the "naturalistic" theory, emphasize the importance of providing students with reading materials and activities with which they are already familiar. The second explanation, development through stages, is exemplified by several models, one of which is as follows: the student goes through prereading (birth to age 6); initial reading or decoding (ages 6 to 7); fluency (ages 7 to 8); reading to learn (from age 8 on); multiple viewpoints (high school ages); and reconstruction (college-age on).[26] Those who give the third explanation, skill mastery, stress the importance of mastering decoding skills, vocabulary skills, and comprehension skills. Finally, those who explain reading as formal instruction point out that both kinds of learning, natural and formal, are important in the development of competence; and the final product of the interplay between formal and natural instruction is shaped by the mind during the process of reading.

DECODING    Decoding is the process of translating printed words into speech; that is, the process of pronouncing a written word. In the area of decoding, researchers ask questions like these: When a person "reads" a word, does the translation entail direct access to a visual pattern, or is it moderated by a phonological quality (or knowledge of letter sounds)? In those situations in which translation is phonological, does the coding depend on spelling-sound rules or on analogies to familiar words? What can be done to increase the accuracy and fluency of decoding among poor readers? What happens to reading speed during silent reading? Why are some words read more quickly in context than in isolation? How are decoding and comprehension related? What happens to decoding when words are read aloud in context?

Research has shown that both good and poor readers use context to decode; poor readers have a greater need to rely on context than do good readers, yet good readers can rely easily on context when necessary.[27] Further, some studies show that poor readers, when reading orally, are interrupted more frequently by their teachers than are good readers. During instruction with poor readers, the teacher usually pronounces the word for the student or focuses on the letter-sound cues. When teachers stop good readers, they provide corrective pronunciation, but they are also more likely to emphasize the available semantic cues.[28]

VOCABULARY   What does it mean to "know" a word? This depends in part on how the word is related to our experiences and to other words. Meanings of words are often gained from their context. Researchers are exploring how word meaning is learned from context and how best to teach vocabulary from context. How does vocabulary relate to comprehension? These are some of the questions researchers are asking: How well can a student understand a passage when some or many of the words are unknown? How can the student use context to ferret out the meaning of unknown words? What features of a text promote the learning of unfamiliar words? How can students be taught general strategies for handling unknown words encountered while reading?

Researchers also grapple with the problem of how to measure a book's readability for students. Their work involves studying the difficulty level, the familiarity, and the appropriateness of words in textbooks.

READING COMPREHENSION   The type of material being read, the background of the reader, and the purpose behind the reading all affect a student's ability to comprehend what he reads. Research in this area involves the following kinds of questions: What types of written material are students reading—textbooks, letters, comic books, stories? How does a student organize the content in his mind in order to comprehend it? Do oral and silent reading require similar comprehension strategies in both good and poor readers? How does the teacher facilitate reading comprehension? What types of inferences do readers draw? How accurate are they? Were they intended by the author? Various strategies for building effective comprehension have emerged from the research: summarizing, questioning, clarifying, and predicting. How can these strategies best be taught to various types of readers?[29]

Research has revealed some of the characteristics of skilled readers:

1. Skilled readers have a good understanding of such linguistic concepts as word, sentence, paragraph, book, page, story.

2. Comprehension is the main goal for skilled readers, and they employ a variety of strategies to achieve that goal.

3. Skilled readers are good at knowing which comprehension skill to use and when to use it.

4. Skilled readers are adept at monitoring their comprehension: they know when they are not understanding and they have a variety of "fix-up" strategies.

Educators are realizing that the social context in which reading instruction occurs is very powerful. How the teacher explains reading con-

*There are many effective style variations among teachers, characterized as the "intangible art of teaching." But art alone does not make a good teacher. Complementing this must be a specialized set of skills grounded in a professional knowledge base. Together they comprise the science of teaching. It is the combination of art and science that makes a professional teacher.*
—Lovely H. Billups and Marilyn Rauth

cepts, how she models reading, and how other students read affect how the child develops his reading skills. How students are grouped for reading within the classroom is important because teachers tend to treat high- and low-ability groups differently. Students in the high group tend to be given more time to answer questions, and the questions asked call for more analysis than those asked in low-ability groups. Students in low-ability groups get interrupted more often by other students and the teacher when they make reading errors, and they are given more clues about letter sounds. Further, the teacher focuses low-ability students on decoding skills and oral reading, whereas she directs high-ability students toward comprehension and silent reading.[30]

Research is beginning to suggest that the reader, much like the writer, is constantly composing messages, planning, and evaluating. To develop such "active" reading, the teacher needs to encourage students to actively process information presented in the text, to make predictions, to draw inferences, and to evaluate the quality of the material they are reading.

WHOLE-LANGUAGE APPROACH TO READING   The whole-language approach, which brings together a particular view of language, learning, and the interaction between students and teacher, is one recent attempt to develop active readers. It is a movement back to basics in the real sense, setting aside basals, workbooks, and tests. Students learn to read and write by reading and writing about things important to them in their world.[31]

Children's interests and concerns are the focus in whole-language classrooms. In lieu of spending time with basal readers in formal reading groups, students read books of interest to them, often silently or to one another. Much of the content of their reading arises from their own written stories and compositions. Thus, language becomes a tool enabling students to learn about and communicate their intrinsic interests.[32]

READING AND WRITING ACROSS THE CURRICULUM   At the upper elementary, middle, and high school levels, three main emphases have been "reading across the curriculum," "writing across the curriculum" and "the development of thinking skills." "Writing across the curriculum," a term coined by James Britton in 1975, represents an effort to make writing an integral part of learning in all courses.[33] The same holds with reading. One leading writer has identified the pervasive role of these skills:

Obviously, there are definite advantages to focusing on reading as a separate body of skills. However, there are also drawbacks from isolating reading instruction. Only recently has there been an awareness that both reading and writing should be taught in all parts of the educational process. Such an idea is for the good of all subjects. Both writing and reading are ways of "coming to understand," and teachers of all subjects, if they hope to have their students gain dominion over the content, need to use writing and reading to benefit their own content.[34]

Teachers use a variety of approaches in teaching reading and writing across the curriculum, requiring students to write such things as personal journals, responses to films, oral histories, limericks, logic problems, and written interviews and to implement reading strategies such as SQ3R (survey, question, read, recite, and review). Such activities assist students in clarifying and presenting their views effectively:

> Of all the ways to straighten out one's ideas and feelings about any topic, writing is one of the most powerful. It is a way of clarifying what has heretofore been fuzzy, nebulous, vague, and for this reason, writing is important in every subject matter discipline, not just in the language arts. Teachers of science, social studies, mathematics, homemaking, and other subjects should not feel that their concern with writing is merely a support of English instruction. The sure grasp of concepts and their relationships promoted by writing contributes to the learning of all subject matter. . . . Writing is thinking.[35]

READING AGENDA FOR THE FUTURE   Reviewing progress made in reading instruction between 1971 and 1984, the National Assessment of Educational Progress suggested continued attention to disadvantaged and minority children and increased emphasis on higher-level reading skills for children at all educational levels. What was a satisfactory level of literacy in 1950 will be only marginal by the year 2000:

> To foster higher-level literacy skills is to place a new and special emphasis on thoughtful, critical elaboration of ideas and understandings drawn from the material students read and from what they already know. They must learn to value their own ideas and to defend as well as question their interpretations in the face of alternative or opposing points of view.[36]

## Writing

The teaching of writing has risen during the 1980s from a relatively neglected school subject to one of lively attention. It is capturing the interest of a widening group of people: psychologists, educators, anthropologists, linguists, and English teachers. Researchers quest after answers to perennial questions about writing: Why is writing so difficult to teach? What roles do teachers play in teaching writing? Why does interest in writing continue at a low ebb?

© *The Picture Cube*

Traditionally, writing instruction has been characterized by the following pattern:

1.  Students write only when teachers assign them to write.

2.  It is the teacher who decides the student's purpose for writing and what format the writing will take.

3.  The teacher's main response to the student's writing is a grade after the project has been completed.

4.  The teacher spends most of his or her time making comments about mechanics rather than meaning.

5.  Students are given little or no help during the actual writing process.

6.  Students are given very little time for the actual writing process. During that time, it is the subject of few if any conversations with other students or the teacher.

7.  Students spend little time writing their first draft, and they rarely revise it.

8.  Most student compositions are read only by one person, the teacher.[37]

On the basis of research to date, teachers can improve their teaching of writing by attending to the following:

1.  Devote more time and effort to first drafts.

2.  Encourage the student to select his or her own purposes for writing.

3. Coach the student *during* the writing process rather than coming in at the end as an evaluator.

4. Encourage the student to consult with other students and the teacher during the writing process.

5. Help the student with the composing process rather than merely attending to grammar.

In comparison with mathematics, where there is plenty of explaining, demonstrating, and teaching of rules, very little instruction of the writing process itself takes place; rather, teachers spend their time on punctuation, parts of speech, and grammar. Textbooks also contribute to this indirectness by addressing the mechanical, outward parts of the writing process: gathering material, outlining, creating a draft, revising, footnoting. This focus on mechanics during the writing process does not correspond with the mental processes students actually engage in as they write.

Educators are moving toward more direct teaching of writing skills. A teacher might say, for example, "Class, today I am going to show you *how* to compose a story—I will teach you some actual composing skills." This teacher views writing as a cognitive process, and she explicitly teaches students cognitive strategies: procedures for developing their thoughts and methods of using them to compose. Students are not simply sent, comments in hand, back to the drawing board to "try again."[38]

Here are some of the more specific trends and research areas emerging over the past decade:

1. Research is being done on how young children invent their own unique spellings and other personal symbols to convey meaning in the absence of a standard writing system like the one adults possess.

2. Traditionally, teachers have focused on the sentence and its various parts. The newer research looks at the principles that tie sentences to one another.

3. Research is taking place on how children think up and structure their stories.

4. Interest is being shown in "adult beginners"; that is, older students who display an extreme lack of development of writing ability.

5. Studies are looking at how teachers can help students learn to generate and elaborate thoughts about the content of their compositions.

6. Researchers have identified an anxiety trait that affects how well students write and how they feel about the process of writing.

7. Rather than taking simple surveys, researchers are conducting more in-depth analyses of the teaching of writing as it occurs in the classroom.

8. Typically, teachers make brief written comments on student's compositions. New and different kinds of teacher feedback are being studied, such as conferencing and interactive journal writing.

9. Researchers are studying what goes on in the student's mind during the composing process.[39]

One interesting approach to the study of writing has been to identify differences between expert and novice writers. Researchers have found the following differences:

1. Expert writers have abstract notions in their minds (opinions, positions, major points) that help them work out an overall structure for their writing. For novice writers (young children), these abstract notions are not well developed and are more difficult to access.

2. While writing, mature writers generate more content than they can use; novices have trouble coming up with enough to say, and they have more difficulty accessing it.

3. Expert writers are better at searching their memories for what information is there (though not necessarily in retrieving it) than are novices.

4. Expert writers have their spelling and punctuation largely "automatized" so they can concentrate on the content of their writing. Very young writers are somewhat handicapped by having to devote so much attention and energy to the mechanics; e.g., "Let's see, how is that word spelled?" and "Do I need a comma or a period now?"

5. Expert writers translate large writing goals into workable subgoals; young writers show only the beginnings of this translation skill.

6. Expert writers can "reprocess" a draft, translating it into new material, rather than simply adding to it. But this is a difficult skill. Even college students, when asked to "rethink" or "completely rewrite" a first draft, do little more than proofread, making small, grammatical revisions. Among novice writers, this reprocessing skill is not at all developed.

## Mathematics

As described in Chapter 4, mathematics instruction has remained remarkably unchanged over the years. Educators have found at least three drawbacks to the traditional teaching of mathematics:

1. Mathematics is portrayed to students as a static, bounded discipline, divorced from science and the other disciplines. It is separated into subjects such as arithmetic, algebra, geometry, and trigonometry. These in turn are broken down into specific topics, facts, and skills. Everything is fragmented. But this is not how mathematics appears in real life. Our daily uses of mathematics—inventing, abstracting, proving, applying—are not taught in traditional math instruction.

2. Students are "absorbing agents." They sit through classes and store up information that is mostly isolated from purposeful activities in the student's own life. Students absorb what other people have done rather than coming to an understanding by themselves.

3. Curriculum guides and textbooks are so completely structured that the teacher's role is managerial. Teachers have little freedom to select or omit material, pursue alternatives, or make significant curricular decisions: their job is to assign lessons to their classes of students, start and stop the lessons according to some

*Comprehension alone is not sufficient. The usefulness of knowledge lies in its value for judgment and action.*—*Lee S. Shulman*

schedule, explain the rules and procedures of each lesson, judge the action of the students during the lesson, and maintain order and control throughout.[40]

Despite these drawbacks, how have students been performing in math? The results of the Third National Mathematics Assessment showed that declining math scores have leveled off, with some improvement in particular age groups, such as 13-year-olds. In all age groups, students are at their best in solving traditional problems in standard ways, but they do poorly trying to solve nonroutine problems—those requiring deeper conceptualizations and applications.[41]

Why is this the case? In looking for answers, researchers started studying the strategies students use to solve problems, their reasons behind the strategies, and the types of errors they make. Results showed that students had weak and fragmented understandings, they often had misconceptions, and they made consistent and predictable errors.

In studying students' misconceptions, researchers discovered that students do not merely sit back and passively receive mathematical information, as previously believed. They actively construct their own meanings and interpretations of what they are learning and use them as a guide in performing mathematical operations.

Research suggests that students differ in their ability to gather, process, and retain information. For example, when faced with a math problem that lacks an explicit question, some students quickly come up with an *intended* question. Others are unaware of any hidden question and they end up focusing on the particulars of the problem. Some students have good "reversibility"; that is, they can recognize inverse relationships between operations such as squaring and finding the square root.

Some students do more rereading of the problem, distinguish between relevant and irrelevant information, and use a wide variety of strategies for comprehending and solving the problem. They can also generalize across problems. In contrast, other students proceed quickly, often on irrelevant clues, tend to apply a single operation throughout, rely on memorized rules, and have difficulty generalizing.

On the whole, female students experience greater difficulty than males in math, although there is some evidence that sex differences are decreasing. There is a tendency in young women toward a pattern called *learned helplessness* (a tendency to believe that nothing you can do will affect your successes or failures). Some research on performance in mathematics shows that girls are more likely than boys to explain their successes as a result of effort rather than ability, and their failures as a result of inability and task difficulty. This pattern might explain why girls show less confidence in their mathematical ability and less persistence in learning math.[42]

## Science

In the study of the teaching of science, three major areas of concern have emerged: How well do students learn science? How competent and well prepared are science teachers? How can science teaching be improved?

The answer to the first question is "not very well." Standardized test performance continues to decline, as does enrollment in science courses. Students can successfully memorize formulas and pass science courses, yet still fail to apply scientific concepts in solving straightforward everyday problems.

Researchers have explored students' misconceptions of science concepts. For example, when asked what happens when a nail rusts, Robert, who had completed four months of high school chemistry, responded, "The coldness reacts on it [the nail] . . . plastic doesn't rust because coldness doesn't cause the same reaction . . . rusting is a breakdown of the iron because it [coldness] brings out the rusting . . . it [coldness] almost draws it [rust] out, like a magnet." Robert was satisfied with this explanation; it *made sense* to him. We know that nails rust when they are left in cold, damp places, so isn't coldness responsible for the rusting process? On their own, students construct theories that help them explain familiar things in the world even before they begin any formal science instruction.

In being introduced to new concepts in a science course, students cannot simply add new knowledge to what they already know. Frequently they must abandon some of their personal theories in favor of new ones that are often counterintuitive. If they cannot replace old conceptions with new ones, their only alternative is to memorize the new information without understanding it. No wonder learning science is so hard!

Science labs are helpful in developing skills used in scientific processes, such as measuring, but have not been very effective in producing conceptual change in students. Traditionally, labs have been places where students "follow recipes," conducting experiments without understanding their underlying purposes. Increasingly, however, labs are being used to arouse interest and to teach problem-solving skills.

Teachers engage primarily in didactic teaching (telling students), which is geared toward rote memorization rather than toward understanding and changing concepts. Textbooks do supply information about science concepts, and they do provide teaching strategies for the teacher, but they lack specific information about students' misconceptions and how to change them. Thus, neither current teaching approaches nor current textbooks concentrate on one of the most fundamental goals of science: to attack students' inaccurate conceptions and replace them with more scientific ones.[43]

Many aspects of science teaching have been researched: effects of advance organizers (information given at the outset that provides an overview of what is to be learned and also aids that learning) and behavioral objectives on students' learning; classroom interaction between the teacher and students; the degree to which teachers structure the class; the types of questions teachers ask and their impact on students' understanding; how science texts are designed (for example, the use of line drawings versus photographs); and students' attitudes toward science and how these attitudes affect their learning of science concepts. Indeed, much work is going on in the study of science instruction.[44]

## Social Studies

As we pointed out in Chapter 4, an overarching goal of social studies is the development of good citizens. Subgoals are acquisition of knowledge, mastery of skills, development of certain attitudes and values, and participation. Factual knowledge has always been a staple of social studies, but controversy exists about what the content of that knowledge should be. "Skills" refers to finding, organizing, and making use of the knowledge. Some form of values education has always been an integral part of social studies instruction. For example, the study of United States history is traditionally associated with patriotic values. According to the National Council for the Social Studies, the six root values embedded in all social studies content are justice, equality, responsibility, freedom, diversity, and privacy. Participation is a relative newcomer to the social studies curriculum. Learning by doing has long been seen as an effective way of learning. Participation is considered a duty of good citizenship. However, in recent years, leading social studies educators have insisted that active participation in public affairs be strengthened in the social studies curriculum.[45]

Many social studies classrooms of today differ little from those of twenty years ago, despite the expenditure of millions of dollars and the involvement of many creative minds working on innovative curricular materials. Teacher talk continues to dominate in the classroom; the conventional social studies textbook remains the primary source of course content; vital social issues are not on the classroom agendas; and students tend to be generally apathetic toward social studies.

Social studies units do not usually appear to be making a significant dent in students' political knowledge and attitudes. Some units are not very effective in helping students (1) recognize and value either their own constitutional rights or those of others, (2) respect people who are different from themselves, or (3) develop a knowledge of government, the political process, and international affairs.

Teachers themselves often impede productive changes in the teaching of social studies. Suppose a teacher were handed a new social studies unit designed to teach students to question and engage in problem solving. If, through his own experiences, he had not learned to be a good problem solver, he would feel insecure implementing this unit. Or suppose he had always believed that students should merely accept rather than evaluate new information. Changing his view and teaching students to become inquirers might be difficult because it would run contrary to his belief about the role of students.

But research is showing that some teachers are breaking away from textbooks, substituting current and controversial issues, and, through discussion, working to change students' attitudes.[46] Researchers, for their part, are asking questions that affect the teaching of social studies: How do teachers' questions affect students' attitudes? What are some effective ways to deal with controversial issues? What beliefs do students construct from their social studies curriculum? How can teachers influence students to identify and analyze social issues? What processes do students employ in attempting to solve current social problems?[47]

# TEACHING SPECIAL TYPES OF LEARNERS

## Creative and Gifted

> I can hardly sit through Wilkes's anthropology class any more. I'm coming to believe it has no substance, and it certainly poses no challenge. I used to ask questions to get us into something worth talking about. That led nowhere. He wouldn't budge. One day I told him I'd learned everything I could from him and that I wanted out. He smiled and handed me a set of "expansions." What a joke. Same old busy work.

Since the mid-1970s, programs for gifted and talented learners have proliferated, moving more toward meeting individual needs. These programs have included summer classes, early school admission, college courses for high school students, enrichment activities in regular classrooms, clubs and extracurricular activities, acceleration, individual tutoring, and parent programs.

Now available are career-education programs for gifted students and programs for the culturally different gifted, the learning-disabled gifted, and the female gifted. Further, there are programs for teaching gifted children leadership skills, computer technology, futuristic thinking, and research skills.

Research on gifted and talented students suggests a need for the following:

1. The early identification of various types of giftedness in children.
2. Greater involvement of the gifted student in making decisions about his or her academic experiences.
3. Provision for greater interaction with other gifted students of similar ability and interests.
4. Attention to emotional as well as academic needs of the gifted student.

5.   The development of educational acceleration programs, sometimes radically accelerated.

6.   Increased expenditure of energy on training the gifted in thinking skills rather than merely providing enrichment experiences.[48]

Some educators have assumed that highly gifted students need no special training in learning how to solve problems or to think creatively. However, research shows that highly intelligent students are sometimes ineffective thinkers—poorer at problem-solving than average-ability students. In responding to these results, teachers of the gifted and talented increasingly include objectives related to the development of problem-solving and creativity skills, forecasting and planning, philosophical thinking, research, inventing, and using the computer.

One example of such a program, the Future Problem Solving Program, advertises the following goals:

1.   Develop rich images of the future.

2.   Become more creative thinkers.

3. Develop and increase communication skills, both oral and written.

4. Develop and increase teamwork skills.

5. Integrate a problem-solving model into daily living.

6. Develop and increase research skills.[49]

## Bilingual Learners

> What a joy! Li Chen is a veritable sponge. He'll be reading at grade level by Christmas. I'll bet his parents make him speak English at home—he probably even teaches them. But José, my little Spanish-speaking boy from Mexico, he's gone into a shell. I can hardly get him to talk to me, let alone the other kids. He's afraid. He thinks they'll make fun of him. He doesn't listen very well, even when I slow down and pronounce my words distinctly. Every time I do, all the kids turn to look at him.

Teachers often ask themselves questions like these: What do I do when a Spanish-speaking student comes into my room? Am I supposed to know Spanish well enough to teach him English along the way so he can understand what's going on? If this is the case, do I teach part of the curriculum in Spanish and part in English? I ask these same questions about my Vietnamese and Chinese students.

These questions reveal the language-speaking dilemma facing educators who teach in modern pluralistic classrooms. There are approximately 5 million students, representing about 10 percent of the entire school-age population in this country, who speak languages other than English as their primary language.[50] All indications are that this percentage is increasing. Many of these children have "limited English proficiency" (LEP). These LEP students, predominantly from Spanish-speaking backgrounds, show lower academic achievement, lower promotion rates, and higher dropout rates than their English-speaking counterparts.

For many years, educators assumed that non-English speakers would pick up English simply by being in an all-English environment. Thus, these students were not provided formal instruction in English. Eventually, parents began bringing suits against school districts, claiming discrimination since their LEP children were not being taught English. In *Lau* v. *Nichols* the Supreme Court ruled that school districts have a duty to see that students are not discriminated against because they do not speak English.[51]

Various approaches have been initiated to comply with the courts in solving this discrimination problem. One major thrust has been the "bilingual approach," in which students are taught partly in English and partly in their native language. Bilingual programs have been categorized as follows:

1. English as a second language (ESL). The students are pulled out of class and given special instruction in English.

*One needs to be able to take advice from researchers but also to know what
to do when that advice is contradictory, or when it contradicts knowledge
that can only be gained in a particular context.—Magdalene Lampert*

2.  Immersion. The program "immerses" students in the new language to be
    learned as they study the curriculum in that language. Programs vary in their
    degree of immersion.

3.  Sheltered English. The program simplifies English vocabulary and sentence
    structure to help students understand the regular curriculum.

4.  Transitional bilingual. The program helps students shift from their native
    language to an all-English curriculum.[52]

Most bilingual programs are compensatory in nature, offering the students dual-language instruction *until* they have acquired enough English to
receive all their instruction in English. During this transition period, enough
of the curriculum must be taught in their native language to allow them to
learn the subject matter, and enough English instruction given to enable
them to learn English. A variety of attempts have been made to balance this
instruction. For example, in an "alternate-days" approach, English is spoken
one day and the native language the next. In the "alternate-subjects" approach, reading, writing, and mathematics, for example, are taught in the
students' native language, while social studies, science, and language arts
are taught in English.

Although both parents and educators are attracted to the bilingual approach, evaluations of its effectiveness have to date produced conflicting and
nondefinitive results. On philosophical grounds, the overriding value of bilingual education is that it offers students a chance to survive in school without giving up their cultural identities. However, it takes more than learning
a second language to be truly bilingual. Students must hang onto their native
culture as they learn English. Far too many have lost it. The problem, finally,
is not that students will not be able to learn English—they will learn it because they know they must survive in an English-speaking society. The
problem is that, in learning English, they give up their cultural identity and
cultural resources, which would allow them to contribute more significantly
to the broader American culture.[53]

## Mildly Handicapped Learners

Shari's plenty capable—but you'd never know it. She's badly spoiled. Her parents have overcompensated for her handicap. By now, she's quite manipulative.
She co-opts most of my kids into waiting on her hand and foot. So I have not
only her handicap problem but the problem she creates with other students.
Seems like every week I'm pulling someone aside and telling them to be about

their own business: "Look, start treating Shari like any other student. Stop trying to be there every minute to offer help."

*Mildly handicapped* is a term frequently used to describe children who have been diagnosed as educably mentally retarded, learning disabled, behavior disordered, mildly emotionally disturbed, or having minimal brain dysfunction. How do these children learn? How do they perceive themselves? How do other students react to them in the regular classroom? These are the types of questions researchers have been studying.

One area of particular interest to the regular teacher is "mainstreaming," or, as this term is more broadly formulated now, providing the "least restrictive educational opportunity," or simply "integrating students." Since the enactment of Public Law 94-142, many handicapped learners have been placed in regular classrooms, generally considered their "least restrictive environment." The intent is to maximize opportunities for handicapped children to interact with nonhandicapped children and to learn in a regular classroom.

Studies have investigated questions like these: What impact does the mainstreaming or integrating of handicapped students have on other students? Should mildly handicapped students be placed with age peers, where they will likely fall behind in achievement? Or should they be placed in a younger class, where they are older but will achieve at about the same level? Does the mildly handicapped student perform better in a regular classroom than in a special classroom?

The results of mainstreaming have not been as bright as educators had hoped they would be. The original assumption was that greater familiarity would bring greater acceptance—that handicapped students would become more valued by the nonhandicapped once they were together in the same classroom. Results show that, in comparison with nonhandicapped students, the handicapped students are less well known and less accepted and often exhibit lower self-esteem. Academically, mildly handicapped students have not been very successful in learning, either in regular or in special classrooms.[54]

## Learners from Low-Income Families

"If you don't get a child started off on the right foot, he never recovers—not even by high school!"

"That's quite an extreme statement. Surely you don't actually believe that?"

"Absolutely. Kids from uneducated families are already behind when they come into my first grade. I've watched them struggle in every grade after that. What do you think'll happen in high school? They'll finally drop out because they can't take the embarrassment, or the hassle. No, when kids come into first grade they'd better already be out of the starting blocks."

In Chapter 1 we sketched several educational movements in the United States. The War on Poverty, a major movement during the 1960s and 1970s, produced a number of federally funded "intervention" programs for low-income children. The theory was that if youngsters from low-income homes began early enough, they would prosper in their later schooling. Early results showed that Head Start children did score higher than their counterparts on intelligence and school readiness tests, but those advantages washed out by the end of the first year in school.

Enter the Follow Through programs. Their goal was to provide a continuous program from kindergarten through third grade. Children in these programs did score higher on achievement tests than their counterparts. However, overall progress from both Head Start and Follow Through was meager, and by the late 1970s funds had been drastically reduced.

Several long-term studies were conducted on these programs. Their graduates experienced a particular brand of success: as youngsters, they were less often retained in any grade and less often placed in special education classes than their counterparts. As teenagers they were less likely to drop out of school and more likely to graduate from high school.

Twenty-two Follow Through programs were implemented across the country. Of those, two continue in operation: the Parent Education Follow Through Program and the Direct Instruction Follow Through Program. The first combines help from the home with the child's schooling. Parents are guided to interact with their children in specific and supportive ways that promote learning. For example, when a child begins a project in the home, parents might ask the child to explain what she is going to do, ask her questions that have more than one correct answer, get her to ask questions, and give her time to think about the problem.

The Direct Instruction Follow Through Program was designed to help lower-income children in kindergarten through third grade acquire basic skills in arithmetic, develop effective use of language, and master visual symbols and basic color concepts. Materials were developed for reading, spelling, language arts, math, science, and music.

Important implications flowed from studies of the two programs: family participation helps foster positive attitudes toward school; in turn, these attitudes encourage children to be persistent and successful in school. Further, structured, carefully sequenced programs for young low-achieving children help them succeed academically in high school.

As an outgrowth of Head Start and Follow Through programs, two new moods appeared across the country. The first engendered a commitment to a wider range of the nation's children. Rather than targeting special programs for low-income children, administrators and educators leaned toward implementing programs in *regular* classrooms for *all* children. The second mood was one of greater optimism about the educability of children, regardless of their age. The early view had been that disadvantaged children must be given a "head start" during the first five years of life or it would be too late—they would be forever doomed to a life of low academic achievement. Later research suggested that this was not necessarily the case; children at all age levels have derived benefits from intervention programs.

# ADAPTING CLASSROOM INSTRUCTION

As part of the continuing study of teaching, educators and researchers have developed a wide range of instructional adaptations. Here we illustrate two of them: mastery learning and cooperative learning.

Mastery learning, introduced in Chapter 1, assumes that *nearly all* students (upwards of 90 percent), given sufficient time, can learn the basic school curriculum. According to this approach, students differ not so much in achievement levels as in the time required to learn a given task. The goal of mastery learning is to increase the proportion of students mastering the curriculum. To be sure, some will take longer (in many cases much longer) than others and will perhaps need special types of instruction.

The mastery concept was robust enough, and certainly had popular appeal, but it was difficult to implement. In addition, one question always arose: How do I establish the *level* of mastery? Overall, teachers who attempted to implement this system did not give it a ringing vote of confidence, although they did report mildly positive effects on students' attitudes and achievement.

Cooperative learning, like mastery learning, is a program designed for all students in a regular classroom. Students work in small groups of four to six and receive rewards based on group, rather than individual, performance. The goals of this program were to raise the academic performance of individual students, teach students to be cooperative rather than competitive, improve the learning of both high and low achievers, and improve race relations in the classroom. Benefits of cooperative learning programs were similar to those of mastery learning: mild improvement in attitudes and achievement. In sum, neither mastery learning nor cooperative learning produced convincing academic superiority over more traditional approaches.[55] Nevertheless, educators remain unswervingly committed to coming up with increasingly effective instructional adaptations.

# CONCLUSION

Undeniably, you are stepping into a profession that is in flux, one under vigorous study. As recently as 1980, few people would have described education as "fluid" or "dynamic." Although much teaching practice does remain unchanged, the *study* of teaching is unrelentingly propelling educators into a new age. Teaching is fast acquiring an empirical "cutting edge," becoming a field of which professionals must "keep abreast." There is an excitement about standing on the leading edge—and a responsibility.

## Expansions

1.   One relatively new area of research is teachers' planning. How do you expect your own planning will change as you gain experience?

2.   Visit with two teachers. How do they plan for the beginning of the school year? for each unit? for each day? Contrast their styles of planning. What accounts for the differences?

3.   Do you see yourself attributing the successes and failures of your students primarily to you? Explain.

4.   Note these two different instructional goals: (a) helping students learn subject matter and (b) teaching students how to learn. What are some of the advantages of pursuing each goal?

5.   Describe your own model of the teaching/learning process.

6.   As a student all these years, you can sense how busy and complex classrooms are. What are your feelings about overseeing such a beehive of activity?

7.   For what purposes might you consider using teacher questions?

8.   Suppose you taught middle school math. How would you increase reading comprehension of your students?

9.   Suppose you taught high school biology. How would you increase writing skills among your students?

10.   How would you work with a mildly handicapped student in your classroom?

11.   Some teachers say that having an up-to-date knowledge of their subject area is not all that important since they do what their own experience tells them anyway. What are your feelings about this?

## Notes

1.   F. Elbaz, *Teacher Thinking: A Study of Practical Knowledge* (New York: Nichols, 1983), p. 133.

2.   C. S. Witherell and V. L. Erickson, "Teacher Education as Adult Development," *Theory into Practice* 17 (1978), pp. 229–238.

3.   S. Feiman-Nemser and R. E. Floden, "The Cultures of Teaching," in M. C. Wittrock (Ed.), *Handbook of Research on Teaching,* 3rd ed. (New York: Macmillan, 1986), pp. 505–526.

4.   P. W. Jackson, *Life in Classrooms* (New York: Holt, Rinehart & Winston, 1968).

5.   National Institute of Education, *Teaching as Clinical Information Processing,* report of Panel 6, National Conference on Studies in Teaching (Washington, D.C.: National Institute of Education, 1975).

6.   C. M. Clark and P. L. Peterson, "Teachers' Thought Processes," in M. C. Wittrock (Ed.), *Handbook of Research on Teaching,* 3rd ed. (New York: Macmillan, 1986), p. 257.

7.   C. M. Clark and R. J. Yinger, *Three studies of teacher planning,* Research Series No. 55 (East Lansing: Michigan State University, 1979).

8.   Clark and Peterson, "Teachers' Thought Processes," pp. 255–296.

9.   Adapted from M. G. Wodlinger, *A Study of Teacher Interactive Decision Making,* unpublished doctoral dissertation, University of Alberta, Edmonton, Canada, 1980.

10.   R. J. Shavelson and P. Stern, "Research on Teachers' Pedagogical Thoughts, Judgments, Decisions, and Behavior," *Review of Educational Research* 51 (1981), p. 482.

11.   For example: J. M. Darley and R. H. Fazio, "Expectancy Confirmation Processes Arising in the Social Interaction Sequence," *American Psychologist* 35 (1980), pp. 867–881; P. L. Peterson and S. A. Barger, "Attribution Theory and Teacher Expectancy," in J. B. Dusek (Ed.), *Teacher Expectancies* (Hillsdale, N.J.: Erlbaum, 1984), pp. 159–184.

12.   Clark and Peterson, "Teachers' Thought Processes," pp. 255–296.

13.   M. C. Wittrock, "Students' Thought Processes," in M. C. Wittrock (Ed.), *Handbook of Research on Teaching,* 3rd ed. (New York: Macmillan, 1986), pp. 297–314.

14.   D. A. Norman, "Cognitive Engineering and Education," in D. T. Tuma and F. Reif (Eds.), *Problem Solving and Education* (Hillsdale, N.J.: Erlbaum, 1980), p. 97.

15.   C. E. Weinstein and R. E. Mayer, "The Teaching of Learning Strategies," in M. C. Wittrock (Ed.), *Handbook of Research on Teaching,* 3rd ed. (New York: Macmillan, 1986), p. 316.

16.   Adapted from Weinstein and Mayer, "Teaching," p. 316.

17.   Weinstein and Mayer, "Teaching," pp. 317–324.

18.   W. Doyle, "Classroom Organization and Management," in M. C. Wittrock (Ed.), *Handbook of Research on Teaching,* 3rd ed. (New York: Macmillan, 1986), pp. 392–431.

19.   Ibid., p. 398.

20.   Adapted from Doyle, "Classroom Organization," p. 396.

21.   J. Shultz and S. Florio, "Stop and Freeze: The Negotiation of Social and Physical Space in a Kindergarten/First Grade Classroom," *Anthropology and Education Quarterly* 10 (1979), pp. 173–174.

22.   P. French and M. MacLure, "Teachers' Questions, Pupils' Answers: An Investigation of Questions and Answers in the Infant Classroom," *First Language* 2 (1981), pp. 31–45.

23.   Adapted from J. L. Lemke, "Classroom Communication of Science," final report to NSF/RISE, April 1982 (ED 222 246).

24.   R. Walker and I. Goodson, "Humor in the Classroom," in P. Woods and M. Hammersley (Eds.), *School Experience: Explorations in the Sociology of Education* (London: Croom Helm, 1977), p. 206.

25.   Adapted from Educational Testing Service, *The Nation's Report Card: Who Reads Best,* report of the National Assessment of Educational Progress (Princeton, N.J.: Author, 1988).

26.   J. S. Chall, *Stages of Reading Development* (New York: McGraw-Hill, 1983).

27.   K. Stanovich, "Toward an Interactive-Compensatory Model of Individual Differences in the Development of Reading Fluency," *Reading Research Quarterly* 6(1) (1980), pp. 32–71.

28.   R. L. Allington, "Content Coverage and Contextual Reading in Reading Groups," *Journal of Reading Behavior* 16(2) (1984), pp. 85–96.

29.   R. Calfee and P. Drum, "Research on Teaching Reading," in M. C. Wittrock (Ed.), *Handbook of Research on Teaching,* 3rd ed. (New York: Macmillan, 1986), pp. 804–849.

30.   T. E. Raphael, "Research on Reading: But What Can I Teach on Monday?," in V. Richardson-Koehler (Ed.), *Educators' Handbook: A Research Perspective* (New York: Longman, 1987), pp. 26–49.

31.   Adapted from K. Goodman, *What's Whole in Whole Language?* (Portsmouth, N.H.: Heinemann, 1986).

32.   Adapted from D. R. Reutzel and P. M. Hollingsworth, "Whole Language and the Practitioner," *Academic Therapy* 23(4) (1988), pp. 405–416.

33.   J. Britton et al., *The Development of Writing Abilities* (London: Macmillan Education, 1975), pp. 11–18.

34.   W. Loban, "A Deepening Understanding of Reading and Writing," in M. P. Douglass (Ed.), *Claremont Reading Conference: Forty-Ninth Yearbook* (Claremont, Calif.: The Claremont Reading Conference, 1985), p. 13.

35.   Ibid., p. 17.

36.   National Assessment of Educational Progress, *The Reading Report Card: Progress toward Excellence in Our Schools,* Report no. 15-R-01 (Princeton, N.J.: Educational Testing Service, 1985), pp. 7–9.

37.   Adapted from S. Florio-Ruane and S. Dunn, "Teaching Writing: Some Perennial Questions and Some Possible Answers," in V. Richardson-Koehler (Ed.), *Educators' Handbook: A Research Perspective* (New York: Longman, 1987), pp. 50–83.

38.   M. Scardamalia and C. Bereiter, "Research on Written Composition," in M. C. Wittrock (Ed.), *Handbook of Research on Teaching,* 3rd ed. (New York: Macmillan, 1986), pp. 778–803.

39.   Adapted from Scardamalia and Bereiter, "Research," pp. 778–803.

40.   T. A. Romberg (Ed.), *Toward Effective Schooling: The IGE Experience* (Lanham, Md.: University Press of America, 1985), p. 5; T. A. Romberg and T. P. Carpenter, "Research on Teaching and Learning Mathematics: Two Disciplines of Scientific Inquiry," in M. C. Wittrock (Ed.), *Handbook of Research on Teaching,* 3rd ed. (New York: Macmillan, 1986), pp. 850–873.

41.   National Assessment of Educational Progress, *The Third National Mathematics Assessment: Results, Trends and Issues,* Report No. 13-MA-01 (Denver: Education Commission of the States, 1983).

42.   J. Confrey, "Mathematics Learning and Teaching," in V. Richardson-Koehler (Ed.), *Educators' Handbook: A Research Perspective* (New York: Longman, 1987), pp. 3–25.

43.   C. W. Anderson and E. L. Smith, "Teaching Science," in V. Richardson-

Koehler (Ed.), *Educators' Handbook: A Research Perspective* (New York: Longman, 1987), pp. 84–111.

44. R. T. White and R. P. Tisher, "Research on Natural Sciences," in M. C. Wittrock (Ed.), *Handbook of Research on Teaching*, 3rd ed. (New York: Macmillan, 1986), pp. 874–905.

45. I. Morrisett (Ed.), *Social Studies in the 1980s: A Report of Project SPAN* (Alexandria, Va.: Association for Supervision and Curriculum Development, 1982).

46. J. P. Shaver, "Implications from Research: What Should Be Taught in Social Studies?," in V. Richardson-Koehler (Ed.), *Educators' Handbook: A Research Perspective* (New York: Longman, 1987), pp. 112–138.

47. B. J. Armento, "Research on Teaching Social Studies," in M. C. Wittrock (Ed.), *Handbook of Research on Teaching*, 3rd ed. (New York: Macmillan, 1986), pp. 942–951.

48. Adapted from E. P. Torrance, "Teaching Creative and Gifted Learners," in M. C. Wittrock (Ed.), *Handbook of Research on Teaching*, 3rd ed. (New York: Macmillan, 1986), pp. 630–647.

49. A. B. Crabbe, "Creating a Brighter Future: An Update on the Future Problem Solving Program," *Journal for the Education of the Gifted 5* (1982), pp. 2–11.

50. L. M. Baca and H. T. Cervantes, *The Bilingual Special Education Interface* (Santa Clara, Calif.: Times Mirror/Mosby, 1984).

51. *Lau* v. *Nichols*, U.S. S.Ct. 414, U.S. 563 (1974).

52. Adapted from G. D. Borich, *Effective Teaching Methods* (Columbus, Ohio: Merrill, 1988), pp. 271–296.

53. L. W. Fillmore and C. Valadez, "Teaching Bilingual Learners," in M. C. Wittrock (Ed.), *Handbook of Research on Teaching*, 3rd ed. (New York: Macmillan, 1986), pp. 648–685.

54. D. L. Macmillan, B. K. Keogh, and R. L. Jones, "Special Educational Research on Mildly Handicapped Learners," in M. C. Wittrock (Ed.), *Handbook of Research on Teaching*, 3rd ed. (New York: Macmillan, 1986), pp. 686–724.

55. J. A. Stallings and D. Stipek, "Research on Early Childhood and Elementary School Teaching Programs," in M. C. Wittrock (Ed.), *Handbook of Research on Teaching*, 3rd ed. (New York: Macmillan, 1986), pp. 727–754.

# CHAPTER 11

# TECHNOLOGY IN TEACHING

*Those who inherit the future must be prepared to deal with it.—Unknown*

**MAIN IDEAS**

- Instructional technology is the means by which instruction is formatted, stored, and delivered to the learner.

- To date, the instructional medium itself (for example, film, television) does not appear to influence learning. Rather, the high-quality materials, the novel experiences, and changes in teaching practices required by the medium appear to be the most important factors in producing learning.

- As a tool, the computer acts as an assistant, helping in word processing, database management, calculating, graphics, and communications.

- As a tutor, the computer is used for drill and practice, simulation, and instructional games.

- As tutee, the computer becomes a learner to be programmed by the student.

- Computer-based instruction achieves slightly higher effects when compared with other instructional treatments in experimental settings. Further, instructional time is reduced and favorable attitudes toward computers are developed.

- Computers are being applied to the teaching of such subjects as written composition, reading, science, and mathematics. On the horizon are interactive videodisc, CD-ROM, hypermedia, telecommunications and satellite communications, and artificial intelligence.
- Now is the time for a balanced understanding of what technology can and cannot do for you and your students.

# INTRODUCTION

"Don't bring one of those things in *my* room! They scare me. I can do all I need to do without one. Teachers who want computers ought to have 'em, but don't foist one on me. Frankly, I think they're grown-up toys that people play games on."

"That's not my problem. I'd like to have two or three in my room, especially if they'd help me teach writing. I'd like one with word processing features. But then I think of the time it would take to learn to use one. I don't have that kind of time. Can't you just see me spending my whole summer vacation sitting in front of one of those things?"

"I've had a computer in my room all year. After only a week of tinkering I could do quite a few things. They have nifty little programs that let you keep roll and make out grades. I don't know that I save a lot of time, but I'm sure having fun—makes me feel like I'm part of the technological age! Some of my kids have been on them for years. They walked me through how to boot the system and invoke the programs, and they taught me a few of the commands. From there I learned it on my own."

Surprising comments? Not really. Even though computers (and other technology) have been in classrooms and school buildings for years, many teachers feel resistant, wary, and even threatened. Others, though not threatened, remain unconvinced of the computer's usefulness in the classroom. Theirs is a wait-and-see position. Still other teachers, initially cautious, have become exuberant converts.

Expanding our focus from individual teachers' comments, let us raise some larger questions to which this chapter is directed: What impact is the technological revolution having on the public schools? How would *you* fit into a high-technology school environment? What implications do computers have for your curriculum, classroom management, and record keeping?

Take a peek into the future:

In the communication laboratory at a local high school, Stan and Leslie are working with software (a computer program) that simulates a laser beam at work. They bring up the "laser operation" on the screen and "turn on" the laser with a key on the keyboard. The laser being simulated is of extremely high power. Stan wants to see what would happen if a real laser, run by a trained technician, were aimed at the moon. The computer shows that the laser does in fact reach the moon and that the reflected spot is six inches in diameter. From this simulation, Stan and Leslie learn a principal advantage of lasers—minimal dispersion of the light beam.

"What happens if a commercial airliner flies through the path of the laser beam?" Leslie wonders. She types that question into the computer. Through an artificial intelligence system built into the program, she learns the effects on the aircraft as it moves various distances from the source of the laser beam. Mr. Vigosky, their teacher, marvels at how a $100 computer program can simulate more than ten million dollars' worth of actual equipment—without risk of personal injury or damage.

Also in the lab, students are learning how a computer can control lights and motors on the basis of input from sensors. Teams of students are tackling projects such as model elevators, robots, traffic-control systems, and a two-axis positioning table for use on a drill press. But one team is having a problem connecting their newly created robot to the computer. Yesterday the students posted a request for help on the computer telecommunications bulletin board maintained by the International Technology Education Association in Reston, Virginia. A teacher in Bozeman, Montana, noting their request on his bulletin board, posted his solution in the form of a schematic circuit diagram.

Another group of students is working on the research-and-development phase of a project for their manufacturing class. Using a computer search, they have reviewed the products manufactured by similar classes across the nation over the past five years. They have been particularly interested in the winners of the Stanley-Proto Mass Production Contest, for they hope to compete in the contest this year. Besides containing manufacturing product information, the laser disk the students are using contains a *multitude* of information for both teachers and students. Today the students are browsing through fifteen supply catalogs contained on the disk to see if a particular type of hinge required in one of their product ideas is available. The information they need appears on the monitor less than five seconds after it is requested. Even with the massive amount of information on the disk, more than half of the disk is blank. The teacher suggests that the *Encyclopedia of Technology* might be a good possibility to add to the disk.

A few students are working on the design and construction of a model underground mass transit system. Right now they are having their plans evaluated by a professional construction engineer located more than a thousand miles away. They use voice interaction via telephone along with computer telecommunications technology. Their plan, created on a CAD (computer-aided design) system, is simultaneously displayed on the construction engineer's monitor and on their own. In discussing their plans, students use a blue pointer on their screen while the engineer uses a red pointer on his screen. It is as if the engineer were there, looking over their shoulder as the students make revisions to their drawings.

Finally, in still another part of the lab, Claude is taking a "field trip" through a steel mill. With the appropriate laser disk loaded into the interactive video system, he is in complete control as he "strolls" through various parts of the plant, pausing for a detailed look in one area, then moving on to the next area. He prints out career and technical information related to various aspects of the plant's work that interests him. He will study them in detail later, at leisure.[1]

# INSTRUCTIONAL TECHNOLOGY

Of the large number of fields within "technology," we focus only on *instructional* technology. The Commission on Instructional Technology has defined *instructional technology* as "a systematic way of designing, carrying out and evaluating the total process of learning and teaching in terms of specific objectives, based on research in human learning and communication and employing a combination of human and nonhuman resources to bring about more effective instruction."[2] More simply, instructional technology is the means by which instruction is formatted, stored, and delivered to the learner.[3]

Instructional technology includes a wide range of devices to supplement your teaching or to take over the task of directly instructing your stu-

© *Spencer Grant/Monkmeyer Photo Service*

dents. Many teachers believe that students' motivation and academic performance can be enhanced through the use of media. And each new medium seems to create enthusiasm: more than half the teachers in the United States use television in their classrooms, especially for teaching science and social sciences; 75 percent report using audiotapes and radio; and 62 percent use computers.[4] Indications are that these percentages, particularly for computer use, will continue to rise.

Since 1970, considerable research has examined media's overall instructional impact (for example, does using television increase student learning?), as well as the relative strengths of different types of media (for example, does television produce greater learning than videotapes?). Overall, the results of these studies have yielded little that warrants optimism.[5] Generally, it appears that the medium does not, in and of itself, affect learning. Where dramatic changes in achievement have occurred following the introduction of a medium, it was not the medium per se that caused the change, but the curricular revisions that were necessary to use it; new media are often accompanied by high-quality materials, novel experiences, and changes in teaching practices.

Even the type of research on media has changed. Earlier studies compared one medium with another. Today, researchers are investigating the attributes of a given medium (for instance, a slide projector's capability of "freezing" a picture) that combine with learners' traits (for example, Rowan is slow in picking up information) to produce different kinds of learning (for example, Rowan's long-term retention). The rather unimpressive findings on the effects of instructional media come primarily from research on traditional media such as television and slide presentations. Research on the impact of computers has been slow in coming and is only now under way, so it is too early to report on findings.

## COMPUTERS IN THE CLASSROOM

Within the limitations of a single chapter, we can do no more than outline the effects of computer technology on education. We focus chiefly on the computer itself, since its near-ubiquitous presence has created a "computer revolution." Our sample takes in both traditional and cutting-edge applications of computers and related systems.

Educational applications for computers can be classified into three major categories: (1) tool, (2) tutor, and (3) tutee.[6] As a tool, the computer assumes the role of assistant; as tutor, the role of teacher; and as tutee, the role of learner. Within each classification, we can observe how computers have been and are being designed to enhance student learning.[7]

### Computer as Tool

In its most traditional use, the computer functions as a tool, much like the compass, protractor, ruler, or pocket calculator. As a tool, the computer

© Photo Researchers, Inc.

© The Picture Cube

*When you go to the hardware store to buy a drill, you do not actually want a drill. Instead, you want a hole. They don't sell holes at the hardware store, but they do sell drills, which are the technology to create holes. We must not lose sight that technology, for the most part, is a tool and it should be used in applications which address educational concerns or problems. We should, therefore, focus on the appropriate application of technology, rather than on the tool itself.—Geoffrey H. Fletcher*

does whatever its programs tell it to do: calculate numbers with speed and accuracy, facilitate word processing, retrieve stored quotes and references. In this section, we discuss five major tool applications of computers: word processing, database management, calculating, graphics, and communications. A number of these tool applications have been combined into comprehensive packages, such as Lotus 1-2-3, Appleworks, and Framework.

WORD PROCESSING   Word processing on a computer might best be described as typing with abandon! Students have a flexible typewriter, devoid of all tedium. Hurriedly conceived paragraphs, unrelated thoughts, and misspelled words can all be thrown in with more thoughtful material because corrections and rewrites are so simple. A sentence can be "cut" here and "pasted" there; the first paragraph can be blocked and "lifted" to become the last paragraph. Misspelled and duplicated words can be picked up by the program's spelling checker. A thesaurus helps find that more appropriate word. Formatting is a breeze. Even the old carriage return (signaled by the bell) is carried out automatically, and words "wrap around" so they need not be split in two. Transferring a finished document onto paper can be accomplished with high-speed laser printers.

Word processors allow students to stop thinking of their text as static; it becomes a fluid body of writing that can be shaped and molded under the repetitive editing of the author. Students can now concentrate on the composing process itself.

Teachers, for their part, use computers to prepare syllabi, handouts, and drawings and to write letters to parents.

DATABASE MANAGEMENT   What is a database? Start out by thinking of a recipe file, that bulging box of cards your mother turns to every time a special occasion creeps up. Suppose all her recipes are on 3″ × 5″ cards and, in pulling one at random, we read at the top: "Dessert: pumpkin pie." On another card we read, "Main dish: ham and cheese casserole." In searching for a dessert for Sunday's guests she goes to the tab card "desserts" and thumbs through the cards behind it for possibilities. Her recipe file is a simple database. Contrast your mother's immaculately organized database with your Aunt Grace's helter-skelter recipe file. For years she has thrown different-sized cards and slips of paper into a shoe box. Her retrieval method is to grab a handful of cards and search through them one at a time.

Consider now a computer database. A database is a collection of information stored in a computer. Rather than a recipe box, suppose your modern mom has a computer sitting on the countertop near the microwave. With a few keystrokes she is in her electronic card file and pulls up a list of desserts, then quickly scrolls through them. Or she may conduct a more limited search on "pies." She may start out looking for "casseroles." With a database set up so that the search includes the ingredients on each card, she can even call for "casseroles with ham" (or those *without* ham). Finally, since Aunt Grace is coming Sunday, and she hates rice, your mom pulls up "main dishes *without* rice."

Using a database management system, you can enter, update, organize and retrieve almost any type of information. In seconds, any one record can be searched out, or any group of records in almost any order.

A computer database can be a great help in many places and situations. Computer databases are being used increasingly in education at the national, state, and local levels to facilitate a multitude of tasks. Individual schools are using computer databases to assist with a variety of administrative and instructional responsibilities. For example, your principal uses a database to access information about students' names, addresses, and phone numbers, students' academic progress, grades, class schedules, and bus schedules and routes. You have responsibility to maintain information on student attendance, test scores, grades, lesson plans, handouts, and letters to parents. Students keep information from class lectures, reading assignments, and library research.[8]

CALCULATING   The widely used pocket calculator includes a dedicated microprocessor. With electronic advances, these calculators can now perform a vast number of arithmetic operations. Still, they are limited in capacity and scope. Most modern desktop computers, the kind found in many classrooms, open up new vistas in calculations and data processing in courses such as mathematics, science, and statistics. In the past, teachers have had to contrive simplified forms of a problem to avoid arduous calculations. Times are changing. Students can now be presented with realistic problems whose complex solutions require less calculation time on high-speed computers than did their more simplified counterparts, done manually. Time is therefore available to concentrate on the theory behind and the application of what students are learning, rather than on calculation procedures. Furthermore, students can create their own calculating tools by writing their own computer programs, thereby gaining a deeper understanding of the nature of the algorithms involved.

An electronic spreadsheet is a general-purpose program for processing numerical data and printing them out in columns, rows, or other configurations. Administrators use spreadsheet programs as scratch pads for preparing such summaries as financial reports, cost estimates, and projected budgets. Teachers use them as grade books. Students use them in a variety of ways: bookkeeping and accounting students use them for generating budgets and profit and loss statements; career education students use them in predicting salary schedules ten years in the future; and vocational education students use them to understand relationships between design decisions and costs.[9]

A powerful advantage of electronic spreadsheets is their ability to recalculate all values quickly whenever any formula or single value changes. This capability allows students to view the effects of different variables on the performance of a system, change the values, and update information. Students propose alternate hypotheses and, because of rapid recalculations, quickly see the effect of changes in one variable on the behavior of the overall system.[10]

GRAPHICS   Computer programs are an appealing tool for practicing commercial art and for communicating summary reports in visual form. Sophisticated graphic designs can be created on the screen, then easily transferred to hard copy (printed on a piece of paper). For example, the superintendent's office creates a pie chart showing what percentage of the district's budget goes to capital equipment, teachers' salaries, utilities, and supplies. In a unit on world civilizations, the teacher devises a column chart showing population distributions for various countries. Her business students, working in teams, include scatter charts in their GNP reports, then convert the charts into overhead transparencies for presentation to the class. A high school principal creates a staff organizational chart using a mechanical drawing program. This same program is used by students of architecture to produce plan drawings for a large shopping mall.

What about combining the features of word processing, database, spreadsheets, and graphics into one comprehensive system? It's been done. In education, information from a database can be converted into a spreadsheet, which is then fed into a graphics-generating program to produce charts and graphs. Students incorporate these charts and graphs in their interpretive reports, which are prepared on a word processor.[11]

COMMUNICATIONS   The microcomputer on your desk can be linked with others wherever phone lines can go. Suppose your school district has stored information on all students, teachers, and school finances on its mainframe. Your principal and other authorized personnel can access and update this information from microcomputers on their office desks. Or let's say the mainframe in the state office of education houses a large number of databases, including one on math programs. Your math team has been charged with the responsibility of looking around for any new junior high computer-assisted math programs. Using the computer in the principal's office, you access the mainframe in the state office for descriptions and evaluations of all the math software packages currently on the market. You take a shopping trip for computer programs without leaving the school! Not to be outdone, your students search a computer-based library card catalog for new methods of coal gasification—from their own home computers. If too few sources turn up in the students' search, you guide them to numerous on-line cataloging databases on the mainframe computer at a local college.

If we can have electronic card catalogs, why not electronic bulletin boards? You can post information on your computer system's bulletin board. Suppose you are in a network of schools, all of which have teachers in high school home economics. You want to try out something new in teaching pie crusts. Turning on your computer, you invoke the bulletin board, type in the proper access codes for your school, then type, "Help! Need creative ideas for teaching pie crusts. Feeling a bit flaky." Your request floods out over the network. Three days later, two creative suggestions have been posted for you on the bulletin board. One is signed "Lightly yours from Portland," and the other, "Crusty from New York."

Computers allow your principal to participate in a national leadership conference—from his own office. They enable your students to communicate with students in other schools across the state as everyone prepares for the upcoming competition in self-propelled vehicles as part of National Engineering Week. They can also facilitate reordering of supplies for the lunchroom or book loans from other school libraries.

We have introduced you to but five applications of the computer as a tool. Many more exist. Using an "electronic chalkboard" (a computer connected to a large-screen projection monitor), you can teach while facing your class, calling up information you have prepared in advance and displaying it before the entire class. When questions arise about a concept previously discussed, you simply scroll backward.

Colorful electronic graphics, "transparencies," are also ready to be brought up at the right moment. These are no ordinary transparencies—they are animated. Suppose you are teaching the proper method of titration. Rather than turning students loose in the chemistry lab, where you have little control over how well they are learning, you send them over to the computers to perform simulated titration experiments under the watchful eye of a tutor program. No mess, no hurried cleanups, no broken equipment. After getting the process down, students can, still on the computer, perform six titration experiments rather than one during a single period.

Students can program their computers to operate cranes, plotters, and robots, or, being restlessly creative, they may become involved in projects to build and control their own robots. What about those students uninterested in the world of mechanics? They can compose, record, and play back their own synthesized music.[12]

## Computer as Tutor

As an adjunct to regular instruction, the computer can serve as a marvelous tool in the hands of both student and teacher. But it can also play a more comprehensive role—that of teacher. In tutor applications, the student is tutored by the computer. Tutor applications can be categorized as (1) drill-

© *Elizabeth Crews/The Image Works*

and-practice applications, (2) tutorial applications, (3) simulation applications, and (4) game applications.[13]

**DRILL-AND-PRACTICE APPLICATIONS**   Committing facts to memory is drudgery—but not for the computer. It shines in this task, patiently insisting that students memorize such things as math, factual data, and spelling words: 12 + 6 = 18; the capital of California is Sacramento; the correct way to spell "bridge" is *b r i d g e.*

Drill-and-practice exercises, when directed by the computer, offer a number of advantages. First, and most important, Allyson receives immediate feedback on the correctness or incorrectness of her response. And she is not allowed to proceed until she types in the correct response! No getting away with "I think I know it," or "I can pretty well guess what the answer is." The computer gets the job done. Second, drill and practice are helpful in achieving a range of curricular objectives; so much of the curriculum is simply memorized information. Third, drill and practice are effective with the young and the old, the fast and the slow. Fourth, the computer tracks the types of responses Allyson makes *during* the task, enabling her teacher to chart patterns of responses, diagnose any problems, and provide targeted remediation.

As a teacher, you need to integrate computer drill-and-practice programs carefully into your ongoing curriculum. These programs are a tool to facilitate memory learning. How should they be implemented? Research suggests that several short, spaced drill sessions are more effective than a few long sessions; even fifteen minutes per day can develop an impressive bank of memorized material.

TUTORIAL APPLICATIONS   In tutorial applications the computer carries the full instructional burden, guiding the student to achieve a specified set of objectives. It must (1) gain the student's attention, (2) present the lesson's objective, (3) help the student review prerequisite skills, (4) present the stimulus and provide guidance, (5) elicit responses and provide feedback, (6) assess performance, and (7) facilitate retention and transfer.[14]

Specifically, the tutorial presents new information; gives a question or problem related to the information and awaits a response; evaluates the response according to some previously determined criteria; and, on the basis of the evaluation, provides additional information. The cycle is repeated: more information, questions, responses, feedback.

Ideal tutorial programs tailor the material to the needs of individual students during the teaching process. If a student is having difficulty, the computer branches over to a remedial presentation; if he is breezing along, it skips over elaborations, extra examples, or practice items.

In practice, most tutorial programs fall far short of this ideal. For a tutorial program to outclass a book, it must be *interactive,* sensitive to the student's responses, and relevant to the expected learning outcomes. Further, the tutorial should return responses that help the student understand; simply flashing up "correct" or "incorrect" messages will not do (even when accompanied by smiles and frowns). The tutorial must tell the student *why* the response is incorrect, then give the correct answer.

Uses for tutorials are virtually unlimited. Think of a small, remote rural school with modest resources, or a large city school with insufficient teachers for certain segments of the curriculum, or the chronically ill or homebound student, or even the truant who could become interested in history if allowed to work at her own pace. A sophisticated tutorial becomes an orchestra leader, directing a student through a coordinated program of supporting media: videotapes, drill-and-practice programs, videodisc players, and random-access audio cassettes. Admittedly, the computer's role as tutor—the complete teacher—is circumscribed, limited and, at this point, highly structured and quite inflexible. But who knows what the future holds?

SIMULATION APPLICATIONS

For just under $10,000 an hour, a student can fly a modern high-performance aircraft. For just under $1,000 per hour, a student can operate a full ten-axis cockpit simulator of the same aircraft.

For just under $100 per hour, a student can operate a sophisticated interactive instruction device-based simulator of the cockpit's subsystems. And for just under $10 per hour, a student can receive work-book instruction on the same system.[15]

Through computer simulation programs, students can vicariously experience novel and important educational activities. Sitting at his computer, Rimano "flies" an airplane, "mixes" dangerous chemicals, "explores" the ocean floor. Simulation affords a number of advantages: vicarious experiences offer less risk than real experiences, training costs can be reduced, and simulations offer convenience and versatility. For example, action sequences can be speeded up or slowed down to enhance learning, and a specific aspect of the phenomenon can be focused on.

Despite these advantages, simulations may not be preferred over actual experiences. For example, catching a full whiff of ammonia from a just-opened bottle can be a wholly unforgettable experience! Conducting a litmus test with an attractive lab partner can be far more memorable than seeing a color graphic display of $p$H values on a lifeless computer screen.

GAME APPLICATIONS   Instructional programs with gaming elements are a vehicle to learning. Educational computer games have been developed that teach basic skills such as reading and mathematics operations, and complex computer games are available that teach students more sophisticated concepts. One can also devise individual adaptations to create many more computer games. In part because of the excitement it engenders, computer gaming has considerable attraction for students; it has been found to be particularly appealing to gifted and talented students.

Whether to use a computer game application depends on the teacher's objectives and the most appropriate means to achieve them. Games must be relevant and well integrated into the overall curriculum. By setting the context for the game and showing how it will help reach intended objectives, teachers ensure that games will be instrumental rather than merely pleasurable diversions.

COMPUTER-ASSISTED INSTRUCTION   Everything discussed so far in this section falls under the heading "computer-assisted instruction." More precisely, when the computer is used to teach students specific content on an individualized basis, computer-assisted instruction (CAI) is occurring. In creating software for CAI, programmers attempt to sequence the context according to the logical structure of the subject matter. For example, in creating a math program, they place the addition of whole numbers before that of fractions.

The computer is programmed to handle certain types of errors students predictably make, and is ready to remediate, just as a teacher does. Unlike the teacher, however, the computer has the supreme virtue of unlimited patience. It is tireless—indeed, relentless—in going back over the same instruction until the material is learned.

CAI has its limitations, however. Computers do not think; they only follow instructions. If a student is having a problem learning a concept and continues making incorrect responses, the computer does not "know" the reason for her incorrect responses; however, her teacher might.

Even with newer, more sophisticated efforts to create tailored instruction as the student moves through the program, there are only so many paths, so much flexibility. Once those paths are exhausted, the student receives no new instruction. The ongoing challenge is to upgrade the computer's "intelligence" in tailoring its programs to individual students' needs.

An additional complaint with computer-driven lessons is their inability to draw the right inferences from the student's behavior. For example, one study found that for some arithmetic tasks, students had developed deep-seated but incorrect procedural methods. Since the methods were wrong, students kept coming up with incorrect answers. The computer could only "assume" that the student had not *learned* the correct method, so it continued re-presenting it. There was no way it could draw an alternative inference, namely, that the students were not using the correct method because they preferred their incorrect method. Without "knowing" this, the computer is unable to point out fallacies in students' reasoning and persuade them to switch methods.[16]

Weaknesses notwithstanding, consequential developments are occurring in CAI. New ways of thinking about the computer's role—new models—are being conceived. These models spur researchers to greater sophistication in their program development. The computer has been portrayed as an intelligent tutor that can *build* a model of the student's thinking as the student moves through a computer program and, as a result, can carry on a learning "conversation" with the student—just as an informed teacher would.

The computer has been seen as a diagnostician. John generates his own hypothesis about a particular problem and enters it into the computer. As the computer reads John's hypothesis, it gains "insight" into the depth of his understanding and is able to select situations in which this novel hypothesis can be tested. Here, we conceive the computer to be an intelligent tutor, effectively diagnosing the student's hypothesis, then creating a model of the process the student has used. On the basis of this model, the computer selects new situations in which the hypothesis can be tested and explored.

Breakthroughs in microelectronics have reduced the costs of CAI systems, increasing their feasibility for school and home use. Even with its limitations, CAI claims the following results:

1. CAI, as an adjunct to the teacher, enables students to learn 10 to 40 percent more in a given time period—if objectives are specifically defined, appropriate software is provided, and students are given twelve to twenty minutes of quality instruction four times a week.

2. Student retention rates following CAI are at least equal to those following conventional instruction.

3. When CAI supplements the curriculum, students have higher or equally positive attitudes toward school.[17]

## Computer as Tutee

As tutor, the computer serves as the teacher. But it can also reverse roles. As tutee, the computer becomes the student while the student becomes the tutor, teaching the computer to carry out various tasks. To do this, the student must be able to communicate with the computer in a language that the computer understands. The student must learn how to write computer programs, a process that requires the development of thinking and problem-solving skills (a major educational goal in any classroom). Common programming languages that students learn are Logo, Pascal, and BASIC. Logo is being used to introduce young students to the computer and to the art of programming. Observe how these students, using Logo, are learning mapping and the use of a computer keyboard:

> A large map with roads and houses is on the floor, and two of the houses have pictures on them, one of a lion, the other of a rabbit.
>
> To begin the lesson, the teacher gives the children a toy car with a dog sitting in it. She tells the children that the dog's car can go right, left, forward, and backward. The teacher says that it is the dog's birthday, and his friend the lion has called him to come over to get a birthday present. She instructs the children to work in pairs, practicing getting the car to the lion's house. When the children get the dog to the lion's house, they pick up the present and are told to go the rabbit's house to pick up a present from him.
>
> After pushing the cars around the floor with their hands for a while, the children are ready to use a computer. The teacher introduces a floor robot that can be instructed by their microcomputer to go in the same directions as the car—right, left, forward, and backward. Using the computer, the children instruct the robot which direction to move to get to the houses and pick up the presents.[18]

The computer adds a refreshing touch of variety, flexibility, and challenge to learning problem-solving skills, both as the computer program is being created and as it is being debugged (corrected). Students see the problem-solving task of programming as a challenge to be met with a constructive activity: "Let's get this silly thing working!"

Many writers stress the importance of students' learning to program as a way of developing problem-solving skills; for example,

> If the essence of problem-solving activity is the representation and processing of information and its structures . . . , then computers will affect this activity in critical, direct, and fundamental ways because computers deal exclusively with this essence! They provide dramatic new freedom in doing all the things that are at the heart of problem solving: representation of knowledge, manipulation of knowledge, varying the givens of a problem and their relationships,

## A New Language

Seymour Papert has made important contributions to the field of education through relating computing to the education of young children. Author of *Mind Storms: Children, Computers, and Powerful Ideas* and of numerous articles and research reports, Papert has devoted much of his effort to the development of child-appropriate, Logo-based computing for elementary schools.

Papert has studied learning activities of young children and how to enhance them through the use of the computer. Working with the Swiss psychologist Jean Piaget, Papert developed a keen interest in the early learning of children:

> I believe with Dewey, Montessori, and Piaget that children learn by doing and by thinking about what they do. And so the fundamental ingredients of educational innovation must be better things to do and better ways to think about oneself doing these things. . . . I claim that computation is by far the richest known source of these ingredients. We can give children unprecedented power to invent and carry out exciting projects by providing them with access to computers, with suitably clear and intelligible programming language and with peripheral devices capable of producing on-line real-time action. . . . In its embodiment as the physical computer, computation opens a vast universe of things to do. But the real magic comes when this is combined with the *conceptual power* of theoretical ideas associated with computation [pp. 161–162].

Papert encourages teachers to gain a "grander vision" of an educational system in which technology plays a paramount role. The child uses the computer to manipulate and extend, thereby gaining a greater and more articulate mastery of his world, a sense of the power of applied knowledge, and a self-confidently realistic image of himself as an intellectual agent.

Much of the child's facility with the computer has stemmed from the Logo programming language developed by Papert. Logo was designed to simulate the child's basic mental processes, such as reasoning. Thus, Logo gives the teacher a glimpse of a student's natural thought processes. At the same time, it helps structure his thinking and reasoning as he models the programming language being learned.

Logo teaches children of different ages and abilities to use the computer through graphics displays. The child directs the "turtle," a small triangle displayed by the program, around the computer monitor through commands such as "Right," "Left," "Forward," and "Backward." Children quickly learn to write computer programs that allow them to play simple games, generate and manipulate word lists and sentences, write poetry, and create conversations. A powerful feature of Logo is its capacity to add new commands or extensions to its basic language, thus enabling students to explore a diversity of academic areas. Logo is easy to learn and use, fun, relatively inexpensive, and compatible with most microcomputers.

R. P. Taylor, (Ed.), *The Computer in the School: Tutor, Tool, Tutee* (New York: Teachers College Press, 1980); R. L. Upchurch and J. Lochhead, "Computers and Higher-Order Thinking Skills," in V. Richardson-Koehler (Ed.), *Educators' Handbook: A Research Perspective* (New York: Longman, 1987), pp. 139–164.

computing potential solutions, and so on. In this way computers are fundamentally different from other technologies, [such as] television, that have bounced off the educational enterprise. These other technologies had to do with transmission of information but not very much to do with varying its representation or transforming its structure.[19]

## Computer Use in Schools

Advances in technology always seem to be well ahead of our ability to apply them in society. Such has been the case with computers in education, as portrayed in this colorful quote: "For many years we have been trying to get the ship in the water. Now that it's afloat, we've discovered to our horror that we don't know how to steer it."[20]

How widely are computers being used in schools? What is the extent of their impact on students' learning? These are two questions for which there are not, as yet, clear-cut answers. First off, placing computers in schools does not ensure their use. Thus, studies indicating how many computers were "carried in the front door" tell us little about how much they are used and their impact. For example, The Center for Social Organization of Schools, in an early survey of 2,209 schools across the country, found: "By January, 1983, 85 percent of all high schools, 77 percent of all junior-senior combinations, and 68 percent of all middle- and junior high schools had one or more microcomputers. The corresponding figure for elementary schools rose to 42 percent during the same period."[21]

All indications are that the rate of school acquisition of computers is escalating. But how much are the twenty shiny new computers sitting in classrooms at a given school being used? Who uses them and for what subjects? One study in the mid-1980s found the following:

> How are these computers being used by students? During the 1984 school year, the median use per week (in minutes) for certain activities was as follows: 19 (elementary) and 55 (secondary) for writing programs and "computer literacy," 13 (elementary) and 17 (secondary) for drills, 12 (elementary) and 11 (secondary) for playing learning or recreational games, and 30 (secondary) for word processing and data processing.[22]

Some researchers have found that only a small percentage of students use computers in a given week, and these students tend to be above average in math skills. A major portion of the school population is excluded, including ethnic minorities and females. Additionally, lower-socioeconomic-group and minority students usually receive instruction for computer use in mastering basic skills through drill-and-practice exercises, whereas higher-achieving and ethnic-majority students usually receive instruction in programming and problem solving. Other research suggests that teachers are indeed careful to ensure that all types and levels of students receive opportunities to develop computer literacy. It appears as though the teacher were the critical factor: his own attitude toward computers, how he schedules students on the computer, and how he coordinates the use of computers with his ongoing instruction determine the patterns of use among groups of students.

One summary of research indicates that the following are among the effects of computer use in schools:

1.  Computer-based instruction achieves consistently higher effects than other instructional treatments to which it is compared in experimental situations. The effects, however, are usually small or moderate.

2.  Computer-based instruction results in significant reductions of instructional time. It also produces favorable attitudes toward computers by students.

3.  Computer-based instruction in elementary schools appears to produce higher achievement effects than it does with junior high and high school students.

4.  Computer-based instruction that supplements other forms of instruction seems to produce greater academic effects than when the computer is used by itself.

5.  In reading, small group computer-based instruction produces better results than does individual computer-based instruction.

6.  In math, computer-based instruction which is nondrill produces higher overall results than does drill-type instruction. However, younger and lower-ability students seem to learn better from drill-type instruction, whereas higher-ability students appear to profit more from tutorial-type instruction.

7.  In general, elementary and high school students seem to profit more from computer-based instruction in math than in reading or language arts.[23]

# ON THE HORIZON

Even as we write this chapter, technology is expanding. Let's take a look at what is on today's horizon.

Hinting at "the next computer revolution," one author prophesies the following:

> The way computing has permeated the fabric of purposeful intellectual and economic activity has no parallel. Computing is perhaps the most exciting technological enterprise in history. . . . Imagine being engaged in a field that changes exponentially! And now computing appears to be entering a new passage. In this phase, by means of developments in hardware and software, computing will grow more powerful, sophisticated and flexible by an order of magnitude in the next decade. At the same time the technology will become an intellectual utility, widely available, ultimately as ubiquitous as the telephone. Visual and other natural interfaces will make the machines easier to use, and a flexible high-capacity network will be capable of linking any combination of individuals who need computing. . . . A typical personal computer in the next decade may have an order of magnitude more computing power than today's

© *The Picture Cube*

typical machine, and from 10 to 100 times more storage. Its high-quality, high-speed screen will, in less than a second, reproduce a new image that consists of from one million to four million pixels in from 64 to 256 shades of color. . . . It will be easier to use by accommodating a natural human–machine interaction, recognizing speech and writing. It will display the results of computation in a visually intuitive manner. For example, pie charts and graphs will be augmented by 3D images presented in many shades of color.

Currently computing can amplify only simple, relatively routine mental capacities, but steady progress is being made toward an ability to enhance the more analytical and inferential skills. . . . Computing—through its ability to extend man's mental abilities—is the engine propelling the current and as yet inadequately named revolution. The journey has only begun.[24]

In the future we may expect to see more use in educational settings of simulations, programming and authoring, telecommunications and satellite communications, and eventually robots and artificial intelligence. Several predicted developments, as well as technologies already on the scene, hold special promise for teaching. Let us catch a glimpse at how some of these can affect you.

## Interactive Videodiscs

Recall the special capability of the computer to *interact* with the student: it holds in reserve the instructional information built into or accessed by its program, waits for the student's input to determine what information to

*The new machine will soon be antiquated, the new drug will be outmoded, the new principle will yield to a more profound one, and the revolutional approach will become first familiar and then old fashioned. Everyone must expect constant change and with it new goals to be achieved and new understanding and skill to be mastered.—Cyril O. Houle*

supply, and then delivers that information contingent upon the student's need. This capability makes the computer appear to be "thinking."

A videodisc is a plastic disc resembling a phonograph record. Millions of pieces of information—audio and visual—are embedded on the disk by means of low-intensity laser beams. When called up, this information appears on the display screen (TV monitor).

By attaching a videodisc player to a computer, you can create a powerful computer-based instructional system. The microcomputer/videodisc combination offers, in one system, media capabilities previously available only in very large and expensive multimedia systems. Motion picture sequences, in full color and with stereophonic sound, can be combined with computer-generated instruction.

Still frames, motion sequences, and audio information can be combined and mixed in any sequence on an optical videodisc. The great value of the videodisc as an instructional medium stems from the fact that it can quickly access any single picture or frame, standard film or television programs, or any other type of audiovisual or textual material previously recorded on the videodisc.[25]

Interactive videodisc programs can be used effectively to teach many different subjects in the curriculum. Though currently out of reach for many classrooms because of cost, these programs are definitely on the horizon. IBM and Apple have set aside millions of dollars for the development of courseware for interactive videodisc; other companies are following suit. Huge growth is anticipated as publishing companies approach developers requesting new courseware. Distributors, too, are waiting in the wings, anxious to be part of the act.[26] For a glimpse of a videodisc system at work in a classroom, let's look in on Frank Garcia's high school Spanish class, where students are learning the language with surprising speed—and enjoying it!

> The reason is my interactive videodisc program. Kids are picking up 40 to 50 percent more information in the same amount of time I took using my standard techniques—you know, the old standbys of memorizing a list of words, using them in practice exercises and giving them back on exams, then trying to fit them together during dialogue sessions. For Pete's sake! We've known for years that people living in a foreign country learn the language faster than when it's taught in the classroom. I'm able to simulate a foreign-country experience with videodisc, right here in my classroom!

Interactive videodisc is ideal for language instruction since it provides the visual capacity to "transport" students to the country itself, placing them in a holistic teaching environment. Language programs can be created for both individual students and the entire class, or a combination of the two. Frank Garcia continues:

> Being able to teach the whole class, all at once, is nice. It's also inexpensive. I use only one set of equipment. I can play a segment of "Digame" (the Spanish program), then freeze it and ask students questions about what they just heard, then help them interpret it. If I want to repeat the segment, I can do it instantly—without rewinding like I have to with videotape. I often put the system on "pause" and have each pair of students discuss between themselves the footage they have just seen. They have to watch and listen carefully, since the characters in the documentary are native Spanish speakers. My kids used to be quite passive. Not any more! Now, they've got to pay attention. It's intense. The visual element makes their learning sink in. They learn faster and remember better. Jake is a sterling scholar in languages. He's studied French and German besides Spanish. He raves about the system: "It's really effective. It pulls you out of the classroom and into the video—the country and its language. I know Spanish far better than French and German, even though I've studied them twice as long as Spanish." [27]

With interactive video, a teacher can "author" her own teaching material. For example, a high school teacher prepares the "script" for her interactive videodisc program in French. She selects segments from three French films that have been included on the disk. One segment involves a conversation between an old man and a young girl on a mountainside; another is between a shopkeeper and customer in a clothing store; and a third is between a mother and her son walking in downtown Paris. The teacher enters the segments into the authoring program, using vocabulary and episodes appropriate to the level of her students.

Interactive videodisc programs are at their best as an aid to the teacher, helping her teach the same amount of material in half the time. She must continue deftly to orchestrate the program's use within the context of her overall curriculum. But what an exciting tool!

Videodisc technology is also seeing rapid growth in the business world:

> Training in business with interactive videodisc technology has shown considerable potential. With time, similar benefits could be achieved in education. For example, the Federal Express Corporation has begun installation of a projected 1,300 interactive stations to provide training for its 6,000 customer service and 17,000 courier personnel. Interactive stations are located at service stations and branch offices nationwide and, to track employee progress, are connected to central computers at company headquarters. In studies comparing interactive video to classroom instruction, the number of employee errors was reduced by an average of 30 percent and incorrect student responses were reduced by 40 percent when videodisc was used. A 60 percent reduction in employee training time was achieved with the use of the videodisc. While system and courseware development was projected to cost $40 million over five years, the company estimated that it would result in direct cost savings of over

$100 million in travel, employee time, and training control. Each terminal delivers tests and training for about $25 per day—compared to the $400 per diem cost of sending an employee to regional headquarters for training. Indirect savings are estimated to be greater: a 10 percent improvement in worker productivity and performance could save the company $150 million, not counting the added billings that would come from greater efficiency.[28]

Following are several examples of interactive videodisc applications:

1.    *Interactive Mathematics* (developed by ISC Educational Systems) is designed to instruct students who are not yet prepared for required college-level math courses. The course is composed of seventy-five modules contained on twenty videodisc sides, each module designed to take roughly an hour to complete. Topics begin with whole numbers and progress to lessons on fractions, decimals, percentages, measurements and geometry, graphs and statistics, and pre-algebra. A special module on "life skills" covers the math involved in such everyday activities as preparing a household budget, buying and operating a car, and planning a vacation.

2.    The *Voyager Gallery* (produced by Optical Data Corporation) includes still and motion sequences of NASA space visuals. Side one of the disc is the "Hyper-Video Database," a bank of more than 2700 stills and motion clips of Jupiter, Saturn, Uranus, and their satellites. Side two features digital "Sound Portraits of the Planets" and offers views of Mercury, Venus, Earth, and Mars.

3.    *Attributes for Successful Employability* is a videodisc program designed to train high school students to become better employees through improving such behavioral skills as dependability, diligence, attitude, and punctuality. The "cast" involves supervisors and employees from seven different job locations. Scenarios are developed that challenge the student to make "dependability" decisions about behavior on the job. Supervisors follow each scenario with "expert advice."

4.    *Exploring Chemistry* uses videodisc technology to teach difficult concepts (e.g., kinetics, equilibrium, gases, and chemical reactions) through a step-by-step visual approach. The program has been used in two Illinois high schools and on the University of Illinois campus, where 50 percent of students' lab work is disc-based. Evaluation of the program's effectiveness found that students trained with the videodisc scored significantly higher on achievement tests than did those doing hands-on work in the lab. Seventy-five percent of students using the interactive program indicated that the videodisc lab significantly decreased the amount of time it took them to learn chemistry.

5.    *Doing Chemistry* is an in-service program designed to upgrade skills of underprepared high school science teachers. Supplemented by written materials, the videodisc programs guide the teacher through the various steps of performing an in-class experiment, including how to set up the experiment, what types of questions to ask students, and how to perform the experiment safely.

6.    The potential of videodiscs for helping students develop sensitivity to other cultures is highlighted by two videodisc courses on "cultural diversity" used at the University of Minnesota. The courses help the largely white student body learn about Southeast Asian immigrants and about Minnesota's oldest cultural group, the Ojibway Indians. The programs teach students about race, ethnicity,

communications skills, descriptive statistics, and problem solving in the social services. The Southeast Asia disc includes interviews with refugees, and the Indian disc presents its information in a bilingual format. The student is introduced to situations in which he might find himself (e.g., social work or teaching), is flooded with information, and then is given the opportunity to decide what is important to his particular application.[29]

Videodisc instruction has frequently been evaluated against other types of training, generally resulting in conclusions such as these:

1. Vicarious experience: In comparison with traditional training methods (textbook, lecture, demonstration), interactive videodisc provides concrete, realistic learning experiences for students.

2. Cost: When compared with common simulators and hands-on training with real equipment, interactive videodisc is less expensive.

3. Safety: When compared with training using real equipment, interactive videodisc is safer for students and equipment.

4. Flexibility: When compared with real equipment, simulators, and lecture/demonstrations, interactive videodisc can be readily adapted to meet a particular instructional need.

5. Efficiency: When compared with traditional training methods, interactive videodisc has resulted in a consistent 25 to 50 percent savings in training time.[30]

# CD-ROM

Technology has produced the capacity to store vast amounts of information through optical storage devices read with a laser beam. These devices include laser discs, CD-audio discs, and CD-ROM discs. In 1983, a laser-produced disc called CD-ROM was introduced. These letters stand for *Compact Disc Read-Only Memory*. Information is embedded on these discs with high- and low-intensity laser beams, and the disc is sold "already written on." A person can only read what is on the disc, but not write new material over this information as might be done on a regular floppy disk. However, technology is moving toward the creation of a compact disc that can be both written to and read from over and over without damage.

Each CD-ROM has the capacity to store more than 600 million bytes of information, or approximately 250,000 pages of text. This is equivalent to what a secretary could generate typing eighty words per minute, eight hours per day, for eight years! When stamped in quantities of more than one hundred, these discs cost less than $5 to produce. This incredible volume of storage represents a dramatic leap in storage capacity for small computers.

CD-ROM enables personal computers to access huge databases of information, as large as those of most mainframe computers now in use. These vast databases can be searched and information retrieved in a matter of seconds. The entire Grolier Encyclopedia set was put on one compact disc, with room to spare. In less than two seconds, any topic in the encyclopedia can be searched and accessed with the use of a standard personal computer and a CD-ROM player. The compact disc itself, containing the entire encyclopedia set, costs less than $200. In 1987, Microsoft produced a CD-ROM library of ten reference works for IBM or IBM-compatible personal computers. Called Bookshelf, it costs less than $300.[31]

At a CD-ROM conference in 1986, Sony and Phillips announced "Compact Disc Interactive" (CD-I). This format was intended to be fully interactive, combining all the capabilities of CD-ROM and CD-audio. It would be a self-contained system that would play CD-ROMs featuring music, visuals, and full-motion video on screen. By running a cable to the television set, one could view whole libraries of information. The information could be accessed and manipulated using a simple manual controller such as a joystick.

In 1987, RCA announced "Digital Video-Interactive" (DVI), a technology that would provide sound and full-screen/full-motion video on a monitor. American Interactive Media (AIM) and Interactive Production Associates are producing two CD-I products based on the best-selling book series *Tell Me Why*. The discs will provide answers to hundreds of questions asked by children, incorporating still and animated graphics, audio, and still photographs. These products are designed to educate and entertain children of ages 7 to 13 in a home or school environment.

CD-ROM has the potential for playing a major role in bringing together libraries, publishers, technology companies, and education in developing creative solutions to educational problems. For example, SilverPlatter Information Services has produced PSYCHLIT, a CD-ROM version of the Psychological Abstracts database, and a CD-ROM version of the Educational Resources Information Center (ERIC) database. DIALOG Information Services has produced DIALOG OnDisc ERIC.

Using such large-scale databases, students access almost instantly a wealth of information for reports, projects, and papers. Preservice and inservice teachers search databases for the latest information in various areas, such as assessing particular needs and providing up-to-date remediation:

> Rachael Peterson, a second-grade teacher in a small rural school, is concerned about Stacy and Monica. Both persist in mirror writing (writing as if they were looking in a mirror). During reading, the girls continue to make reversal errors, (for instance, "was" for "saw"). Rachael spends extra time trying to help the girls generalize and transfer, having them practice sounds in words like "cat," "ran," and "fan," hoping they will give appropriate sounds to new words like "fat," "rat," and "can." The girls make circumlocutions, hesitate too long, and make substitution errors such as saying "dog" when shown a picture of a cat.
>
> At a reading convention, Rachael tunes in to a conversation about recent research on dyslexia—and learns of some new approaches teachers are trying. "Maybe I can get some insights into this stuff, for working with Stacy and Monica." She decides to go to the district office to learn more about dyslexia.

Using a personal computer with a CD-ROM, and working with the district audiovisual specialist, Rachael accesses the ERIC database for information on dyslexia in primary-age children.

## Hypermedia

Recall our recipe database. If we search on the category "desserts" we come up with a long list, including such delights as "black bottom pie," "cherry cheesecake," "pumpkin pie," and "Texas chocolate cake." This list does *not* include "ham and cheese casserole" or "crab salad," because our search category is only "desserts." From the search output, you pull up the recipe for Texas chocolate cake. Your recipe tells you how to make this particular cake—nothing more. Suppose, however, that your Sunday guests are so enamored of your elegantly rich Texas chocolate cake that they begin asking questions: "Where did its name come from?" "Did it really originate in Texas?" "Did you use a special type of chocolate?" How nice it would be to have all this information at your fingertips, since it's all related to your Texas chocolate cake.

Let's switch to another context. Dara is reading a CD-ROM article describing Sioux tribal customs. She finds herself in the middle of a massive database! Somewhere it contains such information as habitats of the Northern Plains, audio recordings of Sioux chants, photographs of General Custer, and video newsclips reviewing the Sioux rebellions of the 1870s. But how can she ever find the specific material she wants in this sea of information?

Enter hypermedia. "Hypermedia" refers to software that electronically links information from a variety of different sources. Using hypermedia, a person can jump instantly from information in one area to information in another. After reading about Sioux tribal customs, Dara clicks a key on her computer, and related kinds of information come up; for example, audio recordings of Sioux chants. Click after click bring up more related information. Quickly she amasses a stockpile of information—materials, songs, pictures—*all* related to the Sioux people.

As a wider variety of information is placed on CD-ROM disks, the need for easy cross-referencing increases. In this technological revolution, it's like taking from one library every book, picture, map, cassette tape, videotape, and newspaper, dumping them all onto a CD-ROM disk, and then saying, "Now we'll initiate a super program that ties all this together." One example of such a program is Apple's HyperCard, which allows a person to create stacks of information to share with others, or to read stacks of information created by others. Using HyperCard software, the quest for information has been simplified to a point-and-click activity. This software is a personal tool kit that gives users the power to use, customize, and create new information using multiple information types such as text, graphics, video, music, voice, and animation. Its unique navigational method lets users browse and search quickly through information in a familiar way, by association and context as well as hierarchy.

*Perhaps the most important technological question is, "What does the technology do that cannot be done as efficiently and effectively with other kinds of learning materials?"—Kenneth A. Sirotnik*

Hypermedia is especially true to its name when it links facts across conventional subject boundaries. Here is an example:

> Enrique is studying chemistry at Piedmont Middle School. He wants to study the life of a chemical compound and its creator. One hypermedia link connects that compound with the chemist's biographical information, located in an entirely different reference work. Another link connects the chemical compound with a listing of grocery store products that incorporate the compound. Still another link connects the compound with long-term health studies on the compound. Using the capabilities of HyperCard to jump around in the information, Enrique is free to focus on content and see how one type of information is linked to other types.[32]

Let's take an example at the high school level. An English course features movements such as Neoclassicism, Romanticism, and Victorianism, with authors ranging from Pope and Swift to Wordsworth, Tennyson, and Yeats. The course places these authors and works in their social, religious, political, intellectual, artistic, and technological contexts. Note how helpful the linking concept would be when Marcia decides to study how Romanticism in England, within its political and religious contexts, affected the writings of Shelley.[33]

The combination of CD-ROM and Hypertext (textual material that is linked together through a computer program) is awesome. It means that one can store a vast amount of information and retrieve it through a program such as HyperCard, complete with text, audio, and graphic capabilities—all at an attractive price. These capabilities may include synthesized and digitized sound, clip art, and animation. For example, you are exposing kindergartners to the subjects of hats and horses. You have on your large screen a picture of a cowboy. You place your computer pointer on his hat and click. Immediately, a man in a suit appears wearing a different kind of hat. Click once again on his hat, and a woman appears wearing an unusual hat. Or suppose you place the pointer on the horse and click. Another breed of horse appears. You place your pointer on the saddle and click. Another type of saddle appears. To make the whole sequence more interesting, you have the horse galloping all this time. The possibilities are virtually endless!

## Telecommunications and Satellite Communication

Suppose you are sitting at your desktop computer in Newark, New Jersey. There is a cable running from the back of your computer to the phone jack on your wall. You pick up the phone and dial a sequence of numbers, allowing you to sign on to a communications network. Another teacher, in Baton Rouge, Louisiana, has a desktop computer as well. She too has a cable running from her computer to her telephone jack. Your dialing has opened up the line between the two computers—indeed, among an entire network of computers. Now your computers can "talk" to each other. After having typed in a special set of codes, you type a message that goes out over the network, including to her computer. Coming to school the next morning, she calls up any messages that have been posted, and your message appears on her screen. She types a reply and sends it back to you.

By subscribing to a database or teletext service, you can access a wide range of information on a variety of subjects. CompuServe is the largest telecommunications source accessible from the classroom. It provides access to many educational forums and databases that teachers and students can use to gain information on such topics as educational research, foreign languages, physical disabilities, and information from the Academic American Encyclopedia.[34] Here's what the availability of electronic information networks means to one group of students:

> Recognizing the value of telecommunications in a global society, Waunekee High School in Wisconsin set up a "Futures" class in which students learn to gather information regarding vital problem areas such as drunk driving, nuclear war, and education. Tenth-grade students conduct an on-line search to bring up the latest information on their selected topic. Typing in the topic "drunk driving," they are astonished in seeing thousands of entries.
>
> Theirs is an age of information *processing*—analyzing, synthesizing, evaluating, drawing conclusions—not simply an age of information gathering. They awaken to the importance of sharing ideas, of becoming part of a larger information network, of being part of a team, of adding to other people's ideas as well as learning from them.[35]

Note how educationally useful a telecommunications network can be:

> In response to declining enrollments, teacher shortages in critical areas, and limited curricular and financial resources, four school districts in Carroll County, Illinois, form a telecommunications consortium to transmit and receive live broadcasts of each other's courses. Four schools, one in each district, "wire" themselves together by the local cable television company, allowing them to receive and broadcast television signals. Each school has its own channel, so students and teachers at participating schools can tune in to each other's broadcasts. Everyone can see and hear . . . ; the system is totally interactive. Using telecommunications allows the districts to increase the advanced coursework available to their students. It heightens competition among bright students and stimulates teachers to use technology to become more innovative in their instruction.[36]

Communications satellites are earth satellites that serve as relay stations for communications signals transmitted from earth stations. These satellites orbit the earth once every twenty-four hours, synchronized with the earth's rotation and thus giving the impression of being parked in one spot over the equator. Once in orbit, a satellite is capable of reaching 43 percent of the earth's surface with a single radio signal. Most communications satellites are launched by NASA. Examples are Comstar, Westar, Intelsat V, Satcom, and Marisat.[37]

Satellite communication in the schools is in its infancy, but it has potential. Software could be distributed to schools via satellite: television stations could broadcast the software up to a satellite, and schools could access it through satellite receivers (dishes). Through this process, every school district in the state of New York could access a new computer program; for example, a tutorial on "Dinosaurs Revisited" (an interesting contrast between method and content!).

## Artificial Intelligence

"Artificial intelligence" refers to the capacity of a computer program to perform functions that are normally associated with human intelligence, such as learning and reasoning. One outgrowth of the study of artificial intelligence is the expert system. An "expert" is a system of software and hardware capable of competently executing a specific task usually performed by a human expert.

Expert systems have been used for developing appropriate geometry proofs, brainstorming solutions to urban renewal problems, and diagnosing medical conditions from an array of symptoms. Expert systems are useful in education because these automated consultants are excellent problem-solvers that can show students the correct skills. Students work their way through a problem while the expert works silently at their side. When the student strays from a correct solution path or asks for help, the expert advises him on how to proceed. Two important mechanisms are at work. First, the student and the expert *share* knowledge about the problem-solving process. For example, a geometry expert encourages a student to develop and record conjectures about proofs; the expert system records the conjectures. Second, the expert examines each conjecture proposed by the student. If a conjecture is consistent with a rule in the expert's "head," it remains silent. But the expert jumps in if the student appears to be using an incorrect rule, or if the conjecture cannot be accounted for by any rule. At this point, it may recommend to the student a more fruitful approach.

Many students flounder when their teachers are unable to take time to observe how they work through a problem and then provide remedial help for faulty approaches. Automated consultants do have the time, and they are relatively efficient. Students of the future will carry home not only their assignments but their portable consultants.[38]

# COMPUTER APPLICATIONS IN SPECIFIC SUBJECTS

Technology in general and computers in particular have found their way into virtually every subject in the curriculum. We illustrate with but one or two examples in a sampling of subject areas.

# Writing

Word processing is a general writing tool—and more. Indeed, it is being used in classrooms not just as a text-producing device but as a means to encourage *good* writing. Teachers see the word processor as stimulating the writer to produce more ideas and more text, with greater creativity. This is the approach students typically take to their writing:

> Students' models of the composing process contrast sharply with those of skilled writers. Students strive to make their compositions "right" the first time. Before starting to write, they mentally organize their ideas. Their goal is to tell what they know rather than to refine their understanding or to have a particular effect on the reader. When students write, they start with the first sentence and continue linearly until they are finished. Except for corrections in spelling and punctuation, they rarely modify their texts. . . . Once a draft is written, changes are mechanically difficult. . . . Once a text is written, it may as well be carved in stone.[39]

Contrast the student's strategy with that of a seasoned writer who has altered his style of writing by shifting to a word processor:

> As a result of using a word processor, I can no longer write well with paper and pencil. I used to compose a sentence by thinking for a couple of minutes and setting down a final version that was about 90 percent optimal; I took my one best shot because making changes later would involve massive physical cutting and pasting. Now I write by thinking for half a minute and typing in a sentence that is perhaps 40 percent of optimal, think for another 15 seconds and make a change (now at 50 percent), make another change a few seconds later (65 percent), and so on. The same amount of time is required to get to the 90 percent level, but now my psychological momentum is behind revision and polishing rather than producing a single finished product, and no cognitive dissonance bars the sentence from eventually evolving to optimal.[40]

A word processing program offers the student an electronic sheet of paper upon which writing can be instantly altered. With the tedium out of the way, both student and teacher can concentrate on the process of writing—communicating ideas and beliefs.

Here are some advantages of using a word processor to write:

1.  Students spend more time composing.

2.  Students feel greater freedom in expressing a range of ideas, since deleting ineffective ones is so easy.

3.  Students tend to consider the overall structure of their composition more frequently.

4.  Students tend to revise more aggressively, rather than merely touching up here and there.

5.  Students tend to collaborate more with the teacher and others during the writing process.[41]

*There is no doubt that computers are here to stay in our lives, and our youth, in order to compete in the world, will to some extent need to know how to operate a computer. With word processors, spelling and grammar applications, and spreadsheets for mathematical computations, it could be very easy for an individual to mask the lack of basic reading, writing and mathematical skills by the use of a computer.—R. Sterling Sagers*

But opinions differ. One spokesman will be unabashedly enthusiastic in support of technology as a writing tool: "I have seen a child move from total rejection of writing to an intense involvement (accompanied by rapid improvement of quality) within a few weeks of beginning to write with a computer."[42] Another will be concerned that, by emphasizing technology, we miss the central questions about writing instruction: "In the panic to find a panacea . . . few pursue such essential questions as what makes good writing in the first place, how it has been attained where it has existed, or who can teach it, and how."[43]

Attempts are being made to bridge the gap between the capabilities of word processors and an understanding of writing instruction. Meanwhile, computer projects to teach writing proliferate: teaching children to write before they read (Writing to Read), talking computers (Programs for Early Acquisition of Language), a pen-pal network (Computer Chronicles Newswire), and a community computer site providing computer opportunities for low-income families (Computer House).[44]

## Reading

Computers are chipping away at ingrained strategies for teaching reading, a process that creates a certain amount of tension:

> While computer technology has provided a dizzying array of new potentials, our knowledge of how to teach reading remains geared to older and more stable technologies. Teachers and students often find themselves more comfortable with convenient texts and tasks that are "friendly" if not entirely effective or satisfactory. Nevertheless, the computer "revolution" in reading will probably not be deflected from success. We have had convincing recent demonstration of the effectiveness and the cost effectiveness of computers as instructional intervention devices.[45]

Computerized beginning reading programs are receiving considerable attention. One example is a tutorial approach. The computer presents the child with reading text. When the child comes upon a new or unfamiliar word, she asks for help by pressing a "help" key. Obligingly, the computer pronounces the word for the child. Another type of program provides audio-visual demonstrations of phonic blending and the addition of affixes and inflectional endings.[46] Yet another approach is to have students build their own stories from computer-generated story fragments, or to create a story fully on their own, facilitated by the computer.

One noteworthy comprehensive program is IBM's massive effort Writing to Read. This program, a holistic approach, involves a variety of language experiences: phonics are taught through visual displays on a computer monitor; children make up their own stories and type them into the computer (often employing invented spellings); letters and words are made out of clay; and children read books that contain words they have included in their own stories.[47]

## Language Arts

A newspaper project uses the computer to help teach language arts skills:

> A group of gifted and talented elementary students elect to participate in a school newspaper project. They are first taught basic interviewing, writing and editing skills, then sent out to solicit articles from their classmates. They interview, gather information, and write up articles and news items.
>
> Their work is carried out in the school's computer lab, where, with the help of an expert, they use *Bank Street Writer* to enter articles into the computer. All writing is checked for clarity, grammar and spelling. Articles are cut, pasted, and formatted, and appropriate graphics are developed for each. The newspaper is printed, duplicated and distributed by the students themselves.
>
> Through this project, students gain experience with the computer as a tool, learn the utility and advantages of word processing, develop oral language and interviewing skills, practice their organization and planning, and are intro-

© *Robert V. Eckert, Jr./The Picture Cube*

duced to desktop publishing packages such as *Newsroom,* where they learn combining graphics with text, printing with different fonts, and creating interesting page layouts.[48]

## Science

Here's how one student applies technology in studying nuclear energy:

Michelle, a senior at Hillcrest High, has interests in both science and psychology. She decides to write a research paper entitled "Nuclear Energy: Its Worrisome Effects upon Teenagers." Writing this paper as a middle-school student, she would have gone the old route: searching through books and articles at the school and city library; writing up references and summaries on 5 × 8 cards; creating a first draft; submitting it to the teacher; making corrections; typing the final copy painstakingly on a typewriter.

Today is a different world. Michelle is computer literate. She has access to a computer, software, a modem, and several computer networks (The Source and BRS, a bibliographic search network). In the computer lab she conducts an extensive computerized bibliographic search through databases and wire service reports. She plugs the results of her reading into a computer simulation program, which shows the responses typical teenagers would give to a series of questions about nuclear energy. Based on this simulation, she creates a list of the most dominant worries teenagers have about nuclear energy, and then creates a set of recommendations. Finally, her report is written on a word processor and published on the school's electronic network.[49]

But wait. Consider the comments of a wise superintendent who found himself in the midst of "SmartClassroom," a flashy science classroom in Port Hueneme, California:

This project is not about installing computers in the classroom. It's about improving the education of kids. Sustaining that perspective, one of my science teachers commented: The computers and video equipment were chosen to suit the science curriculum; the curriculum wasn't developed to suit the technology.[50]

Because the computer is turning out to be such a powerful tool for teaching science, it tends to influence what is taught. If, for example, the process of photosynthesis can be vividly displayed through three-dimensional graphics and simulation, it tends to become a major concept in the curriculum.

Science concepts, in general, lend themselves to vivid and clear presentations through the use of technology. For example, a science videodisc developed by Harvard's Educational Technology Center uses simulation as the strategy for studying the role of light on plant growth. Students can alter the variables, replay the video to observe their effects, and record data on a computer chart.

In this high school example, technology helps solve a real-life science problem:

> We are in a high school in a midwestern city serving children in a low-income community. In a lab room ten students are working, a few alone, others in small groups. Computer work stations are scattered about. A lab technician is working with some of the students.
>
> One small group of students is developing a strategy for their full-time, three-week project to assess the toxicity of the pollutants in an open sewer. They have to analyze the chemical and biological composition of the effluent, locate its source, and bring their results to the attention of the appropriate authorities. They are working on the project with the city's environmental agency, a local firm that specializes in the analysis of toxic materials, and their teachers of chemistry, biology, and social studies.
>
> Sarena, one of the students, does a computer search and comes up with some articles that might be used to build a list of possible pollutants, and another search that lists standard computer-based analysis techniques for determining the presence of these pollutants in the effluent. Another student, Jim, whose interests run more toward policy issues, searches the city database to find the names of companies that have been cited over the last few years for violations of the state and local environmental laws. Bill remembers that one of their instructors offered to lend some analysis equipment that the group can use with their school computers. He calls him to arrange for the use of the equipment next week. Sarena calls an assistant director of the environmental agency, who agrees to give the team a briefing on the legal procedures involved in resolving environmental issues.
>
> The computer graphics lab is presided over by Martin Southworth, an engineer on the staff of Applied Infometrics, a local software engineering firm. Martin is a specialist on the uses of computer-based graphics and design tools. We learn that most of the students in the class are planning to go into various technical support roles in the local machine tool industry, but Martin takes particular pride in the fact that several young women in the school, after working in his lab, decided on pursuing engineering careers. He got them hooked on design work and then worked with the lead teachers in the math and science areas to make the courses in that area build on their enthusiasm for design.[51]

Science instruction, as much as or more than any other subject, stands to profit from technological applications. At the same time, when confronted by such exciting possibilities, science teachers are vigorously challenged to maintain their perspective, employing technology as a tool rather than making it the master.

## Mathematics

Using expert software to teach mathematics is an area of major interest. Considerable research has been conducted on the types of errors students make in mathematical calculations. Technicians are developing expert pro-

*We need to form partnerships, not dependencies, with technology tools.*
—Christopher Dede

grams to predict, diagnose, and remediate these errors, programming automated consultants to be "aware" of the errors their students are likely to make and to be prepared to help them over the hurdles.

Another trend is the development of programs that allow students to explore fundamental mathematical concepts. Logo is a good example. Its originator, Seymour Papert, described Logo as creating an environment where students of all ages can actively explore and construct mathematical ideas.[52]

# IMPLICATIONS

The application of technology to teaching holds exciting possibilities. True, some of the examples in this chapter are futuristic and are not yet found in most present-day schools. But the potential is virtually limitless.

In earlier chapters we called your attention to the importance of classroom and school cultures. If your principal is turned on by computers, he will find all kinds of uses for them. His interest is contagious. Teachers in your school will become interested. So will you and your students. Before long you will be involved in a computer-active environment.

But suppose you find yourself the only one in your building excited about using computers. Do not allow anyone to rain on your parade. Some schools are barren of computers, except for one particular teacher's classroom. For example, at Frederick Harte Elementary, there isn't one computer—except in Roz Montoyo's room, where there are four! Students in Roz's classroom are computer literate, continually at a computer for one purpose or another, and are constantly turned on by the latest software packages.

Suppose your principal decides to order a group of computers for your school. Will you have one in your room—and if you do, will you use it? Here are some comments of teachers who have computers in their rooms:

"Everyone wanted to be at the computer during the first couple of weeks. I finally had to make a sign-up sheet. But I was surprised at how bored kids got after the first month. By then, all the kids wanted to do was to play games— and even that got old."

"If I come across the kinds of programs I want, I'll use my computer. Right now, there's nothing out there that'll really help my teaching. But one thing's for sure: no more games!"

"We have a lot of computers in our school. Everyone likes them. It's just that most of what I teach isn't geared for using computers."

These comments reflect the growing pains of a new technology. Currently there is still a mismatch among hardware, software, and teachers' needs. But where money and profit are involved, problems are attacked and solved rather quickly. What about growing pains for the teacher? Brittleness, resistance to change, unwillingness to be creative, fear—these are not software or hardware problems. These are human problems.

Still, the excitement of an exploding technology—particularly computers and their programs—is irresistible to most teachers. Even teachers without an eye toward computer-assisted learning are dazzled by computers, at the very least finding them fun to play with. But times are changing. No longer can a teacher cavalierly comment, "Sure, a computer would be fun to have in my classroom, and I'll probably get one someday. But still, when it comes to getting serious, I'm the teacher and the computer's a piece of equipment."

Look around you; look into the future:

> Seventy-five percent of all jobs in the United States involve computers in some way. By the year 2000, 80 percent of students currently in school will manipulate information technologically in their work. Newer uses of technology that mirror problem solving and enhance thinking skills are giving students the skills they need for optimal employability in an information age.[53]

Merely standing ready to do something about computers will not win the day. So you decide to become proactive—that is, to prepare for, intervene in, or control an unexpected occasion or situation, especially a negative or difficult one. You don't wait until your principal announces in faculty meeting, "We have just received three computers and I'd like to rotate them through your classrooms." You are more forward looking than this. You start building your computer literacy—now. You anticipate and wrestle with questions like the following: If the computer merely does what I'm already doing, do I really need it? Would it compete with what I'm already doing superbly well? What subject matter or skills am I teaching that could be augmented or even taught more effectively through computer technology? What, exactly, do I want the computer to do?

The time for technological bandwagons has come and gone; so has the time for fearful resistance. Overzealous commitment, like fierce rejection, is unhealthy. Now is a time for balanced understanding of what technology can and cannot do to enhance thinking and learning among your students.

# CONCLUSION

Experts have built the computer magnificently. They are creating ingenious and awe-inspiring programs. But only you, with the intuitions of a teacher and an understanding of students, possess the knowledge to craft the ultimate combination of learner and technology.

## Expansions

1.   How well do you see yourself fitting into a hi-tech teaching environment?

2.   What would be your reactions if your principal wheeled three new computers into your classroom and said, "Make good use of these"?

3.   What purposes do you think television would best serve in your classroom?

4.   For what purposes might you use a database management system in your teaching?

5.   How do you anticipate that word processing will affect your students' style of writing and the way you teach writing?

6.   Computers are likely to have an impact on some subject matter or topic you plan to teach sometime in the future. Explain this probable impact.

7.   Visit a school where computers can be found in at least some of the classrooms. Find out teachers' perceptions of advantages and disadvantages of using these computers.

8.   How do you react to the following concern expressed by some teachers? "I fear that one day computers will take over the really important aspects of my teaching."

9.   What aspects of your teaching could be aided through the use of computers?

## Notes

1.   Adapted from J. E. LaPorte, "A Vision of Computers in Technology Education, *The Technology Teacher* (May/June 1987), pp. 5–7.

2.   S. G. Tickton (Ed.), *To Improve Learning: An Evaluation of Instructional Technology* (New York: Bowker, 1970), p. 12.

3.   T. Schwen, "Professional Scholarship in Educational Technology: Criteria for Inquiry, *AV Communication Review* 25 (1977), pp. 35–79.

4.   J. A. Riccobono, *Availability, Use and Support of Instructional Media, 1982–83: Corporation for Public Broadcasting* (Washington, DC: National Center for Educational Statistics, 1984).

5.   R. E. Clark, and G. Salomon, "Media in Teaching," in M. C. Wittrock (Ed.), *Handbook of Research on Teaching*, 3rd ed. (New York: Macmillan, 1986), pp. 464–478.

6.   R. P. Taylor (Ed.), *The Computer in the School: Tutor, Tool, and Tutee* (New York: Teachers College Press, 1980).

7.   P. F. Merrill, M. N. Tolman, L. Christensen, K. Hammons, B. R. Vincent, and P. L. Reynolds, *Computers in Education* (Englewood Cliffs, N.J.: Prentice-Hall, 1986).

8.  Ibid.

9.  Ibid.

10.  R. L. Upchurch, and J. Lochhead, "Computers and Higher-Order Thinking Skills," in V. Richardson-Koehler (Ed.), *Educators' Handbook: A Research Perspective* (New York: Longman, 1987), p. 156.

11.  Ibid., pp. 156–157.

12.  Merrill et al., *Computers,* p. 195.

13.  Merrill et al., *Computers.*

14.  R. M. Gagne, and L. J. Briggs, *Principles of Instructional Design,* 2nd ed. (New York: Holt, Rinehart & Winston, 1979).

15.  V. Reeve, and R. Miller, SALT Orlando. *The Videodisc Monitor* (1988), 6(4).

16.  J. S. Brown, and R. B. Burton, *Diagnostic Models for Procedural Bugs in Basic Mathematical Skills,* Tech. Rep. No. 3669 (Cambridge: Bolt, Beranek & Newman, 1977).

17.  C. L. Blaschke, *Computer Assisted Instruction (CAI): The Bottom Line* (Falls Church, Va.: Educational Technology Systems, Inc., 1985); M. D. Roblyer, *Measuring the Impact of Computers in Instruction: A Non-Technical Review of Research for Education* (Washington, D.C.: Association for Educational Data Systems, 1985); M. N. Tolman and R. A. Allred, *What Research Says to the Teacher—The Computer and Education* (Washington, D.C.: National Education Association, 1984).

18.  Adapted from R. I. Arends, *Learning to Teach* (New York: Random House, 1988), p. 520.

19.  J. J. Kaput, personal communication (1983) cited in Upchurch and Lochhead, "Computers," p. 143.

20.  A. Luehrmann, quoted in Upchurch and Lochhead, "Computers," p. 162.

21.  *School Uses of Microcomputers: Report from a National Survey* (Baltimore: Johns Hopkins University, 1983), p. 2.

22.  J. Rogers, "Computer Use in Precollege Education," *Computer* 17(4) (1984), pp. 46–52.

23.  Roblyer, *Measuring.*

24.  A. Peled, "The Next Computer Revolution," *Scientific American* 257(4) (October 1987), pp. 57–64.

25.  Merrill et al., *Computers.*

26.  L. Gale, personal communication, May 1988.

27.  Adapted from L. Gale, "Research Shows Videodiscs Helpful in Language Training," *Y News* (Brigham Young University), 12(42) (1987).

28.  R. L. Miller, "Federal Express Goes Interactive," *Videodisc Monitor* 6(4) (1988), p. 1.

29.  Reeve, and Miller, "SALT Orlando," pp. 18–23; R. L. Miller, "Computer Software Released with Consumer Videodiscs from ODC, Pioneer," *Videodisc Monitor* 6(4) (1988), p. 7.

30. Adapted from T. C. Reeves, "Evaluation Review," *Videodisc Monitor* (April 1988), pp. 24–25.

31. J. S. Blanchard, G. E. Mason, and D. Daniel, *Computer Applications in Reading,* 3rd. ed. (Newark, Del.: International Reading Association, 1987).

32. Adapted from D. Goodman, *The Complete HyperCard Handbook* (New York: Bantam Books, 1987).

33. R. Strukhoff, "IRIS Eyes," *CD-ROM Review* (May 1988), pp. 18–21.

34. Blanchard, Mason, and Daniel, *Computer Applications.*

35. Adapted from "Telecommunications in the Classroom," *Computers in the Classroom,* Public Broadcasting System television series, May 19, 1988.

36. P. C. West, R. S. Robinson, and K. Collins, "A Teaching and Telecommunications Partnership," *Educational Leadership* 43(6), (1986), pp. 54–55.

37. D. E. Spencer, *Spencer's Computer Dictionary for Everyone,* 3rd. ed. (New York: Scribner's, 1985).

38. H. M. Halff, "Instructional Applications of Artificial Intelligence," *Educational Leadership* 43(6) (1986), pp. 24–31.

39. J. H. Kane, *Computers for Composing,* Technical Report No. 21 (New York: Bank Street College of Education, 1983), p. 1.

40. C. J. Dede, "Empowering Environments, Hypermedia and Microworlds," *The Computing Teacher* (November 1987), p. 22.

41. Adapted from Kane, *Computers,* pp. 7–8.

42. S. Papert, *Mindstorms: Children, Computers, and Powerful Ideas* (New York: Basic Books, 1980), p. 30.

43. M. Freedman "Those Futile Attempts to Legislate Literacy," *Chronicle of Higher Education* (February 1984), p. 80.

44. S. Florio-Ruane and S. Dunn, "Teaching Writing: Some Perennial Questions and Some Possible Answers," in V. Richardson-Koehler (Ed.), *Educators' Handbook: A Research Perspective* (New York: Longman, 1987), pp. 50–83.

45. M. L. Kamil (1987), cited in Blanchard, Mason, and Daniel, *Computer Applications,* p. vi.

46. D. Clements, *Computers in Early and Primary Education* (Englewood Cliffs, N.J.: Prentice-Hall, 1985).

47. P. Hawkins, "Retired Educator + IBM + 300 Talking Personal Computers + 600 Selectric Typewriters + 10,000 Kindergarten and First Grade Students = a Test of the Theory That Children Could Learn to Read by First Learning to Write," *IPD News* 1(3) (1982), pp. 1–7.

48. Adapted from B. Harris, M. K. Arntsen, R. Thurman, and P. F. Merrill, "Computers, Gifted Students and the Development of an Elementary School Newspaper," *The Computing Teacher* 15(2) (1987), pp. 11–13.

49. Adapted from Arends, *Learning,* pp. 520–521.

50. R. Rescigno and R. Miller, "Hueneme School District, General Telephone Create World's First 'SmartClassroom'" (Port Hueneme, Calif.: Hueneme School

District, 1987); T. Conlon "Science Class Special," *Press-Courier* (Port Hueneme, Calif.), October 1, 1987.

51.   Adapted from Carnegie Forum on Education and the Economy, "Schools for the 21st Century: A Scenario," in *A Nation Prepared: Teachers for the 21st Century,* Report of the Task Force on Teaching as a Profession, May 1986, pp. 45–49.

52.   Confrey, J. "Mathematics Learning and Teaching," in V. Richardson-Koehler (Ed.), *Educators' Handbook: A Research Perspective* (New York: Longman, 1987), p. 19.

53.   G. M. Valdez, et al., *Information Technology Learner Outcomes* (St. Paul: Minnesota Department of Education, 1985).

# SECTION FOUR

# YOU, THE TEACHER

# CHAPTER 12

# YOUR CHALLENGES

*The teacher is a person besieged by other people's expectations.—Magdalene Lampert*

**MAIN IDEAS**

- Current educational reforms, changes in the basic structure of the family, influences of society, your working conditions, and your curriculum—all create challenges in your professional life and stress in your personal life.

- Taking the measure of the challenges you face in a modern classroom prepares you psychologically and emotionally to meet them. Doing so enables you to define your options—and knowing your options enlarges your confidence.

- Acquire perspective. View these challenges within the overall context of a satisfying teaching career.

# INTRODUCTION

It's time to glance back over our shoulders and see how far we've come. Thus far the journey has introduced you to your teacher education program, your first year of teaching, your students, your relationships, the curriculum, the workplace, and the law. You've encountered effective schools and classrooms, knowledge about teaching, and technology. In each of these areas you sensed some of the challenges that surely await you. For example, in contemplating the reality of "mainstreaming," you might have gasped, "Twenty-two *normal* kids. My upper limit! How on earth could I cope with two handicapped students on top of that?" In our discussion of abused children in Chapter 7, you might have wondered, "What would I ever say to a child-abusing parent sitting across the table from me?" Reading through Chapter 4, you might have wondered, "What if they gave me an AIDS unit to teach? Could I do a sensitive job?" In Chapter 9, you might have sensed the difficulty in maintaining high-quality engaged time with a group of rowdy youngsters or restless teenagers.

These are examples of the types of challenges you will face—some, you imagine, with ease and confidence, others with fear and self-doubt. In this chapter we introduce you to additional examples of professional and personal challenges.

Think you're not up to any more challenges? Maybe you feel as if you'd already heard enough, and more might dampen your enthusiasm, if not actually frighten you away. That's a fair concern. Still, going in with your eyes open breeds confidence during those early days, a nice commodity to have. Taking the measure of the challenges you will face in the modern classroom is one way of psychologically and emotionally preparing for them. Awareness of realities defines your options, and knowing your options promotes confidence.

We have selected five professional challenges to introduce and describe: educational reforms, changes in the family, influences of society, your workplace, and your curriculum. We also discuss one personal challenge: stress. As we conclude the chapter, we'll talk about perspective, to help you view these challenges within the overall context of a satisfying teaching career.

# PROFESSIONAL CHALLENGES

## Educational Reforms

By "reforms" we mean changes prescribed for schools with the intent of improving the quality of education. Attempts to improve the quality of edu-

© *Miriam Reinhart/Photo Researchers, Inc.*

cation often take the form of working to improve students' learning, constructing more efficient school buildings, increasing teachers' salaries, and improving working conditions. What challenges do past, current, and future reforms pose to teachers?

**THE FIRST WAVE**   In recent years, there have been a number of movements aimed at "raising the rigor of American education." To improve schools, the argument has been, we need heavy investments of time, money, and energy. Standards must be raised, students and teachers must be held more accountable, the school day must be lengthened, and the number of years students stay in school must be increased. In sum, the first wave was a "more-of-the-same" philosophy: conduct classes in the same manner but add ten minutes to each; teach biology as usual but add two more units; add another math and science course to the graduation requirements; require two years of foreign language rather than one.

Schools responded in various ways. Some faithfully added time and coursework to their schedules, believing that significant changes in achievement would occur. Others assumed their token efforts constituted the called-for reforms. By adding fifteen minutes to their homeroom period, they could claim "flexible scheduling." By taking turns lecturing to one large class, teachers announced their "teaming" approach. By altering several math units, a school now sported a "modern math" curriculum. But, as educators soon discovered, these were merely Band-Aid efforts that failed to treat the more serious problems connected with teaching and learning. Tinkering with the external trappings of schooling did not result in serious changes in students' learning. Further, more of the same did not improve learning to a significant degree (sometimes learning was impeded!). More fundamental changes were needed.[1]

THE SECOND WAVE Simply adding more classes to a student's list of graduation requirements, adding ten minutes to each school day, and calling for greater "rigor" in the curriculum failed to achieve desired results. Problems persisted. Students were still memorizing and promptly forgetting small and unrelated bits of information. What's more, they were being asked to attain goals that would have little significance in five to ten years' time. Teachers were still suffering from feelings of isolation, loss of control, and lack of freedom in making decisions about curriculum. Small adjustments—tightening a nut here and there—failed to produce fundamental changes in the engine itself, the overhaul that leading spokespersons claimed was desperately overdue.

This second wave of reform was a coming together of disparate social and political forces, all of which had the common goal of reforming education. Governors assigned education a number-one priority in their states. They increasingly acted "as strong and eager partners in education reform," providing greater discretion to educators willing to take responsibility for outcomes, and working to increase funding for education—as long as they could show the public that those funds had a positive impact on student retention and achievement.[2] Universities were considering massive reforms in their teacher preparation programs. Business was calling for better-educated workers. Teachers' associations (the National Education Association, for one) started realizing that, if they failed to take the lead, others outside the profession would make decisions for them.

All these groups, converging on education with diverse perspectives, had one thing in common: a desire for complete *restructuring* of schools. They wanted to change the way schools were organized, the way the curriculum was set up, and the way teachers taught. Indeed, this second wave began plumbing our most basic philosophical beliefs about teaching and learning and about the training of teachers.

The second wave continues. Pockets of progress can be observed. Many school districts are surrendering decision-making power to individual schools. The traditional grade structure K–12, use of school time, organization of classes, curricular offerings—all are being revamped. In some schools, teachers are being empowered to make major decisions about the curriculum, their students, and their own working environment. For example, four teachers team-teach a group of eighty students for the equivalent of four periods, then spend the remainder of their day planning and preparing. Meanwhile, the students take electives from "specialist" teachers.

Teachers also assume an active role in planning and conducting their own professional development. Experienced, competent mentor teachers officially take new teachers under their wing, providing systematic training during the first two years. With help from their principals, teachers restructure the school's environment to foster teacher autonomy, flexibility, and trust. Learning goals are formulated to concentrate more acutely on higher-order thinking and on those skills that will make a genuine difference in the lives of students five or ten years down the road.[3]

The first wave of reform focused on students, but many of the initiatives in the second wave have focused on teachers. One outgrowth is the felt need to examine teachers' competence. Not surprisingly, policy makers have come to see teacher exams as a key in reforming education, improving the quality of the teacher corps, and reassuring the public that prospective teachers have the requisite skills and knowledge. As evidence of this trend, seventeen states currently require prospective teachers to take the NTE (formerly called the National Teacher Examination, now referred to as the NTE Program), a test developed by the Educational Testing Service (ETS). Another seventeen states administer their own tests, such as the Pre-Professional Skills Test (PPST), which measures basic proficiency in reading, mathematics, and writing, and the California Basic Educational Skills Test (CBEST), which measures reading, writing, and mathematics. Three states (Arkansas, Texas, and Georgia) now require experienced teachers to pass an examination before they can be recertified. Other states are considering similar testing plans.

Competency exams like the NTE are used to (1) screen potential applicants who apply to teacher education programs, (2) certify teachers at the end of their teacher education program, and (3) recertify veteran teachers who are currently teaching. The National Education Association and the American Federation of Teachers (the two major teachers' unions) would prefer to test only prospective teachers.

The exams themselves are of two basic types, generic tests and subject-matter tests, both typically in a multiple-choice format. Generic tests assume that *all* teachers should have acquired certain general knowledge and skills. Subject-matter or area tests assess knowledge specific to certain certification areas, such as English, mathematics, and music.

These teacher exams have been surrounded by controversy. Essentially, critics question whether measuring a person's knowledge *about* teaching on a multiple-choice test correlates with his or her teaching skills in the classroom. As of now, there is little or no evidence that these tests do in fact predict good teaching. Also, the tests are often accused of being overly narrow in what they cover, and biased against minority-group teachers. On the other side, test proponents argue that no teacher should be allowed to teach a subject about which he or she has below-minimum knowledge.[4]

But a new trend is beginning to appear. Efforts are being made to design more fair and comprehensive evaluations of a prospective teacher's overall competence. With the establishment of the National Board for Professional Standards, teachers may one day go before an evaluating board much like that in such professions as architecture, law, and medicine. Future assessments of teachers will be conducted immediately upon completion of training and during different stages of their careers, and they will be made up of "tests of knowledge and reasoning, systematic documentation of ac-

*There are a growing number of generic principles of effective teaching, and they have already found their way into examinations such as the National Teachers Examination and into state-level assessments of teaching performance during the first teaching year. Their weakness, that they essentially ignore the content-specific character of most teaching, is also their strength. Discovering, explicating, and codifying general teaching principles simplify the otherwise outrageously complex activity of teaching. The great danger occurs, however, when a general teaching principle is distorted into prescription, when maxim becomes mandate. Those states that have taken working principles of teaching, based solely on empirical studies of generic teaching effectiveness, and have rendered them as hard, independent criteria for judging a teacher's worth, are engaged in a political process likely to injure the teaching profession rather than improve it.—Lee S. Shulman*

complishments of both teachers and students and even parents, and analyses of performance at assessment centers and in the work place." Not only will paper-and-pencil tests be used but videotapes of actual teaching and portfolio documents of students' work, teachers' accomplishments, and statements by principals, parents, and fellow teachers.[5]

The second wave of reform has likewise turned on teacher education programs, examining critically the values being instilled in teachers-to-be, the assumptions underlying the training of teachers, and the types of skills, attitudes, and orientations being engendered. The Holmes Group[6] and the Carnegie Task Force on Teaching as a Profession[7] are examples of groups that have taken the responsibility of examining and restructuring their own profession.

THINKING ABOUT THE CHALLENGES   Within your own school building, you will be invited, encouraged, pressed—sometimes co-opted—to participate in reform. State initiatives and mandates, district commitments, your principal's earnestness, other teachers, parents, and even your students will apply pressure for you to join in the reform effort. Once you have become grooved into a teaching pattern, these intrusions can be bothersome, as they are to some teachers:

"Just as I was feeling good about my social studies units, whammo! We're told to start all over, writing them for a team approach."

"My principal keeps pulling me in to plan the *new* humanities program. I wish he'd stop jumping on every bandwagon that comes by. I haven't time to redo my units every year!"

"This year it's the new mentoring program—what'll be next?"

Learn to act flexibly within your own carefully planned curriculum. Be prepared to make productive changes. At the same time, stand fast on your well-tested approaches in the face of pressures created by dazzling but soon-to-die fads. Keep your classroom door open. Important movements and events are taking place outside your room, your school, your district. Gear up for the inevitable, ongoing changes in your profession and become party to the restructuring process. Authentic classroom reforms, those that *do* make a difference, can be carried out only by you.

## Changes in the Family

For purposes of clarity and readability, we have described challenges arising from the home in one section of the chapter and those arising from society in another. In reality, however, these are inextricably intertwined. The influences of society pervade the home and those of the home extend into the larger society. For example, teenage pregnancy can often be traced to factors within both the home and the society. We begin with a chilling case:

> Fifteen-year-old Eric was a loner in his 8th grade class. As a youngster, he had been diagnosed as "hyperactive" and took Ritalin to control his disruptive behavior in class. Teachers described him as unhappy in school. Later, they would note that he always tried very hard to please. In junior high school Eric was a tense, anxious youngster who was obsessed with militarism and teased by his schoolmates. He spent much of his time playing "Dungeons and Dragons." One summer afternoon he hanged himself. There was no apparent reason.[8]

No doubt an intricate combination of factors accounted for Eric's tragic and unnecessary death. Whatever role friends, TV, and school ultimately played, the problem began at home. Let's review recent changes in the family and look at classroom challenges posed by those changes.

The American family, averaging 5.79 persons in 1790, shrank to only 2.62 persons by July 1, 1988.[9] Women are having fewer babies. Several reasons account for this decrease: (1) a large number of women never marry, (2) women are postponing marriage until a later age, leaving fewer childbearing years, (3) many married women are postponing childbearing until their careers are established, (4) many couples are choosing not to have children, and (5) many women prefer to pursue careers rather than rearing children. Indeed, "traditional" families in which the father works while the mother stays at home with her two or three school-age children constitute but 7 percent of current U.S. households.[10]

Divorce and separation have increased dramatically. Twice as many marriages—nearly half—end in divorce today as was the case in 1960, and the number of children affected by divorce now exceeds 1 million annually. Predictions are that 38 percent of first marriages of women in their late twenties will end in divorce.[11]

An increasing number of children are being raised by a single parent. In 1984, 14 percent of all white children and 50 percent of all black children under age 18 lived with their mother only, in comparison with 8 and 29 percent, respectively, in 1970.[12] If current trends continue, between 42 and 70

*The simple truth is, we expect schools and teachers to do what our homes and communities and churches have not been able to accomplish; but the school is not the most imperiled institution—it is the family structure in this country, and the school is absorbing the shock waves of a family structure in transition.—Ernest L. Boyer*

percent of white children and 86 to 94 percent of black children born around 1980 will spend some time in a one-parent family before reaching age 18.[13] In 1984, 24 percent of the Hispanic children under 18 lived with only one parent, their mother. In that year, more than 1.5 million American children under the age of 18 were living with *neither* parent.[14]

Poverty is increasing among school-age children, resulting largely from the increase in single-parent families. Many single parents do not possess adequate job skills or access to training, thus finding it difficult to support children. Currently, 17 percent of American school-age children live below the poverty level.[15]

More women are taking employment outside the home. In 1985 half of all women with children under age 3 were in the work force, up from one-third in 1975—a 47 percent increase in just ten years.[16] As a result of this increase, the number of children whose mothers are employed continues to climb. The proportion of children under age 6 with employed mothers (currently half) is expected to reach two-thirds by 1995, and the proportion of school-age children with employed mothers (currently three-fifths) may rise to three-fourths over the next ten years.[17] The big shift in child care for working mothers is away from the home and away from relatives to child-care centers.

EFFECTS IN THE CLASSROOM    How are these changes in the family reflected in your students? What challenges do they pose?

The fact that women are having fewer children might suggest that children receive greater attention and more abundant opportunities, especially when both parents are working. Further, children in your classroom will have traveled more, having greater familiarity with different cultures and people. Perhaps they are also more tolerant of people whose values are different from their own, and who are less fortunate than they.

A lower birth rate might imply that your classes will be smaller. But this decrease has occurred primarily among middle-class white women. More realistically, it means an increase in the proportion of ethnically different children in your classroom—an increase in diversity.

What of the dramatic increase in divorce? Mothers are more often awarded custody of the children and therefore pressed into the labor market to help support themselves and their children. Whether the child goes with mother or father, the single parent often experiences a drop in disposable income. More significant is the emotional trauma often accompanying divorce when one parent leaves the home: anxiety, aggressiveness, loneliness, depression, exaggerated needs for acceptance and recognition. In many instances, the parent works during the day and the nearest relatives are hundreds of miles away, leaving the child to return to an empty house. Schoolwork suffers. By default, teachers experience an added emotional drain, serving as nurturing parent surrogates.

Teachers stand the possibility of having more poverty-level students. Whereas a class of ten years ago might have included two or three such students, today a class of twenty is likely to have five or six in this category. Problems of lingering flu, stomach ailments, hunger, and poor diet often accompany these children.

During empty afternoons and early evenings, students typically watch television. They may come into your classroom well informed on a variety of subjects: national and world events, exploration, nature, sports, and politics. On the down side, because of television, students carry into the classroom unrealistic expectations of a flashy performance from the teacher and a desire to be entertained constantly with an uninterrupted succession of extravagantly attention-getting activities.

Divorce and the profusion of single-parent families affect the school calendar. When established many years ago, the nine-month school year nicely accommodated school-age children (90 percent) who were living on a farm with two parents. The three-month summer vacation allowed children to work in the fields. Today, less than 3 percent of the families in the United States live on farms. With their parents working outside the home, children with three months of nothing to do become listless and bored and their parents have to arrange for their care during working hours.

THINKING ABOUT THE CHALLENGES   Twenty years ago teachers enjoyed ample support from the home—a strong backup system. Then, the teacher's role was largely confined to helping kids learn. Now, as part of their enlarged role, teachers must provide increasing emotional support for a sizeable percentage of their students. Suppose you balk at this expectation:

> I don't want that big a role! I resist taking over what parents are supposed to do. I can't be responsible for picking up pieces from a broken marriage. I can't prevent emotional scarring, I can't put marriages back together, I can't follow these kids home. I don't have the skills—and I don't have the time or energy. If I tried jumping in, who'd do my job? Who'd teach them to read and write?

There may be a middle ground. Give it some thought.

## Influences of Society

Identifying society's impact on students in classrooms is a complex, indeed controversial, undertaking. What role, for example, does society play in our soaring dropout rates? How does it contribute to the increasing incidence of

© *John Veltri/Photo Researchers, Inc.*

bulimia and anorexia nervosa? sexual promiscuity? AIDS? In this section we will sample some of society's influences and problems as they affect your classroom. Here's a glimpse of the way youngsters absorb elements of their culture:

> My husband and I went to visit my parents for the holiday; also visiting were my grandmother, and my two nephews, ages five and ten. While we were sitting in the living room talking, the five-year-old came running in with a toy gun shouting, "I'll blow you away, Grandma." My shocked husband said, "That's not a very nice thing to say." The five-year-old, in turn, said, "Then I'll blow you away—I'll blow you to bits like Rambo with a grenade." [18]

Sociologists and educators have long pointed out that schools are a microcosm of society. The values, interests, ambitions, intolerance, and friendliness of the community are mirrored in the classroom culture. Let's look at society's influence in your classroom—and at the challenges it poses.

RACE AND IMMIGRATION Immigration policies and racial attitudes find their way into your classroom. Today there are 14 million immigrants in this country, 80 percent having come from South America and Asia. In the 1920s, we also had 14 million, but they were mostly from Europe. Immigrants represent enormous diversity. Some have no formal education; some, such as adult Asians, tend to have a high level of education. There is a new middle class emerging in America: blacks and Hispanics. Though historically *black* meant *poor,* blacks now spread across the entire continuum of economic prosperity. Many live in suburbs, own their own homes, drive luxury cars. The same is happening with Hispanics. In the future, the youth of America will be steadily more Asian, more Hispanic, slightly more black, and less white. The word *minority* will give way to *plurality,* since if a city's population is more than fifty percent black (or Hispanic or Asian), one could hardly call that group a minority.

**THINKING ABOUT THE CHALLENGES**  Think pluralistically. Stereotyped thinking begins to break down: blacks, Asians, Hispanics, and other ethnic groups will not necessarily be poor, nor will they necessarily be low achievers. This reality means that students from every ethnic background can reach their potential. Meeting the challenge begins with the not-too-unreal assumption that all children in your class can succeed, regardless of ethnic background.[19] Study American cultures, if not their languages. Prepare to accommodate (or at least respond to) diversity among your students: in reading materials, in selection and emphasis of curricula, in assignments, and in establishing classroom goals.

### ALCOHOL, TOBACCO, AND DRUGS

> Darlene, a 17-year-old college-bound senior, was riding home after a movie with two friends when a car driven by Mitch, another senior, crashed into her vehicle from behind, propelling it 100 feet into a tree. Darlene was killed instantly. Her companion, 18-year-old Marily, died a few hours later, while another companion escaped with minor injuries. Mitch, partying and drinking after a football game victory, was sentenced to five years in the state penitentiary.[20]

Blame the home environment? parent models? television? peer group at school? A variety of sources can contribute to the use of alcohol, tobacco, and drugs in the schools, threatening, for one thing, the quality of school performance. Hear the comments of today's educators:

> Because it is readily available and because it holds a unique and ambivalent place in our collective lives, alcohol is the most dangerous drug in our society; yet—precisely because its use is so pervasive—it is the most difficult to teach about. . . . We need the courage to send a strong message to our young people that use of alcohol and other drugs is neither expected nor accepted in our schools and communities. . . . We must reject the idea of teaching responsible use of alcohol. Alcohol is illegal for underage people, and there can be no responsible use of an illegal substance. . . . The most dangerous myth is that alcohol use is a rite-of-passage into adult society. If we continue to convey our expectation that children will use alcohol, they will continue to meet that expectation. . . . The gifted athlete, the honor student, and the school leader are

© *David S. Strickler/Monkmeyer Press Photo Service*

equally vulnerable to drug abuse and addiction. The standard joke is there are two kinds of kids who can have trouble with alcohol: boys and girls.[21]

A typical assumption about young people who use drugs is that they do not understand the harmful consequences of their use. . . . Often they know even better than nonusers the negative and positive effects of drug use.[22]

Let's look briefly at some statistics. The average age of beginning alcohol users is 12.5 years. Half of all high school students are "regular" drinkers; one out of three drinks heavily at least once a week; one out of four has a serious drinking problem. Researchers estimate that approximately 4 million youth under the age of 17 are alcoholics, and children as young as 9 years old are being treated for alcoholism.[23]

The early use of "gateway" drugs (alcohol, marijuana, tobacco, smokeless tobacco) is followed by harder drugs (cocaine, PCP, and heroin). Some 80 percent of high school seniors have used marijuana, and two-thirds of American children will have used an illicit drug other than marijuana and alcohol before they graduate from high school.[24]

Of the 28 million children of alcoholics in the United States, 12 to 15 million are students. Children living in an alcoholic home often manifest a variety of academic and behavioral problems, such as a proneness to learning disabilities, attention-deficit disorders, anxiety, and compulsive overachievement. They bring their role in the family into the school. However, a role that permits survival in the alcoholic home typically turns out to be dysfunctional in the classroom. Some of these children will not allow themselves to make mistakes, some are disruptive and unable to concentrate, some are class clowns demanding excessive attention, and some are quiet isolates, going unnoticed by their teachers and peers. Further, these children can show signs of neglect in their appearance and health, extreme fastidiousness, fatigue and listlessness, hyperactivity and emotional outbursts, tardiness, poor attendance, and undue concern for getting home after school. They may demonstrate excessive concern with pleasing authority and avoiding conflict and home–school contact. Actually, no single criterion can identify these children; to identify them, a teacher needs to observe their behavior over time.[25]

Aggressive programs are under way to attack alcohol and drug problems in the schools. Across the nation, a slow but steady movement is growing to ban student use of tobacco on school campuses. On January 1, 1987, for example, a California law went into effect that banned students' use of all tobacco products on all California high school campuses or at any school-sponsored activity under supervision of school district employees. In essence, the law repealed the authority of local school boards to permit smoking and possession of tobacco products on school campuses or during school functions.[26] On another front, the National School Boards Association is spearheading a program to establish nonsmoking in schools as a norm: "Tobacco-Free Young America by the Year 2000."[27] Local school districts, too, are successfully initiating smoking-cessation programs.

**THINKING ABOUT THE CHALLENGES**    In today's classrooms, teachers are becoming more sensitive to danger signals of emotional and psychological problems: hyperactivity, withdrawal, runny eyes, excessive thirst, and frequent use of a bathroom, to name but a few. You too need to develop this special sensitivity. Do not be reluctant to bring others in to help: your principal, parents, the nurse, the school counselor.

Today's classroom problems are complex and pervasive. Your brightest student, your warmest socialite, your best athlete, your "from-a-good-home" student—as well as your down-and-outers—may in reality be suffering from problems of alcohol and drug abuse.

As you seek help, resist writing off or classifying students as "my problem kids," "my AA group," "my normals," or "my heads-on-straight kids." A defeatist attitude or a set of simplistic classifications helps no one.

**SUICIDE**    Educators are deeply concerned about the alarming rise in the incidence of teenage suicide and about the school factors that may be contributing to it:

> When you ask . . . students aged 11 to 15, "Where in school do you feel important?," they look at you as if to say, "That's ridiculous! Of course you don't feel important in school." Students never feel important in classrooms. It's al-

ways in extracurricular activities: athletics, drama, music. In the classroom, only a few of even the top students feel important. Students have strong needs for power and belonging. The decision to be less than careful about sex and pregnancy is the result of both a lack of belonging and a lack of power . . . regardless of their homes, girls who find school satisfying and do well will have little inclination to get pregnant. What's more, they'll also pay attention to what the school teaches about avoiding venereal diseases and AIDS. Unfortunately, disinterested students don't listen to what's going on in the classroom, so it does little good to teach them the facts about AIDS, drugs, or pregnancy. . . . I'm saying that unless we pay attention to what students need we will continue to have trouble teaching the basics successfully.[28]

Our schools are now acknowledging that fostering the socialization of students must be counted among their primary goals. . . . For schools beset by high dropout rates, teenage pregnancy, and subgroups that feel disenfranchised, a greater emphasis on basic academic skills is unlikely to reduce the number of students "at risk" for problems of adulthood—unless they include similar efforts to improve students' socialization and sense of "connectedness."[29]

But many cannot "take the slings and arrows of life without caving in, becoming immobilized, or exploding." Their vulnerability causes them to seek escape in one form or another. They see themselves as outcasts in school.[30]

THINKING ABOUT THE CHALLENGES   The quoted statements carry a recurring message: in addition to basic skills such as reading, science, and math, every teacher should teach interpersonal skills—how to become "connected" in meaningful ways to other people. Learning how to identify at-risk students and learning how and when to make referrals to appropriate agencies can greatly enhance the success of your efforts. You realize, in crafting your goals, that the intellectual pursuits of your students are strongly interconnected with their emotional well-being and their abilities to bond with other students. A supportive classroom atmosphere goes a long way toward moderating the effects of a broken home or an unloving family.

SEXUAL ISSUES   Sexual issues arise in many areas of teaching. Although it is true that national attention is focused on such news-catching stories as sexual abuse, teen parenthood, sexual promiscuity, and AIDS, there are other issues of sexuality that affect *all* students.

Teachers, both elementary and secondary, are usually nervous teaching about—or even commenting on—areas of human sexuality: male and female bodies and how they function differently, how reproduction occurs, and the issues of morality surrounding abortion, unwed motherhood, and extramarital relationships. To be sure, teachers can avoid these sensitive issues by remaining silent; but in doing so, they can lose valuable teaching moments. A teacher's nervousness arises from such factors as personal embarrassment, fear of intruding into the parents' domain, not wanting to reveal personal feelings about sexuality, and lack of understanding about the subject. Not only is there a reluctance to discuss sexual issues but even traditionally acceptable physical contacts have become suspect. One educator laments our anxiety about behavior that could have sexual overtones: "Sadly, fear often inhibits friendly touching and hugging between teachers and children. Teachers know that touching students in a friendly way may be considered sexual abuse or harassment. Similarly, they are afraid to allow students to touch one another because of taboos related to sexual attraction." [31]

Within a classroom, the teacher's responses to students can be influenced by sexual attractiveness—or fear of becoming sexually attracted. For example, a male teacher favors sexually attractive girls with higher grades; a young female teacher, finding herself attracted to a senior athlete, spends inordinate amounts of time nursing him through her course; one male teacher admits, "If a pretty student didn't like me, I'd resent her." On the other side, a teacher's fear of becoming sexually attracted can impede positive learning experiences: a wary male teacher, feeling attracted to a pretty coed, maintains a cold distance despite her pleas for help.

Sexual stereotyping occurs with considerable frequency. For example, a teacher may expect a girl to be less curious about sex than a boy, but at the same time more responsible for putting a damper on a boy's sexual advances. Or a teacher may discriminate against homosexual students, pregnant teenagers, and teenage mothers.

Sexual discrimination occurs in the curriculum as well. Materials are often inaccurate or sexist, portraying the male as dominant, successful, more knowledgeable about math and science, and better able to cope with disruption and emotional stress. Girls are often portrayed as having greater sensitivity, better manual dexterity, and stronger verbal skills and as being more easily manipulated. Sometimes by simply following textbook outlines and suggested materials, teachers innocently convey inaccurate and demeaning sexual roles.

Sexual promiscuity is a much larger issue, to a large extent reflecting prevailing values of our society. The average age of a first sexual experience may be well below 16. Some 40 percent of the 29 million teenagers in the United States have had sexual intercourse (about 5 million girls and about 6.5 million boys). As sexual activity among teens increases, so do the pregnancy and childbearing rates among unmarried girls. Until 1965, barely 15 percent of the teenage girls who gave birth were unmarried; by 1983, 50 percent to 75 percent of them were unwed. Among the 15- to 19-year-old group in the year 1983, 37 percent of the white girls and 87 percent of the black girls giving birth were unwed. More than 715,000 children were born to unwed mothers in 1982. [32] Society continues to look for solutions:

> American teenagers face a tough time today. On the one hand, the age at which young women mature sexually (i.e., are able to bear children) has declined since the turn of the century by about a year, from 13.5 to age 12.8. On the other hand, the average age at which they marry has risen to historical highs. This means an increased period of time in which young people are interested in sex and capable of reproduction, but are neither married nor prepared

for childbearing. The proportion of sexually active teens has, in fact, increased 66 percent since the early 1970s. The U.S. has taken several approaches to the issue, perhaps reflecting our pluralistic tradition. Contraception has become available through hospitals and clinics, and there is substantial evidence that family planning programs reduce teen pregnancies. More recently, formal programs have been established to encourage teens to delay engaging in sexual intercourse, but the success of these programs has yet to be evaluated through rigorous scientific testing. Although sex is widely depicted on every television screen across the U.S. every night of the week, neither contraception nor the consequences of its nonuse are similarly depicted. In addition, parents do not appear to be the major sex educators for their children. Ambivalent attitudes towards sexuality and contraception in the U.S. may contribute to the inability of sexually active American teenagers to use contraception consistently and well.[33]

**THINKING ABOUT THE CHALLENGES**   Sexuality, and issues surrounding it, will appear regularly in your classroom. The physiology of human reproduction is increasingly easy to teach. Units, materials, and special films have been sensitively and accurately prepared for you. More difficult to handle are questions like these:

"What are the pros and cons of having sex before marriage?"

"Will a boy respect a girl if she goes to bed with him?"

"What if a boy says, 'If you really love me you'll go to bed with me?' What should a girl say to him?"

"How does a boy react to a girl who flaunts her body—someone who's just trying to get recognition?"

"If a girl gets pregnant, is the boy obligated to marry her?"

"What do you think about girls who have abortions?"

"How do sexually active people keep from getting AIDS?"

These questions are asked both openly and privately, both fearfully and dispassionately. *All* of them involve moral issues. Students are interested in *your* answers.

### AIDS

Ryan White, a 14-year-old hemophiliac who acquired AIDS as a result of a blood transfusion, was prohibited from attending Western Middle School in Kokomo at the start of the school year. The boy was given home instruction via a telephone hookup to his classroom. The mother brought suit against the district. The court ruled that Ryan must be permitted to attend classes under P.L. 94-142, the Education for All Handicapped Children Act (the school district must educate Ryan in the least restrictive environment). The Kokomo school board voted unanimously to appeal the ruling. "I made the decision [not to admit Ryan] last summer," said James Smith, superintendent of Kokomo's Western School Corporation. "We don't admit any child with tuberculosis, whooping cough, measles, or mumps. And AIDS is one of the most horrendous communicable diseases known."

John McCarthy, superintendent of schools in Swansea, Massachusetts, claims that he was the first superintendent in the U.S. to openly acknowledge the fact that an AIDS victim was enrolled in his school system. "A few parents withdrew their children," he said. "But they are all back in school now." That AIDS victim still attends classes in Swansea today, with no reported problems. "The students have been overwhelmingly supportive," McCarthy said. "He is one of their own. If you saw the child walking down the street, you wouldn't know he was different from any other 13-year-old." An organization in Swansea even raised $9000 to help the family with medical expenses.

A female student at Dundalk Senior High School in Baltimore County, Maryland, donated blood at a Red Cross bloodmobile. Routine screening revealed that she carried the AIDS virus. The principal decided to keep the girl in school and not to reveal her identity—until health officials advised him otherwise.[34]

Junior high school students rallied around a student who has tested positive for the AIDS virus, shouting down a small group protesting his admission to the school. "Go home!" students yelled at the eight people protesting 12-year-old DeWayne Mowery's attendance at Clinton Junior High School. Police twice had to separate the eight protesters from about 200 angry students and parents. Wand Webber, whose son is a ninth-grader, slammed on her brakes and got out of her car to deride the protesters as "disgusting." Members of the group "do not know what they are talking about," she said. "They are shaming the town. They are shaming this community. They are showing the whole world how ignorant they are. Ignorance and petty fear, that scares me more than AIDS," she said.[35]

This is but a sample of the cases now appearing before school boards and courts. Two reactions to AIDS are emerging: (1) AIDS is not technically a communicable disease, since the medical community agrees that it is not spread through casual contact; therefore, individuals who suffer from AIDS have every right to be in school; (2) AIDS is clearly communicable, and school officials have every right to protect the school environment from it.

Educators have picked up on various reports and statistics concerning AIDS. Here is a sample:

The majority of children with AIDS were either infected at birth by their mothers (who may or may not have known that they had AIDS) or they received contaminated blood or blood products in transfusions. . . . A senior scientist with the American Medical Association in Chicago . . . said, "We need to be realistic. . . . We are talking about a small number of children who have been infected. Of the 200 or so children who have had AIDS, 100 have died. Of those who remain, 50% are too sick to attend school. That leaves 50 children with AIDS in America who are able to attend school, or one per state."[36]

Contrary to what one might believe after reading the lay press, the issue of AIDS communicability is clear: no case of casual transmission of AIDS has ever been reported between family members, school children, or children in a day care center. . . . As transfusion-borne AIDS is eliminated, so too will be the majority of instances of younger children with AIDS. . . . The group that will become proportionately more significant is the older AIDS-afflicted student, and this is the population that educators need to assist.[37]

In the midst of controversy, and with the possibility of having to face decisions about students with AIDS, a number of states have established guidelines for educators similar to the recommendations released by the Centers for Disease Control in November 1985. These guidelines suggest that a child with AIDS be educated in an unrestricted environment, unless the child is a preschooler or neurologically handicapped and likely to bite and lose control of bodily functions, or has uncoverable, oozing lesions. In such instances, "a more restricted environment is advisable until more is known about transmission in these settings." For most infected school-aged children, the benefits of an unrestricted setting would outweigh the risks of their acquiring potential harmful infections in the setting and the apparent nonexistent risk of transmission of HTLV-III/LAV (AIDS).[38]

The Centers for Disease Control further recommend that a minimum number of people be told of a child's AIDS diagnosis, that screening blood tests for AIDS not be required for school entry, and that routine procedures for handling blood and body fluid spills be adopted.

Other organizations such as the National Education Association, the National Association of Independent Schools, and the American College Health Association have adopted similar guidelines. Usually these policies suggest that AIDS victims not be automatically barred from attending school, but be treated on an individual basis by a review committee.

THINKING ABOUT THE CHALLENGES  The likelihood of your having a known AIDS-carrying student in your own classroom is small. Likewise, the possibility that one of your fellow teachers or building workers will become an AIDS victim is small. Yet parental and public concern will continue unabated. Students and parents will be raising questions: "What is the school policy about handling AIDS students? How would you treat one of your students known to have AIDS?"

Fortunately, you do not have to make decisions without the help of a committee including a physician, parents, and your principal. But become informed beforehand. Carefully documented reports of our current knowledge about AIDS are appearing with greater frequency. For example, in June of 1988 a brochure entitled *Understanding AIDS: A message from the Surgeon General* was delivered to every home in the United States. Prepared by the U.S. Surgeon General and the Centers for Disease Control, U.S. Public Health Service, the brochure provided factual information about frequently asked questions concerning AIDS.

Think through your own position, fears, and biases, for questions will surely arise:

"Who can kids talk to about AIDS?"

"Can people get AIDS by using public toilets?"

"I feel sorry for homosexuals! What's your opinion about them?"

"If a guy is shooting drugs and goes to bed with a girl, can she get AIDS?"

"Where do people go to find out if they have AIDS or not?"

"Can you get AIDS from kissing?"

Your greatest challenge will be in educating your students and their parents, not in having a student with the AIDS virus.

## Your Workplace

Challenges arising from a changing family life and from a complex society originate in a sphere somewhere beyond your control. But other challenges arise right within your own working environment—your school. The

© *Elizabeth Crews/The Image Works*

sample we offer consists of challenges we consider to be especially trouble-some to teachers.

STUDENT ABSENTEEISM AND DROPOUTS   The dropout rate during elemen-tary school is very small, but it escalates into a major problem and a source of discouragement for many teachers at the high school level. In Phila-delphia the dropout rate in high schools is 38 percent; in Boston it is 43 percent. Nearly half of the Mexican-American and Puerto Rican students who enroll in public high schools drop out before they receive a diploma. In Chicago more than half of the students who should have graduated from high school dropped out before graduation in the year 1984. Dropout is a problem not only in large urban areas but also in suburban America and in small cities and towns.

   Although home and society factors also contribute to dropout, we will focus on factors *within* the school. The great majority of dropouts have low expectations of getting either good grades or good schooling. They have low self-esteem, commonly originating in early home experiences and fos-tered by a history of school failures. Much of the time these students feel they have lost control of their future. They perceive teachers to be unin-terested in them and uncaring, and they see the system as unfair and ineffective.

THINKING ABOUT THE CHALLENGES   Roll up your sleeves rather than wash-ing your hands. In keeping with the expanded role of the modern teacher, go after the dropout and the habitual truant. Tailor assignments so they are doable. High expectations, realistic work assignments, corrective feedback, and ample caring breed success among dropout-prone students. Developing good diagnostic skills enables you to spot and begin rerouting the potential dropout into an avenue of successful experiences. Students rebuild lost self-esteem through academic successes—lots of them. Whereas tasting success for the first time will not erase a backlog of failures, it establishes a powerful starting point. Negative self-images are jarred loose even with just several weeks of successful performance.

ISOLATION   The new teacher's feelings of isolation were discussed in Chap-ter 1. Overcoming these feelings continues to challenge the most experi-enced teachers. Recall that by "isolation" we mean the walling off (physi-cally and psychologically) of a teacher from other adults during the day. Typically, a teacher heads straight for her room in the morning and, with the exception of several short breaks, remains there for the entire day. After school she solos again in preparing for the next day. Late in the afternoon she leaves the building alone, to return the next morning and repeat the cycle.

THINKING ABOUT THE CHALLENGES   Reforms are afoot to restructure schools, physically as well as instructionally. Working to break down teach-ers' isolation, new physical configurations appear: redesigned classrooms

## Dropouts

One million students per year drop out of American high schools. In the words of Ezra Bowen, *Time* writer, this is "the equivalent of dumping the entire pupil population of New York City, biggest in the U.S., onto the nation's trash heap every year. Very few ever drop back in. Most of the others are lost forever, not only to the school system, but to society at large." The problem of dropouts is particularly acute in the nation's large cities. Boston, Chicago, Houston, and Los Angeles report an average of 45 percent dropouts, students who enter ninth grade but leave before completing four more years.

"In many cases the school was the most stabilizing factor in their lives" for those dropouts, says Alcena Boozer, head of an outreach program for dropouts in Portland. "Then that's gone, and nothing's there." What can be done to prevent this loss to individuals and to society? Bowen says, "Old-style pedagogy simply does not work when the climate both inside and outside the schoolhouse is one of paralyzing despair." Educators in inner-city schools point to the low expectations of ghetto students, creating a "ghetto mentality." Students quickly learn to match these low expectations. Michael Timpane, president of Teachers College, Columbia University, observes, "It's only in the past generation that we've had the challenge of trying to succeed with individuals who didn't want to succeed or didn't even want to be in the classroom."

Even in some of the roughest districts, however, some schools have managed to become islands of excellence. They have done this mainly through establishing high expectations and getting across the conviction that their stu-dents can and will meet those expectations. These schools have bold, enduring principals with effective management and leadership skills. The principals are able to maintain or restore order without abandoning the students who are in trouble. Cooperation rather than confrontation is the touchstone of their leadership style. As William Kristol, formerly chief of staff for William Bennett, Secretary of Education under former President Ronald Reagan, explains, "Every good school has a good principal. He can set the general tone, the spirit, the ethos if you will, of the school. He can give it a sense of order, enthusiasm for learning and high expectations."

These principals succeed through setting and carrying out priorities. At the top of the priority list is the establishment and maintenance of rules, which are mixed with demanding classes. High-quality teachers are recruited and are treated with respect. The principal and teachers often create special incentives to motivate students. Parental participation is another priority. Principals also work to fight student anonymity in large urban schools by working on person-to-person contact, not only from faculty to student but among the students.

Citing the need for all schools to combat ghetto mentality and the problem of dropouts, Albert Holland, a high school principal in Boston, says, "Schools can't educate alone. They used to be isolated, but now the problems are so magnified that it takes the family, it takes the school, it takes the community all working together to make education possible."

"Getting tough." Bowen, E., Beaty, J., Ludtke, M., and Simpson, J. C. *Time*, Vol. 131(5), Feb. 1, 1988, pp. 52–58.

and hallways that offer a sense of community; interconnected teachers' offices and work stations that establish a sense of cooperative effort. Cooperative planning and teaming among faculty members are coming onto the scene. With greater autonomy and decision-making power at the building level, staffs bond together in pursuing their shared goals.

But restructuring poses personal challenges. Can you de-isolate yourself? Falling into a comfortable routine is natural: "Being left alone is not so bad—in fact, I function better that way." Before long, isolation becomes a state of affairs to be protected, not to be rescued from! Will your thirst for cooperation, your promises of it, hold up? Will you want to remain isolated in a gleaming, cooperatively designed building?

LACK OF EMPOWERMENT   By "empowerment" we mean providing teachers with permission, authority, and responsibility to carry out their teaching role. Though the term is a recent arrival on the educational scene, concepts underlying it have been around for many years.

The recent emphasis on teacher empowerment arose from literature on teacher dissatisfaction, teacher autonomy, professionalization, and shared decision making. Research has shown that "the conditions under which teachers work are often set up in such a way as to deny teachers a sense of efficacy, success, and self-worth."[39] In the past, teachers were often given responsibility without authority. They were not consulted in decisions directly affecting their work, decisions that at times actually undermined their judgment and professional expertise. Additionally, too few teachers were given recognition for their accomplishments. This lack of empowerment has been decried by a leading educational spokesman:

> What we need is a revolution, a radical departure from the way we structure our schools and think about teaching, if we are to attack a problem too serious for mere tinkering. . . . Teachers have very few ways to incorporate the wisdom gleaned from classroom experience into solutions to school problems. The top-down command structure of American schools subjects them . . . to regulation by higher authority. Frequently teachers must respond to administrative fiat. . . . Too often, they must follow rules and regulations that run contrary to wisdom. . . . Thus, they practice selective obedience and sometimes outright resistance. . . . The way to make schools better is to ask the teachers. . . . But the new breed of teacher—a highly skilled, board-certified professional—clearly must have a decisive voice in the areas of his or her expertise. The old top-down management system and the new teacher-professional are incompatible.[40]

Another leading educator, voicing the need for empowerment, maintains that "the school must be largely self-directing. The people within it must develop a capacity for effective renewal and establish the mechanisms for doing this."[41]

Research in this area clearly indicates that the empowerment of teachers has a positive impact on their professional image, on their commitment to the mission of their school, and on their decision to remain in teaching. Less clear is the impact of teacher empowerment on student outcomes.[42]

THINKING ABOUT THE CHALLENGES   How much decision-making power do you really want? Are you ready to accept the power reformers want to bestow upon you? As a result of becoming socialized into the teaching profession, you may believe that teachers are there to teach, not to make decisions like those principals make. Such a restricted conception of your role—when others are trying to empower you—impedes your ability to teach effectively. Go with your new levels of empowerment—eagerly!

**EDUCATING THE SPECIAL STUDENT**   Reform reports, federally funded programs, state laws, and parents all converge in drawing attention to the needs of the "special" student. Providing education for these students is both costly and labor intensive. These are some of the problems involved in educating special students, particularly within regular classrooms:

> We continue to segregate special education students into disjointed programs and we continue to be inconsistent in classifying and placing these students. The "special," "compensatory," and "remedial" programs that have proliferated over the past 20 years have been initiated independently of other ongoing programs. . . . The widely used "pull-out" approach—removing students with special learning needs from regular classes—has been the predominant strategy for structuring programs to improve the educational attainment of students with special learning needs. Although well intentioned, the pull-out approach neglects the larger problem: regular classroom learning environments have failed to accommodate the educational needs of many [of these] students.[43]

**THINKING ABOUT THE CHALLENGES**   Cooperate with the special education teacher as you both work to attain mutual goals for your students. Be accommodating and flexible while relentlessly pursuing your own curricular goals for all your students. You may be asked to follow up and reinforce skills learned during pull-out instruction. Do it—creatively.

**YEAR-ROUND SCHOOLS**   Many educators feel the September–June calendar has outlived its usefulness. Originally, its purpose was to accommodate the prevailing agricultural economy of the late nineteenth and early twentieth centuries. Children and teenagers were needed on the family farm during the summer months. Today, only a small fraction of American students live on farms, and modern equipment has greatly reduced labor needs.

Those arguing for year-round schooling believe that a long summer vacation disrupts the continuity of a student's learning. Each year, teachers are forced to conduct extensive reviews during September and October, following a summer's worth of forgetting. Extended reviews eat up valuable days that could be spent learning new material. Over the student's schooling career, this accumulated review time takes its toll on overall academic growth. Figure 12-1 illustrates a sample of year-round configurations.

Here are some of the purported advantages for the learner in a year-round school:

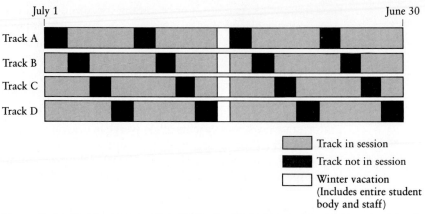

*Figure 12-1    Multitrack year-round calendar* (C. Ballinger, "Rethinking the School Calendar," *Educational Leadership* 45(5) (1988), p. 59.)

1.   Learning is continual over the entire year.

2.   By shortening the summer vacation, there is less memory loss among students.

3.   Remedial help can be offered throughout the entire year rather than sending the distraught student to summer school after nine months of failure and frustration.

4.   Instructional periods fit better into a year-round calendar than a nine-month calendar.

5.   Multitrack versions of year-round schooling are cost effective; they allow considerable savings in both operational and capital outlay costs.[44]

Another argument for the year-round calendar is that greater numbers of students are coming into the classroom from homes where English is not the primary language, and learning English is seriously impeded by long summer breaks:

> For most students, the language of the summer is going to be the language of the community, whether it is English or not. Three months away from formal instruction is not helpful to students learning a new language, whether they are English-speaking students learning Spanish or Spanish-speaking students learning English.[45]

On the other side of the ledger, many teachers and parents argue against a year-round schedule:

1.   Teachers express a need for a three-month break, a thorough renewal for the upcoming school year ("I need that long to recharge my batteries!").

2.   With some year-round plans, a teacher may not have a clearly assigned

room, one that is "my very own for the whole year." This "nest" disruption can be anxiety producing, causing a loss in feelings of ownership.

3. Teachers, especially at the elementary level, are geared to be with one group of students for the entire nine months. But on a multitrack year-round program, teachers are required to work with different combinations of students over the school year ("Just when I get these students working well together, a bunch are shipped off and I have to start over again.").

4. When parents have children in both elementary and high school, vacation times are difficult to synchronize; when one is off the other is on, and vacations suffer.

5. Summer is the traditional time for camping, baseball, swimming, hiking, and travel ("My daughter has to be in school when all her friends are out enjoying life." "Who wants to take a vacation in the dead of winter?").

THINKING ABOUT THE CHALLENGES   As you find yourself on a year-round schedule, there are a number of things to consider. If your school moves onto a year-round schedule, long, leisurely vacation periods will need to be replaced with shorter, more frequent breaks. The frequent recombining of different groups of students with whom you will be working for shorter periods of time challenges your emotional and physical stamina.

Year-round teaching can augment your income. In a multitrack system, you may elect to teach in another track during your break; or you may elect to go on a year-round contract. In both cases, you can generate additional income.

CAREER LADDER PROGRAMS   In principle, the "career ladder" concept offers stages of responsibility and salary that are commensurate with the teacher's competence and seniority. This staging approach attracts better-qualified, career-oriented people and it creates greater effort, ambition, and identification with the teaching profession. It is an attempt not only to encourage the continuous growth of a teacher but to provide differentiation among teachers by rewarding excellence rather than separating the competent from the incompetent.

Career ladder programs represent a legitimate start in restructuring the teaching profession. For years, critics have attacked teaching on grounds that the twenty-year veteran is hardly different from the beginning teacher in salary, responsibilities, and privileges. However, those within the profession know that the seasoned veteran, if a master teacher, can be invaluably helpful to the beginner. Through mentoring, the entire profession upgrades itself.

For illustration, let us think of three categories of teachers: the beginning teacher, the regular teacher, and the master teacher. The career ladder program provides an internship for the beginning teacher, a development program for the regular teacher, and training in mentorship for the master teacher. A teacher moves from one rung of the ladder to the next through

*The truth is that we usually give our newest and least experienced teachers
the most difficult jobs in our schools.—Carl D. Glickman*

experience and expertise, acquiring more responsibility and higher salary
with each upward step. However, there may be tradeoffs. For instance, excellent teachers moving into the master category may be required to give up
their own classrooms in order to help new teachers.

Tennessee was one of the first states to adopt a statewide career ladder
program. Under that program, teachers are free to choose whether or not
they will participate. Those electing to do so create a portfolio, or professional vita, containing such items as instructional plans, descriptions of
classroom management procedures, methods for evaluating students, and
leadership and professional development activities. An evaluation team,
made up of the teacher's peers, examines the portfolio and then turns to the
teacher's actual teaching competence: planning, teaching strategies, classroom management, evaluation procedures, leadership, and ability to communicate with students. Evaluations are gathered through direct observation, dialogue with the teacher, student questionnaires, a principal
questionnaire, the teacher's own written reflections, and a written test.
Every attempt is made to gather data on as many characteristics as possible,
and from as many sources as possible. On the basis of all information
gathered, the evaluation team makes decisions regarding the teacher's advancement up the ladder.

To date, career ladder programs have often sputtered from lack of
funds and "working out the procedural details." Nonetheless, the career
ladder is a genuine teacher-incentive program and is destined to become an
integral part of the restructuring of education.[46]

THINKING ABOUT THE CHALLENGES   Peer review! Even the prospect is
frightening: "I'd just die if a group of teachers came in and evaluated my
teaching! And they'd probably wince at having to do so. I like the way we do
things now. The principal comes in, observes, then tells me about my contract for next year." Teachers are not, as a group, highly competitive. Although nearly all teachers wish for higher salaries, they are surprisingly reluctant to get ahead at the expense of someone else: "We're in this together.
Everyone works hard and earns their salary; we're all pretty equal in what
we do." Moving up the ladder, you run the risk of alienating colleagues.
Some refuse to participate because of that possibility.

But run the risks! Jump into the program, not only to improve your
salary but to upgrade yourself—and the profession. Peer review is an unusual blessing of which too few teachers avail themselves. How often do you
have the chance to be visited and observed by your colleagues? It is almost
always a respectful process. Think of the helpful feedback they can provide.
Think, also, of the evidence they will gather of your *effectiveness*. Couple

this with your systematically developed portfolio—a trail of your accomplishments. Surely your self-confidence will soar! But suppose, after thoughtful evaluation and sensitive discussion, your peers judge you as not being quite ready to assume greater responsibility and increased salary. What now? The evaluation you've just gone through will have identified your professional goals for the coming year. Finally, you will be ready.

## Your Curriculum

"My kids will have trouble with this stuff. They're three months behind my last year's group. I'll have to go more slowly and I'll have to make things simple. They need lots of examples and really short homework assignments. I wish now we had gone with the simpler text."

"I've got *too* much material to teach! I'll have to cut down a lot. I won't be able to get to some of the units."

"Some of these units I don't like. There's a unit on 'Finishing Edges' that's outdated. Whoever wrote this manual was out of it. I don't like the 'Fashions' section either. My girls won't make those kinds of outfits."

Those are challenges, to be sure. The first teacher has the task of translating the subject matter so it is learnable; the second with deciding what to include and what to omit; and the third, with keeping subject matter up to date. For years teachers have faced traditional curricular challenges such as these. They are important, they demand competent skills, and they confront almost every teacher. But they are readily solvable, in most cases, with appropriate reselection of curricular materials.

We tarry no longer with them. Rather, in this section, we have chosen to focus on a different type of curricular challenge: teaching controversial and sensitive subjects such as sexuality, values, character, and religion. Since sexual issues have been discussed, we turn attention to character education and religious education. The question is not, "Do I exclude the teaching of values and religion?" (You are always teaching values, whether you mean to or not.) Rather, the relevant question is, "What challenges face me when sensitive or controversial subjects arise?"

**CHARACTER EDUCATION**[47]    "Moral" or "character" education in the schools has changed dramatically over the years. In the 1940s and 1950s, the United States and democracy were the great hope against the aggression of communism. Students respected their presidents and their schools. Hard work and love of country were strongly endorsed. Teachers preached to their students about what was right and what was wrong. Students either followed the rules or were expelled. Society expected that of them.

In the 1960s and 1970s things began to go sour. Student aptitude scores, peaking in 1963, declined steadily over the next eighteen years. Student unrest, civil disobedience, vandalism, and violent crimes characterized the mid-1960s. As the 1970s began, distrust of government soared, and

President Kennedy's "Ask not what your country can do for you; ask what you can do for your country" met with only cynical smiles. A president and vice-president resigned. "Don't trust anyone over 30" was the street slogan. In Frederick Wiseman's widely acclaimed documentary, *High School,* a young black student announced to the class, "This school is a moral garbage can!" Students grinned and the teacher looked on in sheepish silence. In the midst of this antiauthority movement and moral confusion, teachers began surrendering their moral authority and retreated to merely conveying information and teaching academic skills. Teachers were confused about moral issues and about what their moral role as teachers ought to be.

Educators, still feeling a sense of responsibility, started trying alternative approaches to the teaching of values. Their hope was to instill values without imposing them on students. "Values clarification" was an approach occurring against a backdrop of disloyalty to the country, premarital sex, abortions, vandalism, alcohol, drugs, and teenage pregnancies. Values clarification attempted, through games and discussions, to enable students to clarify their *own* values (rather than those of the community). Teachers felt more secure assuming a neutral role and were content to organize discussions, raise questions, and summarize, hoping students would work their way through their own "values crises."

Cognitive-developmental theory was optimistically employed to help children reach higher stages of moral thinking through discussing moral dilemmas. Here again, teachers maintained neutrality during the discussions. These and other strategies were employed with considerable enthusiasm, but their success in actually bringing about desired moral behavior in children was meager. One explanation was that children were being taught how to think morally, not how to act morally. Moreover, the neutral role played by the teacher diffused her potential as a role model. The 1980s was a period for regrouping and for generating a return to more traditional values. "Preppy" was in and nihilistic punk on its way out. Family shows and comedy started replacing at least some of television's violence. The headlines during this period read, "Public education in need of reform." We have already discussed the flurry of reform reports of the early 1980s revealing the *academic* failings in our schools. But these reports failed to show our *moral* failings, as evidenced by alcohol and drug abuse, vandalism, extreme behavior in classrooms, physical abuse of students and teachers, and sexual promiscuity.

Although the reform reports shied away from suggesting that schools reassert their traditional role in moral education, the public did not. Seventy-nine percent of the nation's respondents to a Gallup poll favored instruction in the schools that would deal with morals and moral behavior.[48] Educators wrestled with this public mandate to teach moral values in what had now become pluralistic classrooms. But two public officials—William Bennett, secretary of education, and Bill Honig, California state superintendent for public instruction—did not wrestle. They reaffirmed the right and the responsibility of the schools to teach traditional American values of love of country, courage, and respect for parents, teachers, and other adults. Teachers were urged to help children become not only smart but also good.[49]

During the latter part of the 1980s, "socialization," which has always included the teaching of cultural norms, was resurrected as an important vehicle for teaching morality: students should be taught what society has learned about living together in a civilized fashion.

**THINKING ABOUT THE CHALLENGES**   For society's sake, your students need to learn how to act as well as how to think. Parents in the latter part of the 1980s have been urging you to teach basic values of human decency, honesty, and courtesy in your classroom. The neutral position taken earlier by teachers has met with only modest success. Your personal example—how you act in and out of the classroom—is a good starting point. Further, students will want to know what *you* think about honesty, exploitation, caring, greed, respect for others, and loyalty to people and country. Start now deciding what you will value in your own classroom and what character traits you will model. Think, too, about what position you would take on various issues. For example, consider the following questions:

"Are the means I'm using justified if I have the students' best interest at heart?"

"How far do I go in helping a student with deep-seated family problems?"

"I see people climbing over each other all the time. That's just the way life is. What's wrong with getting all you can?"

"I think kids need to know how tough teaching really is. What's wrong with telling them about poor teacher salaries?"

"Isn't it passé to teach high school kids to be courteous?"

"These are federal programs—why not pad our capital equipment requests for all we can get?"

**RELIGION IN THE SCHOOL**   Are you free, as a teacher, to urge students to believe in God? Are you justified in questioning their beliefs about God? Can you teach Catholicism, or Buddhism? Can you hold a "moment of prayer" each morning in your classroom? Is it legal to give students a separate room if they want to have religious discussions during the school day?

These and similar questions can gnaw away at teachers. The vast majority of our country's teachers are sensitive to and respectful of the differing faiths of their students. Few would overstep religious bounds in the classroom. But what are the religious bounds? Because much confusion exists in this area, teachers studiously avoid discussions of religious issues.

Teaching religion—or mandating or allowing religious activities in schools—has always been and continues to be surrounded by controversy. There are no signs of abatement. Battle lines are newly drawn with each generation, sometimes with different opponents who use newer weaponry. We will take a short journey, illustrating some of the religious issues you might encounter: prayer in the schools, a "moment of silence," use of school time and property for religious purposes, creationism, and secular humanism. We start with the First Amendment:

> Congress shall make no law respecting an establishment of religion, or prohibiting the free exercise thereof; or abridging the freedom of speech, or of the press; or the right of the people peaceably to assemble, and to petition the Government for a redress of grievances.

The language of the "religion" clauses of the First Amendment is firm, yet provides no clear guidelines for educational policy makers. The "establishment" clause prohibits government from *assisting* religion; the "free exercise" clause prohibits it from *hindering* religion. The problem comes in deciding precisely what is forbidden and what is allowed or required.

Two Supreme Court judges, early on, gave opposing interpretations to the "establishment" clause. In *Everson* v. *Board of Education,* Justice Black presented the "separation" doctrine:

> The "establishment of religion" clause of the First Amendment means at least this: Neither a state nor the Federal Government can set up a church. Neither can pass laws which aid one religion, aid all religions, or prefer one religion over another. Neither can force nor influence a person to go to or to remain away from church against his will or force him to profess a belief or disbelief in any religion. No person can be punished for entertaining or professing religious beliefs or disbeliefs, for church attendance or non-attendance. No tax in any amount, large or small, can be levied to support any religious activities or institutions, whatever they may be called, or whatever form they may adopt to teach or practice religion. Neither a state nor the Federal Government can, openly or secretly, participate in the affairs of any religious organizations or groups and vice versa. In the words of Jefferson, the clause against establishment of religion by law was intended to erect "a wall of separation between Church and State."[50]

On the other side of the fence, Justice Douglas in *Zorach* v. *Clauson* presented the "accommodation" principle:

> We are a religious people whose institutions presuppose a Supreme Being. We guarantee the freedom to worship as one chooses. We make room for as wide a variety of beliefs and creeds as the spiritual needs of man deem necessary. We sponsor an attitude on the part of government that shows no partiality to any one group and that lets each flourish according to the zeal of its adherents and the appeal of its dogma. When the state encourages religious instruction or cooperates with religious authorities by adjusting the schedule of public events to sectarian needs, it follows the best of our traditions. For it then respects the religious nature of our people and accommodates the public service to their spiritual needs. To hold that it may not would be to find in the Constitution a requirement that the government show a callous indifference to religious groups. That would be preferring those who believe in no religion over those who do believe. . . . But we find no constitutional requirement which makes it

necessary for government to be hostile to religion and to throw its weight against efforts to widen the effective scope of religious influence.[51]

The problem for the Supreme Court has been "to find a neutral course between the two religion clauses, both of which are cast in absolute terms, and either of which, if expanded to a logical extreme, would tend to clash with each other."[52]

Early court decisions about school prayer (*Engel* v. *Vitale*[53] and *Abington School District* v. *Schempp*[54]) made it clear that the establishment clause prohibits the state from *requiring* religious activities in school. A later decision on school prayer (*Wallace* v. *Jaffree*[55]) and the earliest religious instruction case (*McCollum* v. *Board of Education*[56]) make it equally clear that the "establishment" clause prohibits the state from actively *encouraging* religious activities in school. Thus, religious activities can be neither mandated nor encouraged.

Since the 1970s, many states have passed "moment of silence" statutes, and federal courts have been divided over their constitutionality. In the wake of these conflicting decisions, the U.S. Supreme Court ruled on an Alabama law that authorized a minute of silence in all public schools "for meditation or voluntary prayer." In a controversial decision in 1985, *Wallace* v. *Jaffree,* the High Court held the law as unconstitutional. Although this decision did not resolve all the questions surrounding a moment-of-silence law, it solved many, if not most:

- Statutes or school district policies requiring a moment of silence "for prayer" are clearly unconstitutional.

- Those policies providing a moment of silence and saying nothing about prayer will not violate the "establishment" clause.

- Statutes that provide for silent "meditation or prayer" but have no secular purpose are unconstitutional.

- Meditation or prayer laws that have educational purposes will probably be upheld.

The U.S. Supreme Court has ruled clearly that school prayer laws are *unconstitutional,* even if students not wishing to participate are excused. Also, required recitation of the Lord's prayer and reading of the Bible are considered a religious ceremony and are likewise unconstitutional.

In March 1984, the United States Senate and House of Representatives debated a constitutional amendment to overturn Supreme Court decisions prohibiting prayer in public schools. This amendment began, "Nothing in this Constitution shall be construed to prohibit individual or group, vocal or silent prayer, in public schools or other public institutions." The amendment also stated, "No person shall be required by the United States or by any state to participate in prayer. Neither the United States nor any state shall compose or mandate the words of any prayer to be said in public schools." Although the majority of the senators voted in favor of this proposal, it failed to receive the two-thirds vote needed to pass. But supporters promised to try again.

What about students wanting to engage in religious activities at school during the school day? In *Bender* v. *Williamsport,*[57] a group of students wanted to start a voluntary, nondenominational club that would meet for thirty minutes twice a week during school hours "to promote spiritual growth and positive attitudes in the lives of its members." They would read scriptures, pray, and carry on religious discussions. After their first meeting, the students were denied further meetings by the principal and, later, by the school board. They brought suit against the school board in the U.S. District Court, claiming violation of their rights to free expression of religion, freedom of speech, and equal protection. These students wanted to hold religious meetings on the same basis as students who were holding nonreligious meetings. The U.S. District Court upheld their request as constitutional and granted the students the privilege. However, the Court of Appeals for the Third Circuit reversed that decision a year later. The case was then appealed to the U.S. Supreme Court. But the Supreme Court vacated the Circuit Court decision on procedural grounds (by a 5-to-4 vote). Unfortunately, this decision not only avoided the constitutional questions but left the whole issue unresolved.

At the same time, almost to the day, Congress passed the Equal Access Act, which was signed into law in August 1984. That part of the act relevant to educators reads as follows:

> It shall be unlawful for any public secondary school *which receives Federal financial assistance* and which has a limited open forum to deny equal access or a fair opportunity to, or discriminate against, any students who wish to conduct a meeting within that limited open forum on the basis of the religious, political, philosophical, or other content of the speech at such meetings.[58]

The act was designed explicitly to make accommodation of religious meetings *mandatory* in public schools whenever school facilities were opened for other voluntary meetings. The act has several consequences: it subjects school officials to considerable political pressure if they refuse to open their doors to their student religious groups; once their doors are opened, school officials lose their ability to make educational decisions about what happens in these meetings; and, most important, school officials must decide whether they will restrict school time and facilities to purely curriculum-related matters or open them up for noncurricular student expression and associations (such as religious clubs).

Whereas students do not have a right under the "free *exercise*" clause to meet for religious purposes on school premises during school hours, they may have a right to do so under the "free *speech*" clause. If their central beliefs, protected by the "free speech" clause, turn out to be religious in nature, students may be able to hold their meetings.[59]

Following are a number of questions surrounding religious issues, and their answers based on court decisions:

"Can students voluntarily request permission to form a prayer club to meet on the same basis as any other student organization?"
   They *may* have the constitutional right to do so.

   "May schools permit student-initiated prayers at assemblies?"
      Generally, no.

"May schools encourage the reciting or singing of prayers at extracurricular activities?"
   Generally, No.

   "Are Christmas observances unconstitutional in public schools?"
      Not necessarily. It depends on the observance. Generally, they need to have "both a religious and a secular basis."

"Can the government deny tax exemption to religious schools that engage in racial discrimination because of their religious beliefs?"
   Yes.

   "May states provide tax deductions to parents who send their children to religious schools?"
      Probably. Although it is unconstitutional for states to provide direct support for religious education, tax deductions to parents for tuition of dependents can be allowed.

"Is it unconstitutional to teach the Bible in public schools?"
   Not necessarily. In the words of the U.S. Supreme Court in *Abington* v. *Schempp:* "The Bible is worthy of study for its literary and historic qualities" and "when presented objectively as part of a secular program of education" would not violate the First Amendment.

   "Must states requiring the teaching of evolution also require the teaching of creationism?"
      No. In a federal Arkansas case, *McLean* v. *Arkansas Board of Education,*[60] the court ruled that the state's Balanced Treatment for Creation-Science and Evolution-Science Act was unconstitutional. On analysis of the act, Judge Overton found that the bill's sponsor was motivated "solely by his religious beliefs and desired to see the Biblical version of creation taught in the public schools." The court concluded that "it was simply and purely an effort to introduce the Biblical version of creation into the public school curriculum" and therefore had no secular legislative purpose. Under our Constitution, wrote the court, "no group, no matter how large or small, may use the organs of government, of which the public schools are the most conspicuous and influential, to foist its religious beliefs on others."[61]

To this point, we have presented only the constitutional side, which, for the most part, prohibits the practice of religion in the schools. What about the Moral Majority contention that religion needs to be put back into the curriculum? These are comments by leading spokespersons who see evil in the court actions just discussed:

I believe that the decay in our public school system suffered an enormous acceleration when prayer and Bible reading were taken out of the classroom by the U.S. Supreme Court. Our public school system is now permeated with [secular] humanism. The human mind has been deceived, and the end result is that our schools are in serious trouble.[62] ["Secular humanism," by this group, is defined as curriculum that is godless, devoid of anything spiritual.]

The public school system . . . gutted by secular humanism, is literally attacking the home, the family structure in this country."[63]

There are 15,700 school districts in America. When we get an active Christian parents' committee in operation in all districts, we can take complete control of all local school boards. This would allow us to determine all local policy; select good textbooks, good curriculum programs; superintendents and principals. Our time has come![64]

Televangelists are proclaiming that the Lord is not pleased with public education. Many of the members of the religious right see the schools as evil, permeated by a godless ideology of secular humanism. Schools, they argue, should teach only ideologically correct ideas; to explore suspect ideas is to advocate evil.

Considerable wealth and power exist in these so-called Moral Majority groups, which include such organizations as Citizens for Excellence in Education, Eagle Forum, Concerned Women for America, Gablers' Educational Research Analysts, National Association of Christian Educators, and the National Council for Better Education. These people can engineer a million letters on the subject of their choice to any legislator in the nation. One survey of this group showed that 88 percent of the Moral Majority supporters agree that biblical creationism should be taught in schools, and 80 percent agreed that secular humanism undermines Christianity. Eighty-one percent agreed that a major educational problem today is that secular humanists have been allowed to determine the textbooks used in the public school system.[65]

To be sure, religious activism has brought some changes in the curriculum and textbooks through the courts. In *Mozert* v. *Hawkins County Public Schools*[66] a group of fundamentalist Christian families in Hawkins County, Tennessee, charged that a Holt, Rinehart and Winston reading series in use in the county schools offended their religious beliefs. The offensive materials included *The Wizard of Oz, The Diary of Anne Frank,* and topics such as the Renaissance, evolution, pollution, Roman Catholicism, Islam, and Buddhism. A story about Leonardo da Vinci and the Renaissance came under fire because it "talks about the idea that the human mind has unknown capabilities for imagination, intelligence, and creativity." Judge Thomas G. Hull ruled for the parents: their children could be taught reading at home, and they could go to the library or study hall during instruction on subjects that violated their fundamentalist beliefs.

In another case, *Smith* v. *Board of School Commissioners of Mobile County,*[67] several hundred parents charged that the curriculum promotes the "religion of secular humanism," which violates the First Amendment prohibition against the official establishment of religion. They further argued that textbooks censor information about Christianity, in violation of the constitutional right to free exercise of religion. Judge Hand ruled that secular humanism *is a religion,* and that it was being promoted unconstitutionally in the Alabama public schools. He therefore ordered the immediate removal of forty-five history, social studies, and home economics textbooks from all Alabama public school classrooms. In this case, a sizeable portion of the new curriculum was suspect; in the first case, parents objected to a reading series and wanted an alternative.

Religious fundamentalists attack the teaching of evolution on grounds that it fails to support the biblical account of the creation. Likewise, these groups would inhibit discussion of controversial issues such as disarmament, strengths and weaknesses of the American government and economy, and American intervention in foreign wars. Among these groups, there is a prevailing belief that (1) the mere exposure to contradictory ideas will undermine the child's faith, (2) children must be taught to accept rather than question and wonder, and (3) scripture provides *scientifically* valid accounts of natural phenomena like the world's creation.

Fundamentalist groups have also used their accusations of secular humanism as an argument *for* the use of tax credits to private schools. "Tax credits" would allow parents to claim tax deductions for enrolling their children in private or parochial schools. The argument of these groups is as follows: Public schools are clearly funding a religion—the religion of secular humanism. According to the Constitution, the government (public schools in this case) cannot prefer one religion over another—but they are doing so with secular humanism. Therefore, religious schools should also be funded, to ensure "no preference."

How does the government end up doing the funding? Parents pay tuition required by the parochial school. They can afford to do so—they are enticed to do so—because the government exempts them from paying a portion of their taxes; they can use the money saved to pay the tuition. Thus, in effect, the government is giving money to the parochial school through the parent.

What are the effects of this pressure on textbook writers and publishers? They are increasingly reluctant to include controversial topics. Religion, for example, is shortchanged in most American history, government, and civics texts, despite its paramount role in the development of this country. Likewise, evolution is omitted from many science and biology texts. The result is often a bland and sometimes distorted view of both history and science.[68]

**THINKING ABOUT THE CHALLENGES**   As a *public* school teacher, you are responsible not only to transmit cultural heritage but also to accommodate all religious, racial, and ethnic backgrounds of your students. Your challenge is to make sure preferential or derogatory treatment is never given to any religious belief or practice. Your approach to religious instruction should be academic, not devotional or sectarian.

Being sensitive to the pluralistic nature of the faiths in your classroom, how will you handle students' questions and issues related to religion? Imagine yourself responding to questions like these:

"What do *you* believe about God, Mr. Sanchez?"

"I gotta go to a program at my church. Can I miss fifth period?"

"My mom and dad said not to read that book. That book you're using is telling it the wrong way."

"I don't want to pledge allegiance, but I feel dumb not doing it. Can I just wait outside the class until you get through?"

"Do Buddhists worship God?"

In responding to these questions, or in dealing with any issue, use your own good sense. Consult with your principal and know the district's guidelines. Be sensitive to students' beliefs and parental wishes.

# PERSONAL CHALLENGES

Like every other profession, teaching offers its personal challenges, involving being recognized for a job well done, overcoming fear of failure, developing emotional stamina, managing stress, carving satisfaction out of routine, and being respected by students. By its very nature, teaching involves intensely personal aspects of one's life, aspects that breed both fulfillment and despair.

A multitude of personal challenges accompany teaching. However, we discuss only one, stress, since it is almost universal among teachers and is rapidly becoming one of the more serious challenges.

## The Concept of Stress

I've been sick. Partially it's the flu, but it's also the worry. My stomach is in knots. Last night I cried. I actually cried. The lady next door came over. She knocked, and I thought, "What the hell does she want!" I opened the door, and there she stood with a piece of cake and a big bowl of soup. And I cried. I just cried. I hadn't been with anyone to let something out, and I felt so bad because I was feeling so negative and here she was bringing me food. She says, "You haven't eaten in days, I bet." I'm losing weight and I look pale. I'm wiped out. I must get away. Things will be okay.[69]

Picture a car, revved up to 3500 RPM, still sitting in neutral—mobilized to screech out, but not doing so. This is akin to what happens physiologically to the body under stress. Suppose you are called to the phone. An

© *Elizabeth Crews/The Image Works*

irate parent scolds you for your "incompetent" handling of her son's math assignments. You listen and try to respond politely and professionally. But your central nervous system is sending the message "Man your battle stations!" The pituitary and adrenal glands dump into the bloodstream hormones that instantly speed up the heartbeat, blood pressure, and respiration. Your body is mobilized for action! But there is no call on your physical strength—no "fight or flight."

Suppose that sort of mobilization recurs throughout the day in response not only to abusive phone calls but to disruptive students, poor student performance, incompleted assignments, and unending demands for help and support. The body is not built to function for long periods in a state of mobilization. Headaches start showing up, as do prolonged colds, insomnia, gastrointestinal disorders, flare-ups of chronic medical problems (for instance, diabetes or high blood pressure), neck and back pains, and missed menstrual cycles.

Determining whether you are under stress is not simple. You cannot wake up in the morning, look into a mirror, and discover that you've "got stress." Three *general* characteristics seem to make up the stress profile: (1) complete emotional and physical exhaustion, (2) growing disillusionment with one's job, and life in general, and (3) self-doubt and self-blame. These characteristics tend to appear gradually and grow in severity over time. One teacher described her stress this way: "I feel like I'm a huge rubber band that's ready to snap, and there is nothing I can do to relieve the tension." Others describe a sense of futility, as if they were drowning in a stormy ocean or have to move a grand piano all alone. Still others describe their energy depletion using images like limp spaghetti, wilted flowers, or a well run dry. It's not like being temporarily tired. Teachers under stress complain of a "total" fatigue from which they can't seem to spring back. In describing their self-doubt, teachers might say they function like a robot: skills and knowledge remain intact, but the will to perform gives way to mechanical behavior. The faded memory of what they "used to be like" is internalized as guilt, doubt, and blame.

Many teachers try to counteract these negative feelings by trying harder, working longer and more intensely. In their disillusionment, the joy of teaching and interacting with parents and children slips away and is replaced by growing cynicism or a malaise of spirit. A deepening insensitivity toward children and their parents settles in. There is an emotional withdrawal from involvement with people. Further, disillusioned teachers tend to discourage new, energetic workers with disheartening remarks like, "We've tried that before," or, "Slow down. Why knock yourself out? What are you trying to prove, anyway?" Increased irritability, anxiety, yelling, and blaming create a fertile breeding ground for carelessness, mistakes, and overall poor performance. Moodiness, depression, and an overriding sense of sadness commonly pervade behavior at this point.[70]

Stress is, above all else, exhaustion! There is a wearing out, a loss of energy. Accompanying this is a loss of idealism, an irritability, depression, low morale, reduced productivity, and an inability to cope. In terms of school behavior, patterns of tardiness and absenteeism develop; there is a persistent failure to perform required tasks (like paperwork); in meetings, teachers act out behaviors (silent withdrawal, destructive criticism, raising irrelevant issues). Finally, stressed teachers routinely denigrate their colleagues and spread negativism and apathy wherever they tread.[71]

Stressors differ by teacher. The conditions that create stress in one teacher may be the very conditions that invigorate another. Even so, research shows that the following are some of the leading and most common causes of stress among teachers: disruptive students, low motivation of students, overcrowded classrooms, lack of support from the principal and other members of the administration, the opening week of school, threats of personal injury, scarcity of resources and materials, inadequate salary, too much work to do in too little time, and the struggle to uphold values and standards. Additionally, teachers are stressed by not being listened to (by students, parents, administrators), a sense of isolation, not being able to communicate to students, feeling responsible but having little control, feeling undervalued and underappreciated, and role conflicts (teacher, counselor, wife, mother; teacher, husband, father, moonlighter).

*Plaster falling from the ceiling was creating a safety hazard; there were no textbooks in some classes, and a new teacher was told to use old copies of* Reader's Digest *as texts; midterms were canceled because the school ran out of paper.*—*Henrietta Schwartz and George Olson*

STRESS FROM ROLE CONFLICTS   Teachers regularly run into tuggings from several demanding roles, all played concurrently:

"Honey, what am I supposed to do? I agreed to serve as faculty supervisor for the seventh/eighth-grade dance Thursday. It starts at 4:00. Mark has a ball game at that time. I can't be both places at once!"

"There's got to be a better solution—you're running ragged most of the time."

"I agree. I can tell my pressure is affecting the whole family. By the end of the day I'm in sheer exhaustion. I don't want to cook, and I don't want to be with the kids—I've been with kids all day!"

Earlier in this chapter we noted the trend for both parents to be working outside the home. In earlier years, the intent of many young women was to teach for one to five years, then marry and stay at home. This practice is changing: more young women are staying in the profession after marriage and continuing as second breadwinners in the family. Sometimes they delay having children; more often they take time off to have their babies, return quickly, then arrange for daycare help.

There are several reasons for women to have children and continue in their careers: (1) the trend is for women to work outside the home, making use of their training and fulfilling lifelong ambitions, (2) many mothers are able to manage successfully both their teaching and their families, and (3) the rising cost of living forces both parents into the working market ("It takes both our salaries just to make ends meet!").

But the role of homemaker and the role of professional teacher compete for time, commitment, and energy. Often, a teacher experiences feelings of guilt from slighting one role or both. Consider this simple yet real conflict:

Saturday morning. I really need to get to school in the quiet of the weekend and redo my bulletin boards. But everybody's itching to get on the lake. Will my bulletin boards be done, or will I be part of the group?

As a teacher, you are counselor, parent surrogate, friend, and perhaps team leader. In the homemaking role, you are parent, spouse, scout advisor, and room parent in your child's fifth grade. After a long day wrestling with teenage problems, you are too depleted to listen to your own daughter's romantic crisis or to attend your husband's company party. A long, relaxing bubble bath is more what you had in mind.

Often as an outgrowth of conflicting roles, teachers experience stress from not having sufficient time to accomplish all they set out to do. Doing less than their best in either role can generate feelings of guilt and despondency:

> I'm on an endless treadmill! No relief in sight. Every day's one harried experience after another. By week's end, things at home have piled sky-high. I dive in, but never seem to get above water. Bang! It's Monday morning; the cycle starts over. There's got to be more to life than this. Where's the time to curl up with a good book or plant the garden? The minute I start indulging myself a little, I'm on a guilt trip. Oh, we do take some breaks, but they don't slow down the everyday wear-and-tear.

THINKING ABOUT THE CHALLENGES    Because teachers characteristically expect too much of themselves, much of their stress is self-induced. They are uncompromisingly conscientious, caring enough to make sizeable sacrifices both at school and in the home.

There is no magical panacea for managing stress. All methods require patience and perseverance. In developing your own effective stress management plan, most of the time you will need to do at least the following:

1.    *Change your perspective.* Try modifying your view of yourself in your role. For example, you may need to back off from being that eternal perfectionist. The emotional expense is just too great. You cannot be completely prepared for every lesson, always have elegant bulletin boards, create flawless exams, engage in high-quality teaching every moment, and "save" every student.

2.    *Acquire new skills.* Sometimes the old coping strategies become worn out and no longer useful, even though they have served you well in the past. You may have to go on a fitness-for-life program, trade old eating habits for sensible ones, learn to use your time more effectively, and say no and mean it.

3.    *Deal directly with stress-producing people and situations.* Sometimes you must go straight to the source of your stress. Suppose your principal is an authoritarian, ruling with an iron hand. You quietly resent him but never confront him. Instead, you set your teeth while stepping into a hot bath, or go on a relaxing run. These are only temporary measures, reducing stress until you see him the following morning. But there is hope. After gathering courage, you sit down with your principal and, for starters, say, "I'm experiencing considerable stress at the moment. Can we talk about it?"

Rediscovering old but effective skills and, at the same time, learning new ones is a valuable technique:

> Every person, including the burnout victim, has a wealth of stress management strategies at his or her disposal. These skills have been learned and practiced over a lifetime. Some remedies are used often and for many stress-provoking situations—a hot bath, a long run, a good cry. Others may be saved for major crises—blowing up, full-scale retreat, a values overhaul. Others have been for-

*Individuals in control of their lives have a deliberate game plan. They are
well informed, sensitive to the stress indicators in their own behavior, and
realistic in assessing their skills and resources. They have learned to put their
jobs in perspective by adding diversity and interest to their lives. They know
how to organize their time and space effectively, and continuously evaluate
their progress in achieving their goals. Their actions declare they are not
passive about their destiny, not controlled by events. Rather, they are active
in molding their environment to meet their needs.—Paula Jorde*

gotten or have atrophied from neglect—prayer, laughter, deep breathing. In
the case of burnout, people are often out of touch with many of their potential
coping resources, having narrowed their typically-used options to only a few
old standbys that may be out of date, inappropriate to the particular situation,
or minimally effective when used repeatedly. One of the major objectives in
working with burnout victims will be to help the individual rediscover forgotten skills and develop new skills for managing stress, preventing burnout, and
promoting vitality.[72]

Stress management is a highly individualized matter:

Once we really understand stress, each of us will be his own best physician, for
no one can appreciate our mental health needs better than ourselves. Everyone
must learn to measure the stress level at which he personally functions best
and then not go either above or below that. By careful observation we can
gradually develop an instinctive feeling telling us that we are running above or
below the stress level that corresponds to our own nature. . . . You must learn
to balance the pleasures and stimulation of social engagements, trips and successful work against your requirements for peace, solitude and serenity. Everybody will arrive at this aim in a somewhat different manner, always characteristic of his own individuality.[73]

The process of stress management is the process of renewal—a valued
and worthwhile activity.

## CONCLUSION

Let us take a step back. It is easy, when reading a chapter on challenges, to
lose the overall perspective: teaching is a satisfying combination of experiences. An experienced teacher, basking in the twilight of her successful career, illustrates this combination:

Yes, there are the realities—the "challenges"—of teaching. And yes, good
teachers I've known have been confronted with them. But they meet them as
part of their normal teaching lives. I look back on my teaching days as times
filled with pleasurable and rewarding experiences. Overall, my students were

fun; they were a joy to be with and teach. I worked hard but I also had plenty of time for other things in my life.

There's stress, but not that much, and certainly not day after day. Everyone gets a little uptight at the beginning of each school year, but it's also a pretty exciting time. Starting a new year with a brand new group of kids gets me stirred up emotionally, in ways I can't explain—but stress isn't a big part of all that.

I worked at teaching and also ran a home with a family. It was a little tight at times. There were the normal tuggings, and sometimes I felt guilty, but we all survived and nobody seems to be much the worse for wear.

We lived modestly—and still do. There were times when I resented not having a better salary for all my work, but so what? Society regularly misplaces its values. Our family ended up doing most of what we wanted to do; we weren't shortchanged that much. I'd choose teaching again if I had it to do over. Teaching has always been in my blood. What else do I say?

As this teacher's sentiments remind us, it is not so much your circumstance as how you see it that is of primary importance. Thus, a "challenge" looming large and frightful to someone else may appear small and easily conquerable to you—because of how you see it. Perhaps the greatest challenge will be to adopt a productive perception. Isolation can be seen as a depressing dungeon imprisoning you or as a dilapidated partition to be broken through. Year-round schooling can be seen as an imposition on your summer vacations or as an excuse to experiment with new methods. Teaching about sexual issues can be perceived as a topic to flee from or as a new frontier for positive influence. You are largely in control.

## Expansions

1. What professional challenges do you see before you as you enter teaching? What personal challenges do you face?

2. Visit with several experienced teachers. What challenges did they face early in their careers? What challenges confront them at this point?

3. Discuss challenges that might result from having each of these students in your class: a pregnant girl, a child from a divorced home, a drug abuser, a sexually promiscuous boy.

4. Suppose you experienced feelings of isolation and/or lack of empowerment. How would you handle them?

5. What would be your reactions if you were asked to teach in a year-round school?

6. What are some of the advantages and disadvantages you see in a career ladder program?

7. What would you do if a student requested that you give your personal religious views to the class?

8.    What effect might working in the classroom have on the stressors in your life? What new stressors might you anticipate from going into teaching?

9.    How well will your currently successful coping strategies work with the various stressors you encounter in teaching? Explain.

## Notes

1.   K. Michaels, "Caution: Second-Wave Reform Taking Place," *Educational Leadership* 45(5) (1988), p. 3.

2.   J. Nathan, "Implications for Educators of Time for Results," *Phi Delta Kappan,* November 1986, pp. 197–201; L. Alexander, "Chairman's Summary," *Time for Results: The Governors' 1991 Report on Education* (Washington, D.C.: National Governors' Association, 1986), p. 6.

3.   A. Liberman, "Expanding the Leadership Team," *Educational Leadership* 45(5) (1988), pp. 4–8.

4.   G. F. Madaus and D. Pullin, "Teacher Certification Tests: Do They Really Measure What We Need to Know?," *Phi Delta Kappan* (September 1987), pp. 31–38.

5.   B. T. Watkins, "New Tests Expected to Bring Dramatic Changes in the Way Prospective Teachers Are Assessed," *The Chronicle of Higher Education,* 25, (11) (November 9, 1988), p. A36.

6.   The Holmes Group, *Tomorrow's Teachers: A Report of the Holmes Group* (East Lansing, Mich.: The Holmes Group, Inc., 1986).

7.   Carnegie Forum on Education and the Economy, *A Nation Prepared: Teachers for the 21st Century,* report of the Carnegie Task Force on Teaching as a Profession (Washington, D.C.: Carnegie Forum, 1986).

8.   M. Seibel and J. N. Murray, "Early Prevention of Adolescent Suicide," *Educational Leadership* 45(6) (1988), pp. 48–51.

9.   U.S. Department of Commerce, Bureau of the Census. *United States Estimates and Components of Change: 1970–1987.* (Current Population Reports. Population Estimates and Projections. Series P-25, No. 1023). Washington, D.C.: U.S. Government Printing Office, August 1988. (C3.186: P-25/1023).

10.   H. Hodgkinson, "The Right Kids for the Right Schools," *Educational Leadership* 45(5) (1986), pp. 10–14.

11.   R. E. Emery, "Interparental Conflict and the Children of Discord and Divorce," *Psychological Bulletin* 92 (1982), pp. 31–330.

12.   U.S. Bureau of the Census, "Marital Status and Living Arrangements: March 1984," *Current Population Reports,* Series P-20, N. 399 (Washington, D.C.: U.S. Government Printing Office, 1985).

13.   L. Bumpass, "Children and Marital Disruption: A Replication and Update," *Demography* 21 (February 1984), pp. 71–82; S. L. Hofferth, "Updating Children's Life Course," *Journal of Marriage and the Family* 47 (February 1985), pp. 93–115.

14. P. London, "Character Education and Clinical Intervention: A Paradigm Shift for U.S. Schools," *Phi Delta Kappan* (May 1987), pp. 667–673.

15. Hodgkinson, "The Right Kids," pp. 10–14.

16. U.S. Department of Labor, Bureau of Labor Statistics, *Labor Force Activity of Mothers of Young Children Continues at Record Pace,* No. 85-381 (Washington, D.C.: U.S. Bureau of Labor Statistics, 1985).

17. S. L. Hofferth and D. Phillips, "Day Care in the Next Decade: 1985–1995," unpublished manuscript, National Institute of Child Health and Human Development, Bethesda, Md., 1986.

18. K. Naab, "Most Readers Think TV is Too Violent," *Milwaukee Journal TV Cable Magazine* (December 14, 1986), p. 4.

19. Hodgkinson, "The Right Kids," pp. 10–14.

20. D. Watson, "The Greatest Risk of All," *Educational Leadership* 45(6) (1988), pp. 16–17.

21. L. Horton, "The Education of Most Worth: Preventing Drug and Alcohol Use," *Educational Leadership* 45(6) (1988), pp. 4–8.

22. W. B. Hansen, "Effective School-Based Approaches to Drug Abuse Prevention," *Educational Leadership* 45(6) (1988), pp. 9–14.

23. L. Horton, *Adolescent Alcohol Abuse* (Bloomington, Ind.: Phi Delta Kappa Educational Foundation, 1985).

24. L. Johnson et al., *Drug Use among American High School Students, College Students, and Other Young Adults* (Washington, D.C.: National Institute on Drug Abuse, 1986).

25. J. R. Gress, "Alcoholism's Hidden Curriculum," *Educational Leadership* 45(6) (1988), pp. 18–19.

26. S. Totten, "The Myriad Dangers of Tobacco Use: Ignorance Is Anything but Bliss," *Educational Leadership* 45(6) (1988), pp. 28–32.

27. W. Snider, "Moves to Ban Smoking in Schools Gain," *Education Week,* June 4, 1986, p. 12.

28. R. Brandt, "On Students' Needs and Team Learning: A Conversation with William Glasser," *Educational Leadership* 45(6) (1988), p. 39.

29. J. J. Elias and J. F. Clabby, "Teaching Social Decision Making," *Educational Leadership* 45(6) (1988), pp. 52–55.

30. Seibel and Murray, "Early Prevention," pp. 48–51.

31. S. S. Klein, "Sex Education and Gender Equity," *Educational Leadership* 45(6) (1988), pp. 69–75.

32. D. M. Morrison, "Adolescent Contraceptive Behavior: A Review," *Psychological Bulletin* 98 (1985), pp. 538–568.

33. F. Jones, J. Forrest, N. Goldman, S. Henshaw, R. Lincoln, J. Rossf, C. Westoff, and D. Wulf, "Teenage Pregnancy in Developed Countries: Determinants of Policy Implications," *Family Planning Perspectives* 17 (March/April 1985), pp. 53–63.

34. S. Reed, "AIDS in the Schools: A Special Report," *Phi Delta Kappan* 67(7) (1986), pp. 494–498.

35. "Students Rally around AIDS Carrier," *The Daily Herald* (Provo, Utah), May 1988.

36. Reed, "AIDS," pp. 494–498.

37. J. H. Strouse and J. P. Phillips, "Teaching about AIDS: A Challenge to Educators," *Educational Leadership* 44(7) (1987), p. 71.

38. Reed, "AIDS," pp. 494–498.

39. M. W. McLaughlin, R. S. Pfeifer, D. Swanson-Owens, and S. Yee, "Why Teachers Won't Teach," *Phi Delta Kappan* 67 (1986), pp. 420–426.

40. A. Shanker, "Teachers Must Take Charge," *Educational Leadership* 44(1) (1986), pp. 12–13.

41. J. I. Goodlad, *A Place Called School* (New York: McGraw-Hill, 1984).

42. D. A. Erlandson, "Teacher Empowerment: What Research Says to the Principal," *NASSP Bulletin,* December 1987.

43. M. C. Wang, M. C. Reynolds, and H. J. Walberg, "Rethinking Special Education," *Educational Leadership* 44(1) (1986), 26–31.

44. C. Ballinger, "Rethinking the School Calendar," *Educational Leadership* 45(5) (1988), p. 59.

45. Ibid., pp. 57–61.

46. C. B. Furtwengler, "Lessons from Tennessee's Career Ladder Program," *Educational Leadership* 44(7) (1987), pp. 66–69.

47. Adapted from K. Ryan, "The New Moral Education," *Phi Delta Kappan* (November 1986), pp. 229–233.

48. G. H. Gallup, "The 12th Annual Gallup Poll of the Public's Attitudes toward the Public Schools," *Phi Delta Kappan* (September 1980), p. 39.

49. Bennett, W. (1984). "To Reclaim a Legacy," text of report on humanities in education, *Chronicle of Higher Education,* November 28, 1984; B. Honig, *Last Chance for Our Children* (Reading, Mass.: Addison-Wesley, 1985).

50. *Everson* v. *Board of Education,* 67 S.Ct. 504, 330 U.S. 1, 91 L.Ed. 711 (1947).

51. *Zorach* v. *Clauson,* 72 S.Ct. 679, 343 U.S. 306, 96 L.Ed. 954 (1952).

52. *Walz* v. *Tax Commission,* 90 S.Ct. 1409, 397 U.S. 664, 25, L.Ed. 2d 697 (1970).

53. *Engel* v. *Vitale,* 82 S.Ct. 1261, 370 U.S. 421, 8 L.Ed. 2d 601, 86 A.L.R. 2d 1285 (1962).

54. *Abington School District* v. *Schempp,* 83 S.Ct. 1560, 374 U.S. 203, 10 L.Ed. 2d 844 (1963).

55. *Wallace* v. *Jaffree,* 105 S.Ct. 2479, 472 U.S. 38, 86 L.Ed. 2d 29 (1985).

56. *McCollum* v. *Board of Education,* 68 S.Ct. 461, 333 U.S. 203, 92 L.Ed. 649, 2 A.L.R. 2d 1338 (1948).

57. *Bender* v. *Williamsport,* 106 S.Ct. 1326, 475 U.S. 534, 89 L.Ed. 2d 501 (1986).

58. Equal Access Act, 20 U.S.C. §4071. (Emphasis added.)

59.   J. C. Robbins, *Voluntary Religious Activities in Public Schools: Policy Guidelines* (Fastback 253) (Bloomington, Ind.: Phi Delta Kappa Educational Foundation, 1987).

60.   *McLean* v. *Arkansas Board of Education,* U.S. Dist. Ct. (E.D. Ark.), 529 F.Supp. 1255 (1982).

61.   D. Schimmel, "Controversial Legal Issues of the 1980s," in V. Richardson-Koehler (Ed.), *Educators' Handbook: A Research Perspective* (New York: Longman, 1987), pp. 601–623.

62.   J. Falwell, *Listen, America* (New York: Basic Books, 1980).

63.   J. Swaggart, Television presentation, January 6, 1985.

64.   R. L. Simmonds, fund-raising letter of the National Association of Christian Educators, circa February 1986.

65.   A. Shupe and W. Stacey, "The Moral Majority Constituency," in R. C. Liebman and R. Wuthnow (Eds.), *The New Christian Right* (New York: Aldine, 1983), pp. 104–116.

66.   *Mozert et al.* v. *Hawkins County Public Schools et al.,* U.S. Dist. Ct. (E.D. Tenn.), 647 F.Supp. 1194 (1986).

67.   *Smith et al.* v. *Board of School Commissioners of Mobile County,* U.S. Dist. Ct. (S.D. Ala.), LEXIS Genfed Library, Dist. file (1987).

68.   C. R. Kniker, *Teaching about Religion in the Public Schools.* (Bloomington, Ind.: Phi Delta Kappa Educational Foundation, 1985).

69.   Adapted from K. Ryan, K. K. Newman, G. Mager, J. Applegate, T. Lasley, R. Flora, and J. Johnston, "The Best of Both Worlds," *Biting the Apple* (New York: Longman, 1980), p. 186.

70.   P. Jorde, *Avoiding Burnout: Strategies for Managing Time, Space, and People in Early Childhood Education* (Washington, D.C.: Acropolis Books, 1982), pp. 19–51.

71.   N. L. Tubesing and D. A. Tubesing, "The Treatment of Choice: Selecting Stress Skills to Suit the Individual and the Situation," in W. S. Paine (Ed.), *Job Stress and Burnout: Research, Theory, and Intervention Perspectives* (Beverly Hills: Sage, 1982), pp. 155–171.

72.   Ibid.

73.   H. Selye, *The Stress of Life: A Scientist's Memoirs* (San Francisco: McGraw-Hill, 1976).

# CHAPTER

# GOOD TEACHING

*The deepest personal sorrow suffered by human beings consists of the difference of what one was capable of becoming and what one has, in fact, become.—Ashley Montagu*

**MAIN IDEAS**

- Teaching is scientific, artistic, complex, often unexplainable, and, above all, an intensely human affair.

- *Good* teaching is a lifelong pursuit. Good teachers exhibit characteristics that extend well beyond an ability to produce academic learning—characteristics such as selflessness, sense of proportion, and adaptability.

- We think the following personal characteristics are particularly important for good teaching: (1) a passionate commitment to teaching, (2) a sustained appetite for learning, (3) respect for students, (4) willingness to take responsibility, (5) open-mindedness, (6) and reflectivity.

- Your quest is not to imitate another great teacher but to become the best teacher that it is in *you* to be.

# INTRODUCTION

> "I've always believed that being a top teacher is not all that difficult. Once I get my first year behind me, I'll be on my way. Yes, discipline and lesson plans are important. But I believe good teaching is mostly careful planning and follow-through."

> > "I applaud your confidence—yet how do I convince you there's more, much more to good teaching? How do I talk about glowing satisfactions and bone-weary fatigue, about unbridled laughter and unrelenting stress? I guess I really can't."

Over the past few chapters, you have learned about effective schools, effective classrooms, how teaching is being studied, and technology in teaching. How natural to assume, then, that good teaching is primarily the process of applying knowledge about teaching in your own classroom. This assumption certainly starts you off in the right direction. Many effective teaching practices can be gleaned from current knowledge about teaching. For example, suppose you engage in longer "wait time" after asking your students a question. In many instances, your students' responses will be more productive than if you had not waited. Research knowledge, the kind to which we have been introducing you over the past few chapters, offers a great many hypotheses for you to try out in your teaching.

But teaching involves more than simply applying what you have learned, more than improving achievement in reading, math, and science— far more! It cannot be limited to the achievement of predefined objectives through flashy teaching methods. Teaching, in the fullest sense, is an intensely human activity: the conceptions, intentions, and values of the teacher are in constant interplay with those of the students. As a result, teaching cultivates a much broader range of outcomes than academic achievement and, in the process, brings about heartaches, joys, satisfactions, frustrations, anxieties, and stress.

We can never determine the full measure of a teacher's effectiveness by how well she produces learning in academic subjects, important as this outcome may be. We must, in addition, consider her commitments, values, judgment, experience, selflessness, honesty, and openness—to name a few traits—which have been finely crafted into a unique combination of teaching qualities. Stunningly good teachers "have it all together."

By now, from your reading, you are atop the foothills, where you can gaze at the mountain, "good teaching." *That* mountain takes nearly a lifetime to ascend! The elite group who reach the summit enjoy the great rewards this level of teaching has to offer. But good teaching is not a prize awarded at the summit; it is the climb itself! A few teachers never start the

*Teachers bring their constantly developing experiences, their growing sense of themselves and their work, and their ever-widening knowledge of both content and craft to their work. Much of what they bring is learned on the job, for in teaching, there is only so much you can talk about before immersion in the work itself initiates a never-ending process of training and growing. Teachers accumulate experiences, skills, and techniques. They develop a repertoire that is complex, multilayered, and idiosyncratic.—William Ayers*

trek. Many start, discover that the climb exacts too much from them—more than they are willing to give—and turn back. Others patiently climb the mountain, paying the daily price, and emerge as superbly good craftspeople.

How do you become a good teacher? What kinds of experiences must you go through and what kinds of decisions do you make along the way? These are questions not easily answered. Pointing out good teachers and poor teachers is much easier than describing the process by which they have become what they are. We do know that novice teachers arrive at their first teaching position carrying a briefcase full of values, attitudes, orientations, and intended "ways of doing things." Over time, and through hundreds of teaching experiences, these raw materials are forged into a particular style and pattern of thinking and acting. When people observe this style, we often hear comments like, "There is a superb teacher at work!" Try as they may, novice teachers, attempting to develop the teaching style of these accomplished craftspeople, cannot take a shortcut in achieving quality. The metamorphosis from novice to master is almost always slow, internal, and authentic.

The path to good teaching is often filled with strange and seemingly irrelevant experiences—sometimes experiences of despair, failure, or frustration. For example, a teacher is habitually exasperated because he cannot overcome his vulnerability and need for acceptance from students; a teacher is dismayed with her overbearingness; a teacher feels himself being hemmed in by the school's bureaucracy.

Perhaps the surest way to achieve a sense of what constitutes good teaching is to peek into the lives of teachers, observing their struggles, decisions, and actions.

## PRACTITIONERS OF THE ART AND SCIENCE

As you contemplate what good teaching means to you, we hope you will recognize that teaching is a serious business, and that it is at once scientific, artistic, complex, and often unexplainable. All in the same day, teachers can be wondrous, disillusioned, vulnerable. Yet they can, through commitment and hard work, acquire the ability to tailor, improvise, and empathize.

In Chapter 1, we introduced you to your first year of teaching, showing how the vast majority of new teachers cope, survive, and finally come to realize they have it in them to become good teachers. In this chapter we turn to seasoned teachers. Let's listen to them carefully as they speak for themselves, giving their reflections, their orientations, their feelings, their commitments, their joys and frustrations. Through this exposure, we discover some of the qualities that make good teachers.

## Portrait of a Dedicated Teacher

What do we see when we look at a teacher who has scaled the mountain? We begin with an exchange of letters between Margaret the veteran and Clare the novice.[1]

**ABILITY TO ENJOY TEACHING**   Margaret writes:

> I am almost forty years old, and I'm happier in my job than anyone I know. That's saying a lot. My husband, who enjoys his work, has routine days when he comes home and says, "Nothing much happened today—just meetings." I never have routine days. When I am in the classroom, I usually am having a wonderful time.
>
> I also hate this job. In March I wanted to quit because of the relentlessness of dealing with one-hundred antsy adolescents day after day. I lose patience with adolescent issues: I think I'll screech if I have to listen to one more adolescent self-obsession. I'm physically exhausted every Friday. The filth in our school is an aesthetic insult. The unending petty politics drain me.

© *Bob Daemmrich/The Image Works*

*© Paul Conklin/Monkmeyer Press Photo Service*

Here is an interesting combination of love and hate in teaching. True, Margaret feels the pressures and fatigue of everyday classroom experience. But because she is focusing on those things that matter most, she is capable of experiencing a satisfaction that, in quiet moments, far exceeds the frustration of "antsy adolescents day after day." She has a sense of proportion—of what is important—and she can live with emotional contrasts.

**COMMITMENT**   Margaret continues:

Ultimately, teaching is nurturing. The teacher enters a giving relationship with strangers, and then the teacher's needs must give way to students' needs. I want to work on my own writing; instead I work on students' writing. My days are spent encouraging young people's growth. I watch my students move beyond me, thinking and writing better than I have ever done. I send them to colleges I could never afford. And I must strive to be proud, not jealous, of them. I must learn generosity of heart.

I am a more compassionate person because I have known teachers and students. I think differently about handicaps because I worked with Guy, who is quadriplegic from a rugby accident. Refugee problems have a human face because I've heard Nazmul tell stories about refugee camps in Bangladesh, and

*The mark of a professional is not what you get by belonging; the mark of a professional is what you give as you belong.* —*Gus Baker and Dick Erickson*

I've heard Merhdad tell about escaping from Iran, hidden in a camel's baggage. I have seen the school social worker give suicidal students his home phone number, telling them to call anytime. I have seen administrators bend all the rules to help individual students through personal crises. Every day I hear stories of courage and generosity.

Facing every new class is an act of courage and optimism. Years ago, the courage required was fairly primitive. I needed courage to discipline my classes, to get them into line, to motivate them to work. But now I need a deeper courage. I look at each new class and know that I must let each of these young people into my life in some significant way. The issue is one of heart. Can I open my heart to two hundred more adolescent strangers each year? Put bluntly, can I be that loving?

Clearly, Margaret feels an intense commitment to her students. At the same time, she struggles with her attempts to be selfless, to subjugate her own needs to those of her students. Her life exhibits a poignant contrast: on the one hand, she shows remarkable giving; on the other, she has a desire to have her own needs fulfilled. She has learned to satisfy these personal needs *within* the context of her teaching.

Teaching, to be powerful, exacts great commitment, as Clare reveals:

And yet I have decided to leave teaching. I am feeling too selfish to teach, too possessive of my time and my future. I have decided to work full-time at the publishing company where I have worked afternoons this year, where I work on my own writing with others coaching me, and where my writing is printed, a thousandfold and over. I will earn almost $5,000 less than I would if I taught full-time next year, and I will work all summer with few vacations.

After a strong, satisfying year I left my first teaching job in June because I was afraid of the cycle that had already been established. I taught six classes a day—five writing and one advanced reading—to seventh graders. I taught at an exceptionally demanding, academically rigorous junior high. By February I was exhausted, and by June I had made two friends outside of teaching. Too much of my time outside of school had been spent on papers, or in the library looking for good reasons to teach *Alice in Wonderland*. I spent a lot of time with other teachers from the school—a smart, professional, and fun group of people. But still we talked about school—and our shared exhaustion.

After living for Memorial Day weekend, I found myself with no plans. I realized how completely I'd been absorbed by my job. I also saw myself years from now, a good teacher—better than I am now—but still without plans for a holiday weekend. And each year the kids would move on.

I hope to teach again some day, when I have more in my life and other investments to balance with teaching. I would like to combine my teaching skills with my own writing, perhaps by coordinating a writing program or working with other teachers to promote writing across the curriculum.

© *Robert Kalman/The Image Works*

In my heart I think I'll be back. And I think I'll be a better teacher for having stepped out and indulged my selfishness.

Compare the difference in commitment between Margaret and Clare, who has, realistically, decided to leave teaching. Note, also, how Clare had refused herself the time to cultivate a life outside of teaching. Would she have in the long run been a better teacher for having done so? Perhaps good teaching requires the ability to make fierce commitments to teaching *and* to one's personal life.

**PERSONAL RENEWAL**    Margaret recognizes the importance of taking care of herself:

Sometimes I think I can't do it all. I don't want to be bitter or a martyr, so I am careful to take care of myself. I put flowers on my desk to offset the dreariness of an old school building. I leave school several times a week to run errands or to take walks in order to feel less trapped. Other teachers take courses at local colleges, join committees of adults, talk in the teacher's lounge, or play with computers. In order to give to others, teachers must nurture themselves.

What is being manifested here? Nest building—one of the surest guards against burnout. Margaret engages in small but powerful renewal tactics.

EXPECTING FULFILLMENT FROM TEACHING  Margaret expects much from teaching:

> Clare, when you consider a life's work, consider not just what you will take to the task, but what it will give to you. Which job will give self-respect and challenge? Which job will give you a world of ideas? Which job will be intellectually challenging? Which job will enlarge you and give you life in abundance? Which job will teach you lessons of the heart?

Margaret views teaching as a two-way street: she makes deep commitments to students; in turn, her students make her life with them rich and challenging. She expects teaching to be an *enormously* fulfilling occupation!

FINDING CHALLENGE AMID ROUTINE  Margaret discovers exhilarating challenges in the midst of mundaneness:

> A curious irony exists. I am never bored at work, yet my days are shockingly routine. I can tell you exactly what I have done every school day of the past eighteen years at 10:15 in the morning (homeroom attendance), and I suspect I will do the same for the next twenty years. All teachers get tired of the monotonous routine of bookkeeping, make-up assignments, twenty-minute lunches, and study hall duties. I identify with J. Alfred Prufrock when he says, "I have measured out my life with coffee spoons." My own life has been measured out in student papers. At a conservative estimate I've graded over 30,000—a mind-boggling statistic which makes me feel like a very dull person indeed.
>
> The monotony of my schedule is mirrored in the monotony of my paycheck. No matter how well or poorly I teach, I will be paid the same amount. There is absolutely no monetary reward for good job performance, or any recognition of professional growth or acquired expertise. My pay depends on how long I've taught and my level of education. I work in a school district in which I cannot afford to live. I am alternatively sad and angry about my pay. To most people I am "just a teacher."
>
> But this is the outside reality. The interior world of the teacher is quite different. Teachers change and grow. There is life after student teaching; there is growth after the first year.
>
> Sometimes I am aware of my growth as a teacher, and I realize that finally, after all these years, I am confident in the classroom. On the very, very best days, when classes sing, I am able to operate on many levels during a single class: I integrate logistics, pedagogy, curriculum, group dynamics, individual needs, and my own philosophy. I feel generous and good-natured towards my students, and I am challenged by classroom issues. But on bad days, I feel like a total failure. Students attack my most vulnerable points. I feel overwhelmed by paperwork. I ache from exhaustion. I dream about going to Aruba, but I go to the next class.

I keep going because I'm intellectually stimulated. I enjoy literature, and I assign books I love and books I want to read. I expect class discussions and student papers to give me new insights into literature. I tell students that in exchange for my hard work, they should keep me interested and they should teach me. They do.

To me, teaching poses questions worthy of a lifetime of thought. I want to think about what the great writers are saying. I want to think about how people learn. I want to think about the values we are passing on to the next generation.

Margaret has come to grips with the struggles inherent in teaching. She has wrestled with trade-offs, has made her decisions, and lives with them. The disadvantages are constantly before her but are not allowed to blur her vision. She works creatively within routine and has learned to derive satisfaction from it. Her teaching life reflects proportion and relevance. Students' growth is her focus and, therefore, the seat of her rewards. By having moved to higher levels of competence, she can now see the complexity and subtlety of good teaching. Margaret's description reveals a genuine respect for students and their questions. She takes students as they are— then lifts them.

## The Voice of Experience

**SELF-REFLECTION**   Here is another teacher, reviewing her teaching career. Like Margaret, she recognizes the struggles and challenges, but also the rewards of teaching:

In evaluating my own life, I find many contradictions. For example, I view myself as a woman of power, yet I am dependent on the approval of my students and the recognition of the public.

Anyone whom I have ever taught has very high priority for me. I take seriously the bond established between us and I have a sense of life-long commitment to students. I have educated them to the best of my ability and sent them out into the world, but this does not end my responsibility to them or my interest in their growth.

But I love teaching precisely because it allows me to live in a world of books—reading books and then sharing my thoughts, perceptions, and feelings with my students. I now read everything with a focus on what can be shared with them, which makes reading even more enriching.

Before I knew what teaching was all about, I used to be afraid that it would lose its challenge after a few years and that I would become arid and stale. To avoid even the possibility of stagnation, I change the content of my old courses every year and I am forever designing new ones.

I realize now that I shall never fully master the kind of teaching that I do. It continuously forces me to use and stretch all my talents and abilities. The frontiers of teaching and learning are infinitely broad and receding.

I am especially vulnerable to criticism from my students. One critical comment, especially from a respected student, can undermine my self-confidence

© *Paul Conklin/Monkmeyer Press Photo Service*

for days. The mere presence of one or two silently or openly hostile students in a small class inhibits my ability to enjoy the class and give fully of myself.

But with increasing self-confidence, I find myself more open to criticism, more able to learn from it, more ready to see it in perspective. I now try to be less devastated by student criticism and more philosophical about not being liked or appreciated by every student. It is rewarding to find that, in the process of becoming more open and vulnerable, I have actually become stronger. I no longer interpret criticism as a total invalidation of my worth, but rather as an issue to be examined.

Although teaching is a lonely enterprise most of the time, I feel that great autonomy is one of the most enviable privileges of an educator. Ultimately I can find the key to good teaching within myself: I can use my own power.

I think I was carried away with the hope of convincing students of my particular viewpoint. But once I fully understood their feelings of vulnerability and powerlessness, I became more cautious about the use of power in the classroom, without relinquishing leadership. Eventually I learned to become authoritative rather than authoritarian.

Teachers are in an exposed position, scrutinized and judged daily by hundreds of students. There are days when I grow weary of performing, entertaining, and filling up others' emptiness. There are days when I tire of offering stimulation, encouragement, and comfort, and of being the target of my students' unresolved parental loves and hates. But curiously, as the years go by, those days grow fewer, perhaps because along with being more open, I have also become more detached.

I used to get angry at students who did not meet my standards, and positively dislike and scorn them. I had to relearn the same lesson that motherhood had taught me. Students, like children, must learn and achieve for themselves, not for their teachers. I must take care that my love and concern for my students, like motherly love and concern, does not become a prison.

The teacher role implies distance, authority, evaluation, and objectivity, as well as warmth and nurturance.

As a teacher, I have been forced continually to examine my values and ideas because I must state them clearly. As a model to my students I must live by the values that I teach. Above all, teaching is a way of sharing myself. It is only in midlife that I have found my current, most genuine and autonomous identity as an educator. Finding this identity has given my life new meaning and new drama. It involves my keen and caring interest in people, and my enjoyment of reading, writing, and teaching. It sanctions my wish to be a lifelong learner. It nurtures my creativity. The sheer enjoyment of my work helps to protect me against depression.

Thus I find myself in midlife with a passion for my work. Teaching demands openness to people and absorption with ideas, protection of time and energy, as well as endless commitment to students. It demands skills of objectivity, observation, and involvement, distance as well as intimacy. It demands self-assurance, power, and humility.[2]

This teacher observes paradoxes in her teaching life, one of which is a desire for autonomy yet a need for approval and validation. Both her commitment to lifelong learning and her power of self-renewal are evident. Students' success is high on her list, as is the value of hard work. Her self-confidence has increased over the years, making her less vulnerable to negative feedback from students. She constantly examines her own values, is open to change, and achieves a balance between intimacy and detachment in her life.

**ADAPTABILITY**   The teaching style of this twenty-five year veteran reveals unusual adaptability:

Nancy was like a symphony conductor, posing questions, probing for alternative views, drawing out the shy while tempering the boisterous. Not much happened in the classroom that did not pass through Nancy, whose pacing and order, structuring and expanding, controlled the rhythm of classroom life.

Although as a teacher she maintained tight control of the classroom discourse, her teaching goals were to liberate her students' minds through literacy, eventually to use great works of literature to illuminate their lives. Whichever work she was teaching, she understood how to organize it, frame it for teaching, and divide it appropriately for assignments and activities. She seemed to possess a mental index for these books she had taught so often— *The Red Badge of Courage, Moby Dick, The Scarlet Letter, The Adventures of Huckleberry Finn*—with key episodes organized in her mind for different pedagogical purposes, different levels of difficulty, different kinds of pupils,

© *Spencer Grant/Monkmeyer Press Photo Service*

different themes or emphases. Her combination of subject-matter understanding and pedagogical skill was quite dazzling.

When an observer arrived at the classroom one morning, she found Nancy sitting at her desk as usual. But her morning greeting elicited no response from Nancy other than a grimace and motion toward the pad of paper on her desktop. "I have laryngitis this morning and will not be able to speak loud," said the note. What's more, she appeared to be fighting the flu, for she had little energy. For a teacher who managed her classroom through the power of her voice and her manner, this was certainly a disabling condition. Or was it?

Using a combination of handwritten notes and whispers, she divided the class into small groups by rows, a tactic she had used twice before during this unit. Each group was given a different character who has a prominent role in the first chapters of the novel, and each group was expected to answer a series of questions about that character. Ample time was used at the end of the period for representatives of each group to report to the whole class. Once again the class had run smoothly, and the subject matter had been treated with care. But the style had changed radically, an utterly different teaching technology was employed, and still the students were engaged, and learning appeared to occur.[3]

Nancy's pattern of teaching is neither uniform nor predictable. She responds flexibly to the difficulty and character of the subject matter, the capacities of the students, and her own physical limitations. She *fashions* the subject matter into digestible food for her students. She is adaptable—not just to the exigencies of the moment but to the learners' needs. Because her priorities are straight, student growth, rather than the satisfaction of her own needs, is paramount.

**EMPOWERMENT**   One writer draws similarities between good teaching and the work of a good midwife who, when talking to expectant parents, said, "The things I know can empower you. My job is to empower you, to help you take active control, to aid you in making important choices." In describing Ana, the midwife, the writer observed:

> I think that there is a relationship between Ana's serious dedication to empowerment, her faith in and commitment to others, and her ability to maintain her values and humane perspective on her work. Because she opens herself to surprise and change, she avoids the dulling habits that become the prelude to burnout. Because she assumes a shared world of responsibility and personal meaning, she maintains perspective on accomplishment and fault. I think that meeting people on their own terms is, in part, an act of personal renewal.[4]

Teachers recognize their own importance in the classroom and know that their vital relationship with students is the heart of the educational enterprise. And so, without belittling themselves, they are able to communicate to their students in a thousand ways, "You are of central importance here, your work is honored here, your discoveries and growth are respected here, and in fact you are the very reason we are here." A good teacher, like a good midwife, focuses on empowerment rather than on control. She frees students to learn and to take charge of their lives. Because she works to empower, she is forever respectful of the learner, not manipulating him, but taking him as he is. She knows when to hang back and be silent, when to watch and wonder at what is taking place all around her.

**INTEGRITY**   In her attempts to be at once loving and objective, this teacher struggles with professional integrity:

> Last fall I gave an assignment for kids to keep a journal for a whole semester, three times a week—a record of what they thought about. They weren't to keep diaries of events, and they weren't to keep a whole lot of emotional stuff.
>
> One girl freaked out on me. She was really angry that I knew more about her than she knew about me. She thought that I should have passed out my journal to all 46 of my kids. There was no way I could say, "Jane, sorry, I'm the adult and you're the kid. That's how this works. There's no getting around that. We're not peers here." With adolescents you have to be so fair that you're not fair to yourself.
>
> She also said, "And I don't like that you didn't keep confidences." I said, "What? Jane, I *did!*"

*He who helps a child helps humanity with immediateness which no other help given to human creatures in any other stage of human life can possibly give again.*—Phillips Brooks

It turned out that she was furious about what I said one day in class: "Danielle has the most magnificent imagination I have run across in years." Danielle was dumpy, poor, fat, and ugly. She—Jane—was sleek, popular, rich, well dressed, beautiful, and an only child. There never was a time when she was not the center of attention.

Jane was jealous and, in effect, asking, "Who do you love more?" I couldn't say to her, "Damn it, I don't care if Danielle is ugly and fat and poor, she still has more imagination than you do. What you *want* to accuse me of is not loving you as much, but what you accuse me of is breaching confidences."

The only way out was to back up and apologize and to take on guilt I didn't even own. I really went under on this. I felt so attacked even though I had given and given and given. I had visions of never going back to this class. But you have to say goodbye to a class. You have to make room for the next one. You can't just accumulate—you have to say, "I've loved you and I've known you and goodbye." [5]

This teacher is involved in a complex moral struggle for control, a struggle that reveals the uncertainty in teaching, along with its "messy practicality." It also reveals the ambiguity, irrationality, and conflict that teachers are used to feeling in their bones. Effective teachers are able to resolve such moral struggles in some productive fashion, thus freeing themselves to engage in their best teaching.

## That Extra Mile

TAKING ADVANTAGE OF TEACHING MOMENTS    One beginning intern, believing in the importance of immersing students deeply in their education and bent upon helping them confront the complexities of life, decided to produce a memorable lesson for a group of seventh graders:

The ground being prepared, I now moved to set the scene, drawing the blinds and asking my students to raise their desktops in simulation of high Puritan pews. Reversing my coat and setting a lectern atop the desk, I mounted to deliver in muted Edwardian tones the fire and brimstone of "Sinners in the Hands of an Angry God."

It was a stunning lesson, if I may say so, however flamboyant. When the sermon ended, the students sat gaping and transfixed in their pews. I closed the book, the bell rang, and we were jolted back into our accustomed routines. In my twenty some years of teaching, I do not think I have managed to surpass the impact of that first class. Unfortunately, my supervisors were not so well pleased. There had been no fewer than ten of them sitting at the back of the room, all scribbling madly, anxious to demonstrate their critical training so

© Olive Pierce/Stock, Boston

that they might be authorized to judge rather than to teach. No sooner had the class ended than the arduous critique began.

At first I was cool and confident, secure in the belief that my lesson had hit home. But they were relentless in their queries. What had been my objectives? What had the children learned? How did I propose to measure this learning objectively? Somewhat taken aback, I struggled to explain what had seemed to me self-evident. The students had experienced what it was like to be a Puritan, how ruthless and discomforting the doctrine of predestination could be, how graphic and powerful Edwards was in describing their predicament. But all of this seemed to no avail, and as the minutes crept by, I began to think that Edwards' congregation had not been so badly off. Sensing my gradual retreat, my inquisitors grew more aggressive. What skills had the students employed and what had been my strategy for reinforcing them? Was I aware that I had used *slang?* They swept aside my halting responses and pressed me hard for answers. "But what did the students learn?" In desperation I cried, "I don't know what they learned, but they'll never forget it!" Their victory complete, they let me go.[6]

This teacher discovered the power of a teaching moment, and the fact that it can transcend formal, preplanned objectives and teaching strategies. Even in his first attempt, the teacher exhibited the beginnings of intelligent intuition—that is, the ability to guess accurately when students' interests

*It is a great tribute to an artist to say that he plays Beethoven or Bach, and
puts nothing between them and the audience. But in so doing he becomes
one with the composer and the listener. In the listener's memory he anony-
mously shares the composer's immortality. The teacher, too, is remembered
who is thus forgotten. He lives in what has happened in the minds of his
students, and in what they remember of things infinitely greater than themselves or than himself.—Erwin Edman*

ought to be capitalized on, through whatever strategies seem appropriate at
the time.

Another seasoned teacher reflects back on the power of the teaching
moments that provide some of the unexpected and surprising beauties in
teaching:

> I realize that much of my learning has been in slivers and slices. I call these the
> small moments in learning. Students cannot simply sit back and wait for such
> moments nor can teachers produce them on cue. They are spontaneous, intu-
> itive, surprising, and unpredictable. They appear here and there, disturbing
> the normal ebb and flow of classroom life. They may not affect everyone—
> they are not meant to—nor do they affect every student in the same way.
>
> Once, in graduate school, I was sitting in my class on adolescent psychol-
> ogy when some children were heard running through the outside hallway. A
> student in the first row rose to close the door, but the professor motioned for
> her to sit down. The professor then proceeded to make a point about the chil-
> dren and the student trying to shut the hallway door, instead of continuing
> with his lecture as I thought he would. He said that the children were only
> being children and that the noise would go away. It did. He then observed that
> educators and teachers too often make themselves into policemen, feeling that
> they must control and manipulate all situations involving children. He argued
> that this is a mistake, because if more adults would allow children to solve
> their own affairs, the children would learn to be more independent and would
> not be cast in a negative light. This whole little incident lasted all of ninety
> seconds and was highly unexpected, but I will always remember it.
>
> And often, when these moments arise, they come quietly and subtly. They
> are not accompanied or preceded by proclamations or warnings, or followed
> by a double asterisk or an exclamation point.
>
> They are the odd and quirky moments that spin off from a teacher's love of
> the moment and willingness to improvise, to go on a hunch, to take a risk, to
> deviate a little, to go with one's teaching intuition. They are short and concise
> and have a certain pithiness of language. They are quickly absorbed and, being
> pocket-sized, are easily carried away. They can be hidden in the cracks and
> crevices of one's education and brought out for reference as one needs them.[7]

What do we see in this example of a teaching moment? Here we have
an unexpected event—children in the hallway. The professor, like our intern
in the first example, demonstrated intelligent intuition. Unlike the intern,

the professor focused a wealth of knowledge about children and learning on an unanticipated event. This artistry, this craft knowledge, this uncommon skill of making good things happen during unanticipated moments—this is a subtle yet important characteristic of good teachers.

BEING A RESEARCHER   A high school teacher asked if he could spend some time in a kindergarten teacher's classroom. He brought in paper bags full of show-and-tell items. The children asked all kinds of questions; he was able to use all their ideas, no matter how far off the mark. The kindergarten teacher decided to try his approach:

> I began to copy Bill's style of teaching whenever the children and I had formal discussions. I practiced his open-ended questions, the kind that seek no specific answers but rather build a chain of ideas without the need for closure. It was not easy. I felt myself always waiting for the right answer—my answer. The children knew I was waiting and watched my face for clues. Clearly, it was not enough simply to copy someone else's teaching manner; real change comes about only through the painful recognition of one's own vulnerability.
>
> Then I discovered the tape recorder and knew, after transcribing the first tape, that I could become my own best witness. The tape recorder, with its unrelenting fidelity, captured the unheard or unfinished murmur, the misunderstood and mystifying context, the disembodied voices asking for clarification and comfort. It also captured the impatience in *my* voice as children struggled for attention, approval, and justice. The tape recordings created for me an overwhelming need to know more about the process of teaching and learning and about my own classroom as a unique society to be studied.
>
> The act of teaching became a daily search for the child's point of view, accompanied by the sometimes unwelcome disclosure of my hidden attitudes. The search was what mattered—only later did someone tell me it was research—and it provided an open-ended script from which to observe, interpret, and integrate the living drama of the classroom.
>
> I began using the tape recorder to try to figure out why the children were lively and imaginative in certain discussions, yet fidgety and distracted in others ("Are you almost finished now, teacher?"), wanting to return quickly to their interrupted play. As I transcribed the daily tapes, several phenomena emerged. Whenever the discussion touched on fantasy, fairness, or friendship ("the three Fs" I began to call them), participation zoomed upward: Is it fair that Paul always gets to be Luke Skywalker and Ben has to be the bad guy? Why should the wolf be allowed to eat up the first two pigs? Can't the three pigs just stay home with their mother?[8]

This person is confronting herself as a teacher, actively searching for feedback about her teaching. She co-opts technology as a tool and uses a tape recorder to "freeze" daily teaching episodes for careful study. She has learned the art of observing and analyzing, with a restless curiosity to understand herself in the context of her teaching—looking for relationships between her behavior and her students' learning. Reflection for her is an *integral* part of teaching, as it is for all good teachers.

Here is another example of a teacher acting as researcher. She exhibits a healthy combination of gleaning ideas from others and relying on her own observations:

> My own classroom research has helped me understand the impact of new approaches. As a teacher-researcher I welcome the opportunity to test hypotheses and pay attention to what my experiences teach me. Observing, listening, and questioning keep me alert to my students' needs and help me find ways to improve my instruction. Often this means involving the students in research. I do this by telling them that I, too, want to learn, and by explaining what it is I want to learn. As my students become an active part of my research, we become a community of learners, rather than a teacher-centered classroom. The result is reciprocity in our learning: I learn from my students as they learn from me.[9]

This teacher is constantly searching for better ways to facilitate student learning. She is an active student of her teaching—an astute classroom observer and hypothesis tester.

MEETING SPECIAL NEEDS    A teacher describes her colleague's ability to meet the special needs of one of her students:

> Daryl's third-grade year was more productive than it appeared on the surface. Though he irritated everyone as soon as he stepped outside the threshold of room 312, inside he had Karen's unconditional acceptance. He formed a solid relationship with Karen, his first attachment to an adult in the school, his first to any white adult authority figure, and maybe even his first important attachment to any adult outside his family. Karen communicated to Daryl that he was a valued person whether he fit into the class or not.
>
> Karen's attitude of acceptance extended on into Daryl's academic work. She believed that lasting, significant results occur over the long term, that children cannot be forced to grow like hothouse orchids, and that their growth cannot be quantified. Measurements can identify only trivial, testable gains; but it is the elusive, not-easily-measured gains that really matter. And those, she believed, are nourished by an abundance of time. She felt Daryl needed time, measured in months, to make friends, and time, measured in years, to mature. Time would result eventually in more disciplined behavior and more learning. She was not in a hurry to measure progress, and she did not hurry Daryl to learn faster.
>
> By allowing Daryl to contribute when he was ready and on his own terms, Karen enabled him to change from a silent isolate into someone about whom she could write in her final report, "Daryl has made enormous social growth this year. He is part of and central to the class. He is not on the outskirts, nor does he want to be."[10]

This teacher accepts students as they are when they come to her. Karen is a superb diagnostician. She exhibits wisdom. She views authentic growth from a broader perspective and, as a result, is uncompromisingly patient.

She is unhampered by the school's "packaged" curriculum and its methods of measurement. Taking a long-range view, Karen frees her students to grow at their own pace and in their own way.

## Professionalism

An early childhood teacher, drawing on her beliefs about how children best learn, speaks out against inappropriate curricula:

> Here is Teresa in dress-up clothes—long skirt, flowery hat, and high heels—talking into the toy telephone. I have already given several notices of clean-up time, and she is the only child left in the house corner. I try to signal her to stop talking, but she pretends not to see, pointedly turning her back as she continues her conversation. Finally, rather irritated, I reach my arm around her and hang up the phone, telling her that it is time to end. Teresa is outraged. She flounces out of the house corner to the furthest limits of the room, where she finds an empty spot. There she reaches for an imaginary wall phone, dials into the air, and speaks into her cupped hand. Then she hangs up with an expression of relief and comes back to the group.
>
> I have no idea what Teresa was saying in her call, nor why she was so persistent. I do know, however, that Teresa has grown tremendously over the year in her ability to communicate with other children.
>
> The challenges children take on are far deeper and more complex than what is usually presented to them as "basic skills," just as the academic aims of textbooks, workbooks, and expensive learning kits are generally much lower than the aims of the children themselves.
>
> There is a real danger that in the current educational atmosphere, primary classrooms are being reduced in spirit and scope, with rigid curricula and "teacher-proof" materials turning teachers into technicians and children into products.
>
> If children are not trusted to learn without predigested lessons, and teachers are not trusted to search out their own materials and ways of presenting them, classrooms become constricted, teacher morale drops, and the demanding job of teaching will become even harder to fill.
>
> Unless teachers speak up (and are heard) about their own classroom experience, and assert their hard-won understanding of how children learn, the art of teaching may be further eroded, and our children's potential for serious pursuit of knowledge may trickle away while the public rejoices in each decimal-point rise in standardized test scores.[11]

Here we observe a professional, well informed about her craft. She trusts her own expertise and her students' ability to work at what they need to know. She is unhesitating in taking a stand when the curriculum fails to meet her students' needs. She makes decisions as a qualified professional, communicates those decisions, and acts on them.

A group of high-school teachers met to discuss their teaching and, in the process, became more professional:

*Professionalism demands that the practitioner should be the master of the knowledge and skills necessary to his practice whenever he practices.*
—Peter Jarvis

We kept reading books because we felt that they offered us some protection against a troublesome tendency we had discovered in our earlier conversations to become insular and self-absorbed. Initially, we had thought it wonderful just to know others who felt the same joys and frustrations in their work that we felt, and to share those joys together and vent those frustrations together. But after a few months of sharing and venting, the wonder wore off, and it seemed that we ought to do something more. In fact, after some meetings, we felt worse about our work rather than better, as if by complaining about this or that working condition, we had recognized our bitterness and sealed ourselves in it. Reading books, we discovered, seemed to help with this problem.

We wished not just to learn from these works, but also to critique them. We distrusted the ability of the theorists and polemicists to be truthful about schools, as we see them. Our sense of the "teacher's voice" was a relatively simple one: the sound of teachers talking to each other after a long silence.[12]

As these teachers increased their professionalism, they came to realize that commiserating with colleagues about school problems quickly becomes unproductive, that swapping complaints has no real value. Further, they saw the danger of a teacher's insulating himself from the discussions and insights of colleagues. Teaching improvement, they realized, is not a solitary effort but is best conducted in collaboration with other teachers; it is critical that teachers talk to and learn from each other.

We can learn much from observing a teacher like Naomi, a seasoned and capable professional operating within a pluralistic classroom:

She plants her shoes on the floor and—whether sitting or standing—sort of leans into action; she uses her small, capable hands—sketching, note-taking, sorting, tidying—to garner the worth of every moment; her face flashes kindliness, jollity, intensity, mischief, anger. These all seem physical aspects developed over long years of being both serious and joyous with and about children. Her teaching draws from the experience of mothering her five children in a bicultural family before she became a teacher, as well as from her wide-ranging intellectual interests, which she uses as raw material for her curriculum. Some of Naomi's personality traits—self-confidence (even feistiness), political shrewdness, humorousness, and physical and spiritual stamina—give her an independence and flexibility of opinion and action that many might find unusual in an elementary school teacher.

Her large, full-color reproductions of Matisse paintings and cutouts are posted, along with a photo of the artist, over the whole length of the chalkboard on the corridor side of the classroom. "These are not just decorations," Naomi explains. "I was so clever! I just put them up and waited. One day, Damien—a big, street-wise, held-back black boy who's almost as tall as I am—commented, as we were looking at a book by Maurice Sendak, that the

Sendak pictures were something like Matisse's pictures. So we had a discussion of art history. They asked, 'How old is that man (Matisse)?' They looked that up in the encyclopedia. We talked about pattern in art, from painting to collage. It was breathtaking! I told them Matisse is my hero. That's why I had put his picture up. We did writing about the idea of Hero as opposed to Superhero. It was 40 minutes of writing! We have a collection of modern art books within our classroom library, and someone took the book *Famous Paintings* and found in it one of 'our' Matisses. So I brought to school three of my expensive Matisse books and the children were arguing about who would get to look at the Matisse books. I mean . . . !"

In the math center are boxes of manipulative materials, many organized according to the *Math Their Way* curriculum (which is not the district-approved text). "I try to use interesting objects to teach numeracy." She shows boxes of pebbles, of shells, of keys, of pottery shards, of coins, of tiles, of bottle caps, of petrified wood, and many more. "With this stuff, kids are observing and learning about real things. But my husband goes crazy when we go off on vacation because I'm always picking up things." She grumbles about the math text the district is using; she considers it unrealistic for the ability span in her class. "I'm convinced that our conventional way of teaching math to these young children is really dangerous. Kids get the wrong idea in their heads about what math is, and it's very hard to set them straight."

It's after five o'clock, and Naomi dashes off to a meeting at the teachers' center. She picks up her bookbag: "I bet you can't guess what book I'm reading to the kids." She pulls out Ved Mehta's *Vedi*. "We read things from adult books *about* children. I have this idea that some day I'll make an anthology of parts of adult books to be read to children. Oh! And Eudora Welty—my book would show her idea of the difference between listening to stories and listening *for stories*." Stowing the Mehta book, she says, "I take this home every night to work on the next section and figure what I'm going to read from it tomorrow."

When school finishes, Naomi takes a vacation in London and France, then comes home to lead a seminar at the teachers' center on using literature in the language arts curriculum.[13]

We sense this teacher's knowledge of the emotional and learning needs of her students and her expert skill in tailoring her curriculum to fit these needs. Prescribed curricula, when inappropriate, are set aside. She does whatever is necessary to ensure students' learning! Her wide-ranging reading and cultural and travel interests enable her to provide a rich and broad-based curriculum. Her preparations go on endlessly, regardless of where she finds herself. The distinction between her personal and teaching worlds is blurred. A clear sense of responsibility pervades all aspects of her teaching—responsibility to her students, herself, and her role as teacher.

# HALLMARKS OF GOOD TEACHING

Many characteristics contribute to good teaching. Vignettes of a sample of teachers highlight such characteristics as commitment, adaptability, selflessness, a sense of proportion, responsibility, and a continued thirst for learning.

Are there some characteristics that show up frequently as one takes an overview of good teachers at work? We think so. Of these, we have selected several we think are particularly important:

- a passionate commitment to teaching
- a sustained appetite for learning
- respect for students
- willingness to take responsibility
- open-mindedness
- reflectivity.

Reflect on these characteristics. Decide whether any of them would be important for you to cultivate in your own teaching.

A word of caution: teaching, and good teaching especially, is both complex and idiosyncratic. You cannot simply adopt a group of characteristics lock, stock, and barrel, expecting them to turn you into a good teacher. Only by adapting them to fit your personality and your style of teaching can you capitalize on their potency. Remember, your quest is to become the best teacher that it is in *you* to be, not to imitate someone else.

To describe these characteristics, we were afforded the opportunity of viewing them through the eyes of principals.

## Passionate Commitment to Teaching

This year in my school, I have two teachers who are directly opposite. One of them just gets by. I'd like to convict him for neglect, but he continues to perform at a barely adequate level. His students suffer. Why would he choose a profession like teaching in the first place—knowing the kinds of demands that would be placed on him? He breezes in just before the bell and flies out right at 3:30. I seldom see any preparation, but I'd have to rate him "average" in teaching performance—why in the world does he have to be "average"? What a disservice to students! They know he's a "nine to three"-er. I doubt he makes much of an impact on kids' lives. I've asked about his long-term plans. If you can believe it, he wants to stay in teaching. That's because he can get by with minimal time and effort, and still carry home the same paycheck.

On the other hand, every principal should be entitled to one of my Beckys. She's every kid's all-American. She gives—far more than the kids realize. Walk into her room. It's swarming with good things going on. She prepares long hours and gets pretty tired, but she enjoys what she's doing. Her commitment to kids really shows. She reaches out.

By and large, teachers enter the profession because of their commitment to students. To be committed is to be numbered among legions of teachers; to have a *passionate* commitment is to be numbered among an elite group. These people spend huge amounts of time and energy preparing,

## A Champion of Teachers

Ernest L. Boyer has served as U.S. Commissioner of Education and President of the Carnegie Foundation for the Advancement of Teaching. He continues to be an articulate advocate of educational excellence, equity, and quality teaching. Although he observes that "a rising tide of reports on educational reform is threatening to engulf us" and that "reports on reforming education won't reform education," he himself has been a prime mover behind reform. Along with other leading reformers such as John Goodlad and his *A Place Called School* and Theodore Sizer and his *Horace's Compromise,* Boyer has influenced American education through his *High School: A Report on Secondary Education in America* and *College: The Undergraduate Experience in America.*

Boyer continually attempts to explain the immense complexity of the links between schools and society. He urges legislators, educators, and the public to heed the impact on education of shifting social patterns such as the proliferation of single-parent families, a trend toward having two wage-earning parents, and the need for child care. These forces are altering the fundamental and traditional relationships between school and family, and between parent and teacher, and are transforming American education.

Boyer points out that a culture heavily emphasizing television, computers, and electronic forms of communication has great potential for self-learning on the part of students in America's schools. Adult and lifelong learning will play greater roles, since modern American education must encompass all age groups. New combinations of specialized and interdisciplinary learning will also be needed, as well as the type of education that helps people realize their global interdependence.

Most of all, Boyer is a champion of teachers: "I believe that next to being a parent, next to being a minister of God, there is no greater calling on the planet earth than to influence with care and judgment and reverence the coming generation. That is what we call teaching. An incompetent teacher is worse than an incompetent surgeon; the surgeon can cut up only one person at a time. What makes a great teacher? A great teacher has an important message, can communicate it to students, cares about students, and is open and authentic in his or her behavior. The quality of the encounter lingers on."

G. R. Kaplan, "Shining Lights in High Places: Education's Top Four Leaders and Their Heirs," *Phi Delta Kappan,* September 1985, pp. 7–16; Brigham Young University Summer Graduation, Commencement Address, 1988.

teaching, and working with students—unbegrudgingly! Sacrifices are at once depleting and satisfying. One teacher said it poignantly: "My teaching is my life. I get a lot of satisfaction out of getting kids to work hard, and they do it." Those for whom teaching is a passionate commitment are never far from their work, emotionally or intellectually. For instance, an elementary teacher, while on a restful vacation, goes into a supermarket to stock up on food items. Walking down the aisle, she stops short: "Oh, look—finally! Some containers my kids can store beads in." Her husband, a few feet away, offers a weak smile of support.

A teacher's commitment (or its absence) shows itself in virtually every aspect of teaching: physical organization of the classroom, class rules, visual aids, interactions with students, homework, and handouts. Students are quite astute in picking up their teacher's level of commitment.

*The desire to learn through the whole of the period of professional practice
is intrinsic to professionalism.—Peter Jarvis*

## Sustained Appetite for Learning

It's interesting to listen to my teachers talk in the lunchroom. One guy has all
the answers—too many of them. I suppose that's what happens when people
stop learning. In reality, a person ought to become *more* teachable as he
learns, not less.

Someone could rightfully hang a "not-interested-in-learning" sign around
this guy's neck. Nobody's asking second-grade teachers to become scholars,
but surely they can be expected to keep up in their field. Something happens to
a teacher when he stays in the trenches all day and never climbs out and looks
around. It's too easy to strap your blinders on and rely only on your own experience. It's dangerous.

Not all my teachers are that way. I've got one who's a constant reader. I go
into the faculty lounge and she's got her nose in the newspaper; I go into the
lunchroom and she's got a book propped open on her lunch tray. Coming in
and out of school, she's always got a book under her arm. I mean, that's some
kind of example for third-graders! And it's not just novels or current events.
She knows the social studies texts, she's read up on computer software, she's
always on the lookout for new methods of teaching science. I go to her when I
want to know what's going on! Guess how this affects the kids?

Some teachers provide a teacher-as-learner model for students, as well
as for other teachers and administrators. New articles, books, conferences,
and discussions keep them busy revising, trying out, incorporating, throwing away, updating. A lifelong thirst for learning keeps these teachers well
informed, improves their teaching, and acts as a catalyst, motivating others
to spend more time gathering new information.

## Respect for Students

Do I have problems with "put-downs" in my school? Oh, wow! At least once a
week a student bursts into my office with a story about being embarrassed in
front of the class. These kids are hurting. You'd think intelligent teachers
would be above that. Of course, I realize I'm hearing only one side of the story.
Even so, some of the comments seem pretty damaging. One student told me
her teacher cracked, in front of the whole class, "If you'd start paying attention, you wouldn't be such an airhead!" I admit high school kids can get pretty
flaky and stretch teachers to the outer limit. But that's still not an excuse for
demeaning comments. Sometimes a teacher will say something or do something that tells kids they're low and the teacher is doing them a favor by being
there. I hate to admit this, but sometimes race is a factor; sometimes it's sex;
sometimes it's how much money the kid's parents are making.

*Does it seem too far fetched to picture the young Helen Keller as the symbol par excellence of every student that ever lived? We are all Helen Kellers in some degree—vision beclouded, ears undiscriminating, speech uncertain and untrue. We have all needed at one time or another, to have* TRUTH *spelled out slowly for us, to have our capabilities redefined and reevaluated, and the limitations of our sensations and perceptions suggested. It is no mean epitaph for any teacher to have it said of him that 'He rendered all whom he taught less deaf, less dumb, less blind.'—Houston Peterson*

But let me get positive. It always amazes me what an effect a teacher's respecting kids can have. I have this huge, unkempt teacher who is something to behold. You look at him and say to yourself, "He's big and he's punishing. I'll bet he manhandles those kids." Well, the fact of the matter is, the kids love him. You know why? He respects them. That's right. No matter what a student says or does, he handles the situation with dignity and courtesy. He never makes sarcastic replies or tells thoughtless jokes. He never does anything to make kids feel put down—like they're unimportant. Even the most backward kids feel okay in his class. I've never had a report of him making fun of a single student. Well, you can guess how students treat him—with equal respect.

Showing respect for the learner is a significant and consistently appearing characteristic of good teachers. Respectfulness toward students does not seem to emerge primarily from teacher education programs; rather, it grows out of a person's values and beliefs about her role as teacher, the student as a person and learner, and the learning process itself. Respect for students shows itself in many aspects of teaching, including the quality of a teacher's preparation and presentation, his manner of interacting with students, his questioning techniques, the nature of his assignments and tests, and his casual conversations.

## Willingness to Take Responsibility

Some of my teachers go around blaming everyone and everything for what they are unwilling to do themselves. Others never complain at all; they just get the job done. I've got two good examples. One of my teachers won't face up to his responsibilities. Take his planning, for example. Most of my teachers come in two or three weeks early to get things in gear for the new year. Not this teacher. He frantically flies in the day before school starts. We have meetings scheduled all that day, and he blames me for eating into all his preparation time. That's not all. He blames the custodian for not being around to fix every little problem in his room; he blames other teachers for using up the storeroom supplies. All he's doing is trying to justify himself and make us feel responsible for his lack of planning. When he's not blaming, he's feeling offended—same thing, I guess. There's nothing harder on my faculty than a teacher who goes around feeling wounded. It wears us all down!

I've got another teacher who's just the opposite. What a pleasure to have him around! Nobody offends him; he never feels wounded by what someone has said. He doesn't try shifting his responsibility over to somebody else. When one of his students starts failing, he goes to work on the problem—special tutoring, additional resources, whatever is needed. He takes responsibility for making sure his kids learn. If the custodian's gone or unavailable, he goes ahead and fixes the light or moves the furniture himself. If we get low on paper, he goes out and scrounges some up. The guy does whatever he has to. His attitude is contagious.

Evasion of personal responsibility is not uncommon among groups in our society, including teachers. When teachers try to evade their felt responsibility, they engage in self-justification, blaming, feeling victimized, being offended, and even playing the role of martyr. They try to make their evasion appear justified, or even right. But it never is. Enormous emotional energy is expended in the process, energy that could be better spent improving their teaching.

But contemplate a school in which everyone accepts, fully, his or her responsibility: the teachers, the principal, the parents, the students. There is no blaming, no feeling offended, no defensiveness—only teachers and students, each fulfilling his or her own responsibility.

## Open-Mindedness

I lay out a new plan for our math team, and one of my teachers comes up with five reasons why it won't work. He's a wet blanket. He's brittle, close-minded, and gets his dander up at the drop of a hat. Sometimes it gets to the point where I have to sit him down and say, "This is the way it's going to be. We're going to change math texts because the one we're using is out of date. Now, adjust." When I tell him things like this, he vacillates between surliness and stony silence. The size of the issue doesn't matter; he acts that way with big and small things. It must be something in his basic personality. He's afraid to open up to other people and to new things. I suppose he's afraid he'll fail. But sometimes I think he's just stubborn.

Compare him with another one of my teachers. She's tough-minded but she's open. She's much older than this guy, so I don't think it's age and experience that makes a person close-minded. The two of us seldom see eye to eye on anything, but I always know where she's coming from, and that she'll weigh things carefully. I can go to her and say, "Will you use this new form for a month and let me know how it works?" She'll give it an honest try. She's refreshing because she doesn't get defensive when someone points out a problem or makes a suggestion. If she thinks it's foolish, she'll throw it out; if not, she'll accept it. Open-mindedness in a teacher sure makes life a lot easier—for all of us!

*"What does teaching mean to you?" brings a clarion reply: It is a passion
and paradox, love and hate, routine and excitement—and it always matters.
—Margo Okazawa-Rey, James Anderson, and Rob Traver*

An open-minded teacher entertains and weighs information and opinions, including those that differ from his own. He gives fair hearing to a new idea, program, or policy, avoiding premature closure and snap judgments. Having considerable tolerance for the opinions of others, he does not become defensive or feel threatened by ideas that bump up against his personal beliefs. Francis Bacon observed that one should "read not to refute or take for granted, but to weigh and consider." An open-minded teacher does not indiscriminately adopt every new idea or attitude or become unduly committed to a particular program or set of teaching practices. Rather, he suspends judgment until after careful consideration.

## Reflectivity

I wish all my teachers would think about their teaching as Ramy does. He's always looking into things, trying to figure out how to be a better teacher. For one thing, he keeps a journal about his teaching. I asked him to share part of it during our last faculty meeting. He got up and read a couple of excerpts that went something like, "I notice that in the morning when I'm fresh I tend to move along at a crisp pace, but then I slow down because I get tired. Kids are off task too much in the afternoon and it wears me down trying to get them back on. I think I'll try switching my hardest subjects to the morning." Another comment was something like, "I find myself being impatient with Matthew and Vi. They are so slow! I don't like working with slow kids. What am I going to do? Maybe I'll try some peer tutoring and see what happens."

Ramy's got a lot of insights about his teaching. I'm sure it's because he's always studying it. People like this who reflect on their teaching generally make good improvements.

Many events are occurring simultaneously in the classroom. The teacher, immersed in these events, seems to be in the midst of a "stream of behavior," with unsorted activities occurring right and left on the part of both teacher and students. Only by standing back and reflecting on these events, once gone through, can teachers effectively analyze what took place. As they reflect, they are able to see (or at least hypothesize) relationships between their teaching and students' progress. The results of their reflections can now be applied to their future plans and actions.

Reflecting on one's teaching increases a teacher's awareness of events taking place in her classroom, which in turn empowers her with a wider range of choices. Her teaching effectiveness can be improved as a result of acting intelligently on these choices.

# CONCLUSION

Good teachers make a large difference in the lives of students. Look around and observe examples of good teachers at work. Watching good teachers teach in specific situations reveals some of what characterizes good teaching. You may be attracted to some of these characteristics. If so, fashion them appropriately into your own teaching repertoire. Developing *your* unique combination of good teaching characteristics will enable you to become the best teacher that it is within you to be—a process requiring time, often years. Be patient yet diligent in your quest.

As you contemplate your teaching goals, consider the difference between progressing to a level of adequacy and climbing to excellence. Having struggled successfully through their first years of teaching, some teachers have a tendency to cruise along comfortably, adequately competent, "above average." But some teachers—a select group—continually improve, working their way to higher and more refined levels of excellence.

Contemplate, even now, the good you will do as a confidently able teacher. Think of the number of students' lives you will touch, the number of worthy and significant contributions you will make to society and to yourself—an abundant fulfillment. But contemplate, also, the contribution you would make as a truly *excellent* teacher.

---

# EXPANSIONS

1.   What are some of the problems involved in trying to make yourself into the "ideal" teacher?

2.   What are advantages in working to become the best teacher that it is in you to be?

3.   Observe several teachers. See if you can predict, in each, one or two characteristics that would help that person become the best teacher that it is in him or her to be.

4.   From your present perspective, what seem to be qualities you anticipate developing after years of teaching?

5.   In the section entitled "Hallmarks of Good Teaching," we presented several characteristics we consider to be particularly important in good teaching. After reflecting on them, select the two that appear to you to be most important. Cite reasons for your choices.

6.   Explain this statement: "You are transparent as you stand before your students; you cannot hide yourself."

7.   Throughout this book we have talked of the teacher as a professional. What does "professionalism in teaching" mean to you now?

# Notes

1.   Adapted from M. T. Metzger, and C. Fox, "Two Teachers of Letters," *Harvard Educational Review* 56(4) (November 1986), pp. 349–354.

2.   Adapted from S. Freud, (1980). "The Passion and Challenge of Teaching," *Harvard Educational Review* 50(1) (February 1980), pp. 1–12.

3.   S. Gudmundsdottir, *Knowledge Use among Experienced Teachers: Four Case Studies of High School Teaching. Dissertation Abstracts* 49 (1989), p. 3688-A.

4.   Adapted from W. Ayers, "Thinking about Teachers and the Curriculum," *Harvard Educational Review* 56(1) (February 1986), pp. 49–51.

5.   Adapted from J. P. McDonald, "Raising the Teacher's Voice and the Ironic Role of Theory," *Harvard Educational Review* 56(4) (November 1986), pp. 355–378.

6.   Adapted from D. W. Thomas, "The Torpedo's Touch," *Harvard Educational Review* 55(2) (May 1985), pp. 220–222.

7.   Adapted from D. Meier, "Learning in Small Moments," *Harvard Educational Review* 56(3) (August 1986), pp. 298–300.

8.   Adapted from V. G. Paley, "On Listening to What the Children Say," *Harvard Educational Review* 56(2) (May 1986), pp. 122–131.

9.   C. L. Five, "Fifth Graders Respond to a Changed Reading Program," *Harvard Educational Review* 56(4) (1986), pp. 395–405.

10.   Adapted from K. Jervis, "A Teacher's Quest for a Child's Questions," *Harvard Educational Review* 56(2) (May 1986), 132–150.

11.   Adapted from A. Martin "Back to Kindergarten Basics," *Harvard Educational Review* 55(3) (August 1985), pp. 318–320.

12.   Adapted from McDonald, "Raising," pp. 355–378.

13.   Adapted from K. Devaney, "Sketches toward a Profile of a Professional Teacher," *Education and Urban Society* 17(3) (May 1985), pp. 269–283.

# NAME INDEX

# SUBJECT INDEX